Pocket Guide to Cases of

Collaboration

Roz D. Lasker, M.D.

David M. Abramson, M.P.H.

Grace R. Freedman, M. Phil.

Center for the Advancement of Collaborative Strategies in Health
The New York Academy of Medicine

The New York Academy of Medicine
1216 Fifth Avenue
New York, NY 10029-5293

This project was supported by
The Robert Wood Johnson Foundation and the W. K. Kellogg Foundation.

Library of Congress Cataloging-in-Publication Data
Lasker, Roz Diane
Pocket guide to cases of medicine & public health collaboration / Roz D. Lasker, David M. Abramson, Grace R. Freedman.
    336 p. cm.
    Includes indexes.
    ISBN 0-924143-08-8 (alk. paper)
    1. Public health—United States—Case studies. 2. Medical care—United States—Case studies. 3. Health planning—United States—Case studies.
4. Medical cooperation—United States—Case studies.
        I. Abramson, David M. (David Michael), 1958– .   II. Freedman, Grace R. (Grace Roegner), 1967– .   III. Title.
    [DNLM: 1. Public Health Administration—United States.
    2. Delivery of Health Care--organization & administration--United States.
3. Organizational Case Studies. 4. Organizational Innovation. 5. Interinstitutional Relations.   WA 540 AA1 L3p 1998]
        RA445.L373 1998
        362.1' 0973--dc21
        DNLM/DLC
        for Library of Congress
                                                        98-22071
                                                        CIP

The *Pocket Guide* can be found on the World Wide Web:
http:/www.nyam.org/pubhlth
Text design by Trejo Production

*To the partners in these cases of collaboration,
who are pioneering new strategies for improving
health and the functioning of the health system.*

Acknowledgments

This *Pocket Guide*, like the monograph *Medicine & Public Health: The Power of Collaboration*, depended on the contributions of many individuals and groups. We are deeply indebted to the hundreds of health professionals who provided information about the cases in this book. Their willingness to share their experiences—problems as well as accomplishments—will enhance the capacity of communities around the country to initiate collaborative activities and to sustain existing partnerships.

We also are grateful to the numerous organizations and agencies that facilitated the collection of this information. In addition to our partners—the American Medical Association, the American Public Health Association, The New York Academy of Medicine, The Robert Wood Johnson Foundation, and the W. K. Kellogg Foundation—these organizations included the Agency for Health Care Policy and Research, the American Association of Health Plans, the American College of Preventive Medicine, the American Hospital Association, the American Medical Group Association, the American Nurses Association, the American Osteopathic Association, the Association of Academic Health Centers, the Association of American Medical Colleges, the Association of Community Health Educators, the Association of Schools of Public Health, the Association of State and Territorial Directors of Nursing, the Association of State and Territorial Health Officials, the Association of Teachers of Preventive Medicine, the Centers for Disease Control and Prevention, the Health Resources and Services Administration, the Health Research and Educational Trust, the Institute for the Advancement of Social Work Research, the Medicine/Public Health Initiative Office at the University of Texas-Houston Health Science Center, the National Association of County and City Health Officials, the National Institutes of Health, and the Washington Business Group on Health.

A number of individuals made invaluable contributions to the *Pocket Guide*. Michael Palica, at The New York Academy of Medicine, masterfully coordinated the complex logistics of the project. Copyeditor Carol Chesler reviewed several iterations of the manuscript, enhancing its content and style. Margaret Trejo brought her remarkable talents, and "reader's eye," to the design of the book, and supervised printing and distribution. Special thanks to Denis Prager, who was the first to recognize the need for an indexed case compendium, and to Marilyn Aguirre-Molina, Sue Hassmiller, Nancy Kaufman, and Paul Tarini at The Robert Wood Johnson Foundation, and Thomas Bruce and Robert DeVries at the W.K. Kellogg Foundation, for their encouragement and support. We also are grateful to Jeremiah Barondess and Patricia Volland at The New York Academy of Medicine for providing a nurturing and stimulating environment in which to work.

Finally, we would like to recognize the authors of *Medicine & Public Health: The Power of Collaboration* who were not directly involved the *Pocket Guide*: Christopher G. Atchison, Lester Breslow, Gert H. Brieger, Sherry Glied, Charles C. Hughes (deceased), Bonnie J. Kostelecky, Russell Miller, Thomas R. Reardon, Stanley J. Reiser, Alfred Sommer, and Gail Warden. By developing a practice-based framework for characterizing cases of cross-sectoral collaboration, they laid the groundwork that made this project possible.

Contents

PART III: INDEXES 269

PART IV: KEYS TO ABBREVIATIONS 313

Part I
Introduction

In December 1997, The New York Academy of Medicine published *Medicine & Public Health: The Power of Collaboration.*[1] That monograph, funded by The Robert Wood Johnson Foundation, and jointly sponsored by the American Medical Association and the American Public Health Association, provides readers with a practice-based conceptual framework for thinking about and implementing cross-sectoral collaborations. The book reviews the historical relationship between medicine and public health and examines the current environment, identifying compelling reasons for the two sectors to work more closely together than they have in the recent past. Moving beyond the hypothetical, it analyzes 414 cases of medicine and public health collaboration—most of which involve other community partners as well—elucidating a set of common, and generally applicable, strategies for improving health and shaping the future direction of the American health system.

Recognizing that there is much that people involved or interested in collaboration can learn from each other, The Robert Wood Johnson Foundation and the W.K. Kellogg Foundation have funded this *Pocket Guide to Cases of Medicine & Public Health Collaboration* to give readers direct access to the cases on which the monograph is based. Available in print form and as an interactive, searchable database on the World Wide Web (http://www.nyam.org/pubhlth), the *Pocket Guide* is structured so that users can quickly identify collaborations that share one or more characteristics of interest and network with the people involved. Toward that end, each case is described in a brief narrative abstract, which includes a contact person or literature citation. In addition, the cases are indexed according to the multidimensional framework developed in *Medicine & Public Health: The Power of Collaboration* (i.e., where the collaborations take place, the types of partners involved, the ways the partners combine their resources and skills to achieve certain health and institutional objectives, and the structural arrangements that undergird the partners' relationships). The print version of the *Pocket Guide* organizes the case abstracts geographically, listing all cases that correspond to each index term at the end of the book. The Internet version has special features that allow users to search the database through multiple index terms simultaneously, to search the text of the case abstracts (for example, to identify collaborations dealing with particular health problems, associated with particular foundation- or government-sponsored initiatives, or reported by particular individuals), to connect to relevant parts of the monograph, and to engage in on-line networking. Both versions provide readers with instructions for submitting new cases of collaboration for addition to the database.

---

[1] Lasker RD and the Committee on Medicine and Public Health. *Medicine & Public Health: The Power of Collaboration.* New York: The New York Academy of Medicine. 1997. The monograph is also available on the Internet at http://www.nyam.org/pubhlth.

Cases Included in the *Pocket Guide*

The collaborations included in this edition of the *Pocket Guide* are drawn from the cases that were analyzed in *Medicine & Public Health: The Power of Collaboration*. Those cases were solicited in August 1996 from members of major medicine and public health associations, staff in government health agencies, and participants in potentially relevant foundation- and government-sponsored initiatives. Using a self-administered written or Internet questionnaire, respondents were asked to provide some basic demographic information about themselves and to answer five open-ended questions: What made the collaboration happen? Who was involved? What was the collaboration trying to achieve? What actually happened? What do you think were the critical elements that determined the project's success or failure?

Over 500 cases were collected through this process, of which 414 involved professionals and/or organizations in *both* medicine and public health—a prerequisite for inclusion in the study. These medicine/public health collaborations, which usually involved other community partners as well, were studied to elucidate the models and strategies presented in the monograph. The number and heterogeneity of these cases made them a suitable substrate for such an analysis. The collaborations were geographically well-dispersed, encompassing diverse regions of the country, urban and rural communities, and activities at local, state, and national levels. They were submitted by a broad array of professionals working in virtually every type of venue relevant to medicine and public health. They reflected both short- and long-term partnerships involving all of the domains of the health system: practice, policy, education and training, and research. They included collaborations associated with a broad spectrum of foundation- and government-led initiatives—such as All Kids Count, Community-Based Public Health, Community Care Network, Community Partnerships in Health Professions Education, Comprehensive Community Health Models, Health of the Public, Healthy Communities, Medicine/Public Health Initiative, Models That Work, Reach Out—as well as partnerships unaffiliated with any formal program. And they included not only successful partnerships, but also partial successes and failures. Because of this diversity, the 414 cases likely encompass most of the common types of medicine/public health interactions occurring in the country.

The *Pocket Guide* contains information about 380—or 92%—of these cases. Since the original solicitation assured confidentiality to case respondents, we were able to include only cases for which we could obtain permission to publish or which had been published previously. For the 35 missing cases, we were unable to obtain the necessary permission either because of problems locating the original case reporter (or a suitable substitute), or because the reporter was concerned that inclusion of the collaboration in the *Pocket Guide* would preclude publication of a forthcoming journal article. In spite of these gaps, the 380 cases in the *Pocket Guide* are fully representative—both demographically and by model of collaboration—of the 414 cases analyzed in the monograph.

It is important to point out, however, that the original 414 cases were not a random sample. Therefore, it is not possible to generalize from the frequencies observed.

The narrative abstract and indexing of each *Pocket Guide* case are based on information from a variety of sources. As a starting point, we reviewed the information that had been collected for the monograph analysis: the responses to the 1996 questionnaire, the published articles and reports submitted by case respondents, and notes from extensive telephone interviews that we conducted to clarify information in some of the case reports. Draft abstracts developed from this material were then sent to all case reporters for review. At that time, April 1998, the reporters also were asked to complete a second self-administered questionnaire to validate the way their case had been characterized. The results of this survey were used to confirm case contacts, to update narrative abstracts, and to refine the way cases had been coded. With this additional information, we found that many cases involved a greater range of collaborative activity than initially suspected. As a result, the *Pocket Guide* includes more examples of each model of collaboration than reported in the monograph.

Framework for Characterizing Cases

Cases in the *Pocket Guide* are characterized according to the framework developed in *Medicine & Public Health: The Power of Collaboration*. This framework, which is used to code and index each case, has four dimensions:

- **geography:** where the collaboration takes place
- **partners:** the types of organizations involved in the collaboration
- **synergies:** the ways the partners combine their resources and skills
- **structural foundations:** the partners' organizational relationships

GEOGRAPHY

In the *Pocket Guide*, cases are organized geographically, reflecting whether the collaboration or collaborative program initiative takes place in a particular state, in a multistate region, at the national level, or in a country other than the United States. This geographic information also is incorporated in the unique identifier assigned to each case. (These identifiers begin either with the two-letter postal abbreviation for a **particular state**, or with MST (for **multistate**), NAT (for **national**), or INT (for **international**). This prefix is then followed by a number.) It is important to point out that while some of the collaborations listed under particular states are statewide in scope, the vast majority reflect activity at the local level. Similarly, most of the national program initiatives promote collaboration at local and/or state levels.

PARTNERS

The cases in the *Pocket Guide* bring together individuals with diverse professional backgrounds working in a broad spectrum of organizations—including but also extending beyond the confines of medicine and public health. In the database, partners are coded according to the following scheme, which encompasses government agencies, medical providers/insurers, academia, professional associations, and community groups.

- local health department (LHD)
- other local government agency (L-GOV)
- state health department (SHD)
- other state government agency (S-GOV)
- federal health agency (FEDHLTH)
- other federal government agency (FEDOTH)

- solo or group medical practice (MDPRAC)
- hospital or health system (HOSP)
- community health center or other publicly funded clinic (CLIN)
- managed care organization (MCO)
- health insurance company (INS)
- laboratory or pharmacy (LAB/RX)

- school of medicine (SOM)
- school of public health (SPH)
- academic research center (ARC)
- residency program (RES)
- academic health center (AHC)
- other university-level academic institution or department (U-OTH)

- medical/specialty society or other clinician association (MEDSOC)
- public health association (PHASSN)
- other professional association (PROFASSN)

- voluntary health organization or advocacy group (VHO)
- business (BUS)
- labor organization (LABR)
- school below the college level (SCHL)
- religious organization or clergy (RELIG)
- media (MEDIA)
- foundation (FNDN)
- other community group (C-OTH)

While most of these types of partners are self-explanatory, a few caveats are worth noting. First, depending on the structure of a particular state or local government, governmental partners responsible for mental health, substance abuse, the environment, Medicaid, or social services may be coded as "health department" or as "other government agency." Second, both independent and state-run local health units are coded as "local health department." Third, partners are coded as "academic health center" when they represent an academic health center as a whole rather than any of its component health professions schools or affiliated teaching hospitals. Finally, associations representing any type of clinician (i.e., not only physicians, but also nurses, dentists, social workers, etc.) are coded as "medical/specialty society or other clinician association." Associations representing institutional providers (such as hospitals or managed care organizations), academic institutions or professionals, or professional groups unrelated to health are coded as "other professional association."

SYNERGIES

One of the advantages of studying a large number of cases of collaboration, as was done in the monograph analysis, is that it is possible to move beyond individual experiences to identify common themes and strategies. Although each of the cases we collected is, in some sense, unique, analysis of the collaborations as a whole elucidated a set of models that are applicable to a broad range of localities, health problems, and program initiatives. One aspect of this modeling system relates to the way partners in a collaboration combine their resources and skills. We refer to these types of models as "synergies" because they allow partners to transcend their own limitations and achieve benefits that none of them can accomplish alone.

In the cases in the database, partners contribute an impressive array of assets to collaborative endeavors: technical, scientific, and pedagogic expertise; methodologic tools; individual-level services and population-based strategies; administration and management skills; legal and regulatory authority; convening power; influence with peers, policymakers, and the public; data and information systems; buildings and space; and financial support. These assets are valuable in and of themselves. But they can reinforce each other substantially when combined in certain ways. In the monograph, we describe six reinforcing combinations of resources and skills (synergies), including concrete models that partners use to put each synergy into action. These models are not mutually exclusive; most collaborations, in fact, involve more than one. In the *Pocket Guide*, each case is coded according to the particular synergy model(s) that it exemplifies.

Below, a brief description is provided for each synergy model. (For reference, a key to these synergy models is provided on page 319.) More detailed information about the synergy models can be obtained in *Medicine & Public Health: The Power of Collaboration*, which is electronically linked to the Internet version of the *Pocket Guide*.

Synergy 1: Improving health care by coordinating medical care with individual-level support services

In the first type of synergy, partners in collaborations seek to enhance the success of medical care—and address determinants of health that go beyond medical care—by coordinating a broad array of services directed at individuals. These collaborations link clinical care to: (a) wraparound services, such as transportation, translation, and child care, which help patients overcome logistical barriers to accessing care; (b) outreach services, such as home visits, which are needed to identify problems at an early stage, to help patients and their families deal with complex medical regimens, and to promote adherence with treatment programs; and (c) social services, which help patients obtain or retain health insurance, and obtain needed nutritional and economic supports.

- In **synergy 1a**, partners link medical and support services by bringing *new types of personnel to existing practice sites*, for example, by connecting public health nurses to medical practices providing care for women or children in the Medicaid program.

- In **synergy 1b,** partners establish *"one-stop" centers* that locate a broad range of medical and support services in one place. This type of co-location makes services more convenient to clients and provides a structure for sharing staff, centralizing services, and coordinating the programs of different partners.

- In **synergy 1c,** partners coordinate medical and support services provided in *various locations* throughout the community. This "center without walls" approach assures that wherever an individual shows up, she or he is aware of the full range of services available through the system and has help in reaching and using those services. Some of the more integrated versions of this model use common contracting, centralized purchasing, and system-wide information systems to improve performance and achieve economies of scale.

Synergy 2: Improving access to care by establishing frameworks to provide care for the un- or underinsured

The second type of synergy makes it feasible for the mainstream medical sector to play a more active role in indigent care by overcoming a number of logistical, financial, and legal barriers that stand in the way.

- In **synergy 2a,** *free clinics* are established that provide indigent patients with free or discounted care.

- In **synergy 2b,** *referral networks* are established, which allow mainstream clinicians to provide free or discounted care where they usually work.

- In **synergy 2c,** academic or private medical practitioners are recruited to *enhance staffing at clinics run by government agencies or not-for-profit organizations* (such as community health centers). Often, this type of collaboration provides academic medical centers with additional sources of support for faculty salaries and with new training experiences for residents and students.

- In **synergy 2d,** contractual arrangements are made that *shift the care of indigent patients from public health clinics to private medical practices, hospitals, health systems, or managed care organizations.* Some health departments seeking to strengthen population-based services use this type of collaboration to move away from providing care directly to indigent individuals while continuing to assure the availability of safety-net services.

Synergy 3: Improving the quality and cost-effectiveness of care by applying a population perspective to medical practice

The third type of synergy applies a population perspective to medical practice in order to improve the quality and cost-effectiveness of medical care—as well as the economic viability of medical professionals and institutions.

- In **synergy 3a**, partners make *population-based information to support clinical decision-making more available and useful to medical practitioners.* By working together, they are able to make the content and format of this information more relevant to medical practice, and to reach a wider professional audience.

- In **synergy 3b**, partners *link community-wide screening programs to follow-up medical care.* By identifying patients who can benefit from medical care and then "funneling" these patients to appropriate providers for further diagnosis and treatment, this type of collaboration enhances the cost-effectiveness of public health screening and provides medical practitioners with new patients (many of whom have insurance).

- In **synergy 3c**, *population-based methodologies* (such as clinical epidemiology, cost-effectiveness analysis, or performance measurement) are *applied to clinical practice.* Usually, these tools are used to support quality-improvement activities and strategic planning, or to enable medical practices and organizations to take on and manage financial risk.

Synergy 4: Using clinical practice to identify and address community health problems

A fourth type of synergy takes advantage of what can be accomplished through clinical practice to achieve clinically oriented public health goals, such as immunization or prenatal care. These collaborations are particularly important as clinical preventive services increasingly become covered health insurance benefits, as patients move from one medical practice or managed care organization to another, and as purchasers and communities measure the extent to which Healthy People 2000 and HEDIS objectives have been achieved.

- In **synergy 4a**, partners design and/or implement *community-wide information systems that incorporate clinical data* from hospitals, laboratories, or office-based practices. When the medical and public health sectors design such information systems together, the systems often incorporate innovative features that make them more useful in the field. For example, some collaboratively developed immunization registries provide medical practitioners with information about vaccines, with automatic reminder and recall letters personalized to the clinician's practice, with patient flow charts, and with practice or management software.

- In **synergy 4b**, partners *take advantage of clinical encounters to identify and address underlying health risks in patients.* In some of these cases, supports provided by public health and community partners—such as counseling guides, culturally appropriate patient education materials, and resource directories—make it easier and less time-consuming for clinicians to elicit information about health risks, to counsel patients about personal behaviors that are detrimental to their health, and to connect them to community-based programs. In other cases of this type, partners address social or environmental causes of health problems in patients, for example, by using savings achieved by moving lead treatment from inpatient to outpatient settings to finance environmental strategies that reduce the need for chelation therapy.

- In **synergy 4c,** *partners combine individual-level and population-based strategies to assure the delivery of a particular clinical service in private and public medical practices throughout the community.* These cases involve a broad range of community groups in a variety of activities, including education and media campaigns to increase awareness of the problem among the public, screening programs to identify people in need of the particular clinical service, outreach efforts to address logistical barriers that some patients face in obtaining the service, and supports for clinical practices.

Synergy 5: Strengthening health promotion and health protection by mobilizing community campaigns

A fifth type of synergy moves away from clinical care, demonstrating how diverse groups in the community can work together around population-based strategies. Often, these collaborations address underlying causes of health problems, such as violence, tobacco use, high-fat diets, and physical inactivity. Many strengthen the capacity of health departments to carry out their essential population-based functions. More than any other synergy, these models show how the combined assets of the medical and public health sectors can be reinforced by other public, private, and not-for-profit organizations in the community.

- In **synergy 5a,** partners *conduct community health assessments* to identify health problems in the community. In many of these cases, the involvement of a spectrum of public and private sector partners facilitates the collection of relevant data from diverse sources, the analysis and reporting of data, and the often difficult move from data collection and the identification of health problems to the implementation of community interventions.

- In **synergy 5b,** partners *mount public education campaigns* to make people in the community aware of important health problems and what they can do about them. By involving diverse community groups in these campaigns, messages are more likely to be credible, understandable, and culturally acceptable, and to be delivered through routes and media that are most effective in reaching targeted population groups.

- In **synergy 5c,** partners *advocate health-related laws and regulations,* such as cigarette taxes, seat belt and helmet laws, or restrictions on the sale of firearms. In these cases, collaboration enhances the capacity of partners to gather policy-relevant information and to make a persuasive case to the public and policymakers.

- In **synergy 5d,** partners seek to *achieve particular community health promotion objectives* by implementing multipronged strategies. Often these collaborations include one or more of the activities described above in synergies 5a–5c, as well as voluntary community initiatives, such as those that increase the availability of healthy food choices in schools, workplaces, and restaurants, or that establish incentives, opportunities, and safe environments for exercise.

- In **synergy 5e**, partners *launch "Healthy Communities"-type initiatives.* These collaborations go beyond categorical health promotion activities by establishing a broad-based process to deal with multiple community health issues over a prolonged period of time. Reflecting community perceptions about health problems, and recognizing the importance of socioeconomic determinants of health, these collaborations address issues that go beyond the traditional purview of the health sectors, such as education, jobs, and housing.

Synergy 6: Shaping the future direction of the health system by collaborating around health system policy, health professions training, and health-related research

In collaborations oriented around **health system policy,** partners identify areas of common concern, and then combine their authority, influence, practical experience, and scientific expertise to do something about them. While most of the cases address governmental policy issues, particularly at the state level, some relate to organizational policy as well.

- In **synergy 6a-1**, partners focus on policies that influence *access to care* for the un- and underinsured. Examples include the leveraging of public funds to support safety-net facilities, expansions in the availability of health insurance coverage, or legislative initiatives that give medical practitioners immunity from liability when they provide indigent care.

- In **synergy 6a-2**, partners influence *provider payment* policies, such as the relative amounts that a state Medicaid program pays for pediatric care in emergency departments and medical offices.

- In **synergy 6a-3**, partners influence *insurance benefits* policies, for example, by using established guidelines or cost-effectiveness analysis to expand coverage for preventive services in public or private insurance programs.

- In **synergy 6a-4**, partners influence policies related to the *quality of medical care*, such as the development and application of practice guidelines, quality assurance standards, or performance measures.

- In **synergy 6a-5**, partners influence policies related to the *regional organization of health care services or facilities*, such as perinatal care or trauma services.

- In **synergy 6a-6**, partners influence policies related to the *organization and financing of public health services or activities*, for example, by working together to restructure health departments, boards of health, or particular public health programs, such as those concerned with maternal and child health or mental health.

Another way to shape the future direction of the health system is by changing the way health professionals are educated and trained. While students, residents, and faculty in academic institutions participate in many of the collaborations in the database, cases coded as one of these synergy models bring partners together for the **explicit purpose of promoting education and training that link the perspectives of medicine and public health.**

- In **synergy 6b-1**, a cross-sectoral perspective is incorporated in the *curriculum of health professions degree programs*. The extent of curriculum change in this model ranges from the marginal (e.g., opportunities to participate in extramural programs, or elective courses and rotations to which only a small proportion of students are exposed) to the substantial (e.g., the incorporation of a broad perspective in a school's mission or structure, or the institution of courses, rotations, or practica that are required of all students).

- In **synergy 6b-2**, *dual-degree programs* are established that give students an MD/MPH or an RN/MPH, for example. This model may or may not involve much interaction between the schools or programs in different sectors.

- In **synergy 6b-3**, *formal, functional connections are established between medical and public health schools or academic programs*. In some of these cases, faculty have dual appointments and/or teach courses in schools or departments in more than one sector. In others, students from a range of schools work together in interdisciplinary teams, sometimes for prolonged periods of time. Another example of this type of collaboration is the development of cross-sectoral academic centers.

- In **synergy 6b-4**, *academic training is linked to medical and public health practice sites and/or other organizations in the broader community*. When dual appointments occur in this model, the health professional often serves as a faculty member at a school of medicine and as an official in a local health department. Some cases encourage cross-sectoral links between academia and practice by requiring that faculty devote a proportion of their time to community projects, or that students rotate through health departments, community health centers, or COPC practice sites.

- In **synergy 6b-5**, *cross-sectoral education or training is provided to health professionals in the field*. In this model, perspectives are broadened through continuing education courses, leadership institutes, or degree-granting programs specifically designed for professionals in active practice.

- In **synergy 6b-6**, opportunities are provided for *cross-sectoral networking*, such as collaborative conferences focusing on the interaction between medicine and public health.

A third way to shape the future direction of the health system is by advancing the knowledge base that supports health-related work. While research plays an important role in many of the collaborations in the database, cases coded as one of these synergy models **explicitly bring together multidisciplinary perspectives to strengthen the research enterprise**. This cross-sectoral investigative approach is valuable in identifying important research questions; in designing, implementing, and disseminating research findings; and in obtaining financial support.

- In **synergy 6c-1**, partners *establish multidisciplinary research centers*. Some of these centers bring together diverse types of professionals within a single school. Others connect various schools within an academic health center or connect academic institutions with health departments or other government agencies.

- In **synergy 6c-2**, partners promote cross-sectoral research through other, *less formal*, means.

STRUCTURAL FOUNDATIONS

Combining resources and skills is one aspect of how collaborations work. Achieving these synergies, however, requires structural arrangements that allow partners from the two health sectors—as well as from the broader community—to continue to work within their own organization while, at the same time, linking up with professionals or institutions in other sectors. The analysis in *Medicine & Public Health: The Power of Collaboration* described six distinct models that partners use to establish these relationships. In the *Pocket Guide*, each case is coded according to the particular structural foundation(s) it exemplifies.

Below, brief definitions are provided for each type of structural foundation. *Pocket Guide* abbreviations follow in parentheses. (For easy reference, this key to structural foundations is also provided on page 323.) More detailed information about the structural foundations can be obtained in the monograph, which is electronically linked to the Internet version of the *Pocket Guide*.

- **Coalitions** (Coalition) are formal groups that bring together representatives of autonomous organizations to address a common problem or objective. The authority, responsibility, and capacity to take action lies with the coalition itself rather than with any one partner or external agency. Coalitions are particularly useful in collaborations that benefit from a broad range of community partners, particularly if they do not require equal or consistent involvement on the part of all partners or close coordination of partner activities.

- **Contractual agreements** (Contract) are binding agreements (e.g., legal documents, memoranda of understanding, or verbal agreements) that commit one partner in a collaboration to carry out a function or to provide a service for another partner. Contracts are used in collaborations that depend on certain interactions between partners—usually the delivery of various health services to individuals. These agreements clarify partners' roles in critical interactions and assure that they are carried out.

- **Administrative/management systems** (Adm/Mgmt) are personnel or offices that run some or all aspects of collaborative enterprises, allowing partners to closely coordinate their activities and resources, or to centralize organization or control. Depending on the work involved, such a "system" may be a full-time staff person dedicated to managing a collaboration, a management office within one partner's organization, or a separate, autonomous management office. These arrangements make it possible for collaborations to integrate activities, to reduce duplication of services, and to achieve economies of scale.

- **Advisory bodies** (Advisory) are groups convened to provide an organization in one sector (such as a government agency or research entity) with input or support from other sectors. Advisory bodies may deliberate independently in constructing recommendations, but they do not have the authority to make operational or policy decisions.

- **Intraorganizational platforms** (Intraorg) are structural arrangements that allow a single organization to expand its perspective by bringing in professionals with the skills and expertise of another sector. Examples include a managed care organization that establishes a clinical epidemiology branch to assess quality or outcomes, or a section on public health within a medical society.

- **Informal arrangements** (Informal) are any of a variety of *ad hoc* relationships among partners, which are generally dependent on personal, rather than structured, interactions.

How to Use the *Pocket Guide*

The *Pocket Guide* is a compendium of cases that illustrates the broad range of models of medicine and public health collaboration taking place in the field. It is structured so that users can quickly identify cases that are of particular interest to them and gain access to knowledgeable sources from whom they can obtain additional information. To serve these functions, the *Pocket Guide* consists of two main components: a series of case entries and tools to facilitate case searching.

CASE ENTRIES

The case entries, which are organized geographically in the print version of the *Pocket Guide*, provide information about collaborations in three complementary ways. As can be seen in the sample below, each entry contains a brief narrative abstract, a set of indexing codes that characterize the case, and a case contact or alternative source of information.

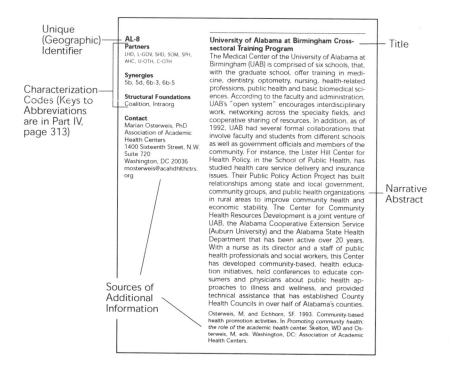

Unique (Geographic) Identifier

Characterization Codes (Keys to Abbreviations are in Part IV, page 313)

Sources of Additional Information

AL-8
Partners
LHD, L-GOV, SHD, SOM, SPH, AHC, U-OTH, C-OTH

Synergies
5b, 5d, 6b-3, 6b-5

Structural Foundations
Coalition, Intraorg

Contact
Marian Osterweis, PhD
Association of Academic
Health Centers
1400 Sixteenth Street, N.W.
Suite 720
Washington, DC 20036
mosterweis@acahdhlthctrs.
org

Title

University of Alabama at Birmingham Cross-sectoral Training Program
The Medical Center of the University of Alabama at Birmingham (UAB) is comprised of six schools, that, with the graduate school, offer training in medicine, dentistry, optometry, nursing, health-related professions, public health and basic biomedical sciences. According to the faculty and administration, UAB's "open system" encourages interdisciplinary work, networking across the specialty fields, and cooperative sharing of resources. In addition, as of 1992, UAB had several formal collaborations that involve faculty and students from different schools as well as government officials and members of the community. For instance, the Lister Hill Center for Health Policy, in the School of Public Health, has studied health care service delivery and insurance issues. Their Public Policy Action Project has built relationships among state and local government, community groups, and public health organizations in rural areas to improve community health and economic stability. The Center for Community Health Resources Development is a joint venture of UAB, the Alabama Cooperative Extension Service (Auburn University) and the Alabama State Health Department that has been active over 20 years. With a nurse as its director and a staff of public health professionals and social workers, this Center has developed community-based, health education initiatives, held conferences to educate consumers and physicians about public health approaches to illness and wellness, and provided technical assistance that has established County Health Councils in over half of Alabama's counties.

Osterweis, M, and Eichhorn, SF. 1993. Community-based health promotion activities. In *Promoting community health: the role of the academic health center.* Skelton, WD and Osterweis, M, eds. Washington, DC: Association of Academic Health Centers.

Narrative Abstract

Case Abstracts

The narrative abstracts are intentionally brief—designed to give readers just enough information to determine whether the collaboration is relevant to their interests and needs. (A key to the acronyms used in the abstracts can be found on page 325.) While space limitations precluded us from telling the "whole story" of each case, we tried, to the extent possible, to include key elements of each collaboration: why it started, when it took place, which partners played major roles, how it illustrates particular collaborative models, and what it accomplished. As mentioned earlier, these narratives are based on information obtained through two surveys, published reports, and, not infrequently, clarifying telephone conversations. Nonetheless, it should be noted that, in most cases, all of this information was provided by a single case reporter. Because of the large number of cases included in the *Pocket Guide*, it was not possible to validate these reporters' descriptions by obtaining multiple partners' perspectives of each collaboration.

Characterization Codes

To the left side of each abstract, readers will find the unique identifier for the case, as well as additional coded information that characterizes the case according to the framework described earlier. These codes, which also are used for indexing purposes, provide information about:

- the types of organizational partners involved in the collaboration
- the particular synergy model(s) by which the partners combine their resources and skills
- the structural foundation(s) that undergird the partners' relationship

For easy reference, definitions and abbreviations for these codes are provided in a set of tables at the end of this book (Keys to Abbreviations on pages 313 through 326). In the Internet version of the *Pocket Guide*, expanded information about each coding term is provided through automatic "hot-links" to relevant sections of *Medicine & Public Health: The Power of Collaboration*.

It is important to point out that the coding of cases in the *Pocket Guide* is not completely uniform. To a large extent, this relates to the evolving nature of many collaborations, which makes it difficult to specify clear boundaries for the enterprise in which partners are engaged. Over time, collaborations commonly develop offshoots or new collaborations, which may complement or replace the original partnership. Consequently, the coding of partners, synergy models, and structural foundations varies depending on whether the case reporter took a broad or narrow view. Other causes of coding variation include differences in the interpretation of certain terms (for example, some case reporters considered funders of collaborations as partners while others did not), and limitations in available information about certain cases, which sometimes made determination of involved synergy models or structural foundations difficult.

Sources of Additional Information

Below the codes, on the left side of the case entry, readers will find an additional source of information for each collaboration. Usually this source is a person—one of the key individuals involved in the case who is willing to be contacted about it. (Due to space constraints, it was not possible to print the names of all knowledgeable and willing contacts for each case.) The case entry includes the name, postal address, and (if available) E-mail address of the contact. The Internet version of the *Pocket Guide* facilitates E-mail communication with these contacts. In cases in which a suitable contact could not be located, did not wish to be listed, or was not directly involved in the partnership, a citation for the case (referring to a journal article, organizational report, or Internet address) is provided instead. (Due to space constraints, it was not possible to list citations other than books for the remaining cases.)

SEARCH TOOLS

Searching cases in the print version of the *Pocket Guide* is facilitated by a series of indexes that follow the case entries. These indexes allow readers to identify all cases in the database that:

- take place in a particular state, a multistate region, at the national level, or in another country (Index 1, p. 271)
- involve a particular type of organizational partner (Index 2, p. 285)
- illustrate a particular synergy model (Index 3, p. 299)
- utilize a particular type of structural foundation (Index 4, p. 309)

The Internet version of the *Pocket Guide* has special features that allow users to search the database through multiple index terms simultaneously and to search the text of the case entries. Through these means it is possible, for example, to identify cases in which particular combinations of partners work together, cases that involve particular models of collaboration in certain parts of the country, cases that are associated with particular health problems or program initiatives, and cases that are reported by particular individuals.

In searching the database—in either print or electronic form—one caveat should be kept in mind. While the database is illustrative of the different types of medicine/public health collaboration occurring around the country, it is *not* a representative sample. Therefore, searches should not be used to estimate the relative frequency of collaborations occurring in different parts of the country, involving different types of partners, or utilizing different types of models.

ADDING NEW CASES TO THE *POCKET GUIDE*

In the course of developing the *Pocket Guide*, we have become aware that considerably more medicine and public health collaborations are occurring around the country—and the world—than are represented in the current database. It is not surprising, then, that many people have expressed interest in the database, not only to obtain information from it, but also to contribute their own cases to it. Individuals interested in participating in this expansion of the *Pocket Guide* can obtain materials to submit their cases in two ways:

- through the *Pocket Guide* Web site (http://www.nyam.org/pubhlth)

- by contacting
  Center for the Advancement of Collaborative Strategies in Health
  Division of Public Health
  The New York Academy of Medicine
  1216 Fifth Avenue, Room 452
  New York, NY 10029
  Phone: 212-822-7250
  Fax: 212-426-6796
  E-mail: pubhealth@nyam.org

New cases of collaboration will be added continually to the Internet version of the *Pocket Guide*. By doing so, we hope to create a "living database" that will become increasingly useful, both as a networking tool and as a sampling frame to study key questions generated by collaboration partners, funders, researchers, and policymakers.

Part II
Case Entries

Collaborations Associated with Particular States (listed alphabetically by postal code)

AL-1

Partners
LHD, LAB/RX, SOM, RES, AHC

Synergies
1a, 2c, 3a, 6b-4

Structural Foundations
Contract

Contact
Michael E. Fleenor, MD, MPH, FACP
Jefferson County Department of Health
1600 6th Avenue South
Birmingham, AL 35233
mfleenor@jcdh.org

Jefferson County STD Prevention Training Center

In the course of establishing a CDC-funded regional STD Prevention Training Center at the Jefferson County Health Department in the early 1980s, public health planners forged a partnership with the academic medical center at the University of Alabama-Birmingham (UAB). The health department needed medical oversight, and the medical school needed a research venue. The university recruited a leading STD researcher/clinician from Johns Hopkins to lead the STD research and training effort, which is targeted at the southeastern United States. He developed a faculty-staffed clinic at the health department with rotations of research fellows and medical students. The health department pays UAB a nominal salary, and in turn the UAB faculty have leveraged their access to a patient base into considerable research grants. The health department provides the clinical space, support staff, nursing services, lab services, and "Disease Intervention Specialists" (outreach workers who do much of the contact-tracing and case finding). The UAB faculty and residents provide clinical oversight for the health department's nursing staff; develop the clinical protocols followed by the nurse-practitioners (which covers 95% of the care delivered in the clinic); provide on-site clinical backup; provide technical assistance in developing and assuring the appropriate use of new technologies; and advise the health department on programmatic aspects of clinic operations.

AL-2

Partners
LHD, SOM, RES, AHC

Synergies
1a, 2c, 6b-4, 6b-5

Structural Foundations
Contract

Jefferson County TB Clinic

Much like the Jefferson County health department's STD Training Center and clinic (AL-1), the TB Clinic was developed in the 1970s as a contractual arrangement by which the medical faculty, residents, and students from the pulmonary and infectious disease departments at the University of Alabama-Birmingham (UAB) supplemented the health department's medical staff at the TB clinic. When the incidence of TB declined in the 1980s, the university pulled its faculty and fellows out of

Contact
Michael E. Fleenor, MD,
MPH, FACP
Jefferson County
Department of Health
1600 6th Avenue South
Birmingham, AL 35233
mfleenor@jcdh.org

AL-3
Partners
LHD, S-GOV, SOM, ARC, RES

Synergies
1a, 1c, 2c, 6a-1, 6a-5, 6a-6,
6b-4

Structural Foundations
Contract, Adm/Mgmt

Contact
Michael E. Fleenor, MD,
MPH, FACP
Jefferson County
Department of Health
1600 6th Avenue South
Birmingham, AL 35233
mfleenor@jcdh.org

AL-4
Partners
LHD, HOSP, SOM, U-OTH

Synergies
1a, 2d, 3c, 6a-4, 6a-5, 6a-6,
6b-6

Structural Foundations
Coalition, Contract,
Adm/Mgmt

the clinic; as TB reemerged in the 1990s, and there was particular research interest regarding multiple drug-resistant TB, the health department was able to entice medical school faculty back. For the TB researchers, the health department has provided a platform at the state level to disseminate research findings and new technologies, such as genetic mapping for TB index case-finding, contact-tracing, and epidemiologic investigation. More recently, UAB has granted adjunct faculty appointments to the health department physicians in recognition of their education of medical students, residents, and fellows. The health department and medical school have co-sponsored CME and clinical practice sessions, exposing physicians-in-training to public health theory and practice.

Jefferson County Maternity and Pediatric Care
The Jefferson County health department provides primary care, family planning, and maternity services to the area's Medicaid and indigent populations. Fifteen years ago, the health department began a collaborative agreement with the pediatric and obstetric departments at the University of Alabama-Birmingham to provide medical staff, and through an additional arrangement with a county hospital, inpatient care. The agreement has expanded over the years to include rotations of pediatric residents through health department clinics, a Medicaid managed care maternity program that accounts for half the county's newborns, and coordination of care for HIV-infected pediatric and maternity patients. One consequence of this partnership has been that almost all of the current pediatric primary care providers were recruited after their initial health department rotations. The system has been supported by fee-for-service funds and dedicated indigent care funds from the county. The emergence of managed care has prompted several new delivery structures (AL-4).

Jefferson County Capitated Pediatric Clinic
In 1994, given the imminent prospect of mandated Medicaid managed care, the Jefferson County Department of Health conducted a utilization review of their pediatric care practice, which is conducted collaboratively by the local health department, the University of Alabama-Birmingham (UAB) Department of Pediatrics, and The Children's Hospital of Alabama (AL-3). To no one's surprise, the per capita cost far exceeded the proposed Medicaid man-

Contact
Michael E. Fleenor, MD, MPH, FACP
Jefferson County
Department of Health
1600 6th Avenue South
Birmingham, AL 35233
mfleenor@jcdh.org

aged care rate. The health department proposed an experiment: it would build a new clinical center and provide Children's Hospital with a global budget to administer and operate all clinical aspects of the pediatric practice. As part of the arrangement, the health department agreed to suspend all of its administrative and clinical protocols if the hospital followed accepted American Academy of Pediatrics guidelines. The hospital would subcontract out to the UAB pediatrics division for medical staff, and the health department would assess the clinic's quality of care using HEDIS 3.0 performance measures. If the operation loses money, Children's Hospital absorbs the loss; if they run a surplus, it will be turned back into further collaborative ventures with the health department. The new clinic will also co-locate health department adult clinics and family planning services in the building.

AL-5
Partners
SHD, MDPRAC, HOSP, CLIN, SOM, SPH, ARC, MEDSOC, PROFASSN, VHO

Synergies
3b, 4a, 6a-6

Structural Foundations
Coalition, Contract, Advisory

Contact
Clifton J. Hataway, MD, MPH
Chronic Disease Prevention Division, Alabama Department of Health
The M A Tower
201 Monroe Street
Montgomery, AL 36130
hata100w@wonder.em.cdc.gov

Alabama Breast and Cervical Cancer Registry
Over a span of six years, a gynecological oncologist worked with women's health groups and the American Cancer Society to lobby the state health department and state legislature for a statewide breast and cervical cancer registry and screening program in Alabama. The physician used his surgical and oncological networks to help advance the cause of the registry and screening program within the medical community. The cancer registry initiative was successful and has since been implemented. The state health department has lent its authority to creating the registry and its technical expertise and neutrality to establishing and managing the database. The screening program, which would have been funded by CDC monies matched by state funds, was rejected by the Governor's Office, but the lobbying effort led to additional state health department funds for mammography screening and treatment programs in selected areas.

AL-6
Partners
LHD, L-GOV, SHD, MEDSOC

Synergies
6a-6

State and County Boards of Censors
In Alabama, the governing body of the Medical Association of the State of Alabama (MASA), known as the Board of Censors, has been delegated responsibilities in the areas of physician licensing and public health by the laws of the state. Similarly, the Board of Censors for each county medical society

Structural Foundations
Contract

Contact
S. Lon Connor
Medical Association of the
State of Alabama
19 South Jackson Street
P.O. Box 1900
Montgomery, AL 36102

AL-7
Partners
LHD, SHD, FEDHLTH, MDPRAC,
HOSP, CLIN, SOM, VHO

Synergies
1a, 1c, 2b, 2d, 3a, 4c, 6a-3,
6a-5

Structural Foundations
Contract
Adm/Mgmt

Contact
Fern M. Shinbaum
Children's Health
Insurance Program,
Alabama Department of
Public Health
201 Monroe Street
RSA Tower, Suite 1362
Montgomery, AL 36130
fshinbaum@adph.state.al.
us

has been delegated responsibilities in the area of
public health at the county level by state law. At the
state level, the Board of Censors of MASA is designated as the State Board of Medical Examiners,
responsible for the credentialing and examination
of applicants for medical licensure in the state.
Also, the elected censors of MASA constitute a majority of the State Committee of Public Health, a
board which exercises overall supervision of the
state health officer. At the county level, the Board
of Censors of the county medical society together
with either the probate judge or county administrator serve as the county board of health. This organizational structure permits the close cooperation of the private practice physician community
and public health professionals in matters related
to public health issues at both the state and local
level.

Alabama Medicaid Freedom of Choice Waiver
The obstetrical community in Alabama was in
crisis—Alabama had the highest infant morality
rates in the nation, obstetrical care for indigent
women was fragmented and hard to access, and
the number of physicians actively delivering babies
was dwindling due to insufficient Medicaid reimbursement and the legal climate of malpractice insurance regulations. The state health officer, a pediatrician with a background in maternal and child
health, widely publicized this problem, and a
change in executive leadership of the Alabama
Medicaid Agency provided an opportunity to act.
The new Medicaid Commissioner worked with the
state health officer to change the reimbursement
strategy with the Medicaid Freedom of Choice
Waiver, which, implemented in 1987, provides
better incentives to physicians to care for underserved women. The Medicaid Freedom of Choice
Waiver allows groups of providers, such as the local
health department and private physicians, to work
together to provide a comprehensive system of
health care for pregnant women and newborns
within single or multicounty geographic areas. The
specific arrangements of care delivery are determined at the local level, and each county-based
system varies. Still, certain components of care are
assured: prenatal care, including physical exams
and health education, hospital delivery, post-
partum care and newborn care, and case management. A federal Maternal and Child Health

SPRANS grant to the Central Alabama System for Perinatal Care provided a framework for the system of care and initial funding, so cash flow problems with Medicaid reimbursement were not a hindrance in setting up the system. A new component, the Medicaid Maternity Waiver Program, began in a few counties in 1997 and is expected to be statewide within a year.

AL-8

Partners
LHD, L-GOV, SHD, SOM, SPH, AHC, U-OTH, C-OTH

Synergies
5b, 5d, 6b-3, 6b-5

Structural Foundations
Coalition, Intraorg

Contact
Marian Osterweis, PhD
Association of Academic Health Centers
1400 Sixteenth Street, N.W.
Suite 720
Washington, DC 20036
mosterweis@acahdhlthctrs.org

University of Alabama at Birmingham Cross-Sectoral Training Program

The Medical Center of the University of Alabama at Birmingham (UAB) is comprised of six schools that, with the graduate school, offer training in medicine, dentistry, optometry, nursing, health-related professions, public health, and basic biomedical sciences. According to the faculty and administration, UAB's "open system" encourages interdisciplinary work, networking across the specialty fields, and cooperative sharing of resources. In addition, as of 1992, UAB had several formal collaborations that involve faculty and students from different schools as well as government officials and members of the community. For instance, the Lister Hill Center for Health Policy, in the School of Public Health, has studied health care service delivery and insurance issues. Their Public Policy Action Project has built relationships among state and local government, community groups, and public health organizations in rural areas to improve community health and economic stability. The Center for Community Health Resources Development is a joint venture of UAB, the Alabama Cooperative Extension Service (Auburn University) and the Alabama State Health Department that has been active over 20 years. With a nurse as its director and a staff of public health professionals and social workers, this Center has developed community-based, health education initiatives, held conferences to educate consumers and physicians about public health approaches to illness and wellness, and provided technical assistance that has established County Health Councils in over half of Alabama's counties.

Osterweis, M and Eichhorn, SF. 1993. Community-based health promotion activities. In *Promoting community health: the role of the academic health center.* Skelton, WD and Osterweis, M, eds. Washington, DC: Association of Academic Health Centers.

[AZ] ARIZONA

AZ-1

Partners
LHD, MDPRAC, RES

Synergies
1a, 2c, 6a-6, 6b-4, 6b-6

Structural Foundations
Contract

Contact
Robert Orford, MD,
MPH, MS
Division of Preventive and
Occupational Medicine
Mayo Clinic Scottsdale
13400 East Shea Boulevard
Scottsdale, AZ 85259
rorford@mayo.edu

Mayo Preventive Medicine Chair Heads Health Department
In 1994, the medical director of Olmstead County's health department resigned. Since the county had a long history with the local Mayo Clinic, which provided medical residents to staff health department clinics, the county approached the Director of the Preventive Medicine Residency Program to develop a collaborative approach to managing the health department's medical programs. The Chair of the Preventive Medicine Division assumed the duties of health department medical director. The opportunity proved timely for the health department, since the Mayo clinician brought expertise in population medicine and managed care. The county saved money by supporting only a part-time salary; the health department received primary care and specialty consultation in its STD, refugee, and adult clinics; and the Mayo Clinic further enhanced community-based training opportunities for its residents. There was even an historical precedent. Dr. Charlie Mayo, the legendary clinic founder, was himself a health department director in the 1920s and 1930s.

AZ-2

Partners
LHD, L-GOV, SHD, FEDHLTH,
MDPRAC, MCO, INS, U-OTH,
C-OTH

Synergies
1c, 4a, 4c, 5b, 6b-5

Structural Foundations
Coalition

Contact
Lisa Kaiser, MSHPA
Maricopa County
Department of Public
Health Services
1845 East Roosevelt
Phoenix, AZ 85006
lkaiser@phservices.
maricopa.gov

Maricopa County Childhood Immunization Campaign
In an effort to boost childhood immunization rates around the state, in 1996 the Arizona state legislature mandated that all health plans interested in being certified as Medicaid managed care plans demonstrate that they have reached an immunization "threshold" for all two-year-olds. The state further required that all childhood immunizations be reported to the state health department. Using a variety of funding opportunities offered by the CDC, the Maricopa County Department of Health Services has been working with private providers and managed care plans to purchase hardware and software to facilitate electronic reporting through physicians' offices. The Maricopa County coalition has focused on six primary areas: coalition building, recruiting additional members (such as birthing hospitals and child-related businesses), linking the immunization projects to WIC programs, developing a media campaign, establishing outreach efforts, and educating providers about the utility of

the electronic registry. The coalition's strategies of performance measurement and epidemiological research are being used to stimulate further public-private partnerships.

AZ-3

Partners
LHD, SHD, S-GOV, HOSP, CLIN, MCO, AHC, U-OTH, MEDSOC, PHASSN, PROFASSN, VHO, RELIG, FNDN, C-OTH

Synergies
3a, 4a, 6b-3, 6b-4, 6b-5

Structural Foundations
Coalition, Advisory

Contact
Douglas Hirano, MPH
Public Health Services
Arizona Department of Health Services
1740 West Adams
Phoenix, AZ 85007
dhirano@hs.state.az.us

Arizona Health Alliance

In September 1996, the Arizona Department of Health Services and the Arizona Medical Association brought together a wide variety of health and public health organizations to view a video conference on the National Medicine/Public Health Initiative. Afterward, attendees discussed moving forward with collaborative activities to improve health in Arizona, leading to the development of the Arizona Health Alliance, a coalition of several state-level associations and agencies representing public health, medical speciality societies, community health centers, and graduate-level education. With an objective to improve health in Arizona through a partnership of medicine and public health, the Alliance is working on several initiatives, including: (1) the development of an integrated health information system; (2) medical and graduate public health education, including supplementing clinical training with population-based health improvement approaches; (3) identifying community-wide areas for health improvement; and (4) strategic planning through the new Turning Point initiative. Though in its early stages, the strength of the collaboration lies in its broad-based membership and committed leadership from the state health department and the state medical association.

AZ-4

Partners
FEDHLTH, MDPRAC, HOSP

Synergies
1a, 1c, 3b, 4b, 6a-2, 6a-4, 6a-5

Structural Foundations
Contract

Contact
Joyce A. Hospodar
The Healthy
Seniors Program
Carondelet Health Network
1120 South Swan Road
Tucson, AZ 85711
jah@theriver.com

Tucson Demonstration Program for the Community Nursing Project

Part of a national study funded by HCFA and mandated by Congress, the Community Nursing Organization (CNO) Demonstration Project was designed to assess the efficacy and cost-effectiveness of using a client/family-centered approach to the coordination of services for Medicare patients. Nurses, called nurse partners, work with Medicare beneficiaries to facilitate their independence and autonomy in the community by using care planning, patient education, and coordination of referrals among physicians and other community services. The Arizona demonstration program covers three counties, includes all the local hospitals, and has over 200 physicians who have patients that are participating in the CNO program. A monthly newsletter is sent to participants in the study, their physicians, and other members of the Carondelet Health Network to keep them abreast of activities geared to seniors. Physicians have been very supportive of the research and the work of the nurses. Overwhelmed by different needs and protocols of insurers and the Medicare programs, the CNO program gives physicians' offices a reprieve from coordinating community services by themselves.

AZ-5

Partners
L-GOV, FEDHLTH, FEDOTH, CLIN, SOM, U-OTH, FNDN

Synergies
1a, 3c, 4b, 4c, 5a, 6b-6, 6c-1

Structural Foundations
Coalition, Contract, Advisory

Contact
Hugh S. Fulmer, MD
Center for Community
Responsive Care, Inc.
90 Cushing Avenue
Boston, MA 02125
copc1@aol.com

Many Farms Clinic on Navajo Reservation

In 1952, an outbreak of infectious hepatitis in the Navajo Reservation led to a request for medical expertise from New York's Cornell University College of Medicine, which had conducted extensive research on the control and treatment of hepatitis. After the outbreak was contained, the consultant team was interested in continuing research and treatment in this Arizona community. The Department of Public Health and Preventive Medicine at Cornell was actively involved in the World Health Program and had developed, in collaboration with the Rockefeller Research Center, isoniazid as chemotherapy for tuberculosis. The Cornell team saw the Many Farms community as a similar environment to India, Africa, and other parts of the world: it had health problems, such as TB and dysentery, closely related to socioeconomic conditions, and a wide cultural gap in terms of acceptance of Western medical techniques. The high dysentery rate among the Navajo was reflected in an infant mortality rate of four times that of the general population and, in 1952, the rate of TB was ten times more prevalent among the Navajo than in the population at large. At this time, the Bureau of Indian Affairs began a Navajo Tuberculosis Control Program in three states, which led to Cornell's development of its pilot demonstration project, the Many Farms Clinic. The Many Farms Clinic project was conducted by faculty from Cornell's Medical College and its School of Nursing and included a team of physicians, field technicians, nurses, interpreters, and behavioral scientists. The Navajo Tribal Government was an active partner in the development of this program, with a physician-liaison, who was also a member of the Tribal Council, and endorsement by traditional healers. The demonstration project was expanded in 1955 when the Indian Health Service was transferred to the US

Public Health Service and lasted until 1960. Many of the techniques and procedures developed there have since become integrated in the Reservation health program, contributing to dramatic decreases in infant mortality and TB rates in Native Amer-ican populations. In 1980, infant mortality among Native Americans was 13.3/1000, comparing favorably to the national rate of 12.6 for all races, and a sharp decrease from the average rate of 85/1000 from 1954 to 1956. Similarly, TB rates dropped from an average of 896/100,000 in 1953 to 1955 to 10.3 in 1980.

Adair, J, Deuschle, K, and Barnett, C. 1988. *The people's health: medicine and anthropology in a Navajo community.* Albuquerque: University of New Mexico Press.

AZ-6
Partners
L-GOV, SHD, FEDHLTH, CLIN

Synergies
1c, 3b, 4b, 5b, 6b-5

Structural Foundations
Coalition

Contact
John R. Kittredge, MD
Tucson Area IHS
7900 South JJ Stock Road
Tucson, AZ 85746

Sells Indian Health Service Unit Domestic Violence Program

In 1996, the Sells Service Unit of the Indian Health Service (IHS), near Tucson, received a grant from the Arizona State Health Department to develop a comprehensive domestic violence program for the Tohono O'Odham Nation. The IHS Hospital's clinical director, nursing director, and emergency room (ER) nursing supervisor are working with the Tribal Department of Human Services to develop a program, which will be placed in the Tucson Center for Women and Children, as well as to gain community support for domestic violence programs in general. The Planning Committee, which includes a wide array of public health and medical specialists, is developing a detailed protocol for screening women about domestic violence. A routine screening procedure, which will be tried first in the ER and the well-child and prenatal clinics of the Service Unit will include a display that prompts the practitioner to ask particular screening questions and to annotate whether the questions were asked. Extensive staff training will be done to stress the importance of screening and to teach effective, culturally sensitive ways of discussing domestic violence in settings that lack privacy, like the ER. In addition, the Committee is creating patient information, such as "safety plan" pamphlets and small cards with phone-referral information.

AZ-7
Partners
MCO

Arizona Partnership for Infant Immunization

A local managed care plan, Pacificare, formerly FHP Health Care of Arizona, contributed staff members and resources to The Arizona Partnership for

Synergies
4c, 5b

Structural Foundations
Coalition

Contact
Geoff Jaroch
Pacificare
P.O. Box 52078
Phoeniz, AZ 85072
tapii@goodnet.com

Infant Immunization. The health plan assisted in the development of communications efforts, such as newsletters, on-line computer services, and brochures, that were designed to promote the importance of immunization for all children. Pacificare's involvement prompted other health plans to contribute personnel, time, and money to the immunization initiative. Over a period of several years, the immunization coverage rates have increased from 52% to 68% among private sector managed care plans in Arizona. Community outreach projects reminding physicians and parents about the importance of immunization are run twice yearly.

[CA] CALIFORNIA

CA-1
Partners
LHD, FEDHLTH, SPH

Synergies
4b, 5b, 6b-6, 6c-2

Structural Foundations
Contract

Contact
Donald Morisky, ScD, SCM, MSPH
Department of Community Health Sciences
UCLA School of Public Health
Box 951772
Los Angeles, CA 90095
dmorisky@ucla.edu

Los Angeles TB Control Research Study
In the early 1990s, students in an advanced community health education class at the UCLA School of Public Health were interested in TB control. The course professor met with the Director of TB Control for LA County and with two infectious disease doctors from the county clinics. As a group, they designed patient education strategies and incentives, and then initiated a randomized study to test the strategies' effectiveness in improving medication compliance and the rate of completion of care. The study, funded by the CDC, revealed significant improvement in compliance behavior, appointment-keeping behavior, and completion of care for those patients randomly assigned to the educational "treatment." Cost-effectiveness analysis further revealed significant reductions in cost; although the costs of the education intervention were higher, since greater numbers of patients completed their treatment, the overall cost to the health system was lower. The project since has developed visually appealing educational materials written in the dialect of local Hispanic males, their target population.

CA-2
Partners
LHD, MDPRAC, HOSP, CLIN, SOM, MEDSOC, FNDN

Synergies
2a, 2b, 2c

Sacramento SPIRIT Program
In the early 1990s, budgetary shortfalls and gaps in coverage for the uninsured within the district of the Sacramento County Health Department spurred the creation of a program called SPIRIT (Sacramento's Physicians Initiative to Reach out, Innovate and Teach)* that helps private physicians donate their time to provide care for the indigent. The pro-

Structural Foundations
Coalition, Adm/Mgmt

Contact
Glennah Trochet, MD
Sacramento County Clinics
Sacramento County
Department of Health and
Human Services
3701 Branch Center Road
Sacramento, CA 95827
gtrochet@ix.netcom.com

CA-3
Partners
LHD, FEDHLTH, MDPRAC, HOSP,
CLIN, MCO, U-OTH, SCHL

Synergies
2c, 3a, 6b-5, 6b-6

Structural Foundations
Coalition, Advisory

Contact
Mark Goodman, MD, FAAP
Long Beach Perinatal
Outreach Education
Program
4100 Long Beach
Boulevard, Suite 201
Long Beach, CA 90807
totsdoc@earthlink.net

ject is a collaboration of private health care institutions, the county health agency, a medical school, and a medical society. Rather than bear the burden of the county's uninsured population individually, the partners agreed to join forces and work with the Sacramento-El Dorado Medical Society to apply for a Robert Wood Johnson Foundation Reach Out grant, to create the program. SPIRIT's coordinating staff match volunteer physicians with uninsured patients at six active clinic sites, and refer patients to a participating specialty network. The program provides free services, including specialty care and surgery, with an estimated value of more than $1 million over a three-year period. One issue has been redefining the roles of the founding partners so that contributions are more equitable in terms of financial and operational impact. The SPIRIT program staff filed for incorporation, and it now operates as a stand-alone, not-for-profit organization.

Long Beach Perinatal Cultural Practices Work Group

Convened by a clinical social worker in 1995, the Perinatal Cultural Practice Work Group is a multidisciplinary and multicultural group of health professionals working on maternal and child health problems in the greater Long Beach area. It was initiated as a result of a needs assessment conducted in 1995 by the Long Beach Perinatal Outreach Education Program, a Regional Perinatal Program of California, supported in part by contracts with the California Department of Health Services' MCH Branch. Members share their professional expertise and differing perspectives in an informal setting, creating a platform to link the organizations and community groups its members represent and to enhance their own professional development. The Task Force has a resource library of research articles and community information, and works collaboratively on grant proposals. It also conducts training sessions on perinatal and maternal and child health issues, especially in regard to enhancing multicultural and linguistic awareness in health systems and community agencies.

CA-4

Partners
LHD, SHD, FEDHLTH, HOSP, CLIN, SOM, RES, AHC, VHO, BUS, MEDIA, FNDN

Synergies
5a, 5b

Structural Foundations
Coalition

Contact
Eliseo J. Perez-Stable, MD
Department of Medicine
University of California at
San Francisco
400 Parnassus Avenue
Room A405
San Francisco, CA 94143
eliseo_perez-stable@ucsf.edu

San Francisco Latino Health Education Campaign

The AHCPR Medical Effectiveness Research Center for Diverse Populations at the University of California at San Francisco's academic health center developed a community education and outreach campaign in 1993 to reach Latinos at risk for cancer. The program, funded through the National Cancer Institute and the National Hispanic Leadership Initiative on Cancer, *En Acción*, first worked with a community-based coalition to identify health behaviors that placed Latinos at risk for breast, cervical, colorectal, prostate, and skin cancers. The coalition then worked with community organizations and small businesses to train volunteer and lay staff workers, produce a media campaign that included print, radio, and TV ads targeting the Spanish-speaking population, and conduct health fairs in Latino neighborhoods. Researchers at the medical school are conducting a cohort study to evaluate the effectiveness of such a community outreach and education campaign.

CA-5

Partners
LHD, L-GOV, FEDHLTH, MDPRAC, MEDSOC, BUS, SCHL, RELIG, C-OTH

Synergies
4c

Structural Foundations
Adm/Mgmt

Contact
Mark Strausberg, PhD
County of Los Angeles
Department of
Health Services
313 N. Figueroa
Los Angeles, CA 90012

Los Angeles Team Immunize

The most recent measles epidemic in Los Angeles led to 38 deaths and 1,800 hospitalizations between 1989 and 1991. Given the extent of such mortality and morbidity, health care providers in Los Angeles were receptive to a community-wide campaign to vaccinate all children. In response to a CDC-funded immunization initiative, the county health department organized the Team Immunize campaign in 1996, a project co-sponsored by the County Board of Supervisors and the county medical association. Over 175 health care providers were recruited to provide free immunizations at a variety of sites throughout the city on Monday evenings and Saturday mornings over a two-month period. The health department organized the recruitment and distribution of vaccines to the providers at private medical practices, clinics, hospitals, churches, community agencies, and schools. As part of the campaign, the county mounted a massive publicity campaign to reach the estimated 300,000 children under six years of age who needed one or more immunizations. All the health care providers who participated in the campaign were recognized for their volunteer efforts.

CA-6

Partners
MDPRAC, SOM, SPH, U-OTH,
MEDSOC, PROFASSN, RELIG,
MEDIA, C-OTH

Synergies
5b, 5c

Structural Foundations
Coalition, Adm/Mgmt,
Advisory

Contact
Ruth Roemer, JD
UCLA School of
Public Health
405 Hildegard Avenue
Los Angeles, CA 90095

California Committee on Therapeutic Abortion

In 1964, a group of physicians, lawyers, clergy, educators, and representative of women's organizations formed the California Committee on Therapeutic Abortion (CCTA) to inform and educate the public concerning the value of therapeutic abortion and its relationship to family welfare. The group prepared and distributed educational literature, conducted public opinion surveys, and supported research into the extent of criminal abortion and its effect on maternal health, family welfare, and the administration of justice in California. To carry out these functions, CCTA began its educational work by mobilizing statements signed by hundreds of medical school deans, obstetricians, gynecologists, pediatricians, lawyers, judges, social scientists, clergy, and other groups, each establishing the perspective of the particular profession on illegal abortion and the need for changing the law. CCTA's advocacy efforts contributed to the enactment of California's Therapeutic Abortion Act of 1967, prior to the 1973 US Supreme Court decision of Roe v. Wade.

CA-7

Partners
LHD, MDPRAC, HOSP, CLIN,
LAB/RX, SOM, MEDSOC, BUS,
FNDN

Synergies
2b

Structural Foundations
Adm/Mgmt

Contact
Tina Ahn, MBA
Operation Access
1409 Sutter Street
San Francisco, CA 94109
operaccess@aol.com

San Francisco Operation Access

In 1994 in the San Francisco Bay Area, a group of surgeons from nonprofit and university hospitals created Operation Access, a nonprofit corporation providing free surgical services to uninsured patients. With funding from The Robert Wood Johnson Foundation's Reach Out Program, Operation Access hired an executive director and coordinator and recruited other volunteer surgeons, nurses, and anesthesiologists. Using the leverage of physician leadership within the hospitals, the organization—which presently includes 7 hospitals and over 100 volunteers—has improved access to outpatient surgery for low-income uninsured patients.

CA-8

Partners
LHD, SOM

Synergies
6b-4

Structural Foundations
Informal

Yolo County Public Health Education for Medical Students

This case is a historical recollection by a "boundary-spanning" physician who was director of the Yolo County health department, as well as an alumnus of the UC-Berkeley School of Public Health and a clinical professor of community health at the UC-Davis School of Medicine. He arranged to have various members of his county health department participate in teaching medical students,

Contact
Herbert Bauer, MD, MPH
Community Health
UC-Davis School
of Medicine
831 Oeste Drive
Davis, CA 95616

CA-9
Partners
LHD, L-GOV, HOSP, CLIN, MCO,
SCHL, FNDN, C-OTH

Synergies
1a, 1c, 2a, 3b, 5a, 5b, 5e

Structural Foundations
Coalition, Adm/Mgmt

Contact
Gary A. Melton
Riverside County Health
Services Agency
4065 County Circle Drive
Riverside, CA 92503
hsa.health1gmelton@co.
riverside.ca.us

and he also enlisted medical students to come to the health department and participate in a variety of public health activities. There was no formal program or contract. The physician recalled that the purpose of such cross-pollination was to demonstrate that medicine and public health had common goals, principally to improve the health of both individuals and populations.

Jurupa Community Partnership
Noticing that a high percentage of students were staying home because of illness, and speculating that this was ill health was also a source of discipline problems, the principal of the Van Buren Elementary School in Jurupa sought to address the connection between the health of school children and their ability to succeed in school. In this low-income, rural community, availability of health services is limited and there is no public transportation or community hospital. The result is poor health of many school children and overuse of emergency room services—both of which could be avoided with primary and preventive care. In 1992, the principal sought to bring additional health and social services to her students and their families by founding the Jurupa Community Partnership, a collaboration of the Riverside County Health Services Agency, the county Department of Public Social Services, the Youth Services Center (a medical provider), and the YMCA. A CCN demonstration partnership funded by the W.K. Kellogg Foundation, the coalition established a school-based health center which uses case management and public health nursing to coordinate care across agencies, across health and social problems, and between the school clinic and home. The Partnership is also working on improving access to other health facilities by running a transportation van, creating a resource list in English and Spanish, and distributing a comprehensive resource directory for community schools. Financial access to health care is also a community concern, and Inland Empire Health Plan, a Medi-Cal full-service, capitated managed care plan, joined the Partnership with an initiative to cover immunizations and well-baby health screenings for the broader community.

CA-10
Partners
LHD, HOSP, VHO, BUS, SCHL,
RELIG, FNDN, C-OTH

El Dorado Divide Wellness Partnership
In the Georgetown Divide, a rural area with high rates of unemployment and poverty, the Divide Wellness Partnership (a CCN demonstration part-

Synergies
1b, 2a, 2b, 5a, 5b, 5e

Structural Foundations
Coalition, Contract,
Adm/Mgmt, Advisory

Contact
Gayle Erbe-Hamlin
El Dorado County Public
Health Department
931 Spring Street
Placerville, CA 95667
gehamlin@innercite.com

CA-11
Partners
LHD, SHD, MDPRAC, LAB/RX,
MEDSOC, PHASSN, PROFASSN,
VHO, C-OTH

Synergies
3a, 4b, 5b, 5c, 5d, 6b-5,
6b-6

Structural Foundations
Adm/Mgmt, Advisory

Contact
Carolina S. Abuelo
Health Partnership Project
California Medical
Association
P.O. Box 7690
Suite 207
San Francisco, CA 94120
cabuelo@calmed.org

nership funded by the W.K. Kellogg Foundation) evolved out of several efforts by key organizations in the area (the local health department, Marshall Hospital, the Divide Community Service Network, and the school district) to gauge and address health problems in the community. A community health assessment revealed that inadequate access to health services and a high need for social services were among the community's top health concerns. The Partnership developed, outfitted, and staffed the Divide Wellness Center using grants and in-kind support of staff, material, and cash. The Center, opened in 1994, is a one-stop location for a wide array of health and social services, including primary and urgent care, case management, preventive and dental screenings, referrals for specialty care, drug/alcohol abuse treatment, and outreach services, such as home visiting. The Center also functions as a community center with parenting and health education, community forums and breakfasts, and it has been "adopted" by many local groups—the Boy/Girl Scouts help maintain the grounds while the local art society has decorated the halls with works of local artists.

California Anti-Tobacco Use
Pharmacy Partnership
The Pharmacy Partnership, created in 1995, is dedicated to reducing the number of pharmacies that sell tobacco products in California; it is supported by funding from the Tobacco Tax Health Protection Act of 1988 (Proposition 99, described in CA-15). A coalition of the California Medical Association, the California Department of Health Services, the California Pharmacists Association and several academic, research, and advocacy centers, the Partnership has developed a comprehensive educational manual for pharmacists, newsletters, in-store posters, and counter-tobacco advertising, all aimed at discouraging tobacco use and sales. Though the goal is to eliminate tobacco sales completely in pharmacies, the Partnership promotes interim steps such as increasing patient counseling on tobacco cessation, reducing pharmacy tobacco sales to minors, reducing open availability of tobacco, and eliminating tobacco promotions or advertising in pharmacies. The Partnership tracks several trends related to tobacco promotions within California and nationally and uses the statistics for education and advocacy. Some findings indicate that chain drug stores are far more likely to carry to-

bacco products than are independents and that they are far less interested in becoming tobacco-free. A 1996 survey of independent pharmacies on policies and attitudes about tobacco sales, commissioned under the Partnership, indicated that 36% of pharmacies have stopped selling tobacco recently (with 88% reporting no change or an increase in business), and over half of the pharmacists whose stores still sell tobacco were interested in strategies to discontinue sales. The Partnership has links to the American Cancer Society, the American Heart Association, and the American Lung Association as well as several community-based organizations, and it refers pharmacists to these organizations to obtain further support of their tobacco cessation efforts at the local level.

CA-12

Partners
LHD, L-GOV, SHD, S-GOV, FEDOTH, MDPRAC, HOSP, CLIN, MCO, SOM, SPH, AHC, U-OTH, MEDSOC, PHASSN, PROFASSN, VHO

Synergies
4c, 6b-5

Structural Foundations
Coalition, Advisory

Contact
Sarah Royce, MD
Tuberculosis
Control Branch
California Department of
Health Services
2151 Berkeley Way
Room 608
Berkeley, CA 94704
sroyce@hw1.cahwnet.gov

California Tuberculosis Elimination Task Force

After decades of decline, TB rates rose in the early 1990s, and California led the nation in the number of reported cases. To deal with the epidemic, the California State Health Department, the California Tuberculosis Controllers Association, and the American Lung Association convened the California Tuberculosis Elimination Task Force in 1992. This broad-based coalition, which represented state and local government, provider groups, public health agencies, volunteer organizations, and affected constituencies, created a detailed strategic plan and action agenda for TB control and elimination over three years. The Strategic Plan identifies five key areas for improvement: (1) to increase and improve identification and reporting of TB; (2) to ensure that all TB patients receive early, appropriate, and complete treatment; (3) to prevent TB infection from becoming overt disease; (4) to develop, implement and evaluate measures to control TB transmission; and (5) to improve TB education of health care providers, policymakers, and communities at risk. The Task Force's Action Agenda outlines specific activities in each of the improvement areas. For each activity, a lead agency is identified, key actions for each partnering organization are outlined (including possible ways to link these activities), and recommendations are made as to how the state health department can best implement and evaluate TB control efforts. Each year the coalition has re-committed itself to the public-private partnership, updating its TB Control Priorities and Action Steps.

CA-13

Partners
LHD, SHD, MDPRAC, HOSP, CLIN, MCO, SOM, ARC, AHC, MEDSOC, PROFASSN, VHO, BUS

Synergies
3a, 4b, 4c, 5b, 6a-3, 6a-4

Structural Foundations
Coalition, Advisory

Contact
Ann Albright, PhD, RN
Division of Chronic Disease
and Injury Control
California Department of
Health Services, Diabetes
Control Program
601 North Seventh Street
P.O. Box 942732
Mailstop 725
Sacramento, CA 94234
annalb@itsa.ucsf.edu

California Diabetes Control Program Coalition

An NIH study released in the early 1990s demonstrated that tight control of blood glucose can bring measurable reductions in the microvascular complications of diabetes. In response, the Diabetes Control Program (DCP) of the California State Department of Health Services convened interest groups from academia, voluntary organizations, medical associations, and patient groups to pursue a vigorous implementation program for prevention and control of diabetes. Convened initially as an advisory group to the state in 1993, the members of the Diabetes Coalition of California soon voted to become an independent body. Their first activity was to work with DCP collaboratively to develop uniform state guidelines for the primary care of diabetes and then to use the Coalition's broad representation to actively market the guidelines around the state to providers, purchasers, and insurers. The Coalition and the DCP also have developed a strategic plan through the year 2000 that lists specific health goals, objectives, and activities to improve service delivery, increase awareness, and create advocacy opportunities. This collaboration benefits from its diverse membership and its foundation in strong science.

CA-14

Partners
LHD, L-GOV, SHD, S-GOV, MDPRAC, HOSP, CLIN, U-OTH, MEDSOC, VHO, BUS, SCHL, MEDIA

Synergies
5d

Structural Foundations
Coalition, Advisory

Contact
Donald O. Lyman, MD
Division of Chronic Disease
and Injury Control
California Department of
Health Services
601 North Seventh Street
P.O. Box 942732
Mailstop 504
Sacramento, CA 94234
dlyman@pacbell.net

California Governor's Council on Physical Fitness and Sports

The Governor of California asked movie celebrity Arnold Schwarzenegger, who had been chair of the President's Council, to set up a Governor's Council on Physical Fitness and Sports. Together, they were able to attract a wide range of participants, such as sports figures, fitness celebrities, and representatives from medicine, public health, and community organizations to the Council. At the same time, the release of data strengthening the connection between physical activity and reductions in cardiovascular disease served to increase interest among the professional community in promoting sports. In 1995, the Council produced a draft report outlining strategies and activities that were being implemented on a community level to encourage physical activity and to improve diet and nutrition. Though the activities are only loosely coordinated, they are taking place throughout the state and are targeted to a wide range of people, including youth, the elderly, employees, and several ethnic groups particularly at-risk for disease. The Coalition also is interested in measuring results and has tied each community-based activity to a Healthy Californians Year 2000 objective.

CA-15
Partners
LHD, L-GOV, SHD, S-GOV, MEDSOC, PHASSN, VHO, LABR, SCHL, RELIG, C-OTH

Synergies
5a, 5b, 5c, 5d

Structural Foundations
Coalition, Advisory

Contact
Donald O. Lyman, MD
Division of Chronic Disease and Injury Prevention
California Department of Health Services
601 North Seventh Street
P.O. Box 942732
Mailstop 504
Sacramento, CA 94234
dlyman@pacbell.net

California Tobacco Control Coalition and Proposition 99

The California Tobacco Control Program is a case of political trade-offs, with differing opinions as to how well the collaboration served medicine and public health partnerships. In 1985, the California State Department of Health Services convened a Cancer Control Planning Group, which subsequently became an independent Tobacco Control Coalition. The Coalition, which had representatives from the state medical association, local and state health departments, and voluntary health associations (American Cancer Society, American Lung Association, American Heart Association among others), lobbied for Proposition 99 as a voter-referendum to increase tobacco taxes (by 25 cents per pack), and the measure was enacted. The referendum designated 20% of the funds to health education and 5% to research, with the remaining 75% going to indigent medical care. With a major economic downturn at this time, the state government removed an additional sum for indigent care from the health education allocation. This action was opposed by the voluntary associations and public health advocates, but supported by the state medical association. The contentious disagreement continued until after an economic recovery when court action forced the return of the health education funds. The return was supported by the state medical association. Nonetheless, the anti-smoking education campaigns that were funded have been innovative and successful (CA-11), easing some of the tensions between public health interests and medical care advocates. Moreover, from 1989 to 1997, California had a 42% reduction in cigarette consumption, and a 32% reduction in smoking prevalence. Environmental exposure was also reduced by the enactment of state laws barring smoking in restaurants and workplaces, and by nearly 90% compliance with a voluntary initiative for families with children under 18 to adopt a "no smoking in the house" policy. The Tobacco Control Program is continuing its activities of ongoing tobacco use assessment, mass media and community campaigns, and health promotion strategies targeting different settings (school, work and public places), and diverse cultural groups.

Novotny, TE and Siegel, MB. 1996. *California's tobacco control saga. Health Affairs.* 15(1):59–72.

CA-16

Partners
SHD, MEDSOC

Synergies
4a

Structural Foundations
Informal

Contact
Lester Breslow, MD, MPH
Department of
Health Services
UCLA School of
Public Health
Room 21253
Los Angeles, CA 90024
breslow@ucla.edu

California Tumor Registry

The California State Department of Health proposed the establishment of a Tumor Registry in 1947, one of the first in the nation. The registry was predicated on physicians reporting specific tumors found in their cancer patients so that public health officials and researchers could document the incidence of these cancers and take action. Interestingly, when the idea of the registry was first promoted, it coincided with a proposal by Governor Earl Warren for universal state health insurance. The California Medical Association, whose endorsement of the registry was critical to its success, at first perceived the registry as a ruse to steal cancer patients for "state doctors." When the state universal insurance proposal died, the medical association reconsidered the registry and ultimately lent its full support and endorsement. The association encouraged leading physicians in key hospitals to approve establishing registries, and such an endorsement proved essential in the development of a statewide system.

CA-17

Partners
MDPRAC, HOSP, MCO, C-OTH

Synergies
3c, 5e

Structural Foundations
Coalition, Adm/Mgmt,
Advisory, Intraorg

Contact
See citation

Kaiser Permanente Community Health Partnership Department

The Kaiser Permanente Northern California Region created a Community Health Partnership (CHP) department in 1989, coinciding with a number of other community efforts in Solano County to resuscitate a primary care clinic on the brink of closure (CA-21). Since access to care and reimbursement for health care services were two key issues affecting primary care in the community, the CHP department began by designing a Medicaid managed care health plan. The CHP department sought input from local physicians, providers, and managers. In addition, the CHP department became the senior partner in a Healthy Communities effort, the Solano Coalition for Better Health (CA-21). The CHP department was responsible for the coalition's initial organization, and has provided resources and personnel to the ongoing administration and operation of coalition activities.

American Association of Health Plans. 1996. *Improving the quality of life in local communities.* Washington, DC.

CA-18
Partners
MCO

Synergies
1b

Structural Foundations
Intraorg

Contact
See citation

Kaiser Permanente Counseling and Learning Center

After the divisive 1966 riots in the Los Angeles community of Watts, a local HMO developed a Counseling and Learning Center to assist children and their families in overcoming educational and psychological barriers. The Kaiser Permanente Counseling and Learning Center developed school outreach services, group and individual therapy programs, preschool and after-school education programs, summer camp programs, educational remediation, SAT preparation, and a Youth Work Preparation Certificate Program that helps high school students make the transition from student to employee. The community center is open to everyone, not only HMO members. Kaiser Permanente provides resources, direction, and guidance to the center, and in over 30 years has allocated over $19 million in direct budget support.

American Association of Health Plans. 1996. *Improving the quality of life in local communities.* Washington, DC.

CA-19
Partners
S-GOV, MCO, VHO, RELIG, C-OTH

Synergies
1c, 4c, 5b

Structural Foundations
Coalition

Contact
See citation

South Central Los Angeles Flu Campaign

The 1993 rate of influenza vaccination among California's Medicare beneficiaries was only 26%, compared with a national rate of 35%. Even more disturbing, the rates of vaccinated African-American seniors were half those of white, non-Hispanic seniors. The California Peer Review Organization (PRO) approached a local HMO in South Central Los Angeles, United Health Plan, to develop a community-wide plan to increase flu vaccination and decrease flu-related morbidity and mortality. Compounding the problems in South Central Los Angeles were the lack of local health care facilities, residents' dependency on public bus transportation, and the constant threat of violence that caused many seniors to barricade themselves in their homes. The HMO made available its provider network in South Central Los Angeles and its mobile health units; developed community and education activities with such local organizations as churches and senior centers; and provided no-cost transportation services to seniors. The HMO also instituted a toll-free "Flu Hotline" staffed by community workers to help facilitate the vaccinations. As the two lead agencies, the PRO and the HMO enlisted the help of a wide range of community organizations and public and private agencies in the campaign. To publicize the vaccination effort, the group developed a media campaign that aired on local radio and television stations.

American Association of Health Plans. 1996. *Improving the quality of life in local communities.* Washington, DC.

CA-20
Partners
LHD, L-GOV, HOSP, MCO, VHO, BUS

Synergies
6a-1

Structural Foundations
Coalition

Contact
See citation

San Francisco Health Summit
In August 1996, San Francisco Mayor Willie Brown convened a "health summit" of policymakers, local media, health care providers, and community leaders to consider alternative solutions to a variety of pressing health issues. The problems facing the public health system included a high HIV/AIDS incidence rate, high substance abuse rates, significant numbers of people with serious mental illness, the second highest rate of homelessness in the country, and a 16% uninsured rate. The city also faced a huge increase in the number of uninsured residents as a consequence of the federal welfare reform act, which would add 26,000 legal immigrants to the ranks of the uninsured. Attendees at the health summit explored a number of possible strategies, including a voluntary, citywide government-managed health insurance plan; tax incentives to lure small businesses into city-run health programs; and efforts to promote San Francisco General Hospital's programs to city workers in order to attract more "paying" clients.

Health Commission of San Francisco. 1996. *Focusing on the community.* Report to The Robert Wood Johnson Foundation Board. San Francisco, CA.

CA-21
Partners
LHD, L-GOV, MDPRAC, HOSP, CLIN, MCO, BUS, SCHL, FNDN

Synergies
1c, 5e

Structural Foundations
Coalition

Contact
See citation

Solano County Coalition for Better Health
In 1989, when a primary care clinic that served many of Solano County's uninsured was about to close, a small group of physicians, government officials, and hospital administrators came together to stave off the closure. Concerned about bearing the costs of delayed medical care, lack of prevention services, and overuse of hospital ER services, the partners all contributed to preserve the clinic, and formed the Solano Coalition for Better Health. The Coalition (a CCN demonstration partnership funded by the W.K. Kellogg Foundation) created the Solano Partnership Healthplan in 1994 as a countywide system of managed care serving 45,000 Medi-Cal enrollees and involving virtually all the county's primary care providers. In addition to expanding existing primary care clinics and opening new community-based clinics, the Health-

plan has used its network of providers and sites to foster appropriate use and continuation of care. One example is a system of cooperation in four hospital emergency rooms to re-direct patients requiring routine care to a primary care provider and to stabilize those with acute conditions and refer them to appropriate follow-up care. The Coalition partnered with Kaiser Permanente on two other projects: The Healthy Vacaville Task Force, a coalition that has created a community dental clinic, re-routed city buses for more efficient access to medical and social services, and translated educational materials into Spanish; and a Community Health Outreach System in which teams of four community health outreach workers headed by a public health nurse make home visits, conduct assessments, and assist families in accessing services and over-coming barriers.

Bogue, R and Hall, Jr, CH, eds. 1997. *Health networks innovations: how 20 communities are improving their system through collaboration.* Chicago: American Hospital Publishing, Inc.

CA-22

Partners
LHD, L-GOV, MDPRAC, HOSP, CLIN, VHO, FNDN, C-OTH

Synergies
1c, 4c, 5a, 5d

Structural Foundations
Coalition, Contract

Contact
See citation

Community Health Plan of Siskiyous

Access to medical care is a critical community need in the remote mountains of Siskiyou County, an area which has large numbers of uninsured and underinsured "working poor," and a scarcity of health professionals. The Community Care Partnership of the Siskiyous (recognized as a CCN finalist partnership by the W.K. Kellogg Foundation) joins two community planning groups—the Community Health Plan and the Health Services Council—and the two medical providers of the region—the Mt. Shasta Medi-Cal Clinic and the Mercy Medical Center Mt. Shasta. Together, they are: (1) developing a local health plan designed to reduce health insurance costs for local employers; (2) expanding access to health care and preventive screening for low-income residents; and (3) designing a care plan for elderly in the community that includes building an assisted living complex with a geriatric clinic and coordination with community services. In addition to expanding medical access and services to the poor, these projects represent employment opportunities for the community and grant opportunities for community service providers. The Partnership is also involved in a wide range of community health promotion activities, including health, fitness, and social programs for the elderly and a newspaper health column. Clinical health promotion activities include, community-wide immunization campaigns and comprehensive prenatal care and new baby services for pregnant teens.

Bogue, R and Hall, Jr, CH, eds. 1997. *Health networks innovations: how 20 communities are improving their system through collaboration.* Chicago: American Hospital Publishing, Inc.

[CO] COLORADO

CO-1
Partners
L-GOV, S-GOV, CLIN, SOM, RES, AHC

Synergies
2c, 5d, 6a-1, 6b-3, 6b-4

Structural Foundations
Contract

Contact
James H. Shore, MD
Department of Psychiatry
University of Colorado
Health Sciences Center
4200 East 9th Avenue
C-249-32
Denver, CO 80262
j.shore@uchsc.edu

Colorado Program for Public Psychiatry

A major focus of the state/university collaborations (NAT-20) has been providing services and manpower from the university to the public mental health system. But these collaborations can also provide valuable educational experiences to the university and its students. Created in 1987, the Program for Public Psychiatry is a collaboration founded upon a 25-year relationship between the Department of Psychiatry at the University of Colorado Health Sciences Center and the Colorado Division of Mental Health. The partnership addressed severe manpower shortages in the 1980s, allowing the state to fully staff two public hospitals and most of its urban community mental health centers. The collaboration also helps fund the research and educational mission of the university, creating new faculty positions and allowing the expansion of programs in forensic psychiatry, developmental disabilities, and child/adolescent psychiatry. The partnership created a required rotation for senior residents in the community mental health centers (CMHCs), a didactic course in public psychiatry, and a protocol for structured supervision of the residents. The relatively low-cost resident workforce allowed the CMHCs to offer community-based programs for underserved groups, such as battered women and prisoners, outreach to the chronically mentally ill, and culture-specific mental health programs. The collaboration has had an impact beyond the immediate program. Psychiatric careers in the public sector now seem a viable career choice to young physicians, psychiatric recruitment and retention have improved and stabilized in all areas of the public sector, and this collaboration is serving as a model for state/university collaborations in other areas of service.

Neligh, G, et al. 1991. The Program for Public Psychiatry: state-university collaboration in Colorado. *Hospital and Community Psychiatry.* 42(1):44–48.

[CT] CONNECTICUT

CT-1

Partners
LHD, L-GOV, HOSP, CLIN, MCO, U-OTH, VHO, BUS, SCHL, RELIG, MEDIA, FNDN, C-OTH

Synergies
1c, 3b, 5a, 5b, 5d, 5e, 6b-6

Structural Foundations
Coalition, Adm/Mgmt

Contact
William C. Powanda
Support Services
Griffin Hospital
130 Division Street
Derby, CT 06418
bpowanda@aol.com

Derby Healthy Valley 2000

Healthy Valley 2000, based in Derby, evolved from a 50-member coalition of health and human services organizations in a six-town region of Southern Connecticut. Led by a hospital/health system, Healthy Valley 2000 has a mission to identify and address broad determinants of the community's health. One of the group's first efforts was to conduct a number of research projects, including a community economic and social profile, a health profile, and a survey of the area's perceived needs. Based on this work, the coalition proposed six major areas in which to collaborate: arts and recreation development; economic development; a community involvement campaign (including voter registration, a community calendar, and a volunteer action center); health campaigns (including assessments and screenings, youth smoking-cessation programs, and centralized intake and referral services); education efforts (including a school-business partnership model); and an Internet information and communication system for the community. The political "weight" of this coalition, anchored as it is by a large hospital/health system, has contributed to its success. The coalition has attracted over $300,000 in external funding, developed an office to provide administrative support to the coalition, and has elicited substantial endorsements and commitments from political and community leaders.

CT-2

Partners
CLIN, SOM, SPH, AHC, U-OTH, VHO, C-OTH

Synergies
2a, 5b, 6b-3, 6b-4

Structural Foundations
Coalition, Adm/Mgmt, Advisory

Yale Community Services Program

In the late 1980s, a number of Yale medical students, chiefly in their first two years, organized a volunteer service program directed at the urban community surrounding the school. A student coordinator position was established in 1991, and by 1992, virtually all first- and second-year medical students participated in the volunteer community service programs. Given the students' interest, and the interest of students in other health professions schools at Yale—public health, graduate nursing,

Contact
Myron Genel, MD
Office of Government and
Community Affairs
Yale University School
of Medicine
P.O. Box 208000
New Haven, CT 06520
myron.genel@yale.edu

and a physicians assistant program—an advisory committee of students, faculty, and administrators from all the schools was established in 1993. The committee oversees a variety of programs. Examples include: an anatomy teaching program in which local high school seniors observe medical students' dissections; the Buddies Just for Kids program, in which Yale students act as navigators and companions for pediatric patients; HOPE, a collaborative effort of all the health professions schools to provide health care and education at homeless shelters; and prenatal care and AIDS projects. Among the challenges the committee is striving to address: how to accommodate new programs arising from community needs assessments and requests; how to foster greater interaction among the students from the different health professions schools; and how to evaluate the community impact of each project.

CT-3
Partners
LHD, SHD, FEDHLTH, MDPRAC,
HOSP, LAB/RX, SOM, AHC,
U-OTH, VHO, BUS, SCHL, MEDIA,
C-OTH

Synergies
4c

Structural Foundations
Coalition

Contact
Nancy C. Sheehan
MD, MPH, FACPM
University of Connecticut
Student Health Services
234 Glenbrook Road
Box U-11
Storrs, CT 06269
nsheehan@shs.heal.uconn.
edu

University of Connecticut Response to a Meningococcal Outbreak

In May 1993, a meningococcal outbreak (three confirmed cases of serogroup C) among University of Connecticut (UConn) students led to the rapid-response mobilization of state, federal, university, and community resources to conduct a massive three-day vaccination program. Targeting over 17,000 people in a short time frame (the week before final exams), this effort, which was the largest of this kind ever in the state, employed medical and support staff from the Red Cross, UConn Health Center, local hospitals, nursing homes, and the private medical community. Volunteers from the community, local businesses, and local media also contributed, with local radio and TV stations donating air time to publicize the effort. Staff from the state and local health departments, CDC, and Student Health Services worked together to locate sufficient vaccines and supplies, to work out logistics of the three-day event, and to control panic with a telephone hotline and by informed discussions with local and university press. The program reached over 70% of the target population, vaccinating nearly 12,000 people over the three days without medical complications or other major incident.

CT-4

Partners
LHD, L-GOV, SHD, S-GOV,
FEDOTH, HOSP, MCO, INS,
U-OTH, VHO, BUS, SCHL, RELIG,
MEDIA, FNDN, C-OTH

Synergies
5b, 5d, 6a-2

Structural Foundations
Coalition, Adm/Mgmt,
Advisory

Contact
Flora Parisky
The Hartford Action Plan
on Infant Health, Inc.
Breaking the Cycle
30 Arbor Street
Hartford, CT 06106
pariskygrp@aol.com

Hartford Breaking the Cycle

In Hartford, the teenage pregnancy statistics are distressing: in 1993, three girls gave birth for every two that graduated from high school, and Hartford's percentage of births to teens, at 23%, was one of the highest in the nation. The Hartford Action Plan on Infant Health (HAP) was created in 1985 when public and private health and social service providers, school and city government, and community and corporate leaders organized to address the root causes of teen pregnancy in their community. Since this health problem is often connected to poverty, abuse, and lack of opportunity, HAP (recognized as a CCN finalist partnership by the W.K. Kellogg Foundation) stresses community-based approaches with emphasis on early intervention, adult involvement, and leadership. HAP, working with the city of Hartford, the Board of Education, and more than 30 community organizations, has developed a five-year citywide program called Breaking the Cycle (BTC) to reduce teen pregnancy rates. The program has worked to define teen pregnancy as a health priority, which enhances the city's ability to receive federal funds, and has helped reinstate arts and music funding in schools. Another intervention is a school-based health education curriculum, known as Postponing Sexual Involvement, which has been tested nationally and found to be effective, that will be given to all Hartford fifth graders. BTC also has a consortium of more than 40 agencies that have agreed to use "best practices" concepts in their prevention programs. The consortium members have committed to implement the provider reimbursement recommendations from a work group of medical providers and insurance payers that relate to health care services for sexually active youth. Coincident with implementation of these efforts, Hartford's teen pregnancy rate decreased to 19.9% in 1997, the lowest figure for the city in 17 years.

[DC] DISTRICT OF COLUMBIA

DC-1

Partners
FEDHLTH, MDPRAC, CLIN, RES,
U-OTH, VHO, SCHL, RELIG,
MEDIA, FNDN, C-OTH

Synergies
2a, 3b, 4c, 5a, 5b, 5d

Mount Pleasant Oral Health Promotion Campaign

In the mid-1990s, a team of public health dental researchers and dental hygienists joined with a Latino community-based organization and several local dentists to organize a dental health promotion campaign in response to a funding opportunity of-

Structural Foundations
Coalition, Adm/Mgmt

Contact
Maria-Rosa Watson
DDS, MS, MPH
Pediatric Dentistry
University of Maryland at
Baltimore Dental School
666 West Baltimore Street
Baltimore, MD 21201
mwatson@umaryland.edu

fered by Oral Health America. The partners' goal was to improve oral health behaviors in the largely Hispanic community of Mount Pleasant by targeting an oral health campaign at mothers and their preschool children. Additional funding was obtained through donations from community groups and dentists, including raffle prizes, toothbrushes, fluorides and sealant material, educational material, and radio and television air time. A community-organized steering committee guided the development of culturally and linguistically appropriate interventions. After conducting a baseline survey to determine the community's oral health knowledge, attitudes, and practices, the researchers designed a series of community interventions: health fairs and screenings, the training of youth health promoters, a multimedia campaign, and a free sealant and fluoride clinic, among others. Based on early evaluations, the pilot project demonstrated the effectiveness of such a community approach in addressing communities not reached by traditional dental care and oral health promotion initiatives.

DC-2
Partners
LHD, SHD, FEDHLTH, FEDOTH,
MDPRAC, HOSP, CLIN, SPH,
MEDSOC, PHASSN, BUS, MEDIA

Synergies
4c, 5c, 5d, 6a-6, 6b-5, 6b-6

Structural Foundations
Coalition, Advisory

Contact
Shay Thomas
Medical Society of the
District of Columbia
(MSDC)
2215 M Street
Washington, DC 20037
thomas@msdc.org

Medical Society Council on Grassroots and Community Activities

The Medical Society of the District of Columbia (MSDC) and its Council on Grassroots and Community Activities (formerly Public Health Committee) have a longstanding relationship with the health department, and the two organizations work on collaborative health initiatives approximately two or three times a year. Two major efforts are a childhood immunization program and a Tuberculosis Prevention Task Force, which was co-chaired by one of the past presidents of the medical society and the health department's Bureau of TB Control. Work is evenly shared in these joint projects, with the MSDC doing administrative management and providing physician and medical student volunteers, while the DOH provides other resources, such as medical supplies and, in some cases, the site facilities for the projects. Other collaborative efforts of these organizations focus on health care in correctional facilities, smoking cessation, brain and spinal cord injuries, and legislative support. The primary goal of these projects is to improve awareness about a particular health concern through education and, secondarily, to build stronger ties between public and private organizations.

[DE] DELAWARE

DE-1
Partners
SHD, S-GOV, FEDHLTH, MDPRAC

Synergies
3a, 6a-1, 6a-3, 6b-5, 6b-6

Structural Foundations
Coalition, Advisory

Contact
Jo Ann Baker
MSN, FNP
Division of Public Health
Delaware Department of
Health and Human Services
P.O. Box 637
Dover, DE 19903
jobaker@state.de.us

Delaware Providers' Partnership
Initiated following a meeting hosted by the American College of Obstetricians and Gynecologists (ACOG) and supported in part by a grant from the federal Maternal and Child Health Bureau (NAT-6), the Delaware Partnership was formed in 1995. Within the Partnership, the Delaware Division of Public Health works with private OB/GYN providers and hospitals to enhance education, information, and support services to pregnant women. The Partnership created a physician education program geared directly for obstetricians and gynecologists, which shared information on services included in the Medicaid managed care plans, on other available wraparound services, and on the best ways to effectively use both types of services in their practices. Subsequent meetings of the Partnership also aided important policy changes. Pregnant women covered within Medicaid managed care can now "self-refer" and go directly to an OB/GYN practitioner without a primary care referral, and the state Medicaid office has approved presumptive eligibility for uninsured pregnant women to facilitate early prenatal care.

[FL] FLORIDA

FL-1
Partners
LHD, L-GOV, HOSP, CLIN

Synergies
3c, 4a, 4b

Structural Foundations
Contract

Contact
Peter Thornton, MPH
Volusia County
Health Department
1350 S. Woodland
Boulevard
DeLand, FL 32720
ehvolco@aol.com

Volusia County Geomapping Data Exchange
In Volusia County, the health department needed clinical data from local hospitals, oncology centers, and clinics in order to analyze the relationship between social and environmental risk factors with particular health outcomes at a neighborhood level. The health department was already geomapping data on contaminants, soils, groundwater, and utilities, but needed comprehensive patient data. In 1996, the health department's environmental administrator arranged with the participating institutions for the clinical information, and in return agreed to provide sophisticated geographic mappings of its partners' patient and population demographics. The health department included information from other sectors in its analysis as well, such as domestic violence data from the sheriff's department and juvenile justice data. In exchange for their clinical data, the hospitals and clinics received the geomapped data services without having to invest in geographic information systems

(GIS) hardware, software, training, or personnel. The two key "selling points" for the participating agencies were that patient confidentiality was rigorously guarded by the health department, and that no proprietary patient or market information would be shared that could give any health care competitor an unfair advantage. The project experienced a considerable delay when a state senator introduced legislation to abolish the three taxing districts in the county. Although the legislation did not pass, the project was stalled for over a year. The project is starting again from the beginning, and the health department has hired a full-time program administrator to develop the programs to their full extent.

FL-2
Partners
LHD, L-GOV, MDPRAC, HOSP, CLIN, MEDSOC, MEDIA

Synergies
2b, 2c, 2d, 6a-1, 6a-2

Structural Foundations
Contract, Advisory

Contact
Gladys Branic, MD, MPH
Manatee County Public Health Unit
410 6th Avenue East
Bradenton, FL 34208
branicg@hrs.state.fl.us

Manatee County Indigent Care Delivery Task Force

By the late 1980s, the pressing needs of uninsured and underinsured patients in Manatee County were making front-page news. Pregnant women without adequate insurance were lining up at two o'clock in the morning outside the community health center in order to schedule a walk-in appointment with one of two overworked obstetricians. The local hospital emergency room (ER) was overflowing with patients in need of primary care, and the hospital was delivering $11 million in uncompensated care annually. The public health department had no obstetricians with hospital privileges, and many of the private obstetricians in the community were refusing to see uninsured patients. The infant mortality rate for nonwhite babies in 1987 was 24.8 for every 1,000 live births. In an effort to address these problems, the local newspaper convened a roundtable discussion that included directors and senior administrators from the local hospitals, the health department, and the community health center. The discussion led to the formation of an Indigent Care Delivery Task Force, which expanded its membership to include the county medical society, public and private physicians, and senior-level nurses. The Task Force developed a plan, which capitalized on a county trust fund that was established when the public hospital was sold. The plan added physicians and nurse-midwives to the public health clinics and community health center, created a referral system for nonemergency patients from the ER to the public clinics, expanded the clinic hours, and increased reimbursement to private physicians for indigent care. The local health department sub-sequently focused on providing an acute-care clinic, and contracted its primary care services out to the community health center. This "triage" system has reduced the burden and cost to the ER, helped the health department and health center expand their capacity, and greatly increased access to care for uninsured patients. All the health care providers share a unified patient information system as well.

FL-3
Partners
LHD, MDPRAC, HOSP, MEDSOC

Synergies
2b

Structural Foundations
Contract, Adm/Mgmt

Contact
Pat Garriton
Charlotte County
Medical Society
Nations Bank Building
3195 Tamiami Trail
2nd Floor
Port Charlotte, FL 33952
garriton@charlottecounty
doctors.com

Charlotte County Physicians for Volunteer Services
In 1993, the Charlotte County Medical Society and the Charlotte County Health Department developed a system for providing specialty medical care to uninsured patients up to 150% of the poverty line. The medical society created the Charlotte County Physicians for Volunteer Services, Inc., a nonprofit organization that coordinates referrals with the help of health department eligibility screening. Since 1994, community physicians have donated over $1 million in services.

FL-4
Partners
LHD, MDPRAC, HOSP, CLIN,
LAB/RX, RES, MEDSOC, FNDN

Synergies
1c, 2b

Structural Foundations
Contract, Adm/Mgmt,
Advisory

Contact
Karen Dany
Florida Department
of Health
1295 West Fairfield Drive
Pensacola, FL 32501

Escambia County We Care Program
In response to an escalating need for specialist care for the uninsured in Escambia County, and its hub city of Pensacola, the local health officer approached county officials in 1992 to establish a referral office in the public health department. At the same time, the health officer approached the medical society to recruit volunteer physicians. This We Care program, modeled on similar efforts in other Florida counties (FL-9), capitalized on state legislation which provided "sovereign immunity" to physicians who volunteered their services to treat the indigent. For physicians already "writing off" charity care, there were significant benefits to registering their patients in the We Care program—all the ancillary services of diagnostic tests, lab work, hospitalization, surgery, chemotherapy and radiation therapy, and medications could be arranged (via donations or special funds) through the We Care office, rather than depending on each physi-

cian and his or her office staff to leverage "favors" from peers. Moreover, the We Care coordinator could serve as a master scheduler and case manager, assuring that no single physician would be unduly burdened by charity care. Over the past six years, We Care has served over 2,000 patients, and at any given time has a caseload of approximately 350 patients. The We Care program has documented over $13 million in donated services, and has developed case histories of patients suffering from chronic pain or a chronic disease whose problems would have gone unresolved or unattended without the We Care program.

FL-5
Partners
SHD, SPH, MEDSOC, PHASSN, PROFASSN

Synergies
6a-6

Structural Foundations
Coalition

Contact
E. Russell Jackson, Jr.
Florida Medical Association
P.O. Box 10269
Tallahassee, FL 32302

State of Florida Department of Health

In 1975, Florida undertook an experiment in public administration on a grand scale. The state legislature reorganized the public health and welfare systems into a single "super-agency," the Department of Health and Rehabilitative Services (HRS). Under the premise that poor and needy individuals often require a combination of health and social services, the state planned to coordinate all its programs through a single agency. Since the agency was built around a "case management model," administrative generalists drawn mostly from the social service ranks replaced specialized health professionals at managerial, regional, and executive levels. A number of public health professionals in the health department were frustrated with the change, and many rebelled against the integrated structure or left the department. Equally unhappy was the Florida Medical Association, which had a long-standing relationship with the public health department and was concerned about the devalued role of health professionals. In 1995 and 1996, the medical association spearheaded a coalition that included the state public health association, the state nursing association, and the state environmental health association in a coordinated lobbying effort to reorganize the HRS. The state legislature was disenchanted with the "super-agency" and receptive to the coalition's proposal to split out public health. As a result, in 1996, the State of Florida Department of Health was reborn. While the final outcome remains to be seen, there were several immediate results of the change: the newly created cabinet position of Secretary of Health was filled by a physician; additional monies were made available for staffing and disease prevention programs; and the county health units were renamed "county health departments," directly reporting to the state administrators.

FL-6
Partners
LHD, HOSP, RES

Synergies
1a, 2c, 6b-4

Structural Foundations
Contract

Contact
Steven A. Hale, MD
Orange County
Health Department
604 Courtland Street
Suite 200
Orlando, FL 32804

Orange County Residency Programs

The Orange County Health Department, headquartered in Orlando, has several programs utilizing medical residents from nearby teaching hospitals. In one program established in the early 1990s, a senior obstetric resident from the Arnold Palmer Hospital staffs a high-risk prenatal clinic at the health department. Patients are referred from a number of public health clinics, which are generally staffed by generalist physicians and nurse-practitioners. The senior resident provides a specialty consultation and triages high-risk patients to the teaching hospital's high-risk maternity clinic. The program has reduced delays considerably by having high-risk patients seen by a specialist, saves the patients unnecessary trips to the hospital if their condition is less than high risk, and establishes an easy linkage to the teaching hospital if needed. In another program, second- and third-year Family Medicine residents from the Florida Hospital System rotate through the public health department for three- and four-week periods. The residents receive clinical experience in the STD clinics, and in-depth orientations to the immunization, tuberculosis control, nutritional, environmental health, and epidemiology programs. Residents also participate in outreach and screening programs, and gain a more intimate understanding of the community resources available to them as local practitioners.

FL-7
Partners
LHD, SHD, MDPRAC, HOSP, CLIN, RES, MEDSOC, FNDN

Synergies
1c, 2b, 2d, 6a-1

Structural Foundations
Contract, Adm/Mgmt

Leon County Pediatrics and Obstetrics Programs

In 1981 in Leon County, categorical federal funds were available for children with special needs, but there was no funding to provide routine primary and preventive health care. The county pediatric society, in cooperation with the county health department, developed a demonstration project to provide primary pediatric care to all low-income children in Tallahassee and Leon County. All the children born in the county are triaged at the hospital, and those who are eligible may enroll to receive all their pediatric needs through private practice pediatricians. The children also receive case management through the publicly funded Talla-

Contact
Arthur P. Cooper, MPH
Leon County Public
Health Department
Florida Department
of Health
P.O. Box 2745
Tallahassee, FL 32316
art_cooper@doh.state.fl.us

FL-8
Partners
LHD, L-GOV, SHD, S-GOV,
FEDHLTH, FEDOTH, MDPRAC,
HOSP, CLIN, MCO, INS, LAB/RX,
SOM, SPH, RES, AHC, U-OTH,
MEDSOC, PHASSN, PROFASSN,
VHO, BUS, LABR, SCHL, RELIG,
MEDIA, FNDN, C-OTH

Synergies
1c, 2a, 2b, 2c, 2d, 4c, 5a,
6a-1, 6a-5, 6a-6, 6b-5, 6b-6

Structural Foundations
Coalition, Contract,
Adm/Mgmt, Advisory

Contact
Jean M. Malecki, MD, MPH
Palm Beach County
Health Department
P.O. Box 29
West Palm Beach, FL
33402

hassee Pediatric Foundation. The program proved so successful that the county health department expanded it to include obstetrical care. For maternal care, the health department conducts the initial eligibility assessment, provides initial laboratory and clinical assessments as well as nutritional counseling and WIC, and then refers the eligible women to participating private practice obstetricians for their maternity care and delivery. Case management is provided by the health department. The two projects involve the efforts of the health department, the local medical society, key community pediatricians, 15 obstetrical providers, the local Family Practice residency program, both community hospitals, and the free-standing Birth Center.

Palm Beach Migrant Health Project

In the early 1950s, the local health officer of Palm Beach was faced with a medically underserved community of migrant farm workers with complex health and social needs. The health officer developed the Migrant Health Project in order to coordinate preventive and curative services for the farm workers, and also to illustrate to county and state officials an expanded role for the county health department. The private medical community endorsed the project because financial, cultural, and social barriers prevented it from adequately addressing the health needs of the migrant workers. The health department created teams within the agency of physicians, nurses, social workers, health educators, nutritionists, sanitarians, and community "liaisons" to provide coordinated care to the difficult-to-reach migrant population. The experiment proved so successful that over the past 35 years the county health department has developed a number of innovative programs in coordination with local officials and the medical community: they expanded the farm worker model to encompass medical services for all the county's medically underserved populations; they established a preventive medicine/public health residency program, a dental public health residency, and an affiliated MPH program, in order to attract skilled health professionals; they created a health care tax district charged with providing ambulatory, preventive, home health, hospital, and trauma services in the county; they developed a capitated Medicaid plan in the 1970s; they expanded the number of community and migrant health centers; and they arranged a program of voluntary physician service through the county medical society. Rather than acting unilaterally, the county health department has cultivated its relationship with local officials and the medical community, furthering a health system that links preventive with curative services.

FL-9

Partners
LHD, SHD, MDPRAC, HOSP, MEDSOC, VHO

Synergies
2b, 3b

Structural Foundations
Coalition, Adm/Mgmt

Contact
Arthur P. Cooper, MPH
Leon County Public
Health Department
Florida Department
of Health
P.O. Box 2745
Tallahassee, FL 32316
art_cooper@doh.state.fl.us

Leon County Breast Cancer Screening Program

In 1989, the Tallahassee chapter of the American Cancer Society invited local health providers to join a campaign to provide breast cancer screening and treatment for uninsured women. The original coalition included the county medical society, county health department, all mammography providers, and the two area hospitals. The American Cancer Society persuaded the state health department to appropriate $10,000 to the project. The group first developed protocols for screening and follow-up, and then designated the health department as the coordination point. The health department determined patients' eligibility for the program, made the appropriate referrals, and provided case management for all the public clinic clients; the county medical society provided case management for the private practice clients. The health department paid for the cost of the mammograms; further diagnosis, treatment, hospitalization or surgery was provided without charge by volunteer physicians and local hospitals. In the program's first seven years, nearly 3,500 women underwent screening, with 91 receiving follow-up care for positive findings. The program ultimately served as a model for a We Care program (FL-4) developed by the local medical society to provide free care to low-income, uninsured individuals.

FL-10

Partners
LHD, MDPRAC, HOSP, CLIN, MCO, RES

Synergies
2c

Structural Foundations
Contract

Volusia County Public-Private Partnerships

In Volusia County, the local health department was seeing over 5,000 maternity and family planning clients and over 500 HIV/AIDS patients each year In 1995. Although the health department had family practitioners and pediatricians on staff, the complex medical problems posed by these patients, and their need for comprehensive primary care, exceeded the health department's resources. Using a combination of federal, state, and county funds, the health department recruited an obstetrician/gynecologist to set up a private practice within the health department, and separately contracted for the services of an HIV specialist at a community-

Contact
Bonita J. Sorensen, MD
Volusia County
Health Department
420 Fentress Boulevard
Daytona Beach, FL 32114
bonita_sorensen@doh.
state.fl.us

based organization's clinic site. The OB/GYN physician had worked at the health department during his residency, was committed to serving the Medicaid and uninsured population, and was interested in establishing a private practice in the community. The health department offered him space, supplies, and staff and guaranteed a minimum revenue in exchange for setting up practice within a newly renovated facility, and he obtained local hospital privileges. Within two years, the health department increased its revenue above cost by 10%, the hospital emergency room experienced a sharp decline in maternity patients using its services for primary care and deliveries, and the physician was exploring the possibility of adding a partner to his practice and establishing a birthing center in conjunction with the local community college. In the case of the HIV specialist, the health department contracted with a private HMO for the services of a physician, who provides care at a community clinic with space and staff paid by the health department. As with the maternity care, the hospital emergency room has seen a sharp drop in inappropriate utilization of its emergency services. Furthermore, the hospital's family practice residency program has approached the HIV specialist to provide clinical training opportunities for its residents. And as with the maternity care, the health department receives in billings more than its HIV program costs. These "excess revenues" are used then to subsidize underfunded core public health functions.

FL-11
Partners
SHD, MEDSOC, PHASSN, FNDN

Synergies
6b-6

Structural Foundations
Coalition

Contact
See citation

Medicine/Public Health Summit

To prepare for a Medicine/Public Health Conference (funded by The Robert Wood Johnson Foundation), and to inform a newly created Florida Department of Health (FL-5), the Florida Medical Association and the Florida Public Health Association convened focus groups in three regions of the state, conducted an analysis of community needs, and held conference calls and interviews with key stakeholders in the medicine and public health communities. The results were published as a white paper and used to formulate the agenda for a statewide conference, held in August 1997. The convening partners also sought to devise a public policy definition of medicine/public health collaboration to assist the state health department and to identify enabling legislation at the state level to promote at least three achievable initiatives that would be chosen. The conference also re-examined medical education and public health training in a framework of collaboration, and identified ways to increase networking among these health professionals.

Florida Medicine/Public Health Summit. August 26, 1997. Conference proceedings sponsored by the Florida Medical Association, et al.

FL-12
Partners
LHD, L-GOV, SHD, MDPRAC, HOSP, MEDSOC, SCHL, RELIG, C-OTH

Synergies
1c, 2a, 2b, 5a, 6a-1

Structural Foundations
Coalition, Contract, Adm/Mgmt, Advisory

Contact
H. Edward Dean
Marion County Indigent Care System
230 NE 25th Avenue
Ocala, FL 34470

Marion County Indigent Care System
The Marion County Commissioners convened a task force in 1989 to examine the issue of indigent health care in their county. The task force conducted a comprehensive community assessment, reported back to the County Commissioners, and at their instigation designed a health care system for uninsured residents. The Marion County Indigent Care System began operation in 1991, functioning as a comprehensive referral network of primary and specialty care physicians who volunteered to see patients in their offices, as well as provide inpatient and outpatient hospital services and staff an urgent care center for minor emergencies. The system was governed by an Oversight Board composed of the CEOs of the two local hospitals, the local health department director, and a state health department regional administrator, with representatives from the Marion County Medical Society, the county's mental health services agencies and its hospital, the county legislature, and the local community. An organization sponsored by local churches, the Interfaith Emergency Services, provided food, clothing, shelter, and counseling services to clients in the Indigent Care System, and the state-funded Children's Medical Services provided the comprehensive medical care for chronically ill children. An evaluation conducted of the system in 1995 determined that in just over three years the cost of indigent care had dropped by 20%, emergency room visits had declined from 389 to 272 per 1,000 people, and there had been a 15% decrease in hospitalizations for conditions suitable for ambulatory care.

FL-13
Partners
LHD, L-GOV, S-GOV, HOSP, U-OTH, BUS, SCHL, MEDIA, FNDN, C-OTH

Healthy Community Initiative of Greater Orlando
In Orlando, what began in 1993 as the vision of one highly placed community activist, has evolved into a public benefit corporation with a $2 million en-

Synergies
5a, 5e, 6b-6, 6c-2

Structural Foundations
Coalition, Adm/Mgmt,
Advisory

Contact
Ronald M. Wilson
Healthy Community
Initiative of Greater
Orlando, Inc.
P.O. Box 561130
Orlando, FL 32856
rmwilson@magicnet.net

dowment. The Healthy Community Initiative of Greater Orlando (HCI) began as a small group of individuals who met regularly for over a year to discuss how best to address complex social and health problems in their area. They concluded that a key element was involving the community in the process and adopting a focus on long-term change. This small initial group, which included a health system executive who had just finished a year of training at The HealthCare Forum's Healthy Communities Fellowship program, enlisted help from experts at the Forum and the National Civic League to form the Healthy Community Coordinating Committee, which included major hospitals, civic leaders, employers, the school system, and a homeless coalition. The next challenge was to go "beyond the usual suspects" to involve a wider range of community representatives. The Committee devised an innovative way to reach out to Hispanic and African-American leaders, and then held focus groups with over 300 residents, many of whom were traditionally underrepresented in planning initiatives. After a community-wide effort to craft an action plan, HCI secured ongoing funding from Florida Hospital and the Orlando Regional Healthcare System and was able to hire staff and become an incorporated nonprofit organization. In 1998, a central focus of HCI is making central Florida a safe and desirable place for children and families. Currently, HCI conducts research, using surveys, focus groups, and coordination of existing community data, and fosters interorganizational communication, acting as a facilitator and providing a neutral forum for collaborative projects. Some recent projects include: the development of a set of 25 quality-of-life indicators for gauging the community's health; the Listening Projects, which consist of key informant interviews with neighborhood residents; and the Center for Trusteeship, which provides a community-based meeting location that hosts an average of ten meetings a week.

[GA] GEORGIA

GA-1

Partners
LHD, SHD, FEDHLTH, HOSP,
CLIN, SOM, SPH, RES, BUS

Synergies
6a-6, 6b-2, 6b-3, 6b-4

Morehouse School of Medicine Preventive Medicine Residency Program

In 1986, the Morehouse School of Medicine in Atlanta began exploring the need for a preventive medicine residency program in conjunction with the state health department. At the time, there

Structural Foundations
Contract, Advisory

Contact
Daniel S. Blumenthal,
MD, MPH
Dept of Community Health
and Preventive Medicine
Morehouse School
of Medicine
720 Westview Drive
Atlanta, GA 30310
danielb@link.msm.edu

had never been a black district health officer in Georgia. The collaboration was initiated by the chair of the newly founded Department of Community Health and Preventive Medicine at the medical school. In addition to the state health department and the private medical school, the residency program works with Emory University's Rollins School of Public Health and the CDC. In the residency program's first ten years, it has graduated 27 physicians, of whom 25 are racial or ethnic minorities. Most are working in the field of preventive medicine at federal, state, and local levels. The state appointed its first black district health officer in 1994.

GA-2
Partners
LHD, L-GOV, FEDHLTH, MDPRAC,
HOSP, LAB/RX, SOM, U-OTH,
PHASSN, SCHL, RELIG, MEDIA,
FNDN

Synergies
1c, 3b, 5b

Structural Foundations
Coalition, Advisory

Contact
Lori M. Harris
Tanner Medical Center
710 Dixie Street
Carrollton, GA 30117

Carroll and Heard Counties Mobile Clinic Project

To improve the availability of affordable medical care in Georgia's Carroll and Heard counties, Tanner Medical Center (TMC) led an initiative to establish a mobile health van service. A primary objective of the Mobile Clinic Project was to increase access to health screenings and improve referral rates of underserved persons to TMC's Community Care medical and dental program. To meet the requirements of a federal Rural Health Outreach grant, a collaborative consortium was formed with representatives from the medical center and from the Carroll and Heard County Departments of Health, Boards of Education, and Departments of Family and Children's Services to oversee the project. Each partner provides input into program administration. The Mobile Clinic began operating in 1995 and provides primary care, preventive screenings, and immunizations at a variety of sites in the two counties, including schools, churches, community centers, shopping centers, and public housing areas. In its first year, there were over 13,000 mobile clinic patients. One specific objective was to improve immunization rates; in 1992, 63% of Carroll County's children were appropriately immunized and the rate had increased to 98.7% by 1997. Additional services have been added to the mobile clinic, such as breast cancer education and screening, cholesterol screening, and health assessment, as additional grant monies have been secured.

GA-3

Partners
L-GOV, S-GOV, FEDHLTH, HOSP, SOM, SPH, U-OTH, VHO, FNDN, C-OTH

Synergies
4a, 4b, 5c, 5d, 6c-1

Structural Foundations
Coalition, Contract, Adm/Mgmt

Contact
Arthur Kellermann, MD, MPH
Center for Injury Control
Rollins School of
Public Health
Emory University
1518 Clifton Road, N.E.
Atlanta, GA 30322
kellerma@sph.emory.edu

Emory University Center for Injury Control

The Emory University Center for Injury Control was developed in 1993 by the Rollins School of Public Health as an institutional platform for injury prevention research, training, and policy development. Led by emergency physicians cross-trained in public health, the Center is supported by staff members who have public health or research training in epidemiology, surveillance, technology assessment, and program evaluation. Its affiliate faculty on the campus include professors of medicine, engineering, and public health, and its off-campus affiliations include public safety and law enforcement agencies. The Center's key program areas are firearm safety, helmet advocacy, and child safety. When the "biker lobby" agitated to repeal Georgia's motorcycle helmet law in 1996, the Center worked with emergency physicians, paramedics, hospital administrators, and public health students to present compelling stories and evidence supporting the helmet law. The helmet law stood. Other projects include: an electronic firearm injury surveillance system, nicknamed "Cops and Docs," which links emergency department data from a five-county area in Metropolitan Atlanta to police reports and medical examiner data; a lobbying effort to mandate that American handguns meet certain safety standards; and the development of a national helmet resource center for promotion and legislative advocacy. Across all of these projects, the Center bridges the private sector emergency departments and emergency medicine groups with its own public health expertise, drawing on resources from the public safety, law enforcement, and engineering communities as well.

GA-4

Partners
SHD, HOSP, MEDSOC

Synergies
3a, 5b, 6b-5

Structural Foundations
Contract, Adm/Mgmt, Advisory

HIV/AIDS Guides

The face of HIV/AIDS was dramatically changing in Georgia in 1987. Over a third of new HIV infections were being diagnosed outside of metropolitan Atlanta, in rural and isolated areas, and physicians in these communities were often unfamiliar with HIV/AIDS resources and emerging clinical options. The state health department's infectious disease director approached the Public Health Committee of the Medical Association of Georgia to collaboratively write a clinician's guide to HIV/AIDS and distribute it to all the primary care doctors in the state.

Contact
Camilla Grayson, MSW
Medical Association
of Georgia
1330 West Peachtree
Street, NW
Suite 500
Atlanta, GA 30309

Despite past differences between the medical and public health communities, the state medical society readily agreed to the partnership. The medical society and the state health department both contributed staff to prepare the book. The writing team gathered research materials from the CDC and obtained input from an advisory board of HIV/AIDS clinicians and infectious disease specialists to describe the clinical elements of care for an HIV-infected patient: the diagnostic process, treatment options, and follow-up guidelines. Moreover, the books described the epidemiology of HIV/AIDS in Georgia; provided the state requirements for informed consent, counseling, and disease reporting; and included a comprehensive resource inventory of medical and social services. The original guide proved so successful among physicians that the group published a revised edition in 1992 and a pediatric guide in 1996.

Kirkpatrick, DJ, Taylor, CG, Klein, ER, Nesheim, SR, et al., eds. 1996. *A pediatric clinician's guide to AIDS and HIV infection in Georgia.* Atlanta, GA.

GA-5
Partners
LHD, FEDHLTH, SOM, SPH, VHO, SCHL, RELIG, FNDN, C-OTH

Synergies
1c, 5a, 5b, 5d

Structural Foundations
Coalition, Contract, Adm/Mgmt, Advisory

Contact
Joyce Essien, MD, MBA
Center for Public
Health Practice
Rollins School of
Public Health
Emory University
1518 Clifton Road, N.E.
Room 664
Atlanta, GA 30322
jessien@sph.emory.edu

Cobb/Fulton County Community Capacity Development

With four-year funding from the W.K. Kellogg Foundation's Community-Based Public Health Initiative, a coalition of community-based organizations, local health departments, a medical school, and a school of public health worked with two communities in Cobb and Fulton counties to build resources and expertise among public housing residents. Faculty members from the Emory School of Public Health and the Morehouse School of Medicine worked with public health officials and community providers to assess and help address health, education, vocational, social service, and recreational needs in the selected communities. The health departments increased their on-site services at the housing projects, and furnished transportation to other health and social services providers. A health professions apprenticeship was developed in the health departments to provide vocational opportunities. The fundamental principle of the consortium was one of community empowerment: the academic and public health partners provided technical assistance and resources in order to develop the community's capacity to gain control over its own health risks.

GA-6

Partners
LHD, L-GOV, MDPRAC, HOSP, INS, BUS, SCHL, FNDN, C-OTH

Synergies
1c, 2a, 2c, 3b, 5a, 5b, 5d, 5e, 6b-4

Structural Foundations
Coalition
Adm/Mgmt

Contact
Nancy J. Kennedy
Northwest Georgia
Healthcare Partnership
P.O. Box 182
Dalton, GA 30722
nghp@ocsonline.com

Northwest Georgia Healthcare Partnership

The Georgia Hospital Association began promoting the concept of "community health partnerships" to its member hospitals in 1992. Two hospitals in Murray and Whitfield counties embraced the idea and began developing a broadly representative community board. Key organizations, such as the local public health departments and the United Way, joined the partnership, which incorporated as the not-for-profit Northwest Georgia Healthcare Partnership. The partners brought in an outside consultant to facilitate their strategic planning. Central to the group's strategy was to recruit the community's experienced leaders and administrators, which allowed for swift decision-making and cohesive leadership. After conducting a public community health assessment, the Partnership designated six working committees to address community needs. The Indigent Care & Accessibility Committee, chaired by the district health director, undertook the following projects: (1) a mobile health van that travels to remote rural areas, public housing projects, trailer parks, and disadvantaged neighborhoods to provide care, and which is staffed by personnel from the county health department and Hamilton Medical Center; (2) a program in which the hospital, the schools, and the health department collaborate to provide staff for school-based health clinics; and (3) a nurse-practitioner scholarship program, which provides funding for the training of family practice nurse practitioners in return for their service at a Medical Access Clinic, a public health department clinic open on evenings and weekends. In another example, as part of their employee wellness and prevention campaign, the Partnership provides screening services to local workers, aggregate data reports to employers, and intervention planning with employers for population-based campaigns on such topics as nutrition/weight management, smoking cessation, prenatal education, or back care. In 1996, the Partnership received funding as a CCN demonstration partnership from the W.K. Kellogg Foundation.

GA-7

Partners
LHD, SHD, FEDHLTH, FEDOTH, MDPRAC, HOSP, CLIN, LAB/RX, SOM, SPH, AHC, MEDSOC, PROFASSN, VHO, MEDIA, FNDN

Statewide Breast and Cervical Cancer Screening Program

To improve cancer screening, treatment, and follow-up among low-income women (as part of the 1990 Prevention Act), CDC offered funding to

Synergies
1c, 2b, 3b, 4c, 5b, 6a-4,
6b-5, 6b-6

Structural Foundations
Coalition, Advisory

Contact
Ruth Schultz, MS, RN
Cancer Control Section
Division of Public Health
Georgia Department of
Human Resources
2 Peachtree Street
6th Floor Annex
Atlanta, GA 30303
rbs@dhr.state.ga.us

state agencies to expand their Breast and Cervical Cancer Early Detection and Control programs. (MI-4 is another example.) The funding was awarded in two stages, first for capacity building and then to provide the actual screening and follow-up. In 1992, a statewide coalition was convened, which included a variety of cancer and women's health care specialists and general practitioners representing the private and public health sectors. These physicians were concerned about the deaths from breast and cervical cancer that could have been prevented, if detected earlier. The coalition became the basis for a network of physicians statewide who supported the program. Its members worked to make their peers aware of the problem and advocated for the intervention. The president of the Georgia Radiological Society, a member of the coalition, was influential in persuading participating mammography facilities to comply with the standards of the American College of Radiology reporting system. In addition, the coalition has conducted educational sessions at hospital staff meetings and meetings of local medical societies. The success of this collaboration is demonstrated in the increased number of private physicians providing services, the increased number of women receiving referrals for screening, and the success rate of connecting abnormal findings to diagnosis and treatment.

GA-8
Partners
LHD, L-GOV, HOSP, CLIN

Synergies
1c, 2a, 2b, 6a-1

Structural Foundations
Contract

Contact
Virginia Galvin, MD
District III
Douglas Cobb Health Unit
1650 County Farm Road
Marietta, GA 30060

Cobb and Douglass Counties Primary Care Partnership
In Georgia, the Boards of Health (BOH) in Cobb and Douglass counties and the WellStar (PROMINA) Northwest Health System have had good working relationships for many years, and they created a partnership that integrates their services in the two counties. Their first formal collaboration, in 1993, was the Cobb Health Futures Alliance (CHFA), created in response to the unmet health care needs of children in the county. Operating from the BOH clinic at the Marietta Community Health Center, CHFA provides preventive primary care services for all children, regardless of insurance status. Children with chronic disease are connected to private physicians in the community, who will treat and manage their care. In five years, over 9,600 children have enrolled in the program. At the same time, the partners of CHFA met regularly on an advisory board to discuss issues and

progress, and there was interest in expanding their partnership to create a comprehensive system of care for the two counties. The health director of Cobb and Douglass counties, who oversees ten community health centers, and leaders in WellStar, which has five hospitals and two Children's' Centers, spent eighteen months planning a system that would provide primary and acute care for all residents of the community. In August 1996, a formal contract was signed, which integrates the primary care service delivery systems of the two entities, maintaining the public health sector's assurance role. In the public-private system, BOH provides primary care services to all eligible individuals of WellStar's system and WellStar accepts all BOH patients into its network regardless of ability to pay, certifies BOH physicians, and assists in the renovation of BOH clinics. This partnership expands access to care among low-income residents, increases the array of services they can receive, and reduces costs to the county government.

GA-9
Partners
SHD, S-GOV, HOSP, SOM, RES

Synergies
2c, 6b-4, 6c-1

Structural Foundations
Contract, Adm/Mgmt

Contact
See citation

Georgia Mental Health Institute

In 1964, the Georgia State Department of Mental Hygiene (SDMH) and Emory University collaborated to create the Georgia Mental Health Institute (GMHI), a facility for training, research, and treatment modeled after the New York State Psychiatric Institute at Columbia University. In the original agreement, Emory was to provide administrative and professional direction for GMHI, but as the facility neared completion, SDMH opposed giving up control of the large budget of this prestigious, new facility. The resolution was that GMHI's superintendent would be a state-appointee who would work closely with the academic chairman from Emory. The original superintendent, a respected psychiatrist/administrator, resigned under pressure from SDMH, which was leaning towards the community-based approach to mental health practice. The next political appointee, though in step with SDMH's community-based perspective, was not a psychiatrist or a clinician, and had no prior experience in combining training, research, and clinical service delivery. This led to tension among the leadership of GMHI and a crisis in its core mission. In the early 1970s, many of GMHI's programs began to unravel as several directors and researchers resigned and the institution had difficulty recruiting qualified faculty and residents. As told in the 1986 account, those involved in the partnership felt that its fate was due to a lack of clearly defined responsibilities for each partner; lack of understanding of the different priorities of each partner; lack of mechanisms or procedures to deal with inevitable tensions in philosophy and interdisciplinary conflicts of status, control, and autonomy; and lack of provisions for continued support and longevity in the face of political and personnel changes. Other issues were insufficient commitment to the endeavor by both sides, such as, no legislative commitment to GMHI, and little interest on the academic side to maintain its integrity in the partnership or to support GMHI with separate funding streams.

Talbott, JA and Robinowitz, CB. 1986. *Working together: state-university collaboration in mental health.* Washington, DC: American Psychiatric Press, Inc. (NAT-20)

[HI] HAWAII

HI-1

Partners
INS, LAB/RX, SPH, MEDSOC, MEDIA

Synergies
5b, 5d

Structural Foundations
Coalition

Contact
Kathryn L. Braun, DrPH
School of Public Health
Center on Aging
University of Hawaii
at Manoa
1960 East-West Road
Biomedical Building C-106
Honolulu, HI 96822
kbraun@hawaii.edu

HealthScope Television Series

In the spring of 1993, the Hawaii Medical Association (HMA) wanted to produce a health education series to highlight the role of its physicians in primary care and disease prevention. They teamed with an independent television producer, whose wife was an associate professor of health education at the University of Hawaii School of Public Health. Together, they persuaded the local NBC-affiliate to air the show as a weekly Friday night series, called *HealthScope*. The format of the show was designed to disseminate a public health message about the community's leading health risks through HMA physicians, to offer specific cues to viewers to act on these messages through HMA-physician-staffed phone banks, and to use the mainstream media to engage the viewers. Each show was tightly scripted by the producer and the public health professor. They used physician and patient role models from the community with whom viewers could identify. Each show opened with a segment focusing on the prevention and treatment of that week's health problem, followed by an interview with an expert physician and then a profile of a patient. Prior to each show, 50,000 fliers advertising the show and promoting the recognition, treatment, and prevention of the "disease of the week" were distributed. During the airing of the ten-week series, which followed the popular *Wheel of Fortune* on Friday nights, five to eight HMA physicians staffed a phone bank to answer viewers' questions. The series was a hit, rated as the number two show in its time slot. The partners also achieved two additional objectives. They educated the local news media about public health issues, and they helped people to think "epidemiologically" about diseases prevalent among various ethnic groups.

[IA] IOWA

IA-1
Partners
LHD, L-GOV, SHD, MDPRAC,
HOSP, CLIN, U-OTH, BUS, FNDN

Synergies
1a, 1c, 2c, 3c, 4c, 5a, 5d,
5e, 6a-5, 6a-6

Structural Foundations
Contract, Adm/Mgmt

Contact
James Faulwell
Grundy County
Memorial Hospital
201 E J Avenue
Grundy Center, IA 50638

Grundy County Health Commission
In 1993, the Grundy County Memorial Hospital in rural Iowa was on the verge of closing its doors. The County Board of Supervisors in the small farming community had bailed out the hospital with a $615,000 loan, but officials were concerned about the hospital's persistent losses. After soliciting opinions from consultants, the state, private not-for-profit hospitals in neighboring counties, and a community task force, the Board of Supervisors created the Grundy County Health Commission. The Commission oversees and administers curative and preventive health care services in the county, including acute and long-term care, home health care, mental health, and emergency medical services. Personnel and administrative functions are shared by the local health department, the hospital, and the county government. The newly created Commission, also a CCN finalist partnership recognized by the W.K. Kellogg Foundation, is partially funded by the neighboring hospitals; the Commission has also received state and federal reimbursements, which have compelled them to pursue integration strategies beyond the county lines. Among the Commission's initiatives: healthcare providers cross-trained to work in multiple sites; a community assessment process to identify health priorities for the farming community; a common case management system that links patients to all health and social services in the county and its environs; and shared support services, such as electronic data processing, purchasing, laundry and linen, and pharmacy and laboratories. One of the Commission's principal goals is to redirect strategic health planning from the more traditional institutional perspective to one focused on the community as a whole.

IA-2

Partners
LHD, SHD, S-GOV, MDPRAC,
HOSP, CLIN, MEDSOC,
PROFASSN, VHO

Synergies
3a, 4a, 6b-5

Structural Foundations
Adm/Mgmt

Contact
Kathie J. Lyman
Polk County
Medical Society
1533 Linden
Suite 100
Des Moines, IA 50309
kjlyman@pcms.org

Des Moines Immunization Registry

As part of a statewide effort to enlist all Iowa physicians in a voluntary electronic immunization registry, in 1996 the Polk County Medical Society and the Hospital Association of Greater Des Moines began working with the Iowa Department of Public Health and a number of community providers to encourage local physicians to use the interactive registry in their practices. Iowa's registry builds on birth certificate data and voluntarily entered immunization data; it is designed to facilitate electronically reported data to the state health department and to enable local physicians and health care providers to more easily identify children who need immunizations. The state provided training and computer software to physicians and their staff, and the medical society and hospital association helped mobilize the health care community. Similar efforts are underway in other Iowa counties, many as part of a Healthy Iowa initiative.

IA-3

Partners
LHD, L-GOV, MDPRAC, HOSP,
U-OTH, VHO, C-OTH

Synergies
5b, 5d

Structural Foundations
Informal

Contact
Teri Walker, RN
Wayne County Public
Health Nursing Service
P.O. Box 102
Corydon, IA 50060

Wayne County Barn-Raising Ethos

With a county population of 7,000 people, all of the practitioners and public health professionals in Wayne County know one another. Following the "barn-raising" ethos that compels the entire community to pitch in on common projects, the public health and medical sectors have collaborated on a number of projects: conducting clinics to provide adolescents with physical exams for sports participation; providing joint prenatal classes several times each year; collaborating on mass household mailings on AIDS education; obtaining community donations to provide immunizations to those not covered by state or federal vaccination programs; and co-sponsoring a county toxic waste clean-up day. The partnerships that arise often involve public health practitioners, physicians, the county hospital, the Cooperative Extension office, and other community service providers.

IA-4

Partners
LHD, L-GOV, SHD, MDPRAC,
HOSP, MCO, INS, RES, BUS,
SCHL, RELIG, MEDIA, FNDN,
C-OTH

Synergies
5a, 5d, 5e

Healthy Linn Care Network

In 1990, a group of community health providers and local leaders conducted a community assessment in response to Healthy People 2000. Although over 200 citizens participated, 23 community health needs were identified, and a series of subcommittees formed, little coordinated action occurred. The local chamber of commerce began a campaign the following year to organize a long-

Structural Foundations
Coalition, Contract,
Adm/Mgmt

Contact
Elizabeth Selk, MS
Healthy Linn Care Network
St. Luke's Hospital
810 1st Avenue, N.E.
Cedar Rapids, IA 52402
easelk@aol.com

term plan for the community. In 1994, the Chamber of Commerce hired facilitators from the National Civic League, who led the community through an assessment process covering a broad spectrum of issue areas, among them health care. Many of the same leaders from the original Healthy Linn 2000 project participated, and by 1995, they had formalized their coalition as the Healthy Linn Care Network. When the group was not successful in obtaining CCN funding, it decided to fund itself, receiving support from the two local hospitals and the health department. A coordinator was hired to help develop a comprehensive community health care delivery system. The network began by conducting a household study, a health and social service provider survey, a community resource inventory, and an environmental health survey. This community health assessment was followed by a prioritization process in which the top ten health problems were identified, work groups established, and strategies developed. As one of its first projects, the network sponsored a Senior Tai Chi program at four senior residences to improve flexibility and balance and reduce falls. The network's inability to obtain external funding was cited by one participant as a key factor in the network's ultimate success, by forcing the partners to provide their own funding and therefore be more invested in its achievements.

IA-5
Partners
LHD, SHD, FEDHLTH, HOSP, INS,
AHC, VHO, SCHL, MEDIA, FNDN,
C-OTH

Synergies
1c, 3c, 5b, 5d, 6a-4

Structural Foundations
Coalition

Contact
Herman A. Hein, MD
University of Iowa
General Hospital
200 Hawkins Drive
Room 214 West
Iowa City, IA 52242
Herman-Hein@uiowa.edu

Des Moines Infant Mortality Prevention Center
A Children's Defense Fund report released in 1991 revealed that Des Moines had the second highest white infant mortality rate in the nation. In response, a citizens group led by a state senator convened to consider how to address this problem. At the same time, the newly formed Blue Cross Blue Shield Foundation of Iowa-South Dakota was looking for worthwhile projects to fund. Working with the Iowa Department of Public Health, the Foundation provided funding for a coordinator to develop and run an Infant Mortality Prevention Center. The state health department contributed office space and secretarial support. The coordinator brought together key community health leaders and providers, including the public hospital and the Visiting Nurse Services. The group reviews data and reports in order to understand the correlates of infant mortality and to identify program deficiencies, and then assigns subcommittees to im-

plement changes. In response, a number of programs have been developed—home visitation services, an extensive SIDS campaign, and a statewide review of infant deaths. Subsequently, both the infant mortality and SIDS rates have dropped in the area.

IA-6
Partners
LHD, L-GOV, HOSP, SOM, VHO

Synergies
5e

Structural Foundations
Coalition

Contact
See citation

Johnson County Healthy People 2000

An independent coalition formed in the early 1990s to assess and develop local public health goals and objectives in Johnson County. Despite strong and enthusiastic coalition membership from a broadly representative group of health care providers, community leaders, academicians associated with the University of Iowa Health of the Public program, and local health officials, the group faced several major obstacles and was periodically in peril of disintegrating from lack of leadership and shifting political winds. The issues which preoccupied the coalition included: who would control the coalition, particularly in regard to the staffing of the coalition office (staffing was initially provided by the local health department using county funds, and was later transferred to one of the local hospitals); what benefit accrued to the coalition members contributing to the process; and what was the relationship between the coalition and the politically appointed board of health. Although board members had a permanent seat on the coalition, during one major political transition the composition of the board of health changed dramatically, and it became clear that the board would not be providing any new resources to the coalition.

Health of the Public National Program Office. 1995. *Community health improvement through information and action: an anthology from the Health of the Public program.* San Francisco, CA.

IA-7
Partners
LHD, MDPRAC, HOSP, RES, U-OTH, FNDN

Synergies
1c, 3c, 5a, 5b, 5e, 6b-5

Structural Foundations
Coalition, Contract, Adm/Mgmt, Advisory

North Iowa Mercy Health Network

Facing a growing need for geriatric services and the increasingly complex administrative needs of the health system today, the North Iowa Mercy Health Network was formed in 1994 to assist health care providers across a 14-county rural area. The Network (recognized by the W.K. Kellogg Foundation as a CCN finalist partnership), encompassing 10 rural hospitals, 8 physician-hospital organizations, 43 primary care clinics, and 1 referral network for geriatric services, focuses on medical care and

Contact
Frances Hoffman
Administrative
Support Services
North Iowa Mercy
Health Center
1000 4th Street, S.W.
Mason City, IA 50401
hoffmanf@mercyhealth.
com

other health services, but uses a population-based, public health perspective to evaluate needs and implement services in the community. The Network is working with local health departments on health assessments for each county, which are being conducted and analyzed by the University of Iowa's Health of the Public program and Iowa State University's Extension Office. The use of these data, plus on-hand mortality and morbidity data and input from community town meetings, will shape program planning for the Network.

[ID] IDAHO

ID-1
Partners
LHD, MDPRAC, HOSP, C-OTH

Synergies
1c, 2b, 3b
Structural Foundations
Coalition, Adm/Mgmt

Contact
Joe Morris, FACHE
Kootenai Medical Center
2003 Lincoln Way
Coeur d'Alene, ID 83814

Coeur d'Alene Voucher Program for Uninsured Patients
In 1990, a local nonprofit organization in Coeur d'Alene opened a free clinic on Tuesday and Thursday evenings to serve uninsured patients. Many of the local physicians, though, did not volunteer to staff the clinic. A local pediatrician, who visited most of the physicians to find out why, discovered that the doctors were willing to donate their time but were uncomfortable in an unfamiliar setting. The pediatrician, in concert with the health department, developed a medical voucher program in its stead. The health department conducts eligibility screenings and distributes vouchers provided by the participating physicians. The health department schedules the office visit and the patient uses the voucher to cover the service. The local medical center provides unlimited laboratory, pharmacy, radiology, and other imaging services using a similar voucher arrangement. The program has fostered far greater physician participation by allowing each physician flexibility in determining the amount of uncompensated service he or she wishes to donate, and by capitalizing on the efficiencies of having physicians provide care in their own offices.

ID-2
Partners
LHD, L-GOV, S-GOV, HOSP, CLIN,
U-OTH, VHO, BUS, SCHL, RELIG,
MEDIA, FNDN

Synergies
5a, 5d, 5e, 6a-6

Southcentral Health Network
In 1992, the Magic Valley Regional Medical Center in Twin Falls recruited administrators from all the area hospitals to form a committee focused on working together to improve community health. Serendipitously, one of the medical center's trustees was the district health director, who coordinated public health activities in eight counties. She asked to join the committee and was wel-

Structural Foundations
Coalition, Contract,
Adm/Mgmt

Contact
Cheryl Juntunen
South Central District
Health Department
1020 Washington Street, N.
Twin Falls, ID 83301
cheryl_j@phd5.state.id.us

comed by the administrators of the competing hospitals, who were wary of one another but willing to allow the health department to serve as the neutral convener for the community health committee. After several months of discussion, the committee broadened its membership to include community members, disconnected itself from the regional medical center, and established itself as the South-central Health Network, with staff support provided by the health department. The network conducted a district wide health assessment using APEXPH in order to identify health priorities in the eight counties, and supplemented that with town meetings and a telephone survey conducted by a local college. Based on these community discussions, work groups were formed in each county to address one of the health priorities: alcohol and other drugs; cancer and heart disease (principally related to tobacco smoking); unintentional injuries from auto accidents; and teen pregnancy. The network received funding from the W.K. Kellogg Foundation as a CCN demonstration partnership. Among the network's early accomplishments: on the basis of the community health assessment, the state health department increased non-categorical funding to the district to address the identified health priorities; a local school district and a community development council used the information as a demonstration of need, which helped obtain additional grant funding; and coalitions have coalesced in the different counties to address the health priorities. As an example, the work group targeting teen pregnancy determined that some of the factors involved are dysfunctional family environments, a history of sexual abuse, limited access to community programs, and inadequate sexuality education. The group has developed a strategy for conducting K–12 sexuality programs in the schools, incorporating a "male responsibility" component; enlisted schools, churches, and parents to participate in the effort; and published a resource inventory of agencies and institutions.

[IL] ILLINOIS

IL-1
Partners
LHD, L-GOV, S-GOV, FEDHLTH,
MDPRAC, HOSP, SOM, RES,
U-OTH, PROFASSN, VHO, BUS,
SCHL, RELIG, MEDIA, C-OTH

Lake County Kids 1st Health Fair
The Kids 1st Health Fair was initiated in 1993 to provide assistance to low-income families residing in Lake County in meeting school health requirements and in obtaining needed preventive health

Synergies
1b, 3b, 5d

Structural Foundations
Coalition, Adm/Mgmt

Contact
Sharon Doney, MSW
Community Health Services
Lake County Health
Department
3010 Grand Avenue
Waukegan, IL 60085

IL-2
Partners
SHD, MDPRAC, MEDSOC, VHO,
C-OTH

Synergies
6a-5

Structural Foundations
Advisory

Contact
Leslee Stein-Spencer,
RN, MS
EMS and Highway Safety
Illinois Department of
Public Health
100 West Randolph Street
Suite 6-600
Chicago, IL 60601
lstein@idph.state.il.us

IL-3
Partners
LHD, S-GOV, HOSP, MEDSOC

services for their children. The Fair is sponsored and organized by the League of Women Voters of Lake County and the Lake County Health Department (LCHD), with medical services provided by volunteer physicians from local hospitals, universities, and private practices. In addition to required physical examinations and immunizations, the children can receive preventive screenings, such as dental exams and tests for speech development, lead level and sickle cell anemia. If further medical assistance is required, LCHD staff make referrals and also follow up with the families to assure that treatment was received. Participating children receive a backpack with age-appropriate school supplies. The Fair also provides families with an opportunity to learn about available services from numerous Lake County agencies and organizations. At the 1997 Fair, over 2,000 children received services, including over 1,000 dental screenings, 670 immunizations, and 900 physical examinations provided by 600 volunteers with the help of 27 major sponsors. The services provided saved families an estimated $85–$185 per examination and $30–50 per immunization, plus $10–25 in school supplies.

Illinois EMS Act
In 1991, a technical assessment team from the National Highway Traffic and Safety Administration evaluated the Illinois emergency medical services (EMS) and trauma systems. The federal team concluded that the state's EMS Act needed major revisions. As a result, the state health department formed an advisory body representing 50 groups, which included physicians, firefighters, and prehospital care professionals, among others. Over a three-year period, the advisory committee rewrote the EMS Act, revising the way local EMS systems are developed, clarifying the designation of trauma centers, providing for supervision of basic life-support services, and creating an EMS Assistance Fund derived from traffic fines and vehicle licensure fees. After several legislative tries, and further revisions by the committee, the revised EMS Act was passed in 1995.

Illinois Domestic Violence Project
In 1995, the Illinois Attorney General's office initiated a domestic violence project with the state

Synergies
1c, 4b

Structural Foundations
Contract, Intraorg

Contact
Nancy L. Carlson, MSW
Violence Against Women
Office of the Attorney
General–State of Illinois
J.R. Thompson Center
100 West Randolph
12th Floor
Chicago, IL 60601

medical society and the Chicago Department of Public Health. Through the program, hospitals throughout the state were surveyed as to their willingness to participate as test sites. Among those who responded positively, a sample was selected. Each participating hospital designated a multidisciplinary team composed of an emergency department physician, nurse, social worker, hospital administrator, and community domestic violence expert. The teams were then trained in instructing their facility staff how to detect battered patients, develop resource materials for patients and staff, and form linkages with appropriate community agencies. Although the program allowed each hospital team to design site-specific strategies for identification of victims of domestic violence and referral mechanisms to assure prompt and confidential treatment and counseling, the program emphasized the need for developing systematic supports for both staff and patients and clear links to existing community services.

IL-4

Partners
LHD, MDPRAC, HOSP, VHO,
C-OTH

Synergies
1b, 2a

Structural Foundations
Adm/Mgmt

Contact
Karen Mayes
Personal Health Services
McLean County Health
Department
200 West Front
Bloomington, IL 61701

McLean County Prenatal Clinic

As poverty rose by 25% throughout the 1980s in McLean County, the local health department noted with concern the increasing number of pregnant women unable to access prenatal care. Having been unsuccessful in an earlier attempt to establish a community prenatal clinic, health department officials convened a group that included private physicians, community agencies, and the county's two hospitals in order to address the problem. Through the group, the private physicians in the community were first persuaded of the need for a community clinic, and then approved a system in which they would staff the clinic on a rotating basis. The health department committed nursing and administrative personnel and one of the hospitals provided space for the clinic. The group then formed a not-for-profit corporation to manage the joint venture and the clinic was officially opened in September 1993. In addition, the health department co-located their Healthy Moms/Healthy Kids and WIC programs at the community clinic in order to better serve both maternal and child health care needs.

IL-5

Partners
LHD, FEDHLTH, MDPRAC, HOSP,
CLIN, RES, FNDN

East St. Louis Health Coalition

In 1990, East St. Louis suffered from a constellation of problems—four of the poorest neighborhoods in America; a murder rate twice that of Washington,

Synergies
1a, 1c, 3b, 3c, 4a, 4c, 6a-5

Structural Foundations
Coalition, Contract,
Adm/Mgmt

Contact
Robert Klutts
Southern Illinois Healthcare
Foundation
8080 State Street
East St. Louis, IL 66203

DC; an infant mortality rate of 20.3 for every 1,000 births; and cerebrovascular, pneumonia and diabetes death rates among African-Americans twice that of the state rate for African-Americans. Compounding the problem was a health care system in disarray—only four primary care physicians to cover 40,000 patients, suburban taxpayers anxious to remove the beleaguered public hospital from the tax rolls, and a local health department reeling from years of mismanagement. The East Side Health Coalition, linking the local health department, the federally qualified community health center, and the community hospital, was formed to coordinate and expand the resources of each partner in this fragmented system. A series of administrative maneuvers strengthened the coalition: the health center director split his duties and became the director of the health department; the health center's medical director adopted the same role for the health department; and the community hospital became a private, nonprofit controlled affiliate of the health center. Personnel were shared among the three agencies and programs were co-located. A seamless system was designed in which patients entering any one of the community-based sites or clinics could be linked to the programs and providers of all three. Each partner contributed specialized skills and resources to the collective system: the health department provided case management services, the health center provided physicians and nurses, and the hospital provided capital expansion resources and clinic space. By 1997, childhood immunizations had risen from 23 to 86% over 8 years, clinic visits increased ninefold from 8,600 to 80,000, and the number of physicians jumped from 4 to 25. The coalition is presently exploring the possibility of becoming a Medicaid managed care plan.

IL-6
Partners
LHD, L-GOV, SHD, HOSP, SCHL,
C-OTH

Synergies
2a, 4b, 5b, 6b-4

Structural Foundations
Contract, Intraorg

Rush-Presbyterian-St. Luke's Medical Center Community Health Promotion

Rush-Presbyterian-St. Luke's Medical Center (Rush) is a large medical center in Chicago that, as of 1992, had several community-based activities for health improvement. Since 1971, Rush had been offering free physicals, preventive care, and immunizations to Chicago public school children. Rush also supported day care centers at public schools and social service agencies that allowed teenage mothers to continue their education. Another pro-

Contact
Marian Osterweis, PhD
Association of Academic
Health Centers
1400 16th Street, N.W.
Suite 720
Washington, DC 20036
mosterweis@acadhlthctrs.
org

ject, the Community Service Initiative Program, trains future physicians to appreciate community health and behavioral medicine and was established by the department of preventive medicine in 1991. Medical students took part in community service as part of their primary care training, in projects such as AIDS education in schools and mental health interventions in inner-city housing projects. Also, the College of Nursing, under contract with the City of Chicago, created ten senior centers with wellness and support activities, and a community health nursing program with ties to the Chicago Board of Health. Lastly, in 1992 Rush founded the Family Violence Center as a crisis intervention program in their emergency department. It was then the only hospital-based center in the state and was funded by the Illinois State Attorney General's office, the departments of nursing and social service, and the women's board of the hospital. Staff of the Center offered services, coordinated care and provided information for victims of violence, with referrals for counseling and support groups, shelter, and legal advice. This Center also provided training to hospital staff and people in the community on early identification and prevention of violence and on available community resources.

Osterweis, M and Eichhorn, SF. 1993. Community-based health promotion activities. In *Promoting community health: the role of the academic health center.* Skelton, WD and Osterweis, M, eds. Washington, DC: Association of Academic Health Centers.

IL-7
Partners
LHD, L-GOV, SHD, FEDHLTH,
FEDOTH, HOSP, SPH, ARC, VHO,
BUS, SCHL, RELIG, FNDN, C-OTH

Synergies
1b, 5b, 5d, 5e

Structural Foundations
Coalition

Contact
Mary Neslon
Bethel New Life
367 North Karlov Street
Chicago, IL 60624
MNelson367@aol.com

Chicago/West Garfield Park Bethel New Life
West Garfield Park in Chicago suffers from many of the economic, social, environmental, and health problems that have plagued inner-city neighborhoods. In the late 1970s, "ruined houses" was one major problem. As the neighborhood housing stock deteriorated, many houses were boarded up and abandoned, and decent places to live became scarce or unaffordable. Using grant funds and leveraging "sweat equity," members of a community-oriented Lutheran church rehabilitated neighborhood housing and helped residents obtain loans for the refurbished properties. More recently, the church members have developed the Bethel Wholisitic Health Center, which provides family health services to over 1,000 residents a month, and they have converted a formerly closed-down hospital campus into a center for elderly and chil-

dren's services. An outgrowth of the Bethel Lutheran Church, Bethel New Life is now an incorporated entity and it leads or is involved in a broad array of community projects dealing with health, jobs and training; economic redevelopment; seniors; and social action. The church center also works with city agencies and other community groups on health promotion, health education, and case management around issues of lead abatement, AIDS education, healthy infants and kids, and supportive housing for the formerly homeless. Bethel New Life is also involved in a collaboration to create a "healthier, more sustainable community" that includes the local hospital, the local health department, schools, other churches, the United Way, and other community groups. This collaboration was chosen by The HealthCare Forum as one of six national demonstration sites in its five-year initiative, Accelerating Community Transformation.

IL-8

Partners
LHD, MDPRAC, HOSP, INS, U-OTH, RELIG, FNDN, C-OTH

Synergies
1c, 5a, 5b, 5e, 6a-2

Structural Foundations
Coalition, Adm/Mgmt

Contact
See citation

Metropolitan Chicago Community Care Alliance

The Genesis Center for Health and Empowerment, which opened in 1995, is a product of the Metropolitan Chicago Community Care Alliance, a partnership of Lutheran General Hospital, Advocate Medical Group, the Cook County Department of Health, Northeastern University and 20 community-based organizations. Funded by the W.K. Kellogg Foundation as a CCN demonstration partnership, the mission of the Alliance was to create a health care center responsive to its low-income, Latino community and to effectively involve the community in the process of building it. In designing the center and its programs, community volunteers were recruited to conduct a door-to-door survey to gauge health concerns and needs of the neighborhood, to develop the sliding fee schedule for the clinic and to help design a resource area for bilingual health education material. In addition to the Health Center, the Metropolitan Chicago Community Care Alliance works with several other Chicago area partnerships for community health improvement: Healthy Community Partnerships, The Des Plaines Health and Empowerment Program, Congregation-Based Health Services, and the Chronic Care Network for Older Adults. The Alliance serves as a common ground for joint program planning and the development of links among the health initiatives of these partner-ships.

Bogue, R and Hall, Jr, CH, eds. 1997. *Health networks inno-vations: how 20 communities are improving their system through collaboration.* Chicago: American Hospital Publish-ing, Inc.

IL-9
Partners
LHD, L-GOV, S-GOV, HOSP, CLIN, U-OTH, VHO, BUS, SCHL, RELIG, FNDN, C-OTH

Synergies
1c, 4a, 5b

Structural Foundations
Coalition, Adm/Mgmt

Contact
See citation

Decatur Community Partnership
The Decatur Community Partnership was founded in 1992 to unite community groups and public and private health service agencies in working together for a healthier community in Macon County. Part-ners included the Decatur Memorial Hospital, the City of Decatur, including the county departments of health, social services, and mental health ser-vices, and an alcohol, tobacco, and drug-abuse prevention program, Communities in Partnership. Awarded a CCN demonstration partnership grant from the W.K. Kellogg Foundation, the Partnership is now working on the Family Investment Project, which uses a "family liaison" case manager to assist families with the available services of 12 health/human service agencies as well as with parenting and employment skills. The Partnership is also in-terested in increasing coordination of services through information technology. Under the Part-nership's direction, touch-screen health information kiosks have been installed in the Decatur Public Li-brary to give members of the community more in-formation on the county's health and humans ser-vice agencies and how to access their services. Approximately 400 people per month use the health kiosks. Another initiative is to establish a Community Health Information Network (CHIN) that uses a single medical form and connects client information among the health/human service agencies on a confidential basis.

Community Care Network Demonstration Program. 1997. *The 25 Community Care Network demonstration partner ships: profiles in progress.* Chicago: Hospital Research and Educational Trust.

IL-10
Partners
LHD, SHD, MDPRAC, HOSP, CLIN, LAB/RX, PROFASSN, VHO, FNDN, C-OTH

Synergies
1a, 1c

Chicago Health Care Linkage Project
Throughout the late 1980s, it had become increas-ingly evident to health planners, providers, and community leaders that Chicago's health care system—particularly those agencies serving poor and minority populations—was inefficient, frag-mented, and unable to provide quality health care reliably. In response to several citywide health sum-

Structural Foundations
Contract, Adm/Mgmt

Contact
See citation

mits that elaborated the problems, in 1990 the Chicago Community Trust funded the Illinois Primary Health Care Association (a group representing many of the city's community health centers) to develop, implement, and evaluate a primary care linkage network among the health centers, the Chicago Department of Health clinics, and area hospitals. The Health Care Linkage Project first began with formal linkages between the health department, which served over one million patients annually at its neighborhood health centers, and the community health centers, which generated approximately half a million patient visits each year. The project funded linkage coordinators, who developed site-specific models linking the health centers and health department clinics. The relationships included: referrals of nonemergent patients from health department clinics to community health centers; the provision of WIC services by health department staff at a community health center one day per week; a health department pharmaceutical dispensary for patients without third-party coverage referred from community health centers; a referral mechanism to community health centers from health department STD clinics; provision of radiology, dentistry, and ophthalmology services at one community health center by health department staff; and a collaborative preventive dental campaign. As a result of the linkage project, the health department and the community health centers documented reductions in waiting times, increased availability of specialty services, better communication among providers, and cost savings as a result of shared diagnostic and pharmaceutical services.

Ferguson, MG, et al. 1992. Health Care Linkage Project: improving access to care. *Henry Ford Hospital Medical Journal.* 40(1,2):9–12.

IL-11
Partners
LHD, CLIN, SPH, U-OTH, VHO, BUS, SCHL, RELIG, MEDIA, FNDN, C-OTH

Synergies
5a

Structural Foundations
Informal

Chicago Near West Side Community Profile
As part of the University of Illinois at Chicago's Great Cities Initiative, and with funding from the Health of the Public program, the university's Health Policy Center published a profile of Chicago's Near West Side community in 1996. The book was designed with three audiences in mind: the university's health professions students; community agencies and providers; and community residents. Rather than relying upon conventional mortality and morbidity statistics to describe the

Contact
Judith A. Cooksey,
MD, MPH
Health Policy Center
(MC 922)
University of Illinois
at Chicago
2121 West Taylor Street
Suite 415
Chicago, IL 60612
jcooksey@uic.edu

health of the community, the authors characterized the inner-city infrastructure—such as the local housing, education, commerce, transportation, and religion—by describing its strengths and resources. As such, the book presents a historical perspective of the neighborhoods that comprise the larger community as well as a documentary of current community redevelopment efforts.

Conrad, K and Cooksey, JA. 1996. *Chicago's Near West Side: a community profile*. University of Illinois at Chicago, Health Policy Center.

[IN] INDIANA

IN-1
Partners
S-GOV, MDPRAC, HOSP, CLIN

Synergies
2b, 6a-2

Structural Foundations
Contract, Advisory

Contact
Donald E. Clayton, MD
Arnett Clinic
2600 Greenbush Street
Lafayette, IN 47904
claytond@arnett.com

Lafayette Medicaid Referral Network
After Indiana instituted a mandatory Medicaid case management program, which required patients to designate a single primary care physician, a group of doctors and clinics in Lafayette complained to the state health department that there was an inequitable distribution of physicians willing to accept Medicaid patients. The state convened a task force with chief executives from the local hospitals and the chairs of the pediatric and obstetric departments. A system was developed that incorporated virtually all pediatricians and obstetricians in the community. The community health clinic determined patients' eligibility, enrolled all the Medicaid patients into its prenatal program, and assigned the women to obstetricians who handled new patients on a rotating basis. Similarly, the Medicaid office assigned children to pediatricians who agreed to accept Medicaid patients up to a certain percentage of their practice.

IN-2
Partners
L-GOV, MDPRAC, VI IO, SCI IL,
RELIG, C-OTH

Synergies
1b, 1c, 2a, 3b, 5a, 5b, 5d

Structural Foundations
Coalition

Tri-County Health Coalition of Southern Indiana
The Tri-County Health Coalition of Southern Indiana is a volunteer organization composed of partnerships, agencies, and individuals. Founded in 1984, it is dedicated to improving the health of the poor, especially minorities and working poor families, in Southern Indiana. Working with the Indiana State Board of Health, the Coalition is particularly concerned with the excess numbers of deaths among minorities and is involved in community health campaigns targeting heart disease, homicide, infant mortality, and HIV/AIDS. Coalition activities include a resource, referral and prevention center, which offers free medical and dental referrals; free acute care medical assistance, in-

Contact
Jesse Floyd, PhD
Tri-County Health Coalition
of Southern Indiana, Inc.
211 East Main Street
P.O. Box 1580
New Albany, IN 47151

IN-3
Partners
LHD, SHD, SOM, U-OTH,
MEDSOC, PHASSN, PROFASSN,
VHO, FNDN

Synergies
6b-6

Structural Foundations
Coalition

Contact
Stephen J. Jay, MD
Indiana University
School of Medicine
Indiana University
Medical Center
Fesler Hall 302
1120 South Drive
Indianapolis, IN 46202
sjay@iupui.edu

cluding pregnancy tests; health education/community development programs, such as support groups, speakers and materials on HIV/AIDS and STD prevention; a food pantry; and a donated-clothes closet. The Coalition is also involved in creating links among community organizations and agencies and in the development of culturally sensitive health education materials.

Medicine/Public Health Forums
With funding from The Robert Wood Johnson Foundation (RWJF), the Indiana Medicine/Public Health Initiative conducted three regional forums (six sessions) in June 1997. Organized in partnership with the Indiana Hospital & Health Association, the Indiana State Medical Association, the Indiana Nursing Association, the Indiana Public Health Association, and Indiana University, the forums involved 109 participants, including the state health department, in discussions around barriers and supports to collaboration between medicine and public health. Evaluation of the forums included analysis of pre- and post-conference surveys, the ranking of future project priorities, and a report summarizing findings from the forums . The conference planning group is currently identifying specific community-based projects to continue the initiative. For instance, its members were planning to collaborate in applying for a RWJF Tobacco-Managed Care Grant.

[KS] KANSAS

KS-1
Partners
LHD, L-GOV, SHD, MDPRAC,
HOSP, LAB/RX

Synergies
2b, 3b, 6a-1

Structural Foundations
Coalition, Contract

Contact
Charles Murphy, MS
Riley County-Manhattan
Health Department
2030 Tecumseh
Manhattan, KS 66502
rchealth@tfsksu.net

Riley County Referral Network
In 1992, the Riley County-Manhattan health department opened up discussions with physicians, hospitals, laboratories, and pharmacies to create a medical care system for the community's uninsured residents. Using state health department funds to provide support staff, the local health department developed a system of health care referrals to the community physicians who volunteered their services. Some patients were seen at the health department clinic while others were seen in physicians' offices. In addition, the health department negotiated donations of diagnostic and ancillary services from the hospitals, pharmacies, and labs in the county. To reward the volunteer effort, the local health department publicly acknowledges all the individuals and institutions involved in the effort.

KS-2

Partners
LHD, L-GOV, SHD, S-GOV,
MDPRAC, HOSP, CLIN, SOM,
SPH, RES, AHC, U-OTH,
MEDSOC, VHO, BUS, SCHL,
RELIG, MEDIA, FNDN

Synergies
5a, 5e, 6b-6

Structural Foundations
Coalition, Contract,
Adm/Mgmt, Advisory

Contact
S. Edwards Dismuke,
MD, MSPH
Department of
Preventive Medicine
University of Kansas
Medical Center-School of
Medicine-Wichita
1010 N. Kansas
Wichita, KS 67214
edismuke@kumc.edu

KS-3

Partners
LHD, MDPRAC, CLIN, MCO,
SOM, RES, AHC, U-OTH, FNDN

Synergies
6b-1, 6b-4

Structural Foundations
Coalition, Contract,
Adm/Mgmt, Advisory

Contact
S. Edwards Dismuke,
MD, MSPH
Department of
Preventive Medicine
University of Kansas
Medical Center-School of
Medicine-Wichita
1010 North Kansas
Wichita, KS 67214
edismuke@kumc.edu

Wichita Public Health Summit

In 1995, the Wichita county health department began holding a series of focus groups regarding community health problems, culminating in a community-wide Public Health Summit, which was attended by city and county elected officials, members of the medical society, all the hospitals, and academic institutions. These participants decided to pursue a community health assessment and health plan collaboratively. A partnership to conduct the assessment was formed by the health department, the Department of Preventive Medicine at the University of Kansas medical school, and the College of Health Professions at Wichita State University. The Kansas Health Foundation contributed $100,000 toward the year-long assessment project. Since the medical school and health professions college jointly run a statewide MPH program, a number of graduate public health students were recruited to help conduct the assessment. Advising the three partners on the assessment project is a broad-based community board, which includes private physicians, the local medical society, and a number of community service providers and leaders.

Primary Care Physician Education Initiative

The Kansas Health Foundation provided the University of Kansas medical school with $15 million over five years, beginning in 1995, to train future primary care physicians to have an understanding of community-oriented primary care. The Primary Care Physician Education initiative follows up on the values and skills promoted through the Health of the Public program, a project devoted to instilling an appreciation of population skills and a community orientation at academic health centers.

KS-4

Partners
LHD, MCO

Synergies
4c

Structural Foundations
Informal

Contact
See citation

Johnson County Operation Immunize

Since 1993, Kaiser Permanente of Kansas employees and physicians have participated in Johnson County's Operation Immunize. Each spring and fall, the clinicians staff weekend clinics alongside public health nurses from the health department to provide free vaccinations to children. In a three-year period, over 1,000 children received the free immunizations.

American Association of Health Plans. 1996. *Improving the quality of life in local communities.* Washington, DC.

[KY] KENTUCKY

KY-5

Partners
L-GOV, S-GOV, INS, SOM, SPH, ARC, U-OTH, VHO, BUS, SCHL, C-OTH

Synergies
5a, 5d, 5e, 6a-3, 6b-4, 6c-2

Structural Foundations
Coalition, Intraorg

Contact
Marian Osterweis, PhD
Association of Academic Health Centers
1400 16th Street, N.W.
Suite 720
Washington, DC 20036
mosterweis@acadhlthctrs.org

University of Kentucky Community-Based and State-Level Partnerships

As of 1993, the University of Kentucky (UK) Medical Center had several active partnerships with state and local government agencies, community service agencies, public schools, and the business community. These links between the academic site and the community provided opportunities for collaboration in assessing community needs, reaching targeted populations, and jointly conducting health promotion activities. Most of these community-based collaborations occurred within individual departments or schools at UK and, in 1993, there was little formal coordination of these activities. At that time, there was growing interest among faculty and administrators to create a coordinating office that would promote and enhance interdisciplinary work across UK's colleges of medicine, nursing, and allied health. (Only the College of Allied Health offers a MPH degree, but it encourages the enrollment of practicing clinicians and medical residents.) In response, the chancellor, who had previously launched a university-wide wellness program, began a planning process for ten multidisciplinary centers of excellence to be located at UK. Three of these centers were active in 1993, the Center on Aging, the Cancer Center, and the Center for Rural Health, and one of the planned centers was explicitly grounded in public health—the Preventive Health Center, which would focus on nutrition, occupational and environmental health, and health promotion and disease prevention. The chancellor of UK had a background in and a commitment to interdisciplinary work. He represents UK in several state-level initiatives on health promotion, such as a research project to assess the feasibility of wellness programs in rural areas for large at-risk populations that is being conducted by the state Blue Cross/Blue Shield Board, and the Healthy Kentuckians 2000 Task Force.

Osterweis, M and Eichhorn, SF. 1993. Community-based health promotion activities. In *Promoting community health: the role of the academic health center.* Skelton, WD and Osterweis, M, eds. Washington, DC: Association of Academic Health Centers.

KY-6
Partners
LHD, CLIN

Synergies
1b

Structural Foundations
Contract, Adm/Mgmt

Contact
Joan B. Dilger
Administration
Family Health Centers Inc.
2215 Portland Avenue
Louisville, KY 40212
jbdiglig01@ulkyvm.
louisville.edu

Jefferson County One-Stop Health Center
With the support and endorsement of the Louisville-Jefferson County Board of Health, the private, nonprofit Family Health Center established itself as a primary care clinic at a former hospital site in 1976. A decade later, the health center seized an opportunity to expand its primary care services with federal funding, and entered into a partnership with the local health department. The two agreed to operate primary care and traditional public health clinics jointly, with staff working side-by-side but under separate governance. The two agencies provided patients with a one-stop health and human services center and a commonly shared case management system. The primary care center could ensure that its patients received family planning, cancer screenings, immunizations, and WIC services, and the public health department could assure primary care access for its patient population. The boards of the two agencies since have considered how to respond jointly to the changing health care marketplace, particularly the reduction in federal and state funding. They have concluded that their emphasis on wellness and prevention, shared purchasing, and reduction of duplication and fragmentation has positioned them to respond to managed care initiatives.

[LA] LOUISIANA

LA-1
Partners
SHD, MDPRAC, HOSP, SOM,
AHC, MEDSOC

Synergies
6a-1, 6a-2, 6a-3, 6a-4, 6a-6

Structural Foundations
Advisory

Louisiana State Government Liaison Committee on Maternal and Child Health
To improve relations between the Louisiana State Maternal and Child Health (MCH) Office and practicing physicians, the state MCH Director and the president of the state chapter of the American Academy of Pediatrics established a Government Liaison Committee in the late 1980s. Composed of physicians, the committee provides advice to the

Contact
Louis Trachtman
Office of Public Health
Louisiana Department of
Health and Hospitals
325 Loyola Avenue
New Orleans, LA 70112
trachman@dhhmail.dhh.
state.la.us

LA-2
Partners
LHD, L-GOV, CLIN, SOM, SPH, U-OTH

Synergies
5b, 5d, 6b-2, 6b-3, 6b-4

Structural Foundations
Intraorg

Contact
N. Kevin Krane, MD
Tulane University
School of Medicine
1430 Tulane Avenue, SL 77
New Orleans, LA 70112
kkrane@tmcpop.tmc.
tulane.edu

LA-3
Partners
LHD, L-GOV

Synergies
1c

Structural Foundations
Adm/Mgmt

Contact
Billie J. Strickland,
MSN, CPNP
State of Louisiana
Office of Public Health
Northeast Regional Office
P.O. Box 6118
Monroe, LA 71211

MCH program on programmatic and fiscal matters, and its primary focus has now shifted from Title V to the Medicaid program. In particular, the Committee facilitated physician input into the state's EPSDT program for Medicaid children. Although the Committee's advisory capacity is informal, it creates a mechanism for the state MCH office to have more physician input related to the care of women and children.

Tulane University Community Service Programs
The Tulane University School of Medicine and its School of Public Health and Tropical Medicine have a number of institutional links, strengthened by the endorsement of the respective deans and the chancellor of the medical center. Some of these involve curricular connections for students pursuing joint MD/MPH degrees or who are part of the Preventive Medicine residency program. Others are targeted at undergraduate medical students. Tulane's program in community medicine, which was situated in the dean of the medical school's office and is being established as a new Department of Family and Community Medicine, coordinates the work of faculty from both schools and serves as an institutional liaison between them. As part of the required "Foundations in Medicine" course for first-year medical students, the community medicine program arranges for public health faculty to teach students clinical epidemiology, health economics, and elements of preventive medicine, and also organizes required community service rotations for the medical students.

Northeast Louisiana Regional Coordination of Home Visits
In the mid-1990s, Northeast Louisiana had one of the nation's highest infant mortality rates caused by child abuse and neglect, in spite of home visit programs run by the health department and the protective services agency. Analysis of the situation revealed that lack of communication between the two programs might be contributing to the problem. Public health nurses were frustrated by their inability to get the protective services agency to act on their reports of substance or physical abuse in children's' homes. Social workers seeing the same patients were being forced to make "life and death" decisions without adequate training to enable them to distinguish biological, social, and

environmental causes of failure to thrive. In 1994, the Regional Administrator of Public Health Nursing approached the Regional Administrator of Protective Services and, together, they developed a plan to have public health nurses and social workers conduct joint visits to families posing a concern for both agencies. The parishes (Louisiana's regional equivalent of a county) have become much more effective in identifying children in abusive or threatening situations and in taking appropriate action quickly. Beginning as a pilot program in one parish, the program later became statewide, with the some of the original developers of the program leading a state-level training session.

[MA] MASSACHUSETTS

MA-1
Partners
SHD, S-GOV, MCO, VHO, SCHL

Synergies
5a, 6a-2, 6a-4, 6a-6

Structural Foundations
Coalition, Contract,
Advisory

Contact
Helen H. Schauffler, PhD
School of Public Health
University of California
at Berkeley
406 Warren Hall
Berkeley, CA 94720
helenhs@uclink2.berkeley.
ed

State Division of Prevention
The Massachusetts Division of Prevention, within the state health department, has a number of formal and informal relationships with the state's Medicaid agency, the Medicaid managed care program, and a number of private HMOs. The Division surveyed all health plans to learn what screening and diagnostic services are provided for chronic diseases, such as diabetes, and participated in a cross-sectoral working group developing clinical preventive guidelines. The Division's school health program has explored ways in which school-based services can be reimbursed by Medicaid managed care plans. The Division has also initiated a statewide group, Partners for Prevention, which seeks to develop a constituency for prevention that extends beyond categorical and programmatic boundaries.

Schauffler, HH, Hennessey, M, Neiger, B. 1997. *Health promotion and managed care.* Report prepared for the Association of State and Territorial Directors of Health Promotion and Public Health Education. Washington, DC.

MA-2
Partners
HOSP, MCO, INS, LAB/RX, SOM,
SPH, ARC, AHC, U-OTH,
PHASSN, VHO, LABR, SCHL,
FNDN, C-OTH

Synergies
6b-2, 6b-4, 6b-6

Tufts University Combined MD/MPH Program
In response to the Health of the Public program, initially funded by the Pew Charitable Trusts and the Rockefeller Foundation, Tufts University School of Medicine developed a four-year combined MD/MPH program in 1987. The accredited program provides medical students with population-based, community-oriented approaches to health

Structural Foundations
Contract, Adm/Mgmt,
Advisory, Intraorg

Contact
Markley H. Boyer,
MD, MPH
Department of Family
Medicine and
Community Health
Tufts University School
of Medicine
136 Harrison Avenue
Boston, MA 02111
mboyer@infonet.tufts.edu

and illness; enhances their health promotion skills; and promotes a keener understanding of the economic, social, and cultural influences that determine the health of individuals and communities. Since Tufts did not have an affiliated school of public health, the program was established in its Department of Family Medicine and Community Health, with public health faculty drawn from other academic institutions, community-based public health practitioners, and medical faculty cross-trained in public health. First- and second-year students take public health core courses: biostatistics, epidemiology, health planning and management, social behavior, environmental health, and public health practice. In their third and fourth years, students in the combined MD/MPH program complete public health rotations and also select advanced public health didactic courses. The total MPH portion of the program is 48 credit hours. While a little over a third of all medical graduates enter primary care, over half the combined degree students have done so. To date, the program has graduated over 100 students.

MA-3
Partners
CLIN, SOM, FNDN

Synergies
6b-1, 6b-4, 6b-6
Structural Foundations
Contract, Adm/Mgmt

Contact
Markley H. Boyer,
MD, MPH
Department of Family
Medicine and
Community Health
Tufts University School
of Medicine
136 Harrison Avenue
Boston, MA 02111
mboyer@infonet.tufts.edu

Tufts University School of Medicine Community-Oriented Curriculum

As part of its Health of the Public program (MA-3), the Tufts University School of Medicine developed a community-oriented curriculum for its medical undergraduates. Required for all first- and second-year students are rotations through a community health center adjacent to the medical school, the South Cove Community Health Center, which cares for a largely poor Chinese population. In addition to providing a community-based setting for ambulatory care training, the community health center also allows the medical students to appreciate and work with cultural, ethical, and linguistic issues. The clinical training is supplemented by small group sessions with the medical students and community-based practitioners, in which specific biomedical problems are linked with broader social factors.

MA-4
Partners
LHD, SHD, HOSP, MEDSOC

Synergies
5a, 6a-4, 6a-5

Massachusetts Perinatal Regionalization

The Massachusetts Department of Public Health convened leaders in the obstetrics community in the late 1960s and early 1970s to develop standards for neonatal and obstetric care. Together with the state health department, they analyzed maternal and perinatal outcomes in an effort to un-

Structural Foundations
Adm/Mgmt, Advisory

Contact
Bernard Guyer, MD, MPH
Department of Maternal
and Child Health
Johns Hopkins School of
Hygiene and Public Health
624 Broadway
Baltimore, MD 21205
bguyer@jhsph.edu

MA-5
Partners
LHD, SHD, FEDHLTH, HOSP,
CLIN, SOM, SPH, AHC, MEDSOC,
PHASSN, PROFASSN, BUS, LABR,
SCHL

Synergies
5a, 5b, 5c, 6b-6

Structural Foundations
Coalition, Advisory

Contact
Myron Allukian, DDS, MPH
Community Dental
Programs
Boston Public Health
Commission
1010 Massachusetts
Avenue
Boston, MA 02118

derstand which systems of care worked and which did not. The group went on to develop standards of care and regionalization of services. The medical community used this process to develop neonatal intensive care units at selected sites and to close down maternal and obstetric units that could not provide appropriate care. As with the development of perinatal and trauma systems in the 1970s and 1980s, a "systems" approach was used by community health planners and the state health department to allocate expensive resources to a regional problem.

Fluoridation Campaign
Although the US Public Health Service and the American Dental Association endorsed the fluoridation of community water supplies in 1950, and a variety of scientific studies had concluded that 50–70% of dental caries could be prevented through fluoridation, by the late 1960s only a handful of Massachusetts' communities had taken that step. A coalition of "pro-fluoridationists" developed in the state, organized by the state dental and medical societies working with a citizen's advocacy group and with the cooperation of the state health department. First, the coalition worked to repeal a mandatory referenda law, which required each of the state's 351 communities to pass a public referendum before the local board of health could order fluoridation. In 1968, after nearly two years of advocacy, the law was repealed. The coalition's next step was to work with the Boston health department on a proposal to regionally fluoridate the state's largest water district, which served Boston and 31 neighboring communities, each with its own board of health. The coalition developed a joint committee to investigate regional fluoridation. The committee was composed of administrators, community organizers, dentists, water supply engineers, health educators, lawyers, physicians, and public health officers. The committee conducted demographic and dental health assessments, community surveys, and regional meetings for local health officials and these communities. By 1971, the committee had convinced a majority of the communities to order fluoridation. Seven years later, after a variety of challenges and appeals had been exhausted, the regional water supply was fluoridated.

MA-6

Partners
LHD, S-GOV, CLIN, SOM, SPH, AHC, FNDN, C-OTH

Synergies
5e, 6a-6, 6b-4, 6b-5, 6b-6

Structural Foundations
Coalition, Contract, Adm/Mgmt

Contact
Miriam E. Torres, RN
Family Health and Social Service Center
26 Queen Street
Worcester, MA 01610
10365313043@
compuserve.com

Community-Based Public Health in Western and Central Massachusetts

A consortium composed of four community-based coalitions in central and western Massachusetts, the local boards of health, the Area Health Education Center, a school of public health, and a medical school was formed with five-year funding under W.K. Kellogg's Community-Based Public Health Initiative in 1991. The premise behind the network was to build sustainable partnerships between academia, communities, local policy bodies, and public health agencies. The consortium sought to improve local capacity to address the needs of both Latino communities and economically depressed blue-collar communities in New England mill towns; to establish a multicultural community-based approach to the training of public health professionals; to promote the capacity of local boards of health to assess and assure the health of their communities; to initiate change in local, state, and national policies affecting their communities; and to evaluate the effectiveness of their consortium. The two principles on which the consortium's work was based involved increasing skills so that work could be done more effectively, and breaking the isolation of organizations working to achieve similar goals.

MA-7

Partners
LHD, L-GOV, SHD, S-GOV, MDPRAC, HOSP, CLIN, MCO, SOM, SPH, MEDSOC, PHASSN, PROFASSN, VHO, BUS, SCHL, RELIG, FNDN, C-OTH

Synergies
1c, 2a, 2b

Structural Foundations
Adm/Mgmt, Advisory

Contact
Janet Slovin, MPA
Worcester Healthcare Outreach
321 Main Street
Worcester, MA 01608

Worcester Healthcare Outreach

The chair of the Worcester District Medical Society's Public Health Committee approached the Central Massachusetts Area Health Education Center (AHEC) and the Massachusetts Medical Society in 1995 to develop a program jointly for linking underserved individuals with health care. The local medical society applied for and received funding from The Robert Wood Johnson Foundation Reach Out initiative. The program, Worcester Healthcare Outreach, refers uninsured individuals to local community health centers for primary care, assists people with applying for government-sponsored insurance programs, runs a weekly, free walk-in clinic, and refers patients to specialists who voluntarily provide care in their offices. In addition, Worcester Healthcare Outreach has developed a program in the local schools to enroll children in state-supported insurance programs, established a fund for free pharmaceuticals, enlisted a local HMO to recruit additional physicians, established a program to provide translators for non-English speaking patients visiting specialists, and solicited the cooperation of local hospitals in providing support services and inpatient care.

MA-8

Partners
LHD, L-GOV, FEDHLTH, MDPRAC, HOSP, AHC, U-OTH, SCHL

Synergies
1a, 4b, 5b, 6b-5

Structural Foundations
Coalition, Contract, Adm/Mgmt

Contact
Elisha Atkins, MD
Massachusetts General
Hospital Chelsea
Health Center
151 Everett Avenue
Chelsea, MA 02150
atkins_elisha@mgh.harvard.edu

Chelsea Asthma Partnership

With funding from AHCPR, Massachusetts General Hospital (MGH) and the city of Chelsea developed a partnership and several programmatic activities to reduce acute asthma episodes in children and adults. Goals of this partnership, which includes a community coalition with representatives of city agencies and health care providers, are to increase primary care access, facilitate public health interventions in the home environment, provide on-going education and support to individuals, and ensure that necessary follow-up services are obtained. First, the partners hired and trained a case manager to provide support, education, and referrals to primary care and preventive services for individuals who presented with an acute asthma episode in the schools or at MGH. Since then, there has been increased coordination of asthma care between the MGH Chelsea Health Center's pediatric unit and the city school health department. Second, they instituted continuing education programs for the staff of the health center's urgent care unit, its adult medicine units, and its ambulatory clinic in order to increase appropriate follow-up care. Third, the partnership has sponsored a community education campaign that emphasizes the need for early identification, environmental remediation, and regular treatment of asthma. Finally, to identify and address environmental risks for asthma, the partners worked collaboratively to train staff of the local housing authority and city inspectors to improve the identification and remedy of asthma triggers in the home. They also contracted with the Work Environment Program of the University of Massachusetts to identify and work with industries whose practices pose a risk of occupational asthma.

MA-9

Partners
LHD, SHD, HOSP, CLIN, VHO, SCHL, RELIG, C-OTH

Boston Medical Center Violence Prevention and Intervention Programs

Violence is a serious public health problem, and homicide is the leading cause of death among young African-American men. Emergency Depart-

Synergies
1a, 4a, 4b

Structural Foundations
Intraorg

Contact
See citation

ments (ED) treat the sequelae of violence, but they also provide an opportunity for prevention and follow-up that can break the cycle of violence in families and communities. As of 1996, Boston Medical Center had several violence prevention programs to address this issue. Project Direction focused on children ages 14 to 21 who were seen in the ED for gunshot injury, stab wounds, or other assault injuries. A violence prevention counselor would speak with the patient while in the ED, then with family and friends, and try to identify the underlying causes of violence in the individual and family. Referrals were made to community agencies, including community health centers, public health departments, medical schools, youth outreach projects, school programs, church groups, and private associations such as Vietnam Veterans Against Violence. Project Direction staff wrote guidelines for counselors and physicians approaching at-risk youth or victims of violence for the first time. The hospital also participated in a statewide Injury Surveillance System established by the Massachusetts State Health Department, in which ED physicians register a detailed report on all gunshot and knife wounds. The state used this data, collected from all 90 of the state's hospitals, to summarize state trends which were periodically reported in a newsletter.

Bernstein, E and Bernstein, B, eds. 1996. *Case studies in emergency medicine and the health of the public.* Sudbury, MA: Jones and Bartlett Publishers. (NAT-18)

MA-10
Partners
LHD, L-GOV, SHD, FEDHLTH, HOSP, SOM, SPH, RES, U-OTH, BUS

Synergies
1a, 3a, 3b, 4b, 6b-5, 6c-1

Structural Foundations
Contract

Boston Medical Center Project ASSERT
In order to give emergency department (ED) staff better strategies for assessing and referring patients with substance abuse problems to treatment, the Boston Medical Center ED created Project ASSERT (Alcohol and Substance Abuse Service and Education for Provider Referral to Treatment) as a collaboration of ED physicians, nurses, community outreach workers, and the City of Boston Department of Public Health Addiction Services. Created in 1994 with a three-year grant from the federal DHHS Center for Substance Abuse Treatment, Project ASSERT links patients with alcohol and other drug-related problems who present at Boston Medical Center's ED with Boston's network of alcohol and drug treatment inpatient and outpatient services. The Massachusetts Department of Health

Contact
Edward Bernstein, MD,
FACEP
Department of
Emergency Medicine
Boston University School
of Medicine
818 Harrison Avenue
Boston, MA 02118
ebernste@bu.edu

provided follow-up data about patients' contact with the substance abuse treatment system after their treatment in Project ASSERT. This information improved estimates of the participants' recovery rates and unmet needs. The grant monies helped the ED create new positions—Health Promotion Advocates (HPAs)—who were drawn from community organizations and trained by Boston University's School of Public Health in a six-week course titled, "HIV and Substance Abuse Health Education." Though the key goal is to identify substance abuse problems, the project team chose to frame drug screening questions as part of broader questions about health and safety. So, the HPAs screen and refer patients for a variety of health concerns in addition to drug treatment, including smoking cessation programs, victim services, STD treatment, prenatal care, breast cancer screening, and primary care clinics. Following the health assessment, the HPAs use a Brief Negotiation Interview to estimate problem severity and readiness to change. Then they make appropriate referrals, providing transportation vouchers when needed, and follow-up with calls to the individual after ten days. Project ASSERT is currently integrated into the ED as a line item financed by Boston Medical Center, which has found the work of HPAs, especially its linkages to primary care, preventive services, and to the substance abuse system to be "value-added services" in the managed care environment. A resolution by the Boston City Council and an award by a respected business group were instrumental in achieving continued funding for the program.

Bernstein, E and Bernstein, B, eds. 1996. *Case studies in emergency medicine and the health of the public.* Sudbury, MA: Jones and Bartlett Publishers. (NAT-18)

MA-11

Partners
LHD, SHD, MDPRAC, HOSP, CLIN,
MCO, LAB/RX, SOM, SPH,
MEDSOC, PHASSN, PROFASSN,
VHO, SCHL, RELIG, MEDIA,
FNDN, C-OTH

Synergies
5b

Structural Foundations
Advisory

Harvard Pilgrim First AIDS Kit

In 1993, the Harvard Pilgrim Health Care Foundation developed a comprehensive package of AIDS education materials for young adults, "The First AIDS Kit," as a joint effort of a pediatrician and a health educator. The project was informed by an advisory group that included young adults, AIDS experts, peer leaders, teachers, and school health experts. The kit, which includes a brochure, a condom key chain, a lifesaver card, and a video for teachers, was distributed to over 26,000 young

Contact
Susan Pauker, MD
Harvard Pilgrim Health
Care Foundation
185 Dartmouth Street
11th Floor
Boston, MA 02116

MA-12
Partners
LHD, L-GOV, HOSP, SPH, VHO, SCHL, FNDN

Synergies
5a, 5c, 5d

Structural Foundations
Coalition, Contract, Advisory

Contact
David Bor, MD
The Cambridge Hospital
1493 Cambridge Street
Cambridge, MA 02139

MA-13
Partners
LHD, L-GOV, SHD, MDPRAC, HOSP, CLIN, MCO, INS, SOM, SPH, RES, AHC, BUS, SCHL, FNDN, C-OTH

Synergies
1c, 6a-1, 6a-5

adults through schools, community centers, and outreach programs in a five-state region. A companion piece to the young adults kit is a "Talk-Listen-Care (TLC) Kit" designed to encourage communication between children ages 4–12 and their parents about issues of self-esteem, sexuality, and AIDS. More than 50,000 of the children's kits have been distributed to libraries, schools, shelters, clinics, and families throughout New England.

Cambridge Health of the City Program
After the Cambridge Health Policy Board conducted a community health assessment in 1994 using APEX*PH*, the list of the top ten preventable health problems was used by the Cambridge Health of the City program to recruit Harvard graduate public health students to address one of the health objectives. A team of three students in the "practice management and community health" course selected teen pregnancy. The students worked with the Health Policy Board's Women's Health Task Force and the clinical director of the Teen Health Center, located at the public high school. The students signed a contract specifying deliverables, procedures to assure confidentiality, ownership of the data, a timetable, and a work plan. They analyzed data from the Teen Health Behavior Survey, reviewed medical charts, and conducted focus groups with post-partum teenage mothers. The students presented their report to the Health of the City Consortium, which included community representatives, the mayor, a city councilor, the superintendent of schools, and the health commissioner. One of the report's recommendations, to make contraceptives available at the Teen Health Center, stirred a great deal of public controversy. Ultimately, the school committee passed the resolution to allow contraceptives to be dispensed at the health center.

Somerbridge Community Health Partnership
The adjacent communities of Cambridge and Somerville face similar urban health challenges—substance abuse, violence, homelessness, teenage pregnancy, and AIDS. There was an opportunity for collaboration across the two cities, especially since many of the agencies providing substance abuse, mental health, legal, and social services served both communities. The current partnership (a CCN

Structural Foundations
Coalition, Adm/Mgmt

Contact
Linda Cundiff
Community Affairs
Cambridge Health Alliance
Somerville Hospital
230 Highland Avenue
Somerville, MA 02143
lcundiff@cphc.org

demonstration partnership funded by the W.K. Kellogg Foundation), which refers to the catchment area of the two communities as "Somerbridge," brings together key health leaders in the two cities (the two hospitals, both local health departments and city human services offices, and community-based organizations) in developing an integrated service delivery plan. The Partnership is developing model programs to coordinate services in the two cities around three challenging health problems: substance abuse, geriatrics, and health care access for recent immigrants. One consequence of these discussions was that the two hospitals realized they had much in common and decided that a merger would benefit their institutions and improve coordination of services between the cities. Merging a public hospital (Cambridge) with a private, not-for-profit one (Somerville) required public dialogue and legislative approval. In the summer of 1996, the Cambridge Public Health Commission was established, a public authority to govern both hospitals, allowing the successful merger of the hospitals.

MA-14
Partners
LHD, SHD, HOSP, CLIN, MCO, INS, VHO, BUS, RELIG, FNDN, C-OTH

Synergies
1c, 2a, 4a, 4c, 5a, 5b, 5d, 5e

Structural Foundations
Coalition

Contact
Frank Robinson, PhD
Partners for a Healthier Community, Inc.
140 High Street
Room 516
Springfield, MA 01199
frank.robinson@bmcsouth.bhs.org

Springfield Community Health Planning Steering Committee
Beginning in 1994 as the Springfield Community Health Planning Steering Committee, a partnership of local health systems and medical providers, the local health department and other government agencies, local foundations, and other community-based groups and individuals was formed to measurably improve health in their community. In 1996, the partnership became a nonprofit organization called Partners for a Healthier Community, Inc., which works with over 75 organizations and has three concrete action plans to improve community health: (1) an immunization program for preschool age children; (2) a comprehensive school health program; and (3) a youth development program for at-risk adolescents. The partnership has been recognized by the W.K. Kellogg Foundation as a CCN finalist partnership and by The HealthCare Forum as a national model for healthy cities and communities. It is also funded by The Robert Wood Johnson Foundation for an outreach program that uses lay health promotion workers.

MA-15

Partners
LHD, L-GOV, SHD, FEDHLTH,
CLIN, PROFASSN, VHO, RELIG,
C-OTH

Synergies
1c, 2b, 4c

Structural Foundations
Coalition, Contract,
Adm/Mgmt

Contact
See citation

Boston Healthy Start Initiative

Throughout the 1980s in Boston, the infant mortality rates among African-American women were three times higher than those of white women in the city. In response, one statewide initiative provided health coverage for uninsured women, and citywide strategies included outreach and home visiting programs to at-risk women and their babies. Despite these efforts, the infant mortality rate remained high. A series of articles in the Boston Globe in 1990 prompted the mayor to convene an Infant Mortality Summit, from which a Maternal Health Commission was empaneled to oversee and coordinate further efforts. Barely two months after the commission was formed, HRSA issued a request for proposals for its Healthy Start Initiative (NAT-9), a five-year multimillion-dollar grant to be awarded to 15 selected cities. The Commission invited three co-conveners—a coalition of black ministers, the Boston Department of Health and Hospitals, and the statewide association representing community health associations—to call the first meeting and begin the grant application process. The actual process of developing a consortium of providers, community leaders, and women from the affected communities, and of crafting a governance structure that shared power and authority equitably over the disbursement of the funds, served to highlight the conflicts and tensions that existed between the city health department and the communities. Notwithstanding the tense planning sessions and grant writing critiques, a consortium was formed and a successful grant application made. The Department of Health and Hospitals (which oversees the public health department) was designated as the fiscal agent to manage the funds and oversee the operation and evaluation of the grant. An Executive Committee was formed, with proportionate representation of the affected communities, and given the responsibility of developing policy, hiring the executive director, and overseeing the process for distributing funds. One persistent problem has been that despite the Consortium's well-developed and equitable governance structure, by virtue of HRSA guidelines in designating a grantee, the Department of Health and Hospitals maintained the ability to override decisions made by the Executive Committee or the Consortium. This reinforced the wariness of community groups skeptical of their ability to truly share power. Despite all these reservations, the Consortium successfully awarded over $3 million to neighborhood-based organizations to implement a number of programs, and the infant mortality rates have decreased throughout the city and among affected communities.

Plough, A and Olafson, F. 1994. Implementing the Boston Healthy Start Initiative: a case study in community empowerment and public health. *Health Education Quarterly* 21(2): 221–234.

[MD] MARYLAND

MD-1
Partners
LHD, MDPRAC, HOSP, LAB/RX, RES, MEDSOC, VHO, FNDN

Synergies
1c, 2b

Structural Foundations
Coalition, Adm/Mgmt

Contact
Carol W. Garvey, MD, MPH
Department of Health
and Human Services
Montgomery County,
Maryland
401 Hungerford Drive
5th Floor
Rockville, MD 20850
carol.garvey@co.mo.md.us

Montgomery County Project Access

Despite being a relatively affluent community with a substantial number of public and private health and human service agencies, Montgomery County still has a substantial population of medically underserved and is under economic pressures to provide for their care. Project Access, funded by The Robert Wood Johnson Foundation (RWJF) through their Reach Out initiative, addresses this issue by creating a referral network that matches medically indigent patients with physicians willing to provide discounted or free care. The program also links extensive support services to the private practitioners' offices. To maximize the effectiveness of medical care provided, and to reduce the frustration experienced by clinicians when patients are unable to get to their appointments or cannot afford needed diagnostic or treatment services, the Project Access system provides transportation, language translation, and low-cost laboratory, x-ray, and pharmacy services as needed. In 1993, the Primary Care Coalition, an incorporated nonprofit organization whose members include the Montgomery County Department of Health and Human Services, the Montgomery County Medical Society, five local hospitals, United Way, and a number of other nonprofit providers of medical and mental health care, developed the concept of Project Access, and jointly pursued funding for it. After receiving the RWJF grant, the Coalition spent the first year planning, hiring a coordinator, and setting up and programming the computer infrastructure. The referral network began operating in 1997, with limited referrals to specific target groups to avoid overwhelming the system. Enrollment has since grown steadily.

MD-2
Partners
LHD, HOSP, RES

Synergies
1a, 1c, 2c, 3b, 6b-4

Structural Foundations
Contract, Informal

Contact
Larry L. Leitch, MA, MPA
Carroll County Health
Department
P.O. Box 845
Westminster, MD 21158
leitchl@dhmh.state.md.us

Carroll County Maternity Care Program
In the early 1970s, the Carroll County Health Department could not find private obstetricians to either staff public health clinics or accept Medicaid or uninsured pregnant women. The local health officer was approached by the chief of OB/GYN at the Greater Baltimore Medical Center, a teaching hospital in search of clinical training sites for its OB/GYN residents. The two quickly established a partnership in which the chief of OB/GYN set up a physician rotation and coordinated in-hospital care and delivery, and the health department provided clinic space and staff for prenatal visits. The medical center provided a neonatal intensive care unit, tertiary level emergency care, social services, and 24-hour physician coverage for any pregnant woman. Senior residents also staffed the health department's family planning clinics, general gynecological clinics, provided genetic counseling services, and also established a breast and cervical cancer screening and treatment program. The partnership, which operated for most of its 28 years on the basis of a handshake before formalizing a contractual arrangement, recently disbanded as Medicaid managed care initiatives depleted the health department's patient base and jeopardized the continuing relationship with the medical center.

MD-3
Partners
LHD, L-GOV, HOSP, MEDSOC

Synergies
2b

Structural Foundations
Coalition, Adm/Mgmt

Contact
Patricia Ford, MPH, MBA
Baltimore County
Department of Health
One Investment Place
11th Floor
Towson, MD 21303

Baltimore County Health Care Project
In 1993, there was growing concern about care for the uninsured in Baltimore County, highlighted by media coverage on national health reform and a Governor's task force on the issue. The president of the county medical association and the health officer of the county health department convened a meeting, bringing together representatives from the medical association, the health department, and the Department of Social Services (DSS). This group launched the Baltimore County Health Care Project, which now also involves five hospitals. Through the partnership, physicians volunteer to provide free consultations to low-income, uninsured patients who are referred to them through the county health department. (Concurrently, the patients are also referred to DSS for more comprehensive assistance and referrals.) In five years, the program has provided over 1,600 medical appointments, many of which included diagnostic tests. In addition, many providers have agreed to continue their relationships with the patients, offering care

at free or reduced cost. Factors in the success of this project are the willingness of the interagency committee to listen and respond to the concerns of the patients and other agencies, a planning process that established mutually agreed upon goals and parameters, proactive ways to address potential problems, and ongoing communication among the principal agencies, partners, and patients.

MD-4

Partners
LHD, SHD, MDPRAC

Synergies
1c, 2d, 3b, 4a, 5a, 6a-1, 6a-5

Structural Foundations
Contract, Advisory

Contact
Nancy S. Luginbill, RN
Health Services
St. Mary's County Health Department
P.O. Box 316
21580 Peabody Street
Leonardtown, MD 20650

St. Mary's County Well-Child Outreach Partnership

When the pediatrician who conducted all the health department's child health clinics retired in 1989, the health officer and nursing director of the St. Mary's County Health Department in Maryland were unsure how they would provide well-child care services to the children. Yet, this crisis also presented an opportunity to change how care was delivered to this group. The Well-Child Outreach program, which has been operating for more than eight years, is a public-private partnership that provides well-child care and preventive interventions such as lead screening and immunizations to uninsured and underinsured children. The partnership involves the county health department, a pediatric group practice, two family practice physicians, and the Maryland State Health Department's Division of Child Health. All children in the county can now access well-child care, and the working relationship between the health department and the private providers is strong. The health department provides case management, tracking, and health education, while private pediatricians provide acute and preventive care. In addition to being more cost-effective, the program has improved access by minimizing financial and geographic barriers and has reduced the fragmentation in care. The health department assures quality of care, contracting with physicians for a regular schedule of exams and tracking these visits with audits. Measurable improvements in the delivery of care have resulted: the "show rate" in the private sector is 95%, compared to the public clinic rate of 55%, and two-year immunization rates have increased.

MD-5

Partners
S-GOV, HOSP, CLIN, SOM, RES

The Maryland Plan

In 1976, the Maryland Mental Hygiene Administration and the University of Maryland's Department of Psychiatry joined forces to better recruit gradu-

Synergies
2c, 6b-4

Structural Foundations
Contract, Advisory

Contact
Walter Weintraub, MD
Department of Psychiatry
University of Maryland
School of Medicine
701 West Pratt Street
4th Floor
Baltimore, MD 21201

ates of psychiatric residency programs into state service. By designing the program collaboratively, the statewide initiative, known as the Maryland Plan, has made public psychiatry more attractive, enhancing the state's capacity to recruit and retain a university-trained workforce. Strategies outlined in the Plan included abolishing the state hospital residency program, placing the Maryland Psychiatric Research Center under university control, sending university residents and faculty to state hospitals and community mental health centers, and offering faculty appointments to state psychiatrists who were teaching residents and medical students. Long-term support for the program was gained by courting state legislators, who needed to understand the importance of successful recruitment for adequate care of the mentally ill, and the mental health constituency groups, which included universities and mental health providers as well as advocacy groups and families of the mentally ill. Over its long history, the Maryland Plan has disproved many myths about public-private collaboration, but also offers several lessons on the difficulties of such relationships, such as: (1) excellent psychiatrists can be recruited without bonuses or increased salaries; instead, job descriptions and responsibilities are important; (2) mandatory state hospital and community health center rotations can be included in training without compromising training or recruitment; and (3) mutually beneficial collaboration can occur without substantial cost on either side. Despite success in some areas, one unanticipated problem was lingering distrust about the Maryland Plan among leaders of the state health department. Other problems were the high-level administrative appointment of some young, "unseasoned" psychiatrists who ended up leaving public service because of political infighting, and the unwitting bias created against foreign medical graduates in the Plan's attempt to demonstrate the need for a better trained workforce in public mental health.

Talbott, JA and Robinowitz, CB. 1986. *Working together: state-university collaboration in mental health.* Washington, DC: American Psychiatric Press, Inc. (NAT-20)

MD-6
Partners
HOSP, SOM, SPH, ARC, FNDN

Baltimore Population-Based Blindness Survey

In 1990, the Dana Center for Preventive Ophthalmology at the Johns Hopkins University School of Medicine and Public Health conducted a popula-

Synergies
3b, 3c, 5b, 6c-1

Structural Foundations
Informal

Contact
See citation

tion-based study to compare visual impairment among Caucasian and African-American residents of Baltimore's inner city. The study had an unexpected result: the leading cause of blindness in both racial groups was unoperated cataract, in spite of the fact that most of the affected individuals had Medicare coverage, lived in close proximity to the medical center, and clearly recognized they were visually impaired. Following publication of the study in 1991, the Center raised funds from a private philanthropist and The Robert Wood Johnson Foundation to conduct a community-based screening and treatment program. Run jointly by the Wilmer Eye Institute and an epidemiologist at the School of Public Health, and involving 150 Baltimore churches, the Sight 'n Soul program trained community residents to conduct visual assessments and to refer those with impairment to the Institute or another source of care. An NIH-funded study, using anthropological and sociological approaches, is attempting to identify the reasons that affected individuals have not sought out care.

Sommer, A, Tielsch, JM, Katz, J, and Quigley, HA, et al. 1991. Racial differences in the cause-specific prevalence of blindness in East Baltimore. *The New England Journal of Medicine*. 325(20):1412–1417.

MD-7
Partners
LHD, L-GOV, MDPRAC, HOSP, INS, MEDSOC, RELIG, C-OTH

Synergies
2b, 2d, 6a-1, 6a-2

Structural Foundations
Contract, Adm/Mgmt, Advisory

Contact
Martin P. Wasserman, MD, JD
Maryland Department of Health and Mental Hygiene
201 W. Preston Street
5th Floor
Baltimore, MD 21201
wassermanm@dhmh.state.md.us

Montgomery County Project Deliver
In 1987, one of the two remaining hospitals in Montgomery County willing to provide labor and delivery services for indigent women refused to continue providing care. The local health department director, who oversaw the prenatal care program, which referred over 1,000 patients to the hospitals' obstetric services, immediately launched a series of meetings with key hospital executives, the president of the local medical society, several eminent community obstetricians, and local elected officials to try and resolve the crisis. When it became evident that the key sticking point was obstetricians' fear of unwarranted lawsuits, the group designed a program, Project Deliver, which would employ the obstetricians for an eight-hour labor and delivery period. This allowed the physicians to be covered under the county's self-insurance, be personally immune from lawsuits, and also capped any successful lawsuit at a maximum of $500,000. The county also negotiated with the

area's largest insurer to exclude indigent patients from the liability premium calculations used for the obstetricians' private practice. As a further incentive for the physicians, the county health department agreed to handle all the Medicaid paperwork for the doctors. Since each of the county's four hospitals was also concerned that it was shouldering a greater burden of uncompensated care, the health department crafted a rotational system that satisfied the hospitals. Although the recruitment of obstetricians to participate in Project Deliver started slowly, in two years' time over 100 physicians had signed up. On the basis of the newly formed relationship with the local health department, a number of the obstetricians began voluntarily providing prenatal care in their offices in addition to the labor and delivery services.

MD-8

Partners
LHD, SHD, SOM, SPH, AHC, VHO, SCHL, RELIG, C-OTH

Synergies
1b, 1c, 2a, 3b, 4c, 5b, 5d, 6b-4

Structural Foundations
Coalition, Adm/Mgmt

Contact
See citation

Baltimore Heart, Body, and Soul

What began in the mid-1980s as an advisory board of public agency leaders and key researchers and providers at Johns Hopkins University and Hospital, evolved in 1989 into Heart, Body, and Soul, Inc., a partnership with the Baltimore clergy coalition CURE (Clergy United for Renewal in East Baltimore). The program, jointly run by CURE and the Johns Hopkins University Center for Health Promotion, provides primary health care, health education, referral and case management services at churches, community centers, schools, clinics, markets, soup kitchens, shelters, in homes, and on the street. The program encompasses five components: (1) Neighborhood Health Resource Centers; (2) community health workers who provide preventive services, screening, health education, referrals, and support services; (3) a training program for the community health workers; (4) access to primary and specialty care in a variety of settings; and (5) curricula and field placement opportunities for medical, nursing, public health, and ministerial students. In one evaluation of the program's effectiveness at fostering control of hypertension, researchers reported that 79% of patients in Heart, Body, and Soul had their hypertension under control after five years as opposed to 50% of a "usual care" group. Likewise, hospitalizations secondary to hypertension were nearly half that in the community model than the "usual care" model of office-based primary care. The partnership was funded for four years under the W.K. Kellogg Foundation's Community-Based Public Health Initiative, and the group's model programs on smoking cessation have been replicated in 15 cities with funding from the American Lung Association and churches.

Health Resources and Services Administration. 1996. Models that Work. URL http://www.bphc.hrsa.dhhs.gov/mtw/.

MD-9
Partners
LHD, CLIN, MCO, SCHL

Synergies
1c, 3b

Structural Foundations
Contract

Contact
See citation

Baltimore School-Based Clinics

The Baltimore health department operates ten school-based health clinics. In the early 1990s, it found that many students coming to the clinics had not received EPSDT exams and appropriate follow-up care. Most of these students were enrolled in Total Health Care, a local community health center with a Medicaid HMO license. After much discussion and negotiation, the HMO and the health department clarified their roles. Candid about their initial mistrust of each other, and of their concerns about losing control over their patients, they jointly developed formal agreements and patient flow charts to manage their patients' care collectively. The HMO agreed to reimburse the health department for EPSDT exams, acknowledging that the school-based clinics were better positioned to reach this population. If such care could be provided in a timely fashion at the community health center, however, the health department agreed to refer the student back to the HMO. The formal agreements and reimbursement schedules helped overcome the barriers of compensation and control, and a series of "field trips" from the school clinics to the health center succeeded in fostering better relationships among the providers. In addition to increasing the number of EPSDT exams performed on the student population by having them conducted at the school clinics, the HMO initiated a health education program at the clinics and also developed three of its own school-based health clinics. The HMO committed further to the collaboration by hiring a part-time nurse coordinator to assist in tracking the clinical care provided at the school-based health centers.

Knight, W. 1996. *Improving the public's health: collaborations between public health departments and managed care organizations*. Washington, DC: The Joint Council of Governmental Public Health Agencies.

MD-10
Partners
MDPRAC, MCO, ARC, C-OTH

Synergies
3c, 4b, 5d

Structural Foundations
Intraorg, Informal

Contact
Gary W. Goldstein, MD
Kennedy Krieger Institute
707 North Broadway
Baltimore, MD 21205

Baltimore Kennedy Krieger Institute
Lead Program

In Baltimore, where over half of the city's housing has lead problems, one of the largest medical providers of lead treatment is using capitated payments to finance a broad multipronged approach. The Kennedy Krieger Institute, a private center for children with brain-based disabilities, sees between 80 and 90% of the lead-poisoned children in Baltimore, including 600 patients at one clinic alone. Traditionally, its lead-toxicity treatment protocol has involved hospitalizing patients and providing chelation treatment. Because of a very restrictive reimbursement structure, the Institute had to hospitalize each child even if it was cheaper to house him or her in a hotel, and social work counseling and housing support were not reimbursed. In 1994, Kennedy Krieger approached a number of managed care organizations and insurers about capitating the lead-toxicity treatment, using a sliding scale that provided higher capitation payments for more severe cases of lead poisoning. For approximately one-third less money than it had received on a cost basis, the Institute was now free to structure its treatment in any way it wanted, with the proviso that it was responsible for the care of the child for one year. Instead of hospitalizing the children, the Institute now moves the family directly into private housing drawn from a registry of lead-free homes, and provides chelation therapy on an outpatient basis. The Institute pays the family's moving costs and supports any other financial needs they have in the move. This often includes paying overdue utility bills, laying out money for utility deposits, and occasionally paying rent if a family falls behind. Kennedy Krieger also conducts lead abatements of lead-poisoned homes, entering them into their housing registry once they are safe. Although the Baltimore health department does not directly provide lead abatement, it maintains surveillance of elevated blood lead levels in the city, regulates landlord compliance, and monitors the provision of lead treatment, such as that provided by Kennedy Krieger. The Kennedy Krieger Institute presently spends more on community services than it does on medical services, and the approach has proven to be a more cost-effective way of treating and preventing lead poisoning in children. Its recidivism rate, once 50%, is now zero.

MD-11

Partners
LHD, HOSP, SOM, BUS, SCHL, FNDN

Synergies
1c

Structural Foundations
Coalition, Contract

Contact
See citation

Baltimore Vision for Health Consortium

In this low-income inner-city area of west Baltimore, the Vision for Health Consortium, formed in 1991, was part of a plan to transform a community that suffers from high unemployment, poor access to health care and preventive services, and many serious health problems such as HIV infection, heart disease, and homicide. This CCN demonstration partnership, funded by the W.K. Kellogg Foundation, will address these issues by creating a coordinated system of care among providers already working in the community. Five major medical providers in the area and the Baltimore City Health Department have signed a "compact" with a private advocacy group, Community Building Partnership, which outlines commitments and responsibilities for developing and operating a new health system with services in adult primary care, children's health, outreach, substance abuse, and violence prevention. The agreement is meant to reduce competitive barriers among the partners to allow them to provide a seamless continuum of care to community residents. The Partnership is also prepared to participate in a Medicaid Managed Care Waiver in order to deliver primary care services in schools.

Community Care Network Demonstration Program. 1997. *The 25 Community Care Network demonstration partnerships: profiles in progress.* Chicago: Hospital Research and Educational Trust.

[ME] MAINE

ME-1

Partners
MDPRAC, HOSP, VHO, FNDN, C-OTH

Synergies
1c, 4a, 5a, 5b, 5e, 6b-5

Structural Foundations
Coalition, Intraorg

Contact
Betsy Kimball
Franklin Community
Health Network
One Hospital Drive
Farmington, ME 04938
bkimball@fchn.org

Maine Franklin Community Partnership

In rural Maine, a key problem is access to high-quality health care, given widespread poverty, lack of education, lack of transportation and a population that is widely dispersed across a geographic area. To address these issues, the Franklin Community Health Network (the parent company of an acute care hospital, a multispecialty group physician practice, a community-based health education organization, and a mental health provider group) joined with a community-based organization, Western Mountains Alliance, and their own Healthy Community Coalition to create the Franklin Community Partnership (a CCN demonstration partnership funded by the W.K. Kellogg Foundation) in the early 1990s. Projects include: (1) the creation of a computer-scannable health card, which speeds registration into the health care system and provides a population database for outreach and targeted health education messages; (2) a mobile health unit, which provides core preventive screening and services, and health education; (3) a program to assess the need for Community Health Educators; and (4) a Youth Rural Leadership program to develop skills of area eighth-graders. Each partner is involved in a variety of community collaborative projects in addition to those funded through the CCN program, including projects with the state health department and the area's public health nurse.

ME-2
Partners
LHD, SHD, MDPRAC, LAB/RX

Synergies
1c, 3c, 4a, 4c

Structural Foundations
Contract, Adm/Mgmt

Contact
See citation

On-Line Pharmacy System for TB Medication

In November 1995, the Maine TB Control program initiated a statewide computerized pharmacy link that allowed patients to fill prescriptions for TB medications at local pharmacies. Prior to that, the state health department had filled all TB prescriptions by shipping them statewide. Under the new program, a physician notifies the TB Control program of a patient requiring medication, and the state creates a computerized pharmacy link. The patient can pick up the medication, for free, at any pharmacy. In addition, the state can monitor medications that have not been picked up within 48 hours and institute outreach activities. The TB Control program also utilizes public health nurses and direct delivery services to get the medication to the patient. Since instituting the system, the TB Control program improved medication delivery time from 5–7 days to under 24 hours; eliminated state responsibility for labeling and mailing TB medication; greatly improved program surveillance; and substantially reduced program staff time.

Benecke, B. 1996. *TB Notes.* Centers for Disease Control and Prevention, Division of TB Elimination, National Center for HIV, STD, and TB Prevention 2:7.

ME-3
Partners
SHD, MDPRAC, MCO

Synergies
3a, 5b, 5c, 5e, 6a-4

Structural Foundations
Contract, Advisory

State Division of Community and Family Health

Although very few of Maine's residents are enrolled in private HMOs (7%), the state health department's Division of Community and Family Health has been developing greater ties with HMOs and Independent Practice Associations (IPAs) in anticipation of the full implementation of Maine's Medicaid managed care program. Together with the managed care organizations, the Division has developed guidelines for breast and cervical cancer,

Contact
Helen H. Schauffler, PhD
School of Public Health
University of California
at Berkeley
406 Warren Hall
Berkeley, CA 94720
helenhs@uclink2.berkeley.
edu

nutritional and cardiovascular education, and participation in a Healthy Communities effort, Healthy Maine 2000. In coordination with the IPAs, the Division has tracked tobacco-related services and in partnership with the HMOs, successfully advocated for the passage of seat-belt legislation. Organizationally, the Division created the Managed Care Workgroup to coordinate efforts between the health department and managed care organizations.

Schauffler, HH, Hennessey, M, Neiger, B. 1997. *Health promotion and managed care.* Report prepared for the Association of State and Territorial Directors of Health Promotion and Public Health Education. Washington, DC.

[MI] MICHIGAN

MI-1
Partners
FEDHLTH, MCO, RELIG

Synergies
5b, 5d

Structural Foundations
Coalition

Contact
Marvella E. Ford, PhD
Center for Medical
Treatment Effectivess
Programs
Henry Ford Health System
1 Ford Place
Suite 3E
Detroit, MI 48202
mford1@biostat.hfh.edu

Detroit Church-Based Asthma Program
In 1996, the AHCPR Medical Treatment Effectiveness Program (MEDTEP) at the Henry Ford Health System identified the need for an adult asthma education program targeting African-Americans in Detroit, particularly since this population was facing increasing mortality and morbidity due to asthma. The health system's researchers spent a year identifying appropriate models of community outreach and education and subsequently developed an asthma education program combined with an empowerment curriculum for African Americans. The researchers and members of the faith community's "health ministry" adapted educational materials to make them more culturally appropriate and publicized the program through church notices and public announcements. The researchers are conducting an evaluation to determine the program's effectiveness. Outcome measures being examined include emergency department use, asthma knowledge, use of peak flow meters and asthma inhalers, perceptions of asthma, and asthma-related quality of life.

MI-2
Partners
LHD, L-GOV, MDPRAC, HOSP,
CLIN, U-OTH, MEDSOC, VHO,
BUS, SCHL, RELIG, MEDIA,
FNDN, C-OTH

Synergies
3b, 4b, 5a, 5b, 5d, 5e

Creating a Healthier Macomb
In the early 1990s, a group of community leaders, public officials, and health care executives began meeting in Macomb County to consider ways of improving the quality of life for the county's residents. After 18 months of planning, in 1994 the group launched its joint project, Creating a Healthier Macomb. By 1996, the group had raised over $1 million from three of the local hospitals and

Structural Foundations
Coalition

Contact
Lisa J. Uchno
Creating a
Healthier Macomb
43421 Garfield
Suite 203
Clinton Township, MI
48038
cahm@ix.netcom.com

MI-3
Partners
LHD, L-GOV, MDPRAC, HOSP,
SOM, ARC, BUS

Synergies
5b

Structural Foundations
Coalition, Contract

Contact
See citation

from a Community Care Network grant from the W.K. Kellogg Foundation. The project built on the principles of the Healthy Communities model—defining health broadly and identifying the foundations of a strong community. In Macomb, that has meant an emphasis on holistic health, family, education, a sense of community, economic opportunities, a strong civic infrastructure, and the environment. The community has established 50 measurable goals. Approximately half are health-related, and the remainder address educational, social, spiritual, economic, and environmental needs. Each goal is overseen by a collaborative work group, which sets annual action plans and publicizes them in the community. Examples include: a cable show on fitness; bike/skate safety rallies and anti-smoking art projects in schools; kits distributed to physicians' offices detailing local health resources on cancer, smoking cessation, and depression; spiritual care month in local churches; an affordable housing initiative; and training of neighborhood women as lay educators for breast and cervical cancer detection. The ongoing community efforts to address the 50 goals are monitored and tracked by a central project office through a computerized database, and made available on the community's electronic bulletin board.

Calhoun County Community Health Information Network

As of 1996, the Calhoun County Health Improvement Program (CCHIP), a collaboration of medicine, public health, academia, business and local government, was working on the development of a Community Health Information Network (CHIN) that would provide consumers with information about health insurance, benefits, and providers using computer kiosks placed in public spaces. The Kalamazoo Center for Applied Medical Informatics (CAMI) was commissioned to assist in the planning, development, and evaluation of the CHIN and worked closely with the Health Network Team from CCHIP. It was planned that the first CHIN program focus on insurance coverage, and CAMI evaluated two existing CHIN prototypes, taking into account input from local consumers, and medical providers on the functioning and "user-friendly-ness" of these systems. By September 1995, CAMI had completed interviews with providers, consumers and payers about the information to include in the system, such as insurance types and claims data, a comparison of potential computer kiosk vendors, and a prototype of the CHIN computer screens. At that time, there were plans to install the CHIN kiosk system and perform a formal evaluation of the program.

Gosbee, J, Ritchie E, and Brunetti, T. 1995. *Health information network design and evaluation for the Calhoun County Health Improvement Program.* Kalamazoo, MI.

MI-4

Partners
LHD, SHD, FEDHLTH, MDPRAC, HOSP, CLIN, LAB/RX, RES, AHC, VHO, MEDIA, C-OTH

Synergies
2b, 3b, 4c

Structural Foundations
Coalition, Contract, Adm/Mgmt, Advisory

Contact
Carol Garlinghouse, MSN, RN
Clinical Service Unit
Cancer Prevention and Control
Michigan Department of Community Health
3423 N. Martin Luther King Jr. Blvd.
P.O. Box 30195
Lansing, MI 48909
garlinghousec@state.mi.us

Statewide Breast and Cervical Cancer Screening Program

Using funds available through the CDC Breast and Cervical Cancer Early Detection Program and supplemented by state tobacco tax revenue, the state health department launched a five-year initiative in 1991 with $4 million per year. The program encouraged local health departments to provide clinical breast exams, Pap smears, pelvic exams, and screening mammograms to any woman over age 40 years old with income up to 250% of the poverty line (GA-7 is another example). To qualify for program funding, the local health departments had to prospectively assure the state that there were adequate referral mechanisms in place to guarantee further diagnosis and treatment for women with breast or cervical cancer regardless of the ability to pay. Twenty-six local health departments joined the program, and most developed partnerships with mammography facilities, laboratories, physicians, and hospitals in order to coordinate the screening and treatment. Since only the screening and program administration were covered by the funds, treatment for uninsured women was donated by the providers. Many of the hospitals in the partnerships shared their expertise in program publicity and coordination, and many provided space for public health clinics so that clients could receive all screenings, including a mammogram, at a single appointment. Since the publicity campaigns were directed at all women, and not only the uninsured, a number of those requiring further diagnosis and treatment would have public or private insurance coverage. The support of state and county medical societies has proved an integral element in recruiting physicians to participate in the programs. As of March 1998, the programs have screened over 45,000 low-income women, and detected breast or cervical cancer in 537 women, who were subsequently treated.

MI-5

Partners
LHD, SHD, HOSP, CLIN, MCO, SCHL, FNDN

Synergies
1c, 2c

Structural Foundations
Contract

Contact
Kate Conway
School-Based
Health Initiative
Henry Ford Health System
1 Ford Place
Detroit, MI 48202
kconway1@hfhs.org

MI-6

Partners
SHD, S-GOV, MEDSOC, PHASSN

Synergies
5c

Structural Foundations
Advisory

Contact
Darlene Burgess
Government Affairs
Henry Ford Health System
1 Ford Place
Detroit, MI 48202
dburges1@hfhs.org

Detroit School-Based Health Centers

Several of Detroit's hospital health systems, including Henry Ford Health System (HFHS), the Detroit Medical Center, St. John, and Beaumont health systems, contracted with the city's schools in 1994 to develop and manage 13 school-based health centers, with much of the start-up funding provided by the W.K. Kellogg Foundation. The health centers are staffed by health system nurse-practitioners and physician assistants, with physician direction and oversight in specific cases or through referrals. Most of the health centers provide comprehensive preventive and primary care services regardless of the student's insurance status. Since there was concern voiced at the program's onset that the health centers might take patients away from private physicians, or from the health systems' providers, the school health center providers have established a communications protocol for involving and informing the student's primary care provider. Since the health systems have absorbed financial losses through the program as part of their charitable and uncompensated care budgets, health administrators are in negotiation with insurance companies, the state, and the local health department regarding financial assistance.

Statewide HIV Informed Consent Law

Since the development of serologic testing for the presence of HIV antibodies in 1985, there has been a persistent tension between the medical and public health communities over public policies regarding HIV testing and informed consent. State and local medical societies and the AMA have favored making HIV testing "routine," at the physician's discretion, and not necessarily subject to prior informed consent by the patient. The CDC has represented the views of many in the public health community by advocating for confidential and voluntary HIV testing. In Michigan in the early 1990s, the Department of Public Health and the Michigan Association for Local Public Health opposed efforts by the Michigan State Medical Society to rescind state law requiring informed consent for HIV testing. A compromise was worked out in Michigan whereby the procedures for obtaining informed consent were streamlined while still maintaining the autonomy of the patient to proactively grant consent.

MI-7
Partners
LHD, HOSP, CLIN, MCO

Synergies
2c

Structural Foundations
Contract

Contact
Melissa Wenzler
Center for Integrated
Urban Health
Henry Ford Health System
1 Ford Place
Detroit, MI 48202
mwenzler@hfhs.org

Detroit Hospitals Adopt Public Health Clinics
Since 1996, the Detroit Health Department has contracted with private hospitals and health systems to provide physicians and mid-level providers for the city's six public health centers. The city funds the initiative under the department's annual $90 million health center budget, most of which comes from state and federal grants. In one example, the Henry Ford Health System (HFHS) provides professional staffing for general primary care clinics for pregnant and postpartum women, children and adolescents, and adults of all ages. One of the reasons for pursuing such a contract with the city is to reduce the number of medically indigent patients using hospital emergency departments for their primary care. In return, the patients receive better coordinated care and access to all of the HFHS's resources.

MI-8
Partners
LHD, SHD, MCO

Synergies
3a

Structural Foundations
Informal

Contact
See citation

Statewide *Guidelines for Lead Screening in Children*
A local HMO, Blue Care Network-Health Central, worked with the Ingham County health department and the Michigan state health department to develop and disseminate *Guidelines for Lead Screening in Children* to all its providers. The protocol has proved useful for testing children in local at-risk populations, and has resulted in the identification and treatment of several children with elevated serum lead levels.

American Association of Health Plans. 1996. *Improving the quality of life in local communities.* Washington, DC.

MI-9
Partners
LHD, FEDHLTH, HOSP, CLIN, MCO

Synergies
1c, 3a, 4a, 4c

Structural Foundations
Coalition, Contract, Adm/Mgmt

Contact
See citation

Detroit Immunization Campaign
According to the National Immunization Survey, in 1994 and 1995 Detroit had the lowest immunization rates among 28 cities and counties. Nor was the problem restricted to the poorest or most disenfranchised. Private practices and HMOs only averaged 55–56% immunization rates for their 2-year-olds, compared with a national rate of 73%. In response, two large area health systems—Henry Ford Health System and the Detroit Medical Center's Children's Hospital—spearheaded a coalition that included other hospitals, community health centers, and the city and county health departments, and were awarded a $7.3 million, five-

year grant from the CDC to address childhood immunization. The Pediatric Immunization Program developed by the coalition will emphasize five key areas: (1) an interactive, electronic immunization registry, which will also alert primary care physicians when their patients need scheduled immunizations; (2) formal linkages between prenatal care and primary and pediatric care, so that there is a continuum of care for mothers and children; (3) a home visit program that will supplement primary care services with immunizations, outreach, and other preventive services; (4) the development of "best clinical practices" for immunization as the product of both community and physician consensus; (5) and policy advocacy to identify and remove local policy barriers to care.

Henry Ford Health System. September 27, 1996. New Release: Henry Ford and Children's Hospitals receive grant to tackle childhood immunization problem in Detroit. Detroit, MI.

MI-10
Partners
LHD, FEDHLTH, HOSP, CLIN

Synergies
1c, 2b, 4b, 5b, 5d

Structural Foundations
Coalition, Adm/Mgmt

Contact
See citation

Michigan Rural Prevention Network

In the early 1990s, the four county health departments in Alcona, Losco, Ogemaw, and Oscoda counties, along with two community health centers and a hospital, formed the Rural Prevention Network. Using federal funds, the network hired five health educators, four volunteer coordinators, and an information and referral specialist. In order to address primary and preventive health care needs in the rural, low-income area, the network developed a comprehensive strategy for chronic disease prevention that included services and programs on smoking cessation, fitness and weight loss, nutrition, diabetes education, and worksite health promotion activities. The network also provided primary care referrals through its toll-free hotline, hosted health fairs, ran media educational campaigns, and published a quarterly newsletter. In enlisting primary care providers to accept patients, the network provided a "dual-direction referral system": network staff could refer community members to primary care providers for treatment, and in return the physicians could refer patients to network staff for behavioral risk factor reduction services.

Health Resources and Services Administration. 1998. Models that Work. URL http://www.bphc.hrsa.dhhs.gov/mtw/.

MI-11
Partners
MCO

Synergies
3a, 6b-5

Structural Foundations
Intraorg

Contact
John J. Wisniewski,
MD, MHSA
Managed Care College
Henry Ford Health System
1 Ford Place
Suite 3C
Detroit, MI 48202
jwisnie1@smtpgw.is.hfh.
edu

Henry Ford Health System Managed Care College

As a strategy for incorporating population-based skills and practices into their organization, the Henry Ford Health System (HFHS) established its Managed Care College (MCC) as a program for continuing education for its medical practitioners in 1993. The program was originally designed for primary care practitioners, but has expanded and now includes practitioners in specialty care as well as administrators, though primary care is still given priority. The curriculum was designed by a smaller subsidiary, which was acquired by HFHS, and the course material changes every year based on feedback from participants and organizational needs. A public health/population-based philosophy is evident in the course materials, but the MCC program has no formal links with outside agencies. Instead, instructors are drawn from internal divisions, such as the Center for Clinical Effectiveness, the Center for Health Systems Studies, Managed Care Services, the Center for Healthcare Quality Improvement, Education and Research, and the Biostatistics Department. Many instructors have dual degrees in medicine and public health or are nationally recognized experts in measuring health outcomes, clinical effectiveness, and system evaluation. The MCC holds its classes on a school-year schedule with weekend courses and workshops as well as intensive seminars on special topics held during the week. Participants can receive CME credit and professional development time to attend these programs, and participation is voluntary. In an evaluation of the MCC program, participants find the course work useful in their practice, and over 80% would strongly recommend the program to a colleague.

[MN] MINNESOTA

MN-1
Partners
LHD, L-GOV, SHD, FEDHLTH,
MDPRAC, HOSP

Synergies
3b, 5b, 5c, 5d

Little Falls Health Promotion Projects

In Minnesota, the state health department gives grants to local public health agencies to publicize the availability of free breast and cervical cancer screening services. To strengthen this activity, in 1993 the Morrison County Public Health Department asked the staff of St. Gabriel's Hospital, a not-for-profit hospital, for ideas on how best to promote the free services. The cancer screening program involves private practice physicians and

Structural Foundations
Coalition, Adm/Mgmt

Contact
Patrick Rioux
St. Gabriel's Hospital
815 SE 2nd Street
Little Falls, MN 56345
emc2@upstel.net

MN-2
Partners
LHD, S-GOV, HOSP

Synergies
5a, 5e, 6b-6

Structural Foundations
Coalition

Contact
Betty Hestekin, RN
Fairview Lakes Regional
Health Care
11685 Lake Boulevard N.
Chisago City, MN 55013
bhestek1@fairview.org

MN-3
Partners
LHD, SHD, HOSP, MCO,
MEDSOC, PHASSN

Synergies
6b-5, 6b-6

hospitals who promote the availability of free services to their patients and assure their follow-up treatment. These partners also collaborated on programs to reduce problem gambling and teen tobacco use. Mid-level professionals in each organization (the health promotion coordinator from the local health department and the community relations director of the hospital) played key roles in these programs.

Chisago County Community Health Assessment

When the community health outreach manager at Chisago Health Services/Fairview Lakes Regional Healthcare learned that the county health department was planning to conduct a state-mandated, countywide community health assessment similar to one planned by the health system, she called her government counterpart to propose they join forces on the project, so as to avoid duplication. They began a collaboration in which work was shared equally and each organization took on roles based on expertise. The health system's outreach manager facilitated the process, and its public relations department wrote and edited the report. Staff at the local health department were responsible for data collection and statistical analysis, and the state health department helped with the design of the assessment instrument. The results of the study were made widely available to local health care providers and agencies and became a resource for the development of a mandated community health plan. The partners continue to work together and are now key facilitators for a Healthy Communities project in the county. Attention to partnership issues was important to the success of this collaboration. The state health department provided facilitation training to the entire group, both organizations were represented while conducting focus groups, and credit was equally shared in the final reports and community presentations of the assessment.

Medicine/Public Health Conference

In 1997, leaders of the Minnesota state medical and public health associations used funding from The Robert Wood Johnson Foundation to organize a statewide conference bringing together leaders from medicine, public health, hospital systems, and managed care organizations. The conference highlighted five collaborative initiatives from around

Structural Foundations
Coalition

Contact
John Oswald, MPH
Center for Health Statistics
Minnesota Department
of Health
114 Burntside Drive
Minneapolis, MN 55422
john.oswald@health.state.
mn.us

the state (MN-4 was one of the featured cases), and focused on ways of expanding such collaborative activity. The cases represented regional planning efforts between local public health agencies, a major tertiary hospital, and a "cooperative" managed care organization to jointly address specific health priorities; community assessments conducted jointly by public health agencies and medical providers; and broad community health campaigns such as hepatitis B prevention among adolescents, bicycle helmet safety for kids, and heart disease reduction. The conference was funded through the Medicine/Public Health Initiative, and capitalized on earlier collaborative efforts coordinated by the Center for Population Health in the Twin Cities of Minneapolis and St. Paul. Representatives from the two associations held subsequent meetings to review opportunities for further collaboration. The group developed a Web site that provides information on collaborative efforts in Minnesota, beginning with a focus on alcohol, tobacco use, and violence issues.

MN-4
Partners
LHD, SHD, HOSP, CLIN, MCO,
INS, SPH, PHASSN, C-OTH

Synergies
4a, 4c, 5c, 5d, 6b-5

Structural Foundations
Coalition, Contract

Contact
Sue Zuidema
Community Health
Department
Hennepin County
Health Department
Health Services Building
525 Portland Avenue South
Level 3
Minneapolis, MN 55415
sue.zuidema@co.hennepin.
mn.us

Minnesota Center for Population Health

In 1994, spurred by state health care reform legislation that called for local public health agencies and health plans to take statutory responsibilities for population health, the Minnesota Public Health Association hosted a series of meetings for leaders in the public and private health services sectors on ways to collaborate to improve population health. This meeting led to the creation of the Center for Population Health, a forum for public and private health organizations to study, discuss, and collaborate on population health improvement. Thirty organizations have since joined the nonprofit, incorporated Center representing all local community health boards and all major health plans and health systems of the area, plus the Minnesota Department of Health, the University of Minnesota School of Public Health, and the United Way. Each has signed a memorandum of understanding, which commits to a joint mission around five functions: assessment and evaluation, policy formation, research, collaborative health initiatives, and professional education on population health. Specific projects include: (1) the creation of a comprehensive immunization registry that connects all birth records and all pediatric immunization providers in the county; (2) a Tobacco Control Workshop, which will coordinate prevention/education interventions, pool data on smoking cessation rates, and monitor and advocate for public policy on tobacco taxes and limiting access to youth; (3) an initiative to provide hepatitis B immunizations for adolescents in schools; and (4) a bicycle safety campaign. The Center has one staff member who, funded by a grant, works on the immunization registry. Partners each pay a small assessment to meet financial needs of the Center or to cover any additional project expenses within their own organization's budget.

MN-5

Partners
LHD, L-GOV, S-GOV, MDPRAC, HOSP, MCO, SPH, ARC, U-OTH, MEDSOC, PROFASSN, LABR, FNDN

Synergies
3a, 3c, 4b, 5b, 5d, 6b-6, 6c-2

Structural Foundations
Contract, Adm/Mgmt

Contact
Janny Dwyer Brust, MPH
Allina Foundation
Allina Health System
5601 Smetana Drive
P.O. Box 9310
Minneapolis, MN 55440
brust@allina.com

Allina Foundation Collaborative Research on Violence Prevention

In 1994, the Minneapolis Department of Health and Family Support released its KIDSTAT report, which revealed an alarming rate of violence experienced by children and adolescents in the city. The Allina Foundation Board of Trustees, working with public health experts, medical providers, researchers, teachers, young people, and their advocates, began developing a multipronged strategy aimed at violence reduction (MN-6, MN-9, MN-10, MN-11, MN-12). Seeing a central role for research in determining what works in violence protection, the Foundation actively supports collaborative research, giving over $300,000 to a Violence Prevention Research Fund, overseen by the medical director for community affairs at the Children's Hospitals and Clinics and the director of the Regional Injury Prevention Research Center at the University of Minnesota. Six research projects were started in 1995, involving the University of Minnesota and professionals from public health, mental health, a nurses' association, and the judicial system. Research topics include measuring the prevalence of domestic violence in rural areas and health-seeking behaviors among rural women, understanding the link between women-battering and child maltreatment, and looking at risk factors and costs related to workplace violence. In addition, research seminars, featuring nationally recognized experts, have been conducted for public health and medical professionals as well as the community. These presentations have provided information on strategies for violence prevention and control, evaluation methods, gun control, and the costs of violence.

MN-6

Partners
LHD, L-GOV, SHD, S-GOV, MDPRAC, HOSP, CLIN, MCO, INS, SPH, ARC, VHO, SCHL, RELIG, FNDN, C-OTH

Synergies
5a, 5b, 5d, 5e, 6b-6

Structural Foundations
Contract, Adm/Mgmt, Advisory

Contact
Janny Dwyer Brust, MPH
Allina Foundation
Allina Health System
5601 Smetana Drive
P.O. Box 9310
Minneapolis, MN 55440
brust@allina.com

Allina Foundation Project REACH

Interested in promoting, and learning from, community-based initiatives, the Allina Foundation designed and funded Project REACH (Research, Education, And Community Health) a four-year, $1 million initiative in 1996, which to date has funded 56 distinct projects. Small grants ($5,000 each) were made available to 34 groups (half of whom are not affiliated with the Allina system) to fund technical assistance, such as conducting needs assessments, planning, implementing or evaluating programs, or assisting with group facilitation or group process skills. Project REACH also funded evaluations for five community-based projects with clinical strategies (totaling over $500,000) and provided funding to 17 Healthy Community teams working in health improvement. Those teams each were given $5,000 to implement an educational strategy that they will evaluate when completed. Strategies include an asthma education program for teachers so that they can intervene at a student's earliest symptoms, and a community-based campaign to improve the image of breast-feeding among African-American women. Project REACH has an advisory council with national and local, private and public health care leaders, which provides information on successful approaches to population-based health improvement, and a review board, composed of local private and public health care experts, which selects the grantees. Key research questions for this initiative include: What population-based strategies are most effective for improving and promoting health? What technical skills are needed by groups working to improve community health to effectively design, implement, and evaluate their strategies? Project REACH staff shares findings, activities, and funding opportunities among groups interested in population health improvement via newsletters and mailings. Further initiatives are planned targeting clinical and community interventions to improve the health of low-income populations in Allina Health System's seven priority areas (cancer, cardiovascular disease, diabetes, pregnancy, asthma, violence (MN-5), and tobacco use).

MN-7

Partners
LHD, SHD, MDPRAC, MCO, FNDN

Prairie Regional Health Alliance

In 1994, the Prairie Regional Health Alliance was founded as a public-private partnership sponsored by the New Pioneer Health Plan CISN. Within the

Synergies
1c, 3c, 4a, 4c, 6a-1, 6a-2, 6b-5

Structural Foundations
Coalition

Contact
Liza Marie Keifer
Network Development
New Pioneer Health Plan
CISN
101 Willmar Avenue, S.W.
P.O. Box 817
Willmar, MN 56201

requirements of the 1992 MinnesotaCare legislation, New Pioneer offers two benefit packages that follow mandated guidelines and have programs that serve publicly insured patients. Early in its development, the Health Plan's parent company, Affiliated Community Health Network (a joint venture of Blue Cross/Blue Shield of Minnesota and Affiliated Community Medical Centers) hired an independent facilitator to assist in developing a regional public health initiative. Bimonthly meetings were held with representatives from public health agencies in the 19-county service area to discuss needs and how organizations in the public and private health care system might collaborate. The group later formalized its mission to promote the health of the population through cooperative partnerships, and has been involved in the development of a regional tracking system for child immunization, a pilot program that uses public health clinics as the access point for child and teen checkups and immunizations for all members in the region, and a population-based prenatal care model that would be operated as a public-private collaboration. When the immunization registry was being developed, the state health department initially identified significant barriers to creating a system, but eventually became more supportive, dedicating staff for technical assistance and funding a pilot program that will expand an immunization registry that currently serves a five-county area. One or two counties will be added each year until the whole region is covered. An important feature of the registry is a reminder card system for both the family and the primary care clinic that triggers public health outreach if a child has not received a scheduled vaccination. The second program, which is testing the reimbursement for clinical prevention services at public health clinics, represents a significant change in contractual policy since Blue Cross/Blue Shield, which will assume operation of New Pioneer in the summer of 1998, has not traditionally reimbursed public health clinics for these services.

MN-8
Partners
LHD, SHD, HOSP

Synergies
1a, 2a, 3b, 4b, 4c

Chisago County Women's Health Evening Clinic
To make it easier for women to obtain routine physicals and preventive screenings, such as breast exams and Pap smears, Chisago Health Services/ Fairview Lakes Regional Healthcare (CHS/Fairview) and the Chisago County Health Department jointly

Structural Foundations
Coalition

Contact
Betty Hestekin
Fairview Lakes Regional
Health Care
11685 Lake Boulevard N.
Chisago, MN 55013
bhesteki1@fairview.org

sponsor the Women's Health Evening Clinic. For five nights a month, three CHS/Fairview clinics around the county are open after normal business hours (until 8:00 p.m.) to provide health services and health education for women. The CHS/Fairview practitioners supply medical services, while the health department's public health nurses offers prevention counseling and education on cancer, osteoporosis, cardiovascular disease, and healthy lifestyles, as well as immunizations and hormone-replacement prescriptions as needed. The health department staff also help low-income and uninsured women apply to receive free mammograms and Pap smears through the Minnesota Breast and Cervical Cancer Control Program. The same sliding scale rates, insurance co-payments, and public subsidies apply whether the appointment is scheduled for daytime or evening, but the evening is "women only" and offers more structured time for education. The State of Minnesota supports the Evening Clinic Program with a provider grant to CHS/Fairview and an outreach grant to the health department. The program has received positive feedback from providers and patients, with women appreciating the convenience, one-to-one attention, and privacy that these clinics afford.

MN-9

Partners
SHD, HOSP, MCO, PROFASSN,
VHO, FNDN

Synergies
3a, 4a, 6b-5, 6b-6

Structural Foundations
Coalition

Contact
Janny Dwyer Brust, MPH
Allina Foundation
Allina Health System
5601 Smetana Drive
P.O. Box 9310
Minneapolis, MN 55440
brust@allina.com

Statewide E-Coding of Violence-Related Injury
Through Minnesota's Health Care Coalition on Violence founded in 1995 (MN-5, MN-10), a community health epidemiologist from the Allina Foundation and a vice president for the Minnesota Hospital and Healthcare Partnership are leading an effort to systematize the state's voluntary collection of injury-related "E-codes." These codes, which are included on billing forms for each patient encounter, provide information about the cause of injury and whether it is violence related. Better tracking of the costs and risk factors associated with violence can assist in planning and monitoring prevention strategies, as well as provide information on the extent and type of violence experienced by individuals in a community. Another project of the Health Care Coalition on Violence is the development of guidebooks for practitioners that review the research literature on the effectiveness of prevention and intervention strategies related to violence.

MN-10

Partners
LHD, SHD, S-GOV, MDPRAC,
HOSP, MCO, INS, ARC, MEDSOC,
VHO, BUS, C-OTH

Synergies
1c, 3a, 4b, 5b, 5d, 6a-2,
6b-5, 6b-6

Structural Foundations
Coalition, Advisory

Contact
Jill S. Heins, MS
Health Care Coalition
on Violence
2829 Verndale Avenue
Anoka, MN 55440
jheins@miph.org

MN-11

Partners
L-GOV, HOSP, MCO, INS, FNDN,
C-OTH

Synergies
1c, 4b, 5a, 5b

Structural Foundations
Coalition, Contract,
Adm/Mgmt, Advisory

Contact
Janny Dwyer Brust, MPH
Allina Foundation
Allina Health System
5601 Smetana Drive
Minneapolis, MN 55440
brust@allina.com

Minnesota Governor's Task Force on Violence and the Health Care Coalition on Violence

In 1995, in response to a state-level report on violence in Minnesota (MN-5, MN-14), the Governor's Task Force on Violence was convened to create a forum for discussion among health care, public health, and community leaders about strategies to reduce violence. The Task Force was especially interested in the role of private health care in violence prevention and issued a report with recommendations for action within the health care industry. To implement the strategies outlined in this report, the Health Care Coalition on Violence was formed. Representatives from health systems, hospitals, health plans, local and state health departments, community organizations, and advocacy groups participate in five committees: (1) Practice Guidelines, Education and Training, which promotes best practices for providers to better identify and act in cases of suspected abuse; (2) Workplace Violence and Abuse Prevention; (3) Data and Research, which works to improve E-coding statewide and review relevant literature on prevention strategies (MN-9); (4) Primary Prevention, which links the health care facilities with community-based home visiting services and prenatal education; and (5) Health Plan Coverage, which examines how reimbursement policies can facilitate effective violence prevention, intervention and rehabilitation efforts.

Minneapolis Day One Project

Patients with social problems usually leave health care settings without referrals to needed social services agencies. The converse is true for clients presenting with medical problems in social service settings. In 1996, the Allina Foundation and United Way of Minneapolis Area created the Day One Project to identify the relationships and tools necessary to ensure that patients and clients receive the right service at the right place and time. Day One focuses on domestic violence to achieve its goals of coordinating health and social services. Three pilot programs are operational. The first streamlines referrals among all 12 Minneapolis/St. Paul domestic violence shelters so that survivors and health providers receive the services they seek in a single call. The second project provides health and social service providers with a database of 2,200 social service providers across the State of Minnesota. The third pilot program integrates this social service database with the largest statewide health care information and referral database, so that referral specialists can address the full continuum of health and social service needs of patients and clients.

MN-12

Partners
LHD, L-GOV, MDPRAC, HOSP, MCO, INS, LAB/RX, ARC, RES, VHO, BUS, SCHL, RELIG

Synergies
1a, 3a, 4a, 4b, 5b, 6b-5

Structural Foundations
Coalition, Adm/Mgmt, Intraorg

Contact
Janny Dwyer Brust, MPH
Allina Foundation
Allina Health System
5601 Smetana Drive
Minneapolis, MN 55440
brust@allina.com

St. Paul Partners for Violence Prevention

The Allina Foundation and the United Hospital Foundation are involved in a $1 million dollar effort, Partners for Violence Prevention, to test anti-violence strategies in St. Paul's West 7th Community. Led by a county commissioner and the co-director of the Initiative for Violence-Free Families and Communities in Ramsey County, who is a family-violence specialist, the project has four major components: (1) improved care and treatment of sexual assault victims at United Hospital's Emergency Department through community-wide protocol development; (2) "safe places" at the United Family Health Center and the emergency room at United Hospital, where on-site advocates are available for people experiencing family violence; (3) a system of improved communication and data collection for emergency responders and the hospital staff regarding the role of violence in a given injury; and (4) the design and implementation of prevention strategies based on the expressed needs of the community.

MN-13

Partners
CLIN, MCO, VHO, SCHL

Synergies
1a, 3c

Structural Foundations
Contract

Contact
Stephanie Mollichoni
Health Partners
CHP-MOD C
Minneapolis, MN 55440

Minneapolis School-Based Care

A Minneapolis-based managed care organization, HealthPartners, entered into a contractual agreement with Health Start, a nonprofit organization managing eight school-based health centers, to provide comprehensive health services to teens at the school health clinics. Health Start provides service to teens in the clinics and bills HealthPartners for the care. HealthPartners' physicians participate in the clinical sessions and provide medical direction for the program. HealthPartners and its hospital (Regions Hospital) also provide in-kind support to the administration of the clinics and for coordination of care after-school hours.

MN-14

Partners
L-GOV, SHD, S-GOV, HOSP, MCO, INS, BUS, FNDN

Minnesota Action Plan to End Gun Violence

In 1994, researchers at Blue Cross/Blue Shield of Minnesota, and its managed care plan, Blue Plus, examined the growing impact of gun violence on its members' health. As a result, the health plan

Synergies
5b, 5d, 5e

Structural Foundations
Coalition, Adm/Mgmt,
Advisory

Contact
Dan Johnson
Community Affairs
Blue Cross and Blue Shield
of Minnesota
3535 Blue Cross Road
Route 459
Eagan, MN 55122
djohnson@bcbsmn.com

spearheaded a statewide campaign involving community leaders, interested citizens, policymakers, health care providers, and advocates (both pro- and anti-gun) to discuss gun violence and steps that could be taken to reduce gun-related mortality and morbidity. In 12 communities across the state, Blue Cross convened community forums that used electronic polling systems to reach consensus about community-level and policy actions. The product of these meetings was the Minnesota Action Plan to End Gun Violence, published as a special insert in a statewide magazine, *Minnesota Monthly*. The action plan recommended an advertising campaign focused on teenagers; a toll-free hotline to encourage students to report guns and crimes in school; a team of teens, school, and park officials working jointly to reduce gun possession by students; and increased access to local social service agencies and conflict resolution programs. The project stimulated the formation of the Governor's Task Force on Violence as a Public Health Problem, which in turn led to the creation of the Minnesota Health Care Coalition on Violence (MN-10). The coalition has prioritized violence as a health care issue, and has focused the attention of health care providers and institutions on supporting or developing programs to address the determinants of violence.

MN-15
Partners
FEDHLTH, MDPRAC, HOSP, SPH,
U-OTH, MEDSOC, VHO, MEDIA

Synergies
5d, 6c-2

Structural Foundations
Coalition, Adm/Mgmt,
Advisory

Contact
See citation

Minnesota Heart Health Program

A ten-year multistate project to develop and test community-wide prevention strategies for cardiovascular disease began in 1980. Supported by the National Heart, Lung, and Blood Institute, the Minnesota Heart Health Program involved three pairs of case-control communities in Minnesota, North Dakota, and South Dakota. Researchers from the University of Minnesota schools of public health, social work, and journalism established local offices and community networks in each of the six cities; developed a range of individual-level and population-wide health education efforts in coordination with the local communities; surveyed a variety of cardiovascular disease endpoints, risk factors, and the effectiveness of the educational strategies; and worked to develop citizen leadership to continue the work after the federal funding ended. The researchers' work built on two seminal community studies from the 1970s: the Stanford Three Communities Study in California, and another study conducted in North Karelia, Finland. Minnesota's multidisciplinary research team shared a simple conceptual base, which emphasized that health behaviors are learned, and that the learning process is influenced by the culture in which people live. Recognizing that secular trends toward more healthful behaviors might provide competitive explanations for the effects of their interventions, the researchers explicitly sought to measure population risk profiles that were more pronounced and experienced earlier in the intervention communities. This case describes the first three years of effort in Mankato, Minnesota, one of the intervention communities. Community involvement included the hiring of local staff for a storefront office, the enlistment of over 190 community leaders as long-term volunteers, and the development of a 21-person community advisory board.

Mittelmark, MB, et al, 1986. Community wide prevention of cardiovascular disease: education strategies of the Minnesota Heart Health program. *Preventive Medicine* 15:1–17.

MN-16

Partners
LHD, L-GOV, MDPRAC, HOSP, CLIN, AHC, U-OTH, MEDSOC, VHO, BUS, LABR, SCHL, FNDN

Synergies
1c, 5b, 6a-5

Structural Foundations
Coalition

Contact
Colleen Swanson
Itasca Partnership for
Quality Healthcare
126 First Avenue Southeast
Grand Rapids, MN 55744

Itasca Partnership for Quality Health Care

The Itasca Partnership for Quality Health Care was formed in response to the challenges of providing adequate care to a sparsely populated, rural area with a large elderly population. The geographic area encompasses 16 rural communities near Grand Rapids, which suffer from high rates of heart disease, cancer, and trauma-related deaths. This CCN demonstration partnership, funded by the W.K. Kellogg Foundation, includes over 50 health care providers, public health and social service agencies, businesses, unions, and government officials. The Partnership is dedicated to developing a community-wide system of health education, health care, and support services that integrates community providers to foster wellness, prevention, and personal health. To meet these goals, the Partnership is developing a Center without Walls initiative and is looking at ways to reverse the trend of outward migration of services from the community, possibly partnering with a large health system or managed care organization to bring local services back. Specific activities of the Partnership have included holding public forums on community health issues and providing advice and support to a local hospital board when the community hospital was recently sold.

MN-17

Partners
LHD, SHD, MCO, VHO, C-OTH

Synergies
4a, 4c, 5b, 5d, 6a-6

Structural Foundations
Contract

Contact
Helen H. Schauffler, PhD
School of Public Health
University of California
at Berkeley
406 Warren Hall
Berkeley, CA 94720
helenhs@uclink2.berkeley.
edu

MinnesotaCare Legislation

As a consequence of the 1992 MinnesotaCare legislation, which mandated Medicaid managed care, all licensed HMOs in the state are required to submit collaboration plans describing how they will assist local public health agencies in achieving public health goals. The process has engendered a close working relationship between health educators at individual HMOs and the state's Division of Family Health. As of 1997, they had collaborated on a number of health promotion initiatives, including asthma education and prevention, diabetes prevention and control, alcohol use prevention, a school health fitness program, and data collection systems. The state also provided a key staff member to develop guidelines for collaborations between public health, licensed HMOs, and community integrated services.

Schauffler, HH, Hennessey, M, Neiger, B. 1997. *Health promotion and managed care*. Report prepared for the Association of State and Territorial Directors of Health Promotion and Public Health Education. Washington, DC.

[MO] MISSOURI

MO-1

Partners
LHD, HOSP, SCHL

Synergies
1a, 1c, 3b, 4c, 5b, 6a-1

Structural Foundations
Coalition, Contract

Contact
George Taylor, RN, BSN
Bates County Health
Department; Director,
Building Healthy People in
Healthy Families
501 North Orange
P.O. Box 208
Butler, MO 64730
rugg@aol.com

Rural Missouri Perinatal Partnership

Public health officials in Bates and Vernon counties, two rural Missouri areas, were faced with high infant mortality rates and high rates of inadequate prenatal care in 1993, attributable in part to the large numbers of teenage pregnancies. In cooperation with the St. Luke's Perinatal Center in Kansas City, the team capitalized on funding from the federal Office of Rural Health Policy to develop a comprehensive health education curriculum and provide better access to services through the public schools. Working with the school districts in the two counties, the group organized high school health education classes, and placed public health nurses in the schools to help identify teenagers who needed medical and psychosocial services. One strategy employed by the public health nurses involved "rudimentary telemedicine"—using a continuous-feed fax machine to send fetal monitor strips to the Perinatal Center in Kansas City. This allowed the high-risk pregnant teenagers to receive sophisticated care without having to travel great distances and miss school. The group reported decreases in infant mortality rates in one county from 17.1 for every 1,000 live births in 1992, to 9.8 in

1994. The rates of access to prenatal care increased correspondingly as well.

MO-2
Partners
LHD, L-GOV, FEDHLTH, FEDOTH, HOSP, CLIN, SOM, RES, U-OTH, VHO, BUS, SCHL, MEDIA, FNDN, C-OTH

Synergies
3b, 4b, 5a, 5c

Structural Foundations
Coalition, Adm/Mgmt, Advisory

Contact
Rodney M. Coe, PhD
Department of Community
and Family Medicine
Saint Louis University
School of Medicine
1402 South Grand
Boulevard
St. Louis, MO 63104
coerm@wpogate.slu.edu

Greater St. Louis Lead Poisoning Prevention Council

The Department of Community and Family Medicine at St. Louis University was only a year old in 1970 when several second-year medical students working on a school project found that 40% of the city's children had elevated blood lead levels. As it was, the department was eager to establish linkages with the local health departments. After the students' findings were independently confirmed, the city health department and the medical school department began organizing a broad coalition of service providers, housing advocates, and public officials to address the problem. The loose-knit group eventually evolved into the Greater St. Louis Lead Poisoning Prevention Council, which focused on establishing screening and treatment programs, developing lead abatement programs, and advocating for stricter enforcement of the city regulations governing lead poisoning. The department has continued its support of the coalition by providing administrative and educational support. The various programs undertaken by the coalition over twenty-five years have waxed and waned, depending on categorical funding, but its advocacy role has persisted because of the group's stable membership and baseline funding from the federal agencies (EPA and HUD), as well as ongoing contributions from the medical school and health department.

MO-3
Partners
MEDSOC, PHASSN

Synergies
6b-6

Structural Foundations
Coalition

Contact
Lorna Wilson, RN, MSPH
Missouri Association
of Local Public
Health Agencies
P.O. Box 31
Jefferson City, MO 65102
lornwilson@aol.com

Joint Committee for Physician/Public Health Relations

The Missouri Association of Osteopathic Physicians and Surgeons approached the Missouri Association of Local Public Health Agencies in the spring of 1996, to work together to improve communication and collaboration between local public health agencies and private medicine. In past years, there had been occasional misunderstandings and disagreements between local public health agencies and private physicians, and there had been no forum for resolving problems. This was the initial purpose of forming the Joint Committee for Physician/Public Health Relations, and subsequently the group added the Missouri State Medical Association to its meetings. The group agreed it would be helpful to understand each others' organizational structures, financing issues, and legal obligations, and also to increase the involvement of local physicians in public health decisions and management. Strategies pursued by the Joint Committee include: presentations at each others' statewide meetings; a draft prototypical agreement for local health departments to use in developing physician/consultant or medical director job descriptions; and joint meetings between the three associations and the state health department to explore ways of funding collaborative efforts between private physicians and local public health agencies. Although relations among the three groups have historically been cordial, there had not been such concerted common planning prior to the formation of the Joint Committee.

MO-4

Partners
LHD, L-GOV, SHD, MDPRAC, SOM, AHC, U-OTH, VHO, SCHL, RELIG, MEDIA, FNDN

Synergies
5a, 6a-5, 6b-4

Structural Foundations
Coalition

Contact
Jane M. Armer, RNC, MSN, PhD
University of Missouri-Columbia
S312 School of Nursing
Columbia, MO 65211
nursarme@showme.
missouri.edu

Howard County Community Health Assessment Research Team

The sole hospital and emergency room in rural midwestern Howard County closed in June 1995, which prompted local community health leaders to consider the citizenry's needs and perceptions. In the process of strategizing how to survey their county, the coalition leaders discovered two important resources: the state health department's five-step protocol, called the Community Health Assessment Research Team (CHART); and a group of willing Health of the Public students from the University of Missouri's schools of medicine, nursing, and health administration. The students collected secondary data, interviewed key informants, conducted surveys of community residents, and administered a mail-back survey to 39 local health professionals. The team's findings were disseminated widely at town and church meetings, published in the local newspapers, and distributed to the key community informants. The report had a great influence on the community's health care leadership. One major finding was that residents were not as concerned about their lack of local access to maternity and surgical services as the health care leaders had presumed, but were concerned about the availability of emergency care. The coalition has since begun working on developing urgent care services, and possibly using the dormant hospital building as a long-term care facility.

MO-5

Partners
LHD, L-GOV, MDPRAC, HOSP,
CLIN, SOM, AHC, U-OTH, SCHL,
RELIG, FNDN

Synergies
5a, 6b-4

Structural Foundations
Coalition

Contact
Jane M. Armer, RNC,
MSN, PhD
University of Missouri-
Columbia
S312 School of Nursing
Columbia, MO 65212
nursarme@showme.
missouri.edu

University of Missouri-Columbia Community Health Resource Guide

As a component of the University of Missouri-Columbia's Health of the Public program, a steering committee was established in 1995 to produce a directory of health care and social service resources. Since previous directories had been unaccessible to community members, and had not been comprehensive in scope, the steering committee developed a survey, which was followed by key informant interviews. Directories were distributed to all participating agencies and providers, and were also made available to the public through the local health department. The steering committee, which included faculty and graduate students from family and community medicine, public health nursing, and health services management, as well as local health department officials, regarded the resource directory as a means of promoting access to existing health and human services in a rural area. They further felt that by developing the directory in consultation with its intended users, the book was more comprehensive and would be used more widely.

MO-6

Partners
LHD, L-GOV, HOSP, CLIN, SOM

Synergies
6a-1

Structural Foundations
Coalition, Contract

Contact
Richard Biery, MD, MSPH
BroadBaker Group, Ltd.
1410 West 50th Street
Kansas City, MO 64112
rmbiery@worldnet.att.com

Kansas City Health Tax-Financed Clinics

In the late 1980s, the board of directors of the Truman Medical Center and Children's Mercy Hospital, with assistance from the dean of the University of Missouri School of Medicine, worked in collaboration with the Mayor and City Council of Kansas City, the Kansas City Health Department, and other community health agencies on a plan to create a source of steady public funding to finance health care for the poor. Together, they were successful in establishing a significant increase to the city's existing health tax levy. The tax levy, which has doubled and is still in effect, provides funding for the Truman Medical Center, Children's Mercy Hospital, the Swope Parkway Health Clinic, the Samuel Rodgers Community Health Center, the Kansas City Free Clinic, and the Cabot Westside Clinic, all of which provide bilingual, primary care for the medically underserved. For more than 30 years, city tax support has been funneled to the medical center, the children's hospital, and the EMS system. The three federally qualified health centers and the free clinic, through contractual agreements with the Kansas City Health Depart-

ment, were added within the last ten years conse-
quent to the favorable vote to increase the tax levy.

[NC] NORTH CAROLINA

NC-1
Partners
LHD, L-GOV, SHD, MDPRAC,
HOSP, CLIN, SPH, BUS, SCHL,
RELIG, MEDIA

Synergies
5a, 5b, 5d, 5e

Structural Foundations
Coalition

Contact
Marc Kolman, MSPH
Anson County Health
Department
P.O. Box 473
Wadesboro, NC 28170
achealth@vnet.net

Healthy Ansonians 2000 Task Force
Invigorated by the leadership of a new CEO, the
Anson County Hospital & Skilled Nursing Facility
(ACH) had been re-thinking its mission and operating practices to include a broader community
perspective. Upon learning about the statewide,
legislatively mandated Healthy Carolinians 2000
project, the CEO of ACH spearheaded a local initiative to create a Healthy Ansonians Task Force in
1997. Co-chaired with the director of the local
health department, and including key leaders from
city and county government, area businesses, and
the directors of the rural health center, county social services, and hospital emergency services, the
Task Force provides a platform for prioritizing and
promoting health objectives. Four areas (STD, maternal and child health, injury prevention, and substance abuse) have been chosen for particular attention, and subgroups are working to identify
opportunities for collaboration among the partners. The Task Force is a certified Healthy Carolinians 2000 initiative and currently is seeking
funding for a mobile wellness vehicle to provide
community health screenings and health education.

NC-2
Partners
LHD, L-GOV, SHD, S-GOV,
MDPRAC, HOSP, VHO, BUS,
SCHL, MEDIA

Synergies
5a, 5e

Structural Foundations
Coalition

Contact
R. Battle Betts, Jr.
Albemale Life Quest
Pasquotank-Perquimans-
Camden-Chowan District
Health Department
P.O. Box 189
Elizabeth City, NC 27909

Chowan County Healthy Carolinians
Chosen as a demonstration community for a
statewide initiative, the Chowan County Healthy
Carolinians Task Force involves key players from
local hospitals, the health department, city and
county government, private medical providers,
businesses, schools and civic organizations. Led
jointly by the director of the health department and
a hospital administrator (both of whose staff helped
coordinate the project), the goals of the Task Force
are to assess present and future health care needs,
to assess community resources in place to address
these needs, to define specific strategies and interventions, and to evaluate the effectiveness of the
process. The Task Force has provided an opportunity to break down territorial boundaries among
the participating organizations and, as a result, the
partners have achieved better coordination on
community health projects.

NC-3

Partners
LHD, L-GOV, SHD, HOSP, VHO, C-OTH

Synergies
3a, 5a, 5b, 5e

Structural Foundations
Advisory

Contact
Susan C. Long-Marin, DVM, MPH
Mecklenburg County
Health Department
249 Billingsley Road
Charlotte, NC 28211
long113w@cdc.gov

Mecklenburg County Health Assessment

In 1993–94, Mecklenburg County conducted a health needs assessment using a modified APEX*PH* protocol with formal endorsement of the Mecklenburg Board of County Commissioners. The assessment group, called the Community Health Advisory Committee, was composed of 42 members representing medical providers, hospitals, county human service agencies, voluntary health organizations, and community and local government leaders. The health department provided epidemiological data and staff, while the Committee identified six priority health concerns. Each area has measurable objectives and specific strategies to meet year 2000 goals. To stimulate continued action around the results of the needs assessment, the county commissioners organized a local Healthy Carolinians Task Force. Recognizing that a key barrier to service delivery was the lack of cooperation among the many community programs already working on the problems, the Committee decided to concentrate on encouraging information exchange and collaboration among existing groups. At this point, some members felt that the Committee's job was completed, and in 1997 leadership of the group shifted to the Human Services Council (HSC), an advisory council for the Board of the County Commissioners. Current projects of HSC include developing consumer health education materials for the six priority areas. This information is communicated through the health department's *Healthy Connections* television program and its Web site, which features community groups working on successful strategies for year 2000 objectives.

NC-4

Partners
LHD, SHD, MDPRAC

Synergies
1a, 1b

Structural Foundations
Contract

Burke County WIC Outreach Office in Private Pediatric Practice

To improve WIC participation among Medicaid families in North Carolina, the state made special outreach money available to local WIC offices if they demonstrated a viable plan to expand caseload and improve accessibility to services. The Burke County WIC program director used the funds to co-locate a WIC clinic with a private medical provider who accepted pediatric Medicaid patients. The clinic, which opened in February 1996 at Mountain View Pediatrics, creates a convenient one-stop center for families to receive both medical care and WIC services. A key element to suc-

Contact
Malinda D. Cecil, MS, RD
Burke County Health
Department-WIC Program
P.O. Drawer 1266
Morganton, NC 28680
bchd@hci.net

cess was the support of a pediatrician who was a former board of health member; he and his partners wrote a letter of support to the state and offered free space at their practice. The clinic is now open three days a week, and an on-site nutritionist works closely with the medical staff to coordinate WIC referrals and to provide nutrition counseling. Though her primary responsibility is to the WIC participants, the nutritionist is available to counsel all the patients of the practice. The WIC clinic has been well received by the medical providers, client satisfaction has increased, and participation in the WIC program is consistently growing.

NC-5
Partners
LHD, SHD, MDPRAC, CLIN, SPH,
FNDN

Synergies
1a, 1c, 3a, 3c, 4b, 6b-6,
6c-1

Structural Foundations
Adm/Mgmt, Advisory

Contact
Peter A. Margolis,
MD, PhD
Department of
Community Pediatrics
University of North
Carolina at Chapel Hill
361 Med School Wing D
Chapel Hill, NC 27599
margolis@med.unc.edu

Pediatric Home Visiting Program
At the beginning of the 1990s, as many as 40% of children in North Carolina did not have a regular physician for short-term and preventive health care. In order to study the feasibility of linking clinical and public health approaches to improving the quality and effectiveness of care for socially disadvantaged children, investigators from several health professions programs at the University of North Carolina at Chapel Hill began a community-wide intervention in 1994. The project involved three strategies targeting children under age five who were at different levels of risk, in order to improve the delivery of clinical preventive services and health outcomes. High-risk children, whose parents' incomes placed them below 100% of the poverty line, were recruited at the community health center to receive intensive home visiting conducted by a team of a public health nurse and an early childhood educator. The home visiting team sought to enhance the health development of the mothers and the children, link families with needed services, and build on the family's social supports. A second intervention, in primary care practices, targeted children at moderate and low risk. The team assisted the practices in measuring the performance of their clinical preventive services. A third intervention sought to assist the community in coordinating home visiting services for high-risk families and in linking practices with public health resources for needed outreach. To date, the interventions have led to improvements in the children's home environments, improved parenting skills, improved maternal health outcomes, and increases in the delivery of clinical preventive services.

NC-6

Partners
LHD, SOM, SPH, U-OTH, FNDN, C-OTH

Synergies
5a, 5d, 6b-3, 6b-4

Structural Foundations
Coalition

Contact
Steven H. Zeisel, MD, PhD
University of North
Carolina at Chapel Hill
School of Public Health
School of Medicine
2212 McGavran-Greenberg
CB# 7400
Chapel Hill, NC 27599
steven_zeisel@unc.edu

University of North Carolina Community-Based Public Health Initiative

As one of seven sites funded in 1992 by the W.K. Kellogg Foundation for its Community-Based Public Health Initiative, the University of North Carolina School of Public Health enlisted the advice and cooperation of four county health departments, community-based groups, and the schools of nursing and medicine at their academic health center. The group's objectives included: creating sustainable models of a "new" public health paradigm; working with the medical school to combine academic and community agency expertise to support community health assessment and planning; and the establishment of an interdisciplinary seminar. In 1996, a seminar, "Community Voices: Partners in Health," enrolled students from medicine, public health, social work, pharmacy, and the social sciences. In addition to the university-based effort, in the four participating counties a number of projects emerged: a center focused on leadership and economic development; funding for administrative help and a health educator at a CBO, Strengthening the Black Family, Inc.; countywide water and sewage planning efforts; and a program to foster community involvement at two housing projects.

NC-7

Partners
LHD, L-GOV, SHD, HOSP, INS, VHO, BUS, SCHL, RELIG, MEDIA, C-OTH

Synergies
2a, 5a, 5b, 5c, 5d, 5e

Structural Foundations
Coalition

Contact
Debi Nelson, MA
Division of Health
Education and Promotion
Caldwell County Health
Department
1966-b Morganton
Boulevard, SW
Lenoir, NC 28645
dnelson@co.caldwell.nc.us

Healthy Caldwellians

Caldwell County, situated at the foothills of North Carolina's Blue Ridge Mountains, is a rural area in which only 8% of the adults possess a college education, the great majority of workers are employed in minimum-wage jobs, and there are a number of environmental and health concerns. In 1995, responding to a statewide Healthy Carolinians 2000 initiative, administrators from the Caldwell County Health Department and the Caldwell Memorial Hospital invited community leaders to meet to consider ways of improving the health and well-being of county residents. The initial meeting brought together county and city government officials, educators, social service providers, law enforcement officials, clergy, and representatives from local industry, banking, and insurance organizations. Within four months, a task force examining health needs and priorities was established, as were six subcommittees on chronic disease, environment, maternal and child health, nutrition and fitness, sexually transmitted disease, and substance abuse. The community group, calling itself Healthy Caldwellians, has formalized its organization by electing officers and adopting a mission statement and by-laws. Among the projects it is developing are a free-care clinic for uninsured patients, a task force developing recommendations to protect the water supply, an "Abstinence Until Marriage" curriculum for the local schools, and Community Health Action Teams staffed by local church members.

NC-8

Partners
LHD, L-GOV, HOSP, LAB/RX, VHO, SCHL, RELIG, C-OTH

Synergies
5b, 5e

Structural Foundations
Coalition

Contact
Jan Stivers, MBA
Richmond Memorial Hospital
925 Long Drive
Rockingham, NC 28379

Richmond County Healthy Carolinians Project

Propelled by the statewide Healthy Carolinians 2000 project, the Richmond County health department and Richmond Memorial Hospital co-chaired a community initiative. The stated goal of the effort was to increase collaboration and reduce duplication of services. The group of community leaders, service providers, interested citizens, and health care providers continues to meet, and has produced a community resource brochure. The group has maintained the project without external funding, a factor cited as limiting the group's capacity.

NC-9

Partners
SOM, SPH

Synergies
6b-3, 6c-1

Structural Foundations
Intraorg

Contact
Steven H. Zeisel, MD, PhD
Department of Nutrition
University of North Carolina at Chapel Hill
School of Public Health
School of Medicine
2212 McGavran-Greenberg
CB#7400
Chapel Hill, NC 27599
steven_zeisel@unc.edu

University of North Carolina Department of Nutrition

The University of North Carolina's Department of Nutrition was established in 1946 in the School of Public Health. In 1993, the department was seeking a new chair. At that time, the schools of medicine and public health both wanted a nutrition department with sufficient depth to address the broad range of nutrition science: from molecular mechanisms to community interventions. To accomplish that, they needed a department that would concentrate not only on biological mechanisms, but also on the epidemiological relationship between diet and disease, the elucidation of strategies to modify the diets of individuals and populations, and the development of practice-based skills for delivering nutrition information to the community and to individuals. The two schools decided to share the new department for several reasons. First, they needed the combined expertise of medicine and public health to achieve the department's mission. Second, the medical school's biochemistry department was losing its metabolic expertise—a gap that could be filled through the nutrition department. Finally, they believed that a shared department would have more prestige within the university, would be more effective in enhancing training opportunities for students, and would be more successful in competing for grants. The collaboration initiated a period of rapid expansion in the size and responsibilities of the department, and enhanced its national recognition. Between 1990 and 1996, the number of primary faculty doubled, and more than 20 faculty were given joint or adjunct appointments. Research support increased tenfold. The Department has become the leader of a national initiative to develop a medical school curriculum in nutrition (with almost $2 million in funding). It was awarded a Doctoral Student Training Grant in Nutrition from NIH in 1992, and was recognized as an outstanding nutrition department by the Bristol-Myers Squibb Foundation in 1995. Consequent to its new-found stature, student applications to its degree programs have doubled since 1990.

NC-10

Partners
LHD, L-GOV, S-GOV, MDPRAC, HOSP, MEDSOC, VHO, FNDN

Synergies
1a, 1c, 2a, 2d, 6a-1, 6a-5

Structural Foundations
Contract, Adm/Mgmt

Contact
Denese R. Stallings, RN, MA
Cleveland County
Health Department
315 Grover Street
Shelby, NC 28150
denese.stallings@
healthnt1.co.cleveland.
nc.us

Cleveland County (CLECO) Primary Care Network

Cleveland County in the early 1990s was experiencing an imminent crisis in primary care. Many county residents relied upon the county hospital's emergency room for their primary care needs, and the burden was driving the hospital's costs up and leading to an attrition of emergency room physicians. Compounding the problem, a local primary care physician who provided care to many of the county's uninsured patients was about to retire. The hospital asked the health department to house a primary care clinic in order to ease the emergency room's burden. Since the health department was interested in developing an integrated system of care that incorporated home visits, preventive services, and primary care services, in 1994 the health department director and the chair of the board of health developed the not-for-profit, Cleveland County Primary Care Network called CLECO. The network's board of directors included representatives from all of the county's health agencies, including the hospitals, mental health agencies, and the medical society. The health department director is the CEO of the primary care network, which operates four primary care practices and eighteen nursing homes and rest homes, contracts with a physician group for medical coverage, and also has a long-term care network, which hires geriatric nurse-practitioners and physicians who visit nursing homes in the region every day. The nursing home visits have resulted in a reduction in EMS transports and emergency room visits for routine complaints. Because the network CEO is the health department director, all the primary care sites offer preventive services through the health department's nutritionists, health educators, and pharmacists. The network provides 24-hour physician coverage and accepts referrals from clinics, hospitals, and the school-based clinics throughout the county.

NC-11

Partners
LHD, L-GOV, MDPRAC, HOSP, VHO, MEDIA, C-OTH

Synergies
3a, 5b, 5e, 6b-5

Structural Foundations
Coalition

Contact
Judith Hill, RHEd
Healthy Carolinians Task Force and Diabetes Today
Bertie County
Health Department
502 Barringer Street
Windsor, NC 27983

Bertie County Community Diabetes Program

The Bertie County Health Department Health Promotion Team determined in 1995 that there was a need for a community-based diabetes awareness and training program. The team received CDC funding through their state health department to assemble a task force composed of community leaders, representatives from service agencies and medical providers, people with diabetes, and interested citizens. The group's objectives were to provide supports for people living with diabetes, such as monthly support groups and educational forums; to mount a community-wide educational campaign raising awareness of the disease and the value of a good diet in preventing diabetes or modifying its effects; and to provide a means for educating local health care providers and service agencies to the value of early recognition and management of diabetes. The group became certified as a Healthy Carolinians Task Force, having adopted the program's principle of involving all segments of the community in jointly surveying and addressing the problem. The CDC and state-provided facilitators helped underscore for the group members, particularly the health care providers, how their work was not inherently competitive but complementary.

NC-12

Partners
LHD, L-GOV, MDPRAC, HOSP, U-OTH, MEDSOC, SCHL, RELIG, MEDIA, C-OTH

Synergies
5a, 5b, 5d, 5e, 6b-6

Healthy Wake County 2000

After the Governor's Task Force on Health Objectives for the Year 2000 issued its report in 1991, an Office of Healthy Carolinians was established to stimulate local partnerships. In Wake County, the local health department took the lead in recruiting a number of community representatives, including clergy, school leaders, civic leaders, and health

Structural Foundations
Coalition, Adm/Mgmt

Contact
Lechelle Wardell, MPH
Wake County
Human Services/
Community Health
P.O. Box 14049
Raleigh, NC 27620
lwardell@co.wake.nc.us

providers, to consider the health needs of the community, particularly those of African-Americans. The health department director and its minority health program manager coordinated the effort, conducted a needs assessment, and convened a community forum. Three areas were selected through the public process: chronic diseases, such as heart disease, cancer, hypertension, stroke, and diabetes; HIV/AIDS and other sexually transmitted diseases; and violence. A formal coalition was formed in 1993, Healthy Wake County 2000, and three subcommittees were established to coordinate agency and community resources and skills to address each problem. Based on morbidity and mortality data, the groups also set targets to reach by the year 2000: a 15% reduction in chronic disease mortality, a 10% decrease in reported cases of STD and HIV/AIDS, and a 5% decrease in violent incidents.

NC-13
Partners
LHD, L-GOV, MDPRAC, HOSP, CLIN, LAB/RX, U-OTH, MEDSOC, BUS, SCHL, RELIG, FNDN

Synergies
1c, 2b, 3b, 5a, 5b, 5d, 5e, 6a-5

Structural Foundations
Coalition

Contact
Paul M. Hugger, MDiv
Wilkes Regional
Medical Center
Wilkes Community
Health Council
P.O. 609
North Wilkesboro, NC
28659
paulhugger@hotmail.com

Wilkes County Community Health Council

With a grant from a local hospital trust, the Wilkes County Community Health Council was created in 1993 with the charge to develop a model for integrating health services in the community to make health care more accessible. With key leadership from the Wilkes Regional Health System, the Council included representatives from the county health department and the department of social services, local medical centers, primary care and mental health clinics, the school and judicial systems, and the religious and business communities. In their first year, the Council surveyed health needs in Wilkes County, opened a telephone information and referral service, launched a prescription drug assistance program, and expanded access to primary care by establishing an after-hours clinic and by working with private physicians to provide care for needy children. Additional community health promotion projects have been started, such as activities to reduce drug, alcohol, and tobacco use among middle school students, and an effort to establish chronic disease screening in workplaces.

NC-14
Partners
S-GOV, FEDHLTH, HOSP, CLIN, SOM, RES, AHC, MEDSOC, PROFASSN

University of North Carolina Psychiatric Residency Program

In the early 1970s, crises related to mental health manpower in North Carolina led to a meeting of the University of North Carolina (UNC) School of Medicine at Chapel Hill and its affiliate North Car-

Synergies
2c, 6b-1, 6b-3, 6b-4

Structural Foundations
Contract, Adm/Mgmt,
Advisory

Contact
Robert N. Golden, MD
Department of Psychiatry
University of
North Carolina
School of Medicine
CB 7160
Chapel Hill, NC 27399
rgolden@css.unc.edu

olina Memorial Hospital, the Dorothea Dix State
Mental Health Hospital, and the State Division of
Mental Health Services. Several important issues
brought them together. First, the Dorothea Dix
Hospital had sufficient funds (in "hard" state
money) but was unable to recruit quality residents,
while UNC's Department of Psychiatry had quality
students, but was losing federal funds. Second, the
medical school had increased enrollment and
needed new training sites, increased faculty and
residents for teaching, and a larger patient pool for
research. Third, the state hospital residents needed
increased exposure to outpatient experiences, liaison services, and neurology training, which the
university could provide, and the university residents needed increased exposure to chronically
mentally ill patients from the public health sector.
To address these needs, the leaders from these organizations created a collaborative psychiatric residency program, based on input from the National
Institutes of Mental Health (NIMH), the American
Medical Association (AMA) Council on Medical Education, and the Residency Review Committee in
Psychiatry. The program assures the quality of service and teaching through joint management of
curriculum design, clinical assignments, and evaluation, and through contracts related to resident
stipends, supervision, and faculty reimbursement
for teaching. Active for over 20 years, the residency
program has improved service by expanding the
number of well-trained psychiatrists working in the
area. Rates of board-certification have improved
for public hospital residents, and program graduates are more likely to remain in the state and to
work in state hospitals or community mental health
centers.

Talbott, JA and Robinowitz, CB. 1986. *Working together:
state-university collaboration in mental health.* Washington,
DC: American Psychiatric Press, Inc. (NAT-20)

NC-15
Partners
LHD, SHD, HOSP, FNDN

Synergies
1a, 1c, 2d, 6a-6

Structural Foundations
Contract, Adm/Mgmt

Mecklenburg County Privatization Initiative
In 1994, the county commissioners authorized the
county manager to explore the privatization of a
number of Mecklenburg County services, including
clinical and population-based public health functions. One year later the county signed a contract
with the Carolinas HealthCare System to assume
responsibility for approximately 80% of the county
health department's staff and resources. Incorporated as a public authority, the Carolinas Health-

Contact
Stephen R. Keener,
MD, MPH
Department of
Public Health
Carolinas HealthCare
System
249 Billingsley Road
Charlotte, NC 28211
ncs0839@interpath.com

Care System had the ability to capitalize on its quasi-governmental status by raising money through bond issues but could otherwise function as a privately run entity. The six-year agreement requires the integrated hospital system to provide: (1) all of the health department's direct clinical services, such as maternal and child care, dental services, WIC, STD and TB clinics; (2) community services, such as school health; (3) public health nursing; (4) case management for children, the elderly, and HIV patients; and (5) health education and outreach for vulnerable populations. The health system also provides public health support services, including administration, laboratory, medical records, budgeting and purchasing, and billing; and public health assessment and policy development activities, such as community diagnosis and needs assessments, epidemiologic surveillance, community-wide planning and agenda-setting, and coalition-building. Consistent with state regulations, the county health department retains the direct provision of the following services: birth and death record registrations; communicable disease control services (principally case-finding and contact-tracing); and the environmental health services of food, water, and waste system inspection and regulation. The county and the integrated health system agreed to a level amount of county funding for the six-year period, equivalent to roughly 60% of the expense budget for these services. The health system also agreed to employ all affected county health department employees at their current salary and provide them with a comparable benefits package. The health system integrated the health department's clinical preventive services with its own primary care services, using the hospital's ambulatory care system. The medical care of most of Mecklenburg County's uninsured patients is provided through this ambulatory care system, and the county provides funding for this purpose through a separate contract. An extensive longitudinal evaluation of the impact of the changeover is underway. Since the agreement began, the health system reports that it has expanded public health services under its jurisdiction while operating under the fixed amount of county funding. This capacity has resulted from reductions in duplication of services; achievement of economies of scale in purchasing, laboratory, and human resources; cost-shifting; and the health system's greater experience in recovering third-party revenue for health care services.

NC-16

Partners
SOM, SPH, ARC, AHC, U-OTH

Synergies
5d, 6b-3, 6c-1

Structural Foundations
Advisory, Intraorg

Contact
Marian Osterweis, PhD
Association of Academic
Health Centers
1400 16th Street, N.W.
Suite 720
Washington, DC 20036
mosterwies@acadhlthctrs.
org

University of North Carolina Health Research Centers

At the University of North Carolina at Chapel Hill (UNC), there is a strong history of formal and informal collaboration across the five schools (dentistry, medicine, nursing, pharmacy, and public health), the Area Health Education Centers Program, and UNC's several prominent, multidisciplinary centers. As of 1992, these centers included the 30-year old Cecil G. Sheps Center, UNC's Injury Prevention Research Center, which was then one of five national centers originally funded by CDC, and the UNC Nutrition Center (NC-9). At that time, the vice chancellor's office played a role in unifying and supporting the collaborative work of these schools, programs, and centers, aided by a supportive culture among the faculty and geographic proximity of these schools and programs to one another on campus. One collaborative venture was the UNC Center for Health Promotion/Disease Prevention, which was created in the early 1980s as a joint enterprise of the vice chancellor's office and each of the five schools. The Center's "critical mass" facilitated research and grants management, and provided opportunities for people interested in collaborative research or education. Each school contributed financial support to the Center, a policy advisory board consisting of deans from each school sets its overall direction, and it was staffed by faculty from each school. All faculty of the Center continued to work in their "home" discipline or school. Specific projects of the Center include the Low-Birthweight Prevention Task Force, the Injury Prevention Task Force, and the Cardiovascular Disease Task Force.

Osterweis, M and Eichhorn SF. 1993. Community-based health promotion activities. In *Promoting community health: the role of the academic health center.* Skelton, WD and Osterweis, M, eds. Washington, DC: Association of Academic Health Centers.

NC-17

Partners
LHD, L-GOV, SHD, S-GOV,
FEDHLTH, MDPRAC, HOSP, CLIN,
MCO, INS, LAB/RX, AHC, U-OTH,
MEDSOC, BUS, SCHL, FNDN

Southeastern North Carolina HealthCare 1999

Established in 1992, HealthCare 1999 (HC99) is a CCN demonstration partnership, funded originally by the W.K. Kellogg Foundation, which is using collaboration as a strategy to create a coordinated regional system of health care that includes services

Synergies
5a, 5e, 6a-5, 6b-5

Structural Foundations
Coalition, Adm/Mgmt,
Advisory

Contact
Anne Lowry
HealthCare 1999
P.O. Box 1510
Pembroke, NC 28372
hc99@papa.uncp.edu

for prevention, treatment, and rehabilitation. By involving over 100 agencies that serve a nine-county area in rural North Carolina, including representatives from commerce, education, government, medical practice, insurance, and an academic health center, the Partnership is working on several initiatives around training, recruiting, and retaining health care providers; improving health infrastructure and financial access to the health system; and assessing health needs in the community. For continuing education of health professionals working in the community, the Partnership is strengthening the region's family medicine residency program, the health science library, and its continuing education programs for nurses, physician assistants, and other allied health personnel as well as promoting health careers among local high school and college students. The Partnership is also working on improving the health of high-risk populations by determining where they live and work, assessing their needs, and then targeting health service interventions directly to them. Lastly, the Partnership is promoting Healthy Carolinians, a state-level initiative to assist communities in developing their own health-focused partnerships. The HC99 region currently has three certified Healthy Carolinians communities and two others working towards certification.

NC-18
Partners
LHD, L-GOV, SHD, CLIN, LAB/RX

Synergies
1b, 3b, 5b, 6a-5

Structural Foundations
Contract, Adm/Mgmt

Contact
See citation

Rural Health Department and Community Health Center Alliance

In response to a perceived community health care crisis after the only local hospital was forced to close in 1985, a local health department and a community health center entered into a cooperative agreement in 1990 to share space and resources. The state rural health office, the county commissioners, the boards of the two agencies, and the agency directors were all involved in the planning and implementation of the alliance. Since the health department faced severe space shortages, and the community health center was committed to providing primary care and urgent care services, the two agencies agreed to co-locate in the former hospital building. The site was renovated to accommodate the health department and a satellite clinic of the health center; the space was color-coded to designate common areas (such as reception and waiting rooms and conference space) and separate autonomous areas. The two agencies agreed to share laboratory and x-ray services and a medical director. A number of clinical and technical personnel were also shared through a variety of contractual arrangements to cover pediatric and obstetric services and information systems. Despite an agreement in principle to share medical records, health educators, case managers, and health promotion activities, as of 1993 there were still considerable barriers to further integration of the two agencies. The boards of the two agencies were reluctant to cede control or autonomy, the agency administrators were concerned about the time involved in managing collaborative activities and in reporting to a separate oversight board, and a number of community residents felt that such integrated programming came at the expense of the local hospital (some felt that the $1.3 million raised by a local bond to renovate the building should have been used to sustain the hospital). Despite the barriers, a variety of informal and programmatic efforts have brought the two agencies closer together, including patient care coordination, co-sponsorship of a health fair and a community screening project, and a number of successful jointly developed grant applications.

Lambrew, JM, Ricketts, T, and Morrissey, JP. 1993. Case study of the integration of a local health department and a community health center. *Public Health Reports.* 108(1):19–29.

[ND] NORTH DAKOTA

ND-1
Partners
SHD, S-GOV, MDPRAC, HOSP, MEDSOC, PHASSN, PROFASSN, VHO

Synergies
3a, 4a, 5a, 5b, 5c, 5d, 6c-2

Structural Foundations
Coalition

Contact
Jonathan B. Weisbuch, MD, MPH
Maricopa County Department of Public Health
1825-45 E. Roosevelt Street
Phoenix, AZ 85007
jbweisbuch@earhlink.net

Motorcycle Helmet Campaign
In 1977, North Dakota's motorcycle helmet law was repealed. The state health department was greatly concerned about the potential increase in death and disability from motorcycle crashes. Under the direction of the state health officer, a group of state and voluntary agencies worked to pool their motorcycle crash data in an effort to reinstate the helmet law. To initiate the program, the State Health Council declared motorcycle crashes a reportable event. The North Dakota state health department then gained the support of the state medical association, highway department, police, hospital association, and statewide ambulance services to gather their disparate information on motorcycle injuries and submit that information to the state health department. The database was maintained by the health department and all data analysis was done by this agency. Although the group's advo-

cacy effort failed and legislation submitted in 1979 to require helmet usage did not pass, the process demonstrated for the partners how cooperative information gathering could serve a common goal. This was particularly noteworthy since the mandatory reporting of crash data was done with the support and cooperation of the clinical and protective services communities.

[NE] NEBRASKA

NE-1
Partners
LHD, MDPRAC, HOSP, MEDSOC, FNDN, C-OTH

Synergies
1a, 1c, 2b, 6a-5, 6b-6

Structural Foundations
Coalition, Adm/Mgmt

Contact
Sheila Bjerrum, RN
Polk County Health
Department
220 North State Street
Osceola, NE 68651
pchd.sb@navix.net

Lancaster County CATCH

CATCH (Community Access to Coordinated Healthcare) was designed in 1994 to assure access to medical care for Medicaid and underserved patients in the region. In response to legislative mandates and economic pressures, a core group of public health providers—five county health departments, a community action agency, a group of rural physicians, and a rural hospital network—joined to develop a model for the delivery of Medicaid Managed Care in 15 counties of rural Southeast Nebraska. CATCH serves as the public health component of a vertically integrated health system (the Rural Comprehensive Care Network of Nebraska (RCCN) formed in November 1997), which also includes a physician network and a hospital network. The CATCH network was developed with support from The Robert Wood Johnson Foundation; the grant was applied for collaboratively and written with assistance from an urban county health department and a medical society.

NE-2
Partners
S-GOV, HOSP, SOM, RES, U-OTH

Synergies
2c, 6b-4

Structural Foundations
Contract

Contact
Susan Boust, MD
University of Nebraska
Medical Center
Department of Psychiatry
Mailstop 985575
Omaha, NE 68198

Nebraska Public Psychiatry Residency Training in Rural Areas

The shortage of well-trained psychiatrists to serve the public sector is even more severe in rural areas (where many state hospitals are located), since universities and other professional resources tend to be concentrated in cities. In rural Nebraska, the state hospital faced workforce shortages just as the state's two medical schools (which had combined their psychiatry programs into one department under a single chairman) faced a lack of training sites and financing for their residents. In response to these pressures, the combined Department of Psychiatry of the University of Nebraska Medical Center and Creighton University worked with the state mental health authority to create a residency training program in 1987 to staff the state hospital,

Hastings Regional Center. At that time, the Hasting Center was a state-of-the-art treatment center with many innovative programs in chemical dependency and chronic mental illness, giving residents opportunities to learn new techniques, such as daily computerized monitoring of patient's cognitive levels. To bridge the 150-mile distance between the hospital and the Omaha campus, the program had requirements that residents attend classes in Omaha once a week, and faculty supervisors flew to the hospital once a week. The Residency Review Committee of the American College of Graduate Medical Education reviewed the training program at Hastings in 1991 and, despite their efforts to bridge the gaps created by distance, the training program was not approved for accreditation. The training program still operates, but as a month-long elective rather than a full, year-long training experience as planned. Even with only brief exposure to the Hastings location, one resident was successfully recruited by the state hospital.

Talbott, JA and Robinowitz, CB. 1986. *Working together: state-university collaboration in mental health.* Washington, DC: American Psychiatric Press, Inc. (NAT-20)

[NH] NEW HAMPSHIRE

NH-1
Partners
SOM, C-OTH

Synergies
6b-1

Structural Foundations
Intraorg

Contact
Russell C. Jones, MD, MPH
154 Main Street
P.O. Box 2456
New London, NH 03257
jone106@wonder.em.cdc.gov

COPC Elective at Dartmouth Medical School

The Dartmouth School of Medicine offers its second-year medical students a six-week elective in Community-Oriented Primary Care. The objective of the course is to introduce the medical students to the world of practical public health and to community assessment and development. Students address a number of topics, including the relationship of the physician to the community, and how that varies by clinical practice arrangements; broad determinants of health; barriers to care attributable to the health system, providers, and to patients; population data, and its usefulness to the clinician; problem-solving and systems analysis; development of community coalitions; strategic program development; and evaluation. Discussions and lectures are complemented by community scenarios, which are based on actual community problems and which present the students with real data sets and community factors with which to work. As in the actual cases, students need to find other data sources to supplement the information they have at hand, and a number of "external forces" emerge—hidden epidemics of child abuse, or insufficient number of translators at a primary care clinic serving a Hispanic population. As taught by a community-based physician who is also a former state health director, the course engages students in the interplay of population and clinical approaches to health, disease, and the forces that impinge on them.

NH-2

Partners
SHD, MCO, INS, MEDSOC

Synergies
6a-3

Structural Foundations
Informal

Contact
Palmer P. Jones
New Hampshire
Medical Society
7 North State Street
Concord, NH 03301
nhmed@aol.com

Statewide Voluntary Vaccination Effort
When New Hampshire decided that it could no longer fund the purchase of vaccines due to tight budgetary restrictions, the state's major health plans were approached by the state health commissioner and the president of the state medical society to provide the funding. There had been discussion among state legislators, public and private health providers, and the governor to mandate vaccinations. Rather than adopt this regulatory approach, the state encouraged the health plans to pursue a voluntary strategy, and the health plans concurred. The health plans have since continued to fund the purchase of vaccines for the state.

[NJ] NEW JERSEY

NJ-1

Partners
SHD, S-GOV, HOSP, MEDSOC,
PROFASSN, C-OTH

Synergies
4a

Structural Foundations
Contract, Adm/Mgmt,
Advisory

Contact
Virginia Dato, MD, MPH
Center for Public
Health Practice
University of Pittsburgh
School of Public Health
125 Parran Hall
Pittsburgh, PA 15261
vdato@aol.com

Statewide Electronic Birth Certificate
In the late 1980s, the state health department in New Jersey wanted the capacity to monitor and record prenatal and birth events electronically. Hospitals throughout the state wanted to be able to submit reports and data electronically. Physicians wanted prenatal and medical information about pregnant women available when they presented in labor at the hospital. The state hospital association wanted a more accurate research database in order to analyze epidemiologic trends, assess risk in different hospital markets, and obtain reliable data for negotiations with insurers. To meet these needs, an advisory group of state personnel, hospital, and community representatives was convened by the state Director of Maternal and Child Health to consider their mutual needs. After diverse views were aired and reconciled, the group decided to develop an electronic birth certificate, which would provide the state health department with aggregate statewide data to support surveillance, vital registries, and epidemiologic investiga-

tions, and would allow each hospital to customize the birth certificate to meet its own needs. The group developed an extensive set of data elements and, with its technology contractor, designed the system in a modular format so that data could be collected at the source, such as at a delivery room or nursery. A final modular component was added that could be customized by each hospital to collect data for its unique needs. Some hospitals wanted to monitor breast-feeding patterns, others wanted to track high-risk babies, and still others wanted to monitor Caesarian section rates and induction indicators. The health department added modules that automatically registered low-birthweight babies for newborn hearing screening exams and a parentage certificate that could be printed and signed by the baby's mother and father. Within two years of implementation, all the hospitals in the state were voluntarily registering their births electronically. (Related cases: NJ-3, NJ-6)

NJ-2

Partners
SHD, S-GOV, FEDHLTH, MDPRAC, MCO, MEDSOC, C-OTH

Synergies
3a, 6b-5, 6b-6

Structural Foundations
Coalition

Contact
Lisa Smith, MS
Division of Women's
Health Issues
The American College of
Obstetricians and
Gynecologists (ACOG)
409 12th Street, S.W.
P.O. Box 96920
Washington, DC 20090
lsmith@acog.org

NJ-3

Partners
LHD, L-GOV, SHD, S-GOV, FEDHLTH, MDPRAC, HOSP, CLIN, MCO, SOM, AHC, U-OTH, MEDSOC, PHASSN, PROFASSN, VHO, RELIG, FNDN, C-OTH

Alliance to Promote Comprehensive Prenatal Care

The New Jersey Alliance to Promote Comprehensive Prenatal Care was formed in the fall of 1995 in response to the American College of Obstetricians and Gynecologists (ACOG) District III Providers' Partnership meeting, which was supported in part by a grant from the federal Maternal and Child Health Bureau (NAT-6). The Alliance, composed of private medical providers and public health professionals, held planning regional meetings across the state to educate obstetricians and gynecologists and their office staffs about the range of programs and wraparound services available within the state's Medicaid managed care system and the best ways to use them in their practices. The Alliance operated for more than a year, but it currently is not active.

Statewide Immunization Information System

When New Jersey suffered a major measles outbreak in 1989-1991, it spurred a number of immunization efforts, much as it did in other states across the country. One strategy was to create a centralized computer database that integrated immunization data so that any authorized health care

Synergies
3a, 3b, 4a, 4c, 6b-6

Structural Foundations
Coalition, Contract,
Adm/Mgmt, Advisory

Contact
Janet DeGraaf
State of New Jersey
Department of Health
and Senior Services
CN 360
P.O. Box 369
Trenton, NJ 08625
jd3@doh.state.nj.us

provider could access a child's immunization history. In 1993, The Robert Wood Johnson Foundation awarded the Department of Pediatrics at the University of Medicine and Dentistry of New Jersey $3 million, under its All Kids Count initiative, to develop the database over three years. The group designing the system assessed different provider practices to see how they did business, soliciting the input of the physicians and clinical office staff for what would be useful to them in their particular clinical settings. A number of practice supports were added to the basic immunization registry as a result of these discussions: the system provides clinicians with immunization status reports for individual patients, and has the capacity to generate phone call or home-visit lists, as well as recall notices and patient reminders that can be mailed to patients on the provider's letterhead. After a successful three-year pilot test in Camden, the Statewide Immunization Information System (SIIS) was implemented in 1997. It has been deployed to 24 county and local health departments and is in the process of being linked to an additional 200 public and private providers throughout New Jersey. The expansion of SIIS has increased the number and diversity of collaborators to include HMO representatives, local advisory board members, representatives from the American Academy of Pediatrics and the American Academy of Family Practitioners, and maternal and child health consortia, among others. One unintended consequence of the registry, at least in Camden, has been an improvement in the relationship between the private practitioners and the local public health department. Whereas physicians once thought that the public health immunization clinics were pulling paying patients away from their practices, the registry provided documentation that only 2% of private patients in Camden were picked up at the health department clinics. With the warming of relations, providers began utilizing the health department outreach workers more often to assist with hard-to-reach patients. (Related cases: NJ-1, NJ-6)

NJ-4

Partners
SHD, FEDHLTH, HOSP, SOM

Synergies
1a, 1c, 3a, 4c, 5a, 6b-5, 6b-6, 6c-1

National TB Center
In response to rising rates of TB in the early 1990s, and particularly the emergence of multiple drug-resistant strains, a group of New Jersey health officials, clinicians, and academic researchers formed the National TB Center in 1993. The Center is a

Structural Foundations
Contract, Adm/Mgmt,
Advisory

Contact
Kenneth L. Shilkret, MA
Tuberculosis Program
New Jersey Department of
Health and Senior Services
University Office Plaza
P.O. Box 369
Trenton, NJ 08625
kls1@cdc.gov

joint project of the University of Medicine and Dentistry of New Jersey, its affiliated University Hospital, and the New Jersey Department of Health and Senior Services. Clinical faculty from the pulmonary division, pediatrics, preventive medicine and community health, microbiology, and molecular genetics worked with the state health commissioner and the state TB Control Program to develop state-of-the-art diagnostic, treatment, and prevention programs. In late 1993, the Center signed a cooperative agreement with the CDC to be a Model TB Prevention and Control Center. As such, the Center also worked to develop new treatments through clinical drug trials and to increase professional skills related to TB through training and education of health care professionals at all levels. Using state public health practitioners as faculty members and consultants, the Center designed a case management team approach, which included directly observed therapy; initiated a toll-free information line (1-800-4TB DOCS) for medical consultation; developed a World Wide Web site with current information on TB, including resources and treatment protocols; conducted community and molecular epidemiological research studies; and developed a statewide training program. The Center has maintained itself with core funding from the state health department, the academic health center, and the CDC.

NJ-5
Partners
SHD, FEDHLTH, MDPRAC, SOM,
MEDSOC

Synergies
3a, 6b-5

Structural Foundations
Advisory

Contact
Carol Ann Genese,
MT, MBA
Infectious & Zoonotic
Disease Program
New Jersey Department of
Health and Senior Services
3635 Quakerbridge Road
Trenton, NJ 08625
cag@doh.state.nj.us

New Jersey Lyme Disease Guide
In 1991, the governor of New Jersey asked the state health department to help educate physicians as to the diagnosis and treatment of Lyme disease. The state epidemiologist approached the New Jersey Academy of Medicine, a not-for-profit institution devoted to providing continuing medical education to the state's physicians, to collaborate on the publication of a monograph. The Academy recruited a writing group from the state health department, practicing physicians representing different specialties, and academic clinical faculty at the state medical school. *Lyme Disease in New Jersey: A Practical Guide for New Jersey Clinicians* was published and distributed to all New Jersey physicians in 1993. The guide provides clinicians with background and history on the disease, its epidemiology, clinical manifestations, diagnostic testing procedures, and effective treatment and prevention strategies.

NJ-6

Partners
LHD, SHD, S-GOV, FEDHLTH,
MDPRAC, HOSP, LAB/RX, U-OTH,
PROFASSN, BUS

Synergies
4a, 6a-6

Structural Foundations
Contract, Advisory

Contact
Carol Ann Genese,
MT, MBA
Infectious & Zoonotic
Disease Program
New Jersey Department of
Health and Senior Services
3635 Quakerbridge Road
Trenton, NJ 08625
cag@doh.state.nj.us

Electronic Lab Reporting

In the early 1990s, the state of New Jersey wanted to upgrade its communicable disease surveillance system. Two committees were empaneled by the state epidemiologist; they included state health officials and representatives from the state hospital association, local health departments, intensive care and infectious disease physicians, pediatricians, and laboratory representatives. One recommendation of the committees was to use electronic laboratory reporting as the foundation for a surveillance system, with physician diagnosis and reporting as a backup. State regulations were revised in 1995 to accommodate the regulatory change. The other key strategy was to piggyback the interactive electronic system on the evolving statewide electronic network (NJ-1, NJ-3). The system, still in development, will allow for easy "two-way" communication between the state and the labs. If a specific antibiotic or drug resistance is encountered, or a particular outbreak emerges, the state will be able to notify the labs immediately and the labs can modify their pathologic screening procedures rapidly and improve the identification of new cases.

NJ-7

Partners
LHD, L-GOV, MDPRAC, HOSP,
MCO, SOM, VHO, SCHL, RELIG,
FNDN, C-OTH

Synergies
1a, 1c, 5a, 5b, 5d, 5e

Structural Foundations
Coalition

Contact
Owen McNally
Community Health
Improvement Services
Our Lady of Lourdes
Medical Center
1600 Haddon Avenue
Camden, NJ 08103

Camden City Community Health Improvement Learning Collaborative

The Learning Collaborative of Camden is designed to connect community-based and culturally sensitive services to low-income women of childbearing age and their families in this inner-city area. This CCN demonstration partnership, funded by the W.K. Kellogg Foundation, began in 1993 and involves medical providers, local church members and community groups, and representatives from county departments of health, social services, education, and housing. They have several initiatives designed to identify health needs and reduce barriers to care in the community. First, community health facilitators (CHFs) help coordinate services for individuals in the community, identify community health needs, and recruit community providers into the partnership. Second, mobile clinic vans provide primary care, coordination, and outreach services. Third, Neighborhood Living Rooms operate as community centers that provide easy access to health promotion, screening, case management, and community outreach. The Partnership also supports school-based programs such as an asthma program, health fairs, clothing drives, and immunization days.

NJ-8

Partners
LHD, L-GOV, MDPRAC, HOSP, U-OTH, PROFASSN, VHO, BUS, SCHL, RELIG, MEDIA, FNDN, C-OTH

Synergies
3a, 3b, 3c, 4c, 5a, 5b, 5d, 5e, 6b-6

Structural Foundations
Coalition

Contact
John F. Marcy
Community and Kimball Medical Center Foundations
99 Highway 37 West
Toms River, NJ 08755
jmarcy@ckhcs.com

Building a Healthier Ocean County

In 1993, the Building a Healthier Ocean County (BHOC) coalition began with an APEX*PH* community health assessment. The motivations of the partners differed—Community Medical Center initiated it as a community benefit demonstration project, and the Ocean County Board of Health and Jersey Coast Health Planning Council became involved to advance their missions of service in community health—but each felt that the data were necessary for planning efforts. After reviewing the results of the assessment, the partners hosted a three-day conference, involving representatives from public and private medical and social service agencies in Ocean County, to discuss health and quality-of-life issues in their service areas. The BHOC coalition evolved from this conference, and task forces were formed to address issues of access and transportation, costs, universal care, family values, prevention and education, technology, and coordination of resources. Currently, the coalition (a CCN finalist partnership recognized by the W.K. Kellogg Foundation) involves all of the hospitals in the area, the original partners, and more than 80 organizations, including the Ocean County Board of Social Services, the Ocean County Department of Human Services, the Ocean County Department of Transportation, and other local agencies and businesses. In 1996, BHOC partners each contributed funds to field a telephone survey of 1,200 randomly selected residents. Data collection, analysis, and sharing of results have been a key mission of the coalition. Recent uses of data in planning include: (1) adolescent initiatives for recreation, substance abuse, and education, (2) use of emergency room utilization data to reduce nonemergency use, (3) the collection of transportation information as part of a statewide initiative, and (4) a childhood immunization initiative. BHOC sponsors many specific clinical, preventive, and community health promotion projects, such as an effort to coordinate cancer screening activities and services, as well as educational conferences targeted for the community and for medical and social service providers. Moreover, the coalition is widely recognized as a vehicle for collaboration and communication among community providers, becoming a "clearinghouse" for health promotion initiatives in the county. The coalition provides a roundtable for gaining feedback and additional resources for these initiatives, as well as a way for members to keep abreast of countywide happenings.

NJ-9
Partners
SOM, U-OTH

Synergies
6b-1, 6b-2, 6c-2

Structural Foundations
Intraorg

Contact
Bernard D. Goldstein, MD
New Jersey Graduate
Program in Public Health
University of Medicine
and Dentistry of New
Jersey-Robert Wood
Johnson Medical School
681 Frelinghuysen Road
P.O. Box 1179
Piscataway, NJ 08855
bgold@eohsi.rutgers.edu

UMDNJ-Robert Wood Johnson Medical School MD/MPH Program

With the development of an accredited public health graduate program designed for working public health practitioners and a joint MD/MPH program that emphasizes clinical prevention and population sciences, the University of Medicine and Dentistry of New Jersey (UMDNJ)-Robert Wood Johnson Medical School, Rutgers University, and the New Jersey Graduate Program in Public Health have shifted the focus of the traditional medical school's curriculum and resources. Consequences of the joint degree program and graduate public health affiliation include: (1) these schools share one of the largest preventive medicine departments in the country, with 40 full-time faculty and over $10 million in funding; (2) the public health perspective is well-integrated into the medical curriculum, represented by over 100 hours of required teaching time of prevention, public health, and population sciences in the first two years of medical school; (3) trained epidemiologists and biostatisticians are available to clinical and research faculty in the medical school; and (4) there is a greater emphasis on the social science disciplines than traditionally seen in health professions training. The chair of the OB/GYN department has offered even to provide the funding for any of his faculty interested in obtaining an MPH degree.

[NM] NEW MEXICO

NM-1
Partners
L-GOV, HOSP, SOM, AHC,
U-OTH, VHO, SCHL, C-OTH

Synergies
1a, 5b

Structural Foundations
Coalition, Intraorg

New Mexico Adolescent Social Action Program

Mortality among teenagers in New Mexico is one-third higher than the national average, and a large proportion of the deaths are related to the use of alcohol and other drugs. The Adolescent Social Action Program (ASAP) was founded in 1982 as a prevention program to reduce mortality and morbidity related to alcohol, tobacco, and other drugs among adolescents. The main objective of the program is to empower and educate teenage participants, so that they can persuade their peers that substance use is unacceptable, as they avoid sub-

Contact
Robert M. Gougelet, MD
Department of
Emergency Medicine
University of New Mexico
School of Medicine
Ambulatory Care Center
4th Floor
Albuquerque, NM 87131
robg@swcp.com

stance abuse themselves. In the past 15 years, the program, based at Albuquerque's University Hospital and with direct links to the University of New Mexico, community-based organizations, the public schools, and local government, has involved 1,300 middle and high school students in 30 at-risk communities across the state and 300 volunteer facilitators. Within the program, small groups of students have a series of visits to University-affiliated hospitals, principally the emergency department, and the Bernalillo County Detention Center, and they interview carefully screened patients in these facilities and learn first hand of the medical, legal, emotional and social consequences of alcohol, tobacco, and other drug use. Facilitators, who are University of New Mexico students with backgrounds ranging from medicine, public health, nursing, sociology, psychology, and health education, receive intensive training in the ASAP method and, in turn, train the adolescent students in active listening and questioning techniques. Both quantitative and qualitative research evaluations have been done on the ASAP program, demonstrating the effectiveness and efficacy of this program in improving attitudes about risk, the ability to make positive life choices, and reduced tendencies to mix alcohol and drug use with driving.

Bernstein, E and Bernstein, B, eds. 1996. *Case studies in emergency medicine and the health of the public.* Sudbury, MA: Jones and Bartlett Publishers. (NAT-18)

NM-2

Partners
SHD, S-GOV, CLIN, SOM, AHC, FNDN, C-OTH

Synergies
5d, 6b-1, 6b-3, 6b-4

Structural Foundations
Coalition, Intraorg

Contact
Marian Osterweis, PhD
Association of Academic
Health Centers
1400 16th Street, N.W.
Suite 720
Washington, DC 20036
mosterweis@acadhlthctrs.
org

University of New Mexico Primary Care Curriculum and Community Health Promotion

Philosophically, the University of New Mexico (UNM) is committed to multidisciplinary education, as illustrated by its Primary Care Curriculum (PCC), a widely studied model for education which has received funding support from the W.K. Kellogg Foundation's initiative in community care, the Pew Charitable Trusts/Rockefeller Foundation's Health of the Public program, and a Robert Wood Johnson Foundation curriculum grant. Since 1981, the PCC program has included a Primary Care Preceptorships component in which students work in one of 35 small communities in New Mexico for four months, spending 15% of their time on a community-based project. In 1991, 70% of the students chose a project related to health promotion and disease prevention in the community. With the PCC program, there is also a Multidisciplinary Collaborative Clinic that integrates population, behavioral, and biological perspectives in health care delivery in order to increase health care effectiveness and improve the quality of education geared to ambulatory services. UNM also encouraged other collaborative partnerships on health promotion activities with community-based organizations, state agencies, and the state legislature. A key contribution of UNM in these partnerships is making sure that health promotion activities have strong evaluation and dissemination components that are well-grounded in theory.

Osterweis, M and Eichhorn, SF. 1993. Community-based health promotion activities. In *Promoting community health: the role of the academic health center.* Skelton, WD and Osterweis, M, eds. Washington, DC: Association of Academic Health Centers.

NM-3

Partners
L-GOV, SHD, FEDHLTH, HOSP, SOM, RES, AHC, U-OTH, VHO, BUS, MEDIA, FNDN, C-OTH

Synergies
6a-5, 6b-4

Structural Foundations
Coalition, Contract, Advisory

Contact
Sandra McCollum
Community Partnerships
University of New Mexico
School of Medicine
Box 715–BMSB
Albuquerque, NM 87131
smccollum@salud.unm.edu

Santa Rosa Hospital Survival

When the sole physician in rural Santa Rosa moved out of town in 1993, the town's 18-bed hospital was forced to consider closing its doors. The hospital served a predominantly Hispanic population in Guadalupe County, the third poorest county in the United States, and treated one to two trauma patients daily. The hospital administrator contacted the state health department, which in turn contacted the University of New Mexico academic health center in Albuquerque. The university immediately mobilized a response team composed of representatives from hospital administration, the Family Practice Department, the College of Nursing, and the Office of Rural Health. Some members of the team were also part of the university's Health of the Public program funded by The Robert Wood Johnson Foundation and the Pew Charitable Trusts. The team arranged for family practice faculty and residents to provide clinical services in the community, and the university's hospital administrators helped the county to apply for rural grants, develop operational policies, and oversee fiscal management. The team also brought a "community encourager" to meet with community leaders and citizens and organize community support for the hospital. In order to demonstrate the impact of the hospital on the local economy, the hospital staff were paid with $2 bills so that the local businesses could directly see the financial impact. As long-term measures, the university recruited two physicians to serve the community, and helped convene a planning consortium that included the local hospital board; community groups; local social service, mental health, and health care providers; and the university. The university has since provided similar "emergency response" services to three other rural counties.

NM-4
Partners
LHD, SHD, CLIN

Synergies
1c, 3b

Structural Foundations
Informal

Contact
See citation

Dona Ana County TB Control Program
Beginning in 1994, the state health department's TB Control program began coordinating its program of isoniazid preventive therapy with that of prenatal care and postpartum follow-up provided at a community health clinic in Dona Ana County. Any woman who had a positive PPD reaction during her prenatal care at the First Step Women's Health Clinic was referred to the state TB Control program. The state public health officials helped formulate a TB treatment plan and returned it to the First Step providers. After the baby was born, a public health nurse would meet the mother at her first WIC appointment, help educate her on TB prevention and treatment, and begin monitoring the isoniazid treatment. An average of ten women per month have been followed through this program. In addition to the direct benefits, the women receive added benefits from referrals made by the public health nurses handling each case, particularly since the Spanish-speaking public health nurses often provide links to services the women had not known about.

Fields, D and Gorjanc, J. 1996. *TB Notes*. Centers for Disease Control and Prevention, Division of TB Elimination, National Center for HIV, STD, and TB Prevention 2:4.

[NV] NEVADA

NV-1
Partners
LHD, SHD, MDPRAC, HOSP, MCO, SOM, MEDSOC, PROFASSN

Synergies
3a, 4a, 4c, 5b

Structural Foundations
Coalition

Nevada Childhood Immunization Initiative
In response to the 1995 National Immunization Initiative, which established the goal of having 90% of all 2-year-old children fully immunized, several Nevada health agencies and associations began working toward an interactive computerized immunization registry. The Nevada State Health Division, the Clark and Washoe County Health Districts, and the Nevada Society of Health Maintenance Physicians began meeting in 1996 to address issues of patient confidentiality, technical logistics of developing such an integrated system, and strategies for capitalizing on immunization opportunities. The Society of Health Maintenance Physicians, whose

Contact
Yvonne Riggan, RN, BSN
Western Region
Sierra Health Services
P.O. Box 15645
Las Vegas, NV 89114
yvonner@sierrahealth.com

members include medical directors and practicing physicians working with Nevada's health plans, also solicited the support and cooperation of other health care associations within the state. The state hospital association and its members have agreed to provide immunization information packets and reminder cards to parents at hospital discharge after the birth of their child. Also, the county medical societies are mounting education campaigns targeted at primary care and emergency physicians in order to maximize every immunization opportunity. Responsibility for the immunization initiative has since shifted to one of two immunization coalitions that formed in Nevada, one in the northern part of the state, the other in the southern. The focus has also broadened to include appropriate immunizations for all ages.

NV-2
Partners
SHD, S-GOV, MDPRAC, HOSP,
MCO, BUS, MEDIA, C-OTH

Synergies
1c, 2b, 4c, 5b, 6a-1

Structural Foundations
Coalition, Adm/Mgmt

Contact
Yvonne Riggan, RN, BSN
Sierra Health Services
P.O. Box 15645
Las Vegas, NV 89114
yvonner@sierrahealth.com

Baby Your Baby Project

A series of serendipitous events led to Nevada's Baby Your Baby prenatal care initiative in 1992. The governor had appointed a Maternal and Child Health Advisory Board in 1989. Given the increasing incidence of low-birthweight babies and rising infant mortality rates, one of the advisory group's first recommendations was to increase access to first trimester prenatal care. At about the same time, the governor's wife—who happened to be pregnant—was having a difficult time accessing early prenatal care in her community because she was considered a high-risk pregnancy. Her statewide prominence further fueled the public debate regarding access problems faced by numerous women. The neighboring state of Utah had developed a model program, called Baby Your Baby, as a public-private partnership to improve prenatal care. When Nevada state health officials called their Utahan counterparts, they discovered that the Kiwanis Club of Las Vegas and Sunbelt Broadcasting had already called for information about the program. Together with the state's First Lady, the group identified a funding mechanism for their state project that would match donations to federal Medicaid dollars. The group recruited a number of private sector sponsors, including several major health systems and medical groups. The initiative provided funding for increased prenatal care services and mounted a statewide advertising campaign urging pregnant women to seek prenatal care as early as possible. An independent evaluation of the program in 1994 reported that the infant mortality rate had dropped, the rate of entry into early prenatal care had increased, and the incidence of low-birthweight babies was on the decline. The partners in the project currently are investigating models of expanding their program to include pediatric primary medical and dental care.

[NY] NEW YORK

NY-1

Partners
LHD, HOSP, AHC, VHO

Synergies
1c, 3a, 3b, 4a, 5b, 6b-6

Structural Foundations
Contract, Adm/Mgmt

Contact
George Hripcsak, MD
Department of
Medical Informatics
Columbia-Presbyterian
Medical Center
161 Fort Washington
Avenue
DAP-1310
New York, NY 10032
hripcsak@columbia.edu

New York City TB and Home Visit Intranet
In 1996, the New York City Department of Health, the Visiting Nurse Association, and Columbia University's primary care network perceived an opportunity to address their overlapping information needs. All three organizations wanted to provide timely health education to their patients and use the data they collected more efficiently. The Columbia University Department of Medical Informatics developed an "intranet" computer network that linked the three partners. The telecommunications technology allowed nurses making home visits to use wireless technology and hand-held computers to transmit their patient assessments directly into the patient's medical center records; created a consumer "health kiosk" at health department clinics, which provided health education material; and provided for automatic reporting of all TB cases diagnosed at the academic medical center and its clinics directly to the health department. The partners benefitted by accurate and timely TB reporting, enhanced patient education materials, better links to patients' primary care providers, and by the reduced threat of TB transmission within the hospital. The partners were able to justify the expense of such a project through the multiple functions it served.

NY-2

Partners
SHD, MDPRAC, HOSP, MEDSOC, PROFASSN

Synergies
3c, 6a-4

Structural Foundations
Contract, Advisory

Obstetric and Neonatal Peer Review Teams
The New York State Department of Health undertook a comprehensive review of obstetric and neonatal services in New York City's public hospitals and their affiliate hospitals following a March 1995 New York Times report on citywide birth outcomes. The articles were critical of the quality of obstetric/neonatal care in New York City's public hospitals, citing higher neonatal mortality rates and anecdotal reports. The state health department engaged multidisciplinary peer review teams to conduct site visits and chart audits at each of the

Contact
Monica Meyer, MD
433 River Street
Suite 303
Troy, NY 12180
mxm02@health.state.ny.us

targeted hospitals. The review teams were composed of two obstetricians, two neonatalogists, two nurse-midwives, one obstetric nurse, and one neonatal nurse, all of whom were practicing providers unaffiliated with the health department. The state recruited these providers in consultation with representatives from the national associations of each of these health profession specialities. Following the site visits, the peer review teams met with hospital staff to review their findings and consider ways of improving care. The state health department adopted this collaborative approach in an effort to engender the trust and cooperation of the hospital community, enhance the credibility of the review process, and elicit optimal strategies for improving obstetric and neonatal services at each hospital. The collaboration also has led the state health department to reevaluate its perinatal database in order to fashion a system that balances the data-reporting burdens with the capacity to monitor accurately the quality of maternal and neonatal care.

NY-3
Partners
LHD, MEDSOC

Synergies
3a, 6b-6
Structural Foundations
Advisory, Intraorg

Contact
James Kelly, MSEd
Erie County
Medical Society
237 Main Street
Suite 1514
Buffalo, NY 14203
kelly@eriemds.org

Erie County Medical Society Public Health Committee

The county medical society and the health department in Erie County have maintained an ongoing cooperative effort over the years to inform community-based physicians about such pressing public health issues as rabies, Lyme disease, tobacco eradication, domestic violence, adult immunizations, and HIV testing. The partnership has been facilitated by having a county health department physician, who is also a medical society member, chair the medical society's Public Health Committee and sit on the executive board. Upon the advice of the Public Health Committee, the medical society notifies its 1,700 members about these issues via articles in the society's monthly bulletin or topical mailings focusing on a particular issue. Initially, the top public health physician was invited to sit on the committee to allay the concerns of private physicians about the perceived encroachment of public health into their practice domains. As trust between the sectors has grown, there is greater understanding as to what each can contribute to improving the health of patients, and a greater rapport between the public health sector and office-based physicians.

NY-4

Partners
LHD, MDPRAC, HOSP

Synergies
2c

Structural Foundations
Contract

Contact
Marvin Thalenberg, MD
Rockland County
Health Department
Sanatorium Road
Building D
Pomona, NY 10970
mthalenberg@mem.po.
com

NY-5

Partners
LHD, MDPRAC, MCO, INS, BUS,
C-OTH

Synergies
5b

Structural Foundations
Advisory

Contact
George Anstadt
Medical Department
Eastman Kodak Company
Mail Code 35023
Building 1, Allen Grove
1st Floor
Rochester, NY 14652
ganstadt@kodak.com

NY-6

Partners
SHD, MDPRAC, MEDSOC

Synergies
6a-1, 6a-2

Nyack Obstetric Group

When the three obstetricians who covered the Rockland County prenatal care clinic resigned in 1991, the health department director approached the local hospital president for help. The community hospital had long hosted the prenatal clinic, which was run by the health department, and had benefitted from referrals to its pediatric and obstetric beds. The hospital president recruited a medical group of four physicians, one of whom was a perinatologist, to cover the clinic as part of their growing practice. The hospital executive and health department commissioner persuaded the county legislature to pay the physicians through the hospital. With the support of public health nurses, community educators, and the hospital's nursing staff, the medical group has delivered over 3,000 babies in five years, and, despite the above-average risk of the women, has demonstrated comparable birth outcomes with their suburban colleagues.

Eastman Kodak Health Information Service

In 1995, the Preventive Services group at Eastman Kodak wanted to test the notion that providing reliable health information to the community could reduce overall health care costs to employers. The group convened insurers, community physicians, business representatives, and government officials, who helped select and advise a commercial vendor to provide general and targeted health information to the HMO members of Rochester's largest employers using a nurse-staffed information phone line. An actuarial analysis conducted for the group did not support their premise that the program would save at least as much as it cost, which was $40 per member in the "pilot" year. The group presently is investigating why such an "RN-line," which was very popular, did not have the measurable positive clinical or financial impact that previous work had suggested it would.

New York State Medicaid Pediatric Reimbursement

The New York State chapter of the American Academy of Pediatrics (NYAAP) worked with the New York State Department of Social Services (DSS) over a contentious payment issue, and the result was a better payment policy for children cov-

Structural Foundations
Contract, Informal

Contact
Philip C. Gioia, MD
Children's Health
Specialists
281 Grant Avenue
Medical Center
Auburn, NY 13021
gioia@relex.com

ered through the Medicaid program. In the late 1980s, DSS began using chart reviews to document Medicaid visits, which led to downgraded payments for office visits and demands for payback on visits that were not properly documented. As a result, medical practitioners were receiving 20–50% of their regular fees for seeing Medicaid patients in their offices, while hospitals were receiving three times that amount for providing the same type of care in emergency rooms. Following an exchange of letters, through which NYAAP pointed out the counterproductive nature of the payment structure, DSS set up a program to give board-certified pediatricians and family practitioners with 24-hour coverage a reimbursement rate close to their private rate for patients less than 18 years of age. This revised policy increased access to medical practitioners for families and facilitated recruitment of primary care pediatricians to the area.

NY-7
Partners
LHD, L-GOV, HOSP, CLIN

Synergies
1a, 2d

Structural Foundations
Contract

Contact
James B. Crucetti,
MD, MPH
Albany County
Department of Health
175 Green Street
P.O. Box 678
Albany, NY 12201
jbc@health.co.albany.ny.us

Albany Partnership for Healthier Communities
Assuring high-quality medical care in Albany's public health clinics was a continual challenge for the county health department, as was recruiting and scheduling part-time physicians to staff its clinics, arranging for after-hours coverage, and paying malpractice insurance. In 1995, the health department contracted with a coalition of two voluntary hospitals and a community health center as the Partnership for Healthier Communities, to provide primary care to the Medicaid and uninsured patients of Albany county. The health department transferred its patients and the clinic sites to the primary care partners, and also assigned a public health nurse and an outreach worker to each site. The public health professionals provided outreach and enabling services, as well as access to the health department's support services. As a result of the partnership, patients have greater access to primary care sites and to the hospital systems' resources—such as social work, specialty care, and diagnostic services—and the hospital systems have seen their "no-show" rate drop considerably in light of the home visits and case management provided by the health department. The health department has broken even on its primary care operation: the lost revenue from Medicaid and indigent care dollars has been offset by savings on *per diem* physician and malpractice costs.

NY-8

Partners

LHD, SHD, MDPRAC, HOSP, CLIN, MCO, SOM, MEDSOC, VHO, BUS, RELIG, FNDN, C-OTH

Synergies

1c, 2b, 3b, 4c, 5b

Structural Foundations

Coalition, Adm/Mgmt

Contact

Bonnie Lewis
Monroe County Women's
Health Partnership
111 Westfall Road
Room 1040
Rochester, NY 14692

Monroe County Women's Health Partnership

After several years of funding hospital-based breast cancer screening programs, in 1992 the New York State Department of Health decided to broaden its reach (NY-10). The state appealed to the local health departments to adopt a coalition-building model to "screen and treat" breast cancer, rather than relying upon individual institutions. As it happened, Monroe County already had much of the community apparatus in place, developed as part of a successful four-year influenza vaccination project (NY-12). Under the leadership of the local health department, the Women's Health Partnership grew to include the Monroe County Medical Society (which initially served as the fiscal agent for the project's funding), several University of Rochester medical departments involved in data analysis and evaluation activities, the American Cancer Society and Cancer Action, the faith community, a number of community-based organizations, and a service-delivery component that involved 41 agencies and over 110 providers. At the heart of the Partnership is an office which oversees budget management, data collection, scheduling and case management of 2,500 clients, report writing, and the coordination of at least eight monthly committee meetings. Through the medical society's and the Partnership's ties to the practice community, every radiologist in the area agreed to participate. As a collective, the Partnership provides a number of support services, such as child care and transportation, to assist women in overcoming barriers to making and keeping their appointments. The Partnership's flexibility and broad community reach has contributed to its success. Since the community-wide campaign began, mammography rates for women ages 50 to 74 in Monroe County have increased from 43% to 62%, with the greatest improvement in those neighborhoods with particularly low rates at baseline. As a result, breast cancer increasingly is being diagnosed at earlier stages. The Partnership is developing similar programs to provide other preventive women's health services as well.

NY-9

Partners

L-GOV, SHD, MDPRAC, MEDSOC, VHO, C-OTH

Establishment of a County Health Department

The relationship between the regulatory authority of the state health department and the "home rule" autonomy of local health officials was a tenuous one in the 1950s in New York State. Although

Synergies
6a-6, 6b-6

Structural Foundations
Informal

Contact
Julius S. Prince, MD, DrPH
7103 Pinehurst Parkway
Chevy Chase, MD 20815
jsprincemd@aol.com

the Public Health Law called for the creation of local health departments in all counties with a population over 100,000, not every county was quick to comply. Local medical practitioners often regarded public health departments as encroachments on their traditional domain. In the Jamestown District in upstate New York, the state district health officer sent to establish a county health department spent 16 years cultivating relationships with local physicians, key county administrators, elected officials, community leaders, and voluntary organizations. He became an active member of the county medical society, and then enlisted the medical society's help and influence to establish an autonomous county health department. During the polio epidemic of the 1950s, the district health officer further established himself with his physician peers by providing much needed supplies and vaccines, and by serving as a communicable disease specialist for several of the local hospitals. He initiated a regular backyard picnic at his farm, which served as the backdrop for his public health promotion and networking efforts in the mostly rural, agricultural county. In 1964, the county board of supervisors established an autonomous county health department, aided by substantial financial support from the state health department.

NY-10
Partners
LHD, SHD, FEDHLTH, MDPRAC, HOSP, CLIN, LAB/RX, MEDSOC, VHO, BUS, LABR, SCHL, RELIG, MEDIA, FNDN, C-OTH

Synergies
2b, 3b, 4c, 5b

Structural Foundations
Coalition, Contract, Adm/Mgmt

Contact
Susan J. True, MEd
Bureau of Chronic
Disease Services
New York State
Department of Health
Empire State Plaza,
Corning Tower
Room 780
Albany, NY 12237
sjt02@health.state.ny.us

New York Breast Health Partnerships
The New York State Department of Health initiated several institution-based breast cancer screening programs in 1988. Although the programs screened over 40,000 women in five years, the state health planners concluded that the populations most in need of access to screening and treatment services—low-income, uninsured, and minority populations—were beyond the reach of most institutions. With the impetus of the CDC's Breast and Cervical Early Cancer Detection Program, the state health department shifted its focus to community-based Breast Health Partnerships (NY-8 is one local example). The Partnerships were intended to be problem-solving groups, charged with bringing the resources of individual partners to the table to coordinate the delivery of comprehensive breast cancer screening services to underserved women. County health units were the first entities approached by the state, with the intent that they would serve as community conveners. The Partnerships were further structured as flexible coalitions, allowing for various partners to partici-

pate with greater or lesser intensity. Across all the Breast Health Partnerships, the coalitions funded by the state were required to provide comprehensive breast cancer screening services to eligible women; ensure that diagnostic testing and treatment were available to all women; use common screening intake and follow-up forms; and negotiate with providers using the same maximum allowable reimbursement rate schedule. In addition, each Partnership had to designate a lead agency to serve as liaison among that state, the Partnership, and the community; a data manager to collect and forward standardized data to the state health planners; and a fiscal contractor to serve as the legal entity for managing the Partnership's funds. In many counties, the health department filled the roles of lead agency and data manager, and the local chapter of the American Cancer Society, or another nonprofit agency, served as the fiscal contractor. While the Partnerships proved more effective than the earlier institution-based programs, many of the funded coalitions reported they could be more effective if they could have funded a dedicated Partnership coordinator or an outreach specialist.

NY-11
Partners
LHD, SOM, AHC, U-OTH

Synergies
5a, 6c-1

Structural Foundations
Contract

Contact
Nancy M. Bennett, MD, MS
Monroe County
Department of Health
111 Westfall Road
Caller 632
Rochester, NY 14692
bennett@prevmed.
rochester.edu

The Center for the Study of Rochester's Health
Capitalizing on a collaborative relationship developed over a number of projects (NY-8, NY-12, NY-22) and contracts between the Monroe County Department of Health and the University of Rochester, the two organizations jointly began developing The Center for the Study of Rochester's Health in 1996. The goals of the Center are to conduct research to help define critical pathways to community health outcomes and to perform intensive and sophisticated evaluations of public health and prevention interventions. Although there is no school of public health at the university, both the medical and nursing schools have historically provided clinical faculty and analytical expertise to the health department; the key administrators developing the research center intend to pool the expertise of the various researchers, clinicians, and public health practitioners who had too often been working in isolation from one another, on separate projects or grants. One of the Center's first projects is an exploration of cardiovascular risk in the community, its epidemiology, and the efficacy of community interventions.

NY-12
Partners
LHD, L-GOV, FEDHLTH, MDPRAC, HOSP, CLIN, MCO, LAB/RX, SOM, ARC, MEDSOC, VHO, RELIG, MEDIA, C-OTH

Synergies
3a, 3c, 4c, 5b, 6a-2, 6c-2

Structural Foundations
Coalition, Contract, Adm/Mgmt, Advisory

Contact
William H. Barker, MD
Department of Community and Preventive Medicine
University of Rochester
Medical Center
Box 644
601 Elmwood Avenue
Rochester, NY 14642
Barker@prevmed.rochester.edu

Monroe County McFlu Campaign

In the mid-1980s, CDC and HCFA selected Monroe County as one of ten sites to evaluate the cost-effectiveness of furnishing influenza vaccine among elderly patients as a Medicare benefit. Since access to a medical practitioner was not the issue for the Medicare population, CDC and HCFA wanted to see if specific Medicare reimbursement for influenza vaccination would lead to a rise in immunization rates and, secondarily, to a decrease in influenza-associated morbidity and mortality. The CDC, in particular, also wanted to encourage partnerships between public health agencies and the medical practice community, with academic medical centers providing the research infrastructure. Investigators at the University of Rochester Medical Center and the Monroe County Health Department, who dubbed their project McFlu, recruited hospitals, nursing homes, labs, and over 80% of all eligible physicians in the county to participate. The project's partners recognized early on that enhanced reimbursement alone was not sufficient, but that a community-wide health promotion strategy would be required. Direct mailings to seniors and multimedia public service announcements promoted the flu vaccines and directed seniors to physicians' offices as well as public clinics for the reimbursable service. The health department distributed and tracked the influenza vaccine and recruited providers and patients; after a number of incomplete Medicare claims were returned to physicians, the health department also took on the role of central claims processing, which dropped the "rejection rate" from 25% to 2% of all submitted claims. The university conducted laboratory-based influenza surveillance, supervised the analysis, and coordinated the entire demonstration project. Overall, McFlu increased immunization rates from 45 to 75% of the eligible population and decreased pneumonia hospitalization rates and nursing home outbreaks. On a national level, the results of McFlu and other influenza demonstration projects around the country led HCFA to amend Medicare reimbursement in 1993, and to include annual influenza immunization as a covered benefit. Locally, McFlu provided a demonstration of community-based strategies that would prove useful as a model for other collaborative efforts (NY-8, NY-11, NY-22).

NY-13

Partners
LHD, L-GOV, HOSP, CLIN, VHO, SCHL, FNDN, C-OTH

Synergies
1c, 4b, 6b-6

Structural Foundations
Coalition, Adm/Mgmt

Contact
Mary E. Haust, MA
Binghamton City
School District
Community Resource
Center
1123 Vestal Avenue
Binghamton, NY 13903
mary_h@bcsd.stier.org

Broome Community Partners

Although the chief executives of several institutions in Broome County had been discussing the impact of welfare, Medicaid, and education reform for several years, their coordinated efforts to address community problems coalesced in response to a funding opportunity. Organizing themselves as the Broome Community Partners, the partnership included the school district, local health department, local mental health agency, Catholic Charities, a community health-planning agency, United Way, and two local hospitals. Upon receiving funding as a CCN demonstration partnership from the W.K. Kellogg Foundation, the partners directed their efforts at coordinating care and services for children ages 0–3. The partners created a universal risk assessment and general intake protocol that was designed by all agencies and providers, and which was tied in to a common client information system and case management program with formal referral linkages. The partners also sought to integrate the work of community health workers, representing many of the community agencies, so that no client "falls between the cracks" of the community's support and service systems. The Broome Community Partners also instituted a Case Conferencing program, which draws together a multiagency, multidisciplinary team to foster early identification of individuals at risk, and which facilitates a central tracking of clients' progress.

NY-14

Partners
L-GOV, S-GOV, FEDHLTH, HOSP, CLIN, ARC, U-OTH

Synergies
3a, 3c, 6a-1, 6a-2, 6a-3, 6a-4, 6a-6, 6c-1

Structural Foundations
Coalition, Contract, Adm/Mgmt, Advisory

Center for the Study of Issues in Public Mental Health

The four-year-old Center for the Study of Issues in Public Mental Health is a cross-sectoral research enterprise that informs mental health policy decisions by using New York State and its counties as research laboratories. The NIMH-funded Center links the Nathan Kline Institute (a state-funded psychiatric research facility), the New York State Office of Mental Health, and the Rockefeller College of Public Affairs and Policy at the State University of New York at Albany. The Center draws researchers statewide from the clinical and basic sciences, such as medicine, pharmacology, nursing, and biochemistry, and the social and policy sciences, including biostatistics, mathematics, ethnography, economics, public health, sociology, and health law. In return for addressing issues relevant to policy and program needs, the researchers are given access to

Contact
Carole Siegel, PhD
Center for the Study
of Issues in Public
Mental Health
Nathan S. Kline Institute for
Psychiatric Research
140 Old Orangeburg Road
Orangeburg, NY 10962
siegel@iris.rfmh.org

comprehensive data sets previously beyond their reach. Using $3.5 million NIMH funding over five years, the Center has almost 30 interinstitutional research projects underway. Examples include a project examining the decision-making processes used by physicians in the treatment and disposition of mentally ill patients who present at psychiatric emergency rooms and an analysis of New York City's program of supported housing for the homeless mentally ill. Studies examining managed care and mental health include evaluations of managed care plans for New York State Medicaid recipients discharged from state psychiatric centers and the development of rate-setting methodologies to account for the "risk" of mental illness among various populations.

NY-15

Partners
LHD, L-GOV, SHD, S-GOV,
FEDHLTH, FEDOTH, HOSP, CLIN,
MCO, INS, LAB/RX, SOM, SPH,
RES, AHC, U-OTH, MEDSOC,
BUS, MEDIA

Synergies
3a, 3c, 4c, 5b, 6a-4, 6b-5

Structural Foundations
Coalition, Contract,
Adm/Mgmt, Advisory

Contact
Raphael P. Nenner, MD
IPRO
1979 Marcus Avenue
Lake Success, NY 11042
nypro.rnenner@sdps.org

New York State IPRO
A research organization dedicated to quality of care, IPRO is the federally designated Peer Review Organization (PRO) for Medicare in New York State and the state's utilization review agent for Medicaid patients. As part of its Health Care Quality Improvement Program, IPRO brings together practicing clinicians, epidemiologists, and other public health professionals to design and implement quality improvement projects. Part of every project's design is a feedback mechanism to provide physicians, hospitals, or public health professionals with information on project results, so that they can quickly make improvements in the delivery of care. Several IPRO projects have resulted in measurable improvements in medical care, such as reduction in rates of radical prostatectomy and an increase in use of prophylactic antibiotics in selected surgical procedures. An ongoing project called Put Prevention Into Practice is focused on increasing specific clinical preventive services in the interest of public health, such as increasing the use of influenza and pneumococcal vaccines among the elderly and the use of mammography among women covered by Medicare. IPRO clinicians and epidemiologists work collaboratively with local health departments, state and county medical societies, consumer groups, and community-based organizations on the health promotion and disease prevention portions of these projects.

NY-16

Partners
LHD, L-GOV, S-GOV, MDPRAC,
HOSP, CLIN, SOM, MEDSOC, BUS

Synergies
5a, 6a-1, 6a-4, 6a-5

Structural Foundations
Coalition, Adm/Mgmt

Contact
Jay A. Gsell, MPA
Genesee County
Government
County Building #1
Main & Court Streets
Batavia, NY 14020

Lake Plains Rural Health Care Initiative

Like many rural areas, this region of upstate New York has concerns about the capacity of its health system. Insuring adequate access to primary care, increasing physician presence at the rural hospitals, and providing preventive education and health care for citizens and employees are among the key concerns of local government and businesses. In 1993, Genesee County government representatives started meeting with two local hospitals and Graham Manufacturing, a multinational firm that is a primary employer in the area, to discuss these issues; they were brought together by their mutual third-party administrator for medical and dental insurance. From this has grown the Lake Plains Rural Health Care Initiative, a three-county collaboration whose goal is to explore jointly ways of keeping rural health care local, accessible, appropriate, and cost-effective. Representatives from Orleans and Wyoming County governments and public health departments, two more local hospitals, and the Genesee County Medical Society were added to the group. The rural network has received two-year funding from the New York State Department of Health. Immediate priorities include: (1) setting up a governance structure that connects physician organizations from the three counties with rural hospitals and county public health departments, and (2) evaluating urban-based health plans in Rochester and Buffalo to propose best models for developing a locally controlled managed care system that protects quality and choice.

NY-17

Partners
SHD, HOSP, RES, AHC, C-OTH

Synergies
1b, 1c, 2a, 3b

Structural Foundations
Contract, Intraorg

Yorkville Common Pantry Clinic for the Homeless

Many of the 150 homeless clients served daily by the Yorkville Common Pantry in East Harlem have substance abuse and/or chronic mental health problems and are at risk for TB, HIV/AIDS, and STDs. In addition, they are averse to using traditional hospital-based clinics and community health centers, and avoid seeing health care providers until they are acutely ill. The Pantry is a soup kitchen and food pantry that also provides case management assistance for social services and referrals to health/mental health care services. They also sponsor a ten-bed transitional shelter program. To better address the medical needs of their clients, the Pantry approached nearby Mount Sinai Hospital to design a program for on-site medical

Contact
Barbara Brenner,
DrPH, MSW
Community Relations
Mount Sinai
Medical Center
The Mount Sinai Hospital
One Gustav L. Levy Place
New York, NY 10029
brenner8@juno.com

and psychiatric care, working through social workers in the Community Relations Department. Over a three-year period from 1994 to 1997, a clinic program was established at the Pantry joining the resources of multiple hospital programs. Using a community psychiatry rotation and weekly medical triage run through the Department of Emergency Medicine, a system of regular psychiatric and physical health services was placed on-site at the Pantry. In addition, linkages were made between the Pantry's case managers and the hospital's social workers to improve resource and entitlement counseling for the clients.

NY-18
Partners
HOSP, AHC, SCHL, FNDN

Synergies
1b, 2a

Structural Foundations
Contract, Adm/Mgmt

Contact
Barbara Brenner,
DrPH, MSW
Community Relations
Mount Sinai
Medical Center
The Mount Sinai Hospital
One Gustav L. Levy Place
New York, NY 10029
brenner8@juno.com

Mount Sinai Grandparent Caregivers Program
The Mount Sinai Pediatric Early Child Health screening program evaluated over 300 preschool children in East Harlem Community School District 4 for developmental delays and psychosocial problems. Staffed by a team composed of a pediatrician, a psychologist, and a social worker, this program identified that many of the children with emotional or development difficulties (approximately one-third) were living in households where both biological parents were absent due to either substance abuse or HIV/AIDS. Many of the children were living with older grandparents (between 40 and 80 years old), who had difficulties with public assistance, Medicaid benefits, and legal problems related to custody of the children. In addition, these older caregivers tended to delay seeking medical care or to overuse emergency room services while experiencing their own medical and psychosocial problems of depression and anxiety. With assistance from a major foundation committed to the needs of older adults, a Grandparent Caregivers program was developed in 1994, with weekly on-site medical care clinics for the grandparents at the children's school, plus parenting and health education, entitlement and benefits counseling, and social and recreational support. Over 100 grandparent-headed households, representing 600 family members, have been involved in the program each year, resulting in lower absenteeism at school and reduced use of inappropriate medical care.

NY-19

Partners
LHD, SHD, FEDHLTH, MDPRAC, HOSP, CLIN, SOM, SPH, AHC, MEDSOC, PHASSN, PROFASSN, VHO

Synergies
3a, 6a-4, 6a-5, 6b-6

Structural Foundations
Advisory

Contact
Jean Pakter, MD, MPH
Columbia School of
Public Health
MCH Program
1175 Park Avenue
New York, NY 10128

New York City Maternal and Child Health Advisory Committees

In 1950, the commissioner of the New York City Department of Health (NYC DOH) convened advisory committees for maternal and child health to act as a bridge between public health and medical professionals working in the city. Physician specialists served on the committees, with a physician chosen by the commissioner as the chair and with representatives from the teaching hospitals of each borough. Committees on obstetrics, pediatrics, nursing, and later, neonatal care, were formed. The advisory committees were very influential in helping the NYC DOH develop policy, and in setting standards of care in the city. For politically contentious issues, the medical sector lent the authority of their clinical expertise as well as practical knowledge of barriers to health care delivery, while the NYC DOH contributed population-based data and the authority to change citywide policy through the NYC Board of Health. For example, the committees were involved in setting standards of care for premature/low-birthweight babies and assisted in the designation of certain hospitals as the centers for this specialized care. Another example was the essential role of the advisory committees in defining standards of care for termination of pregnancy when New York State had passed the legalized abortion law. The committees also provided a forum to share clinical findings (such as the danger of using high concentrations of oxygen on premature babies) or health promotion messages (such as support of breast-feeding) that could improve individual care and population health. The advisory committees continued through the 1980s.

NY-20

Partners
LHD, SOM, SPH

Synergies
6b-4

Structural Foundations
Contract

New York City District Health Centers Location

In the early 1930s, the New York City Department of Health (NYC DOH) made a clear policy decision to locate several new district health centers as close as possible to each medical school in the city. The health centers housed each school of medicine's Department of Preventive Medicine, and the arrangement created an opportunity for close interaction among students and practicing public health professionals. The health department provided office space, labs, and seminar rooms to the schools, and medical students could observe care provided at health department clinics. Bureau

Contact
Duncan W. Clark, MD
The Medical Society for the
County of Kings, Inc.
165 Cadman Plaza East
Brooklyn, NY 11201

Chiefs of the NYC DOH conducted monthly classes for senior students, which aided some of the medical schools (New York University, Cornell, and Long Island College of Medicine) in maintaining required senior clerkships in the health centers. In addition, professors of preventive medicine actively supported and endorsed many NYC DOH initiatives regarding communicable disease control and maternal and child health practices.

NY-21
Partners
LHD, SOM, VHO

Synergies
1c, 6b-4

Structural Foundations
Contract

Contact
Duncan W. Clark, MD
The Medical Society for the
County of Kings, Inc.
165 Cadman Plaza East
Brooklyn, NY 11201

Brooklyn Combined Nursing Program and Medical Student Training
To promote integrated nursing care, the director of the Visiting Nurse Association of Brooklyn (VNAB) and commissioner of the New York City Department of Health (NYC DOH) created a pilot program in the late 1940s that combined the different nursing skills from each agency in their at-home patient visits. VNAB nurses, who were more clinically trained, added patient education to their duties, and NYC DOH nurses, who were more skilled in public health outreach, added bedside nursing to their activities. Together they operated under a special program based on the "combined nursing" model, which lasted about seven years. The chair of Preventive Medicine at Long Island College of Medicine saw this program as an opportunity to demonstrate the importance of a family focus to senior medical students. In a required public health clinical clerkship, medical students accompanied one of these nurses to a family's home for the initial visit and subsequently studied their health concerns, collecting data from the hospital and community agencies on the care the family received. The student then prepared a comprehensive report, which covered the health concerns of the entire family, not just the "index case" to which the nurse was assigned. The student's report identified chronic problems, the need for clinical and preventive medical attention, and an assessment of the quality of care received. With the report, the nursing staff learned about the types of community resources that the family had used in the past. Based on this information, the medical student and nurse discussed the best strategies for moving families into more traditional health care settings and for obtaining needed social services. Though the combined nursing program ended after a short time, VNAB continued to assign nurses to families until 1982. The medical clerkship component re-

mained a mandatory requirement for preventive medicine students for over 20 years, and now operates as an elective assignment.

NY-22

Partners
LHD, SHD, FEDHLTH, AHC, FNDN, C-OTH

Synergies
3c, 5a, 6c-1

Structural Foundations
Contract, Adm/Mgmt

Contact
Mary Paris, MPH
Center for the Study of Rochester Health
University of Rochester Medical Center
601 Elmwood Avenue
Box 644
Rochester, NY 14624
paris@prevmed.rochester.edu

Monroe County Evaluation of Ischemic Heart Disease

Despite recent advances, heart disease remains the leading cause of death in the United States. With funding from the Agency for Health Care Policy and Research and The Robert Wood Johnson Foundation, researchers in the Ischemic Heart Disease Evaluation project in Monroe County have used a "data-driven" approach to better define the burden of illness in the community and to establish a framework for community health planning. A collaborative research team of the Monroe County Health Department and the University of Rochester performed in-depth analysis of population-based data on cardiac risk factors and hospital admissions, procedure utilization, and mortality related to cardiovascular disease. The research team, which includes the deputy health director, will use critical path analysis as a tool for aggregating data from multiple sources and for explaining causal relationships among risk factors and illness. The findings will be disseminated among the key players in the county's health system, including medical and public health professionals, insurers, and health planners, and will inform a community process of program planning around heart disease prevention.

NY-23

Partners
LHD, SHD, MCO, SPH, MEDSOC, PHASSN, VHO, FNDN

Synergies
4c, 5d, 6b-6

Structural Foundations
Coalition

Contact
Ilene Fennoy, MD, MPH
Public Health Association of New York City (PHANYC)
237 Thompson Street
New York, NY 10012
ifl581@aol.com

New York City Medicine and Public Health Collaboration Meeting

In March 1998, the "Medicine and Public Health Collaboration in New York" meeting was co-hosted by the Public Health Association of New York City and the Medical Society of the State of New York, with funding from The Robert Wood Johnson Foundation. The meeting's planning group included representatives from these organizations as well as the private medical sector, managed care, community-based organizations, and the New York City Department of Health. The format of the meeting was designed to encourage specific actions around three health topics: healthy births, child health, and tobacco exposure. Following a morning of background presentations on examples of medicine and public health collaboration, participants met in afternoon roundtable discussions to hear the "medical" and the "public health" perspectives for each topic, and then together explored the potential for interaction between these sectors in New York City. Each group developed a set of recommendations for further action, which they presented to the larger forum at the end of the day.

NY-24
Partners
S-GOV, HOSP, SOM, RES

Synergies
2c, 6b-4

Structural Foundations
Contract

Contact
Yeates Conwell, MD
Department of Psychiatry
University of Rochester
300 Crittenden Boulevard
P.O. Box PSYCH
Rochester, NY 14642

Rochester Integrated Psychiatric Residency Training Program

Like many fields of medicine, psychiatric training has focused on acute conditions rather than on chronic and rehabilitative care. The need for comprehensive care of the chronically mentally ill, especially in community settings, became increasingly important with the deinstitutionalization movement of the 1970s. A nationwide survey conducted in 1980 showed that while 76% of schools of medicine had some training relationship with state mental health hospitals, only 15% had an integrated training system (NAT-20). In response to these concerns, the Department of Psychiatry at the University of Rochester School of Medicine and the Rochester Psychiatric Center (RCP), which is part of the New York State Office of Mental Health, developed collaborative residency training in the 1980s that emphasizes chronic mental disorders and public psychiatry. State hospital rotations offer residents a varied patient population, state-of-the-art training in psychiatric rehabilitation, education about up-to-date drug therapies, and exposure to the administrative side of public psychiatry. Residents also have the opportunity to work for longer periods of time with people who have serious mental illness than is typical for most inpatient training, thus enriching their clinical experience. In return, the state facilities receive needed staffing and augmented in-service training. Although the partners had a long history of working together informally, it took two years of negotiation to devise a formal contract wherein the state supports the training of five residents and two faculty members. For this collaboration to proceed: (1) all parties needed to appreciate that integrated training emphasizing issues related to chronic mental illness and public psychiatry would enhance recruitment of university-trained psychiatrists to the state facility; (2) the state needed to provide funds to support training goals, not just service delivery, with specific contract stipulations clarifying each partner's responsibilities; (3) the university needed to commit its top faculty to the effort and garner support from the full faculty; and (4) the university needed to have total responsibility for recruitment, selection of residents, and development of the curriculum. As of 1998, the training program is still operational.

NY-25

Partners
LHD, L-GOV, FEDOTH, HOSP, SOM, AHC, VHO, FNDN

Synergies
1b, 2a, 3c, 4c, 5a

Structural Foundations
Contract

Contact
George G. Reader, MD
Ambulatory and
Community Medicine
Cornell University
Medical College
1300 York Avenue
New York, NY 10021

Queens-Long Island City Action Program

The Johnson Administration's Office of Economic Opportunity funded the Queens-Long Island City Action Program (QUALICAP) from 1969 to 1973, which, in turn, created a community-based health and social service center that housed family planning and maternal health programs developed collaboratively by Planned Parenthood and New York Hospital-Cornell University Medical Center (NYH-CUMC). As the project was forming, the New York City health commissioner convened a meeting of agencies providing health care services to the Astoria-Long Island City area of Queens. New York Hospital was designated as a key service provider to the QUALICAP clinic. Cornell's Chair of Obstetrics and Gynecology received a grant from the Rockefeller Foundation for family planning and took the lead in establishing a community program. The chief of the Division of Ambulatory and Community Medicine served as a liaison with the community and the health department, and also spearheaded a household health survey and a community provider census funded by the Health Research Council of New York City. Additional funding came from the New York City Human Resources Administration. The collaboration of QUALICAP, the health department, and NYH-CUMC improved maternal and child health care for this low-income community, and provided valuable training to medical students and residents. In 1973, however, when the Rockefeller Foundation grant expired and New York City faced a serious budget crisis, the QUALICAP program and the other collaborative activities ended due to lack of funds.

NY-26

Partners
LHD, L-GOV, HOSP, SOM, AHC

Synergies
1b, 2a, 6c-2

New York City Welfare Medical Care Demonstration Project

In the 1960s, the health and welfare commissioners in New York City were interested in developing a pilot program that would provide a single source of health care for welfare recipients and that would be comparable to the standard fee-for-service care

Structural Foundations
Contract

Contact
George G. Reader, MD
Ambulatory and
Community Medicine
Cornell University
Medical College
1300 York Avenue
New York, NY 10021

these clients usually received. Physicians affiliated with New York Hospital-Cornell University Medical Center responded to the city's request and established a group practice site, with Cornell's chief of the Division of Ambulatory and Community Medicine as a leading organizer. This experimental program was funded through the Health Research Council of New York City. The welfare department randomly assigned new clients to the practice, and the physician group was given prepayment to provide comprehensive care for clients served by them. A formal evaluation of the program demonstrated that a voluntary teaching hospital could provide a full range of medical services in a personalized and coordinated way to welfare recipients, but the length of the observation period made it difficult to detect significant differences in mortality or morbidity or in cost savings. The program was discontinued after the evaluation period.

Goodrich, CH, Olendzki, MC, and Reader, GG. 1970. *Welfare Medical Care: An Experiment.* Cambridge, MA: Harvard University Press.

NY-27
Partners
LHD, SHD, CLIN, SOM, SPH, AHC, VHO, SCHL, C-OTH
Synergies
5b, 5d, 6b-4

Structural Foundations
Coalition, Contract, Intraorg

Contact
Marian Osterweis, PhD
Association of Academic
Health Centers
1400 16th Street, N.W.
Suite 720
Washington, DC 20036
mosterweis@acadhlthctrs.
org

Brooklyn Community Health Promotion
The State University of New York Health Science Center at Brooklyn (SUNY-HSCB) is an academic health center located within an ethnically and culturally diverse inner-city community. HSCB is a major provider of primary care services, public health outreach and prevention activities, and health promotion/disease prevention programs in the community. Its community-oriented primary care focus has led to many partnerships with educational, health, and social service agencies in the community. As of 1992, HSCB had provided technical assistance to the borough president's office, contributed to overall health planning efforts for the community, and assisted in the coordination of health promotion activities across schools and in the community. With funding from the federal government, the New York State and New York City Departments of Health, HSCB's three major areas of service for the community at that time were HIV/AIDS prevention, alcoholism and substance abuse, and prenatal outreach and parenting education. Many activities in this area were done in partnership with local community-based organizations, which increased the value of the programs to community members as well as their effectiveness.

Osterweis, M and Eichhorn, SF. 1993. Community-based health promotion activities. In *Promoting community health: the role of the academic health center*. Skelton, WD and Osterweis, M, eds. Washington, DC: Association of Academic Health Centers.

NY-28

Partners
LHD, MCO

Synergies
1c, 4b

Structural Foundations
Contract

Contact
Patsy Yang-Lewis, MPH
Westchester County
Department of Health
145 Hugenot Street
New Rochelle, NY 10801
pry1@exchange.co.
westchester.ny.us

Westchester County Lead Poisoning Treatment

When Westchester County became one of the first counties in New York State to embark on a mandatory Medicaid managed care program in 1996, the health commissioner arranged with participating managed care organizations to subcontract for lead poisoning treatment services from the local health department. Although the managed care providers were required to take responsibility for all pediatric services, including immunizations and lead screening, it was evident that the number of lead poisoning cases in the county was insufficient to warrant the MCOs developing their own in-house expertise. Since the health department had the requisite expertise and staffing, it contracted with the MCOs to provide home visits, education, and follow-up care for particular children with elevated blood lead levels. The arrangement has worked to the financial benefit of both the MCOs and the local health department.

NY-29

Partners
FEDOTH, MCO, VHO, SCHL,
RELIG, C-OTH

Synergies
5b

Structural Foundations
Adm/Mgmt, Advisory

Contact
See citation

Bronx Health Education Campaign

As a not-for-profit insurance plan serving a culturally and racially diverse indigent population, the Bronx Health Plan recognized that residents in its service area had little access to health education programs, particularly those provided by such issue-specific agencies as the American Cancer Society. The health plan established a program involving participants in the AmeriCorps Volunteers in the Service to America (VISTA) program, who worked as community health outreach workers. The VISTA workers organized over 200 health education workshops in a two-year period and invited voluntary health organizations to provide speakers and materials. The workshops were attended by over 5,000 area residents. As part of the campaign, the health plan provided one full-time staff member to train and supervise the VISTA workers, general oversight by the plan's Community Relations Manager, and office support services. Several consequences of the health education campaign include: VISTA workers parlaying their experience into gainful employment; the Bronx Health Plan becoming more responsive to health needs expressed at the community workshops; the development of a resource guide; and the creation of a community-based Health Education Advisory Council.

American Association of Health Plans. 1996. *Improving the quality of life in local communities.* Washington, DC.

NY-30

Partners
LHD, L-GOV, MDPRAC, HOSP, CLIN, SPH, AHC, VHO, SCHL, C-OTH

Synergies
1c, 5b

Structural Foundations
Coalition, Contract

Contact
See citation

Washington Heights Columbia-Presbyterian Community Health System

Access to affordable health care has long been a critical need in the predominantly poor Latino neighborhood of Washington Heights that surrounds Columbia-Presbyterian Medical Center (CPMC). Working with a network of community-based organizations (Northern Manhattan Collaborates!) and local elected officials in a CCN finalist partnership (recognized by the W.K. Kellogg Foundation), CPMC has worked to develop more programs and practice sites to serve the community, including six off-site practices in the community, five school-based clinics, a 300-bed community hospital, and a program which links more than 60 community-based physicians, the majority of whom are Latin American-born and -educated, to the hospital. CPMC involves the community and community-based organizations in its pediatric asthma project by stressing case management of children and families with asthma and by working with tenants' organizations for targeted community education and outreach.

Bogue, R and Hall, Jr, CH, eds. 1997. *Health networks innovations: how 20 communities are improving their system through collaboration.* Chicago: American Hospital Publishing, Inc.

NY-31

Partners
LHD, L-GOV, SHD, S-GOV, FEDHLTH, MDPRAC, HOSP, INS, AHC, BUS, FNDN

Synergies
1c, 3b, 4a, 6a-1, 6a-2

Structural Foundations
Coalition

Monroe County Community Coalition for Long-Term Care

Monroe County has a large and growing elderly population, and the problems of chronic illness are becoming a health priority in the community. To address this need, the Community Coalition for Long-Term Care was created in 1989 as a public-private partnership of Monroe County government, hospitals, insurers, businesses, and other health providers. Recognized by the W.K. Kellogg Foundation as a CCN finalist partnership, the Coalition uses a comprehensive community database to support coordinated care services for the elderly in Monroe County. The Coalition has also developed a capitated, managed care program for primary,

Contact
Helena Temkin-Greener, MD
Community Coalition for Long-Term Care
311 Alexander Street
Suite 201
Rochester, NY 14604

NY-32
Partners
LHD, FEDHLTH, HOSP, SPH

Synergies
1b, 1c, 3b, 3c, 4b

Structural Foundations
Contract, Adm/Mgmt

Contact
See citation

NY-33
Partners
LHD, HOSP, CLIN, VHO

Synergies
1a, 1c, 2a, 3b

Structural Foundations
Coalition

acute, and long-term care among older Medicaid- and Medicare-eligible individuals and the Independent Living System for Seniors, which provides comprehensive, cost-effective, and client-centered care (now operating as a separate organization). They are also conducting a study on the feasibility of linking the managed care program with long-term care insurance.

Harlem Hospital Model TB Clinic

When several infectious disease doctors started the Model TB Clinic at Harlem Hospital in 1993, the incidence of multidrug-resistant tuberculosis in Harlem was four times the citywide rate. Guided by a medical compliance strategy known as "directly observed therapy" (which requires TB patients to take their medications at the clinic or at home under the supervision of a clinic nurse or outreach worker), the physicians enlisted the city health department's help in screening, referring, and tracking patients. The health department provided public health educators and outreach workers to the Model TB Clinic to find hard-to-reach patients, and also provided diagnostic x-ray services. Another partner in the CDC-funded Model TB Clinic, the Columbia School of Public Health, provided research and evaluation services. One of the school's contributions was linking AIDS and TB registries to facilitate case-finding and outreach. Teams were established at the clinic, staffed by a physician, a nurse, a social worker, and a public health outreach worker. The teams were alerted whenever a TB patient was admitted to Harlem Hospital, and they recruited patients into the clinic. The clinic's goal was to provide each patient with coordinated medical and social service care, as well as education, in one place. The incidence of TB has declined citywide and in Central Harlem each year since 1993.

Abramson, DM. 1994. TB: The resurging illness hits New York in a drug-resistant form. *Columbia Public Health Chronicle* 2(2): 11–17.

Finger Lakes Migrant Health Collaboration

In 1993, the New York State Department of Health used a federal block grant to fund five collaborative efforts between migrant health centers and local health departments. The funding was earmarked for improving the quality and efficiency of care by increasing migrant camp-based screenings and by improving linkages between the migrant

Contact
Margaret Gadon,
MD, MPH
Department of Medicine
Baystate Medical Center
Mason Square
Neighborhood
Health Center
11 Wilbraham Road
Springfield, MA 01109
mgadon@schoolph.umass.
edu

health centers and the local health departments. The Finger Lakes Migrant Health Center worked with five surrounding counties to provide screening for TB, HIV, diabetes, and hypertension. In addition, it provided case management for affected migrants. The screenings were conducted at migrant camps by a team composed of community health workers, a health center physician, and a public health nurse from the local health department. All migrant farm workers with positive TB tests were sent to the local health department for chest x-rays. HIV-positive migrants were seen at one of two local health centers. Further treatment and social services were managed by the health center's case manager, who coordinated care across the migrant clinics, state and community health agencies, and a tertiary referral center. As a result of the collaboration, there was a 300% increase in migrant farm worker screening for TB and HIV over previous seasons, and 828 migrants identified as positive were treated for these conditions through publicly financed programs.

[OH] OHIO

OH-1
Partners
LHD, L-GOV, SHD, FEDHLTH,
SOM

Synergies
1a, 3b, 6b-4

Structural Foundations
Contract

Contact
Marjorie E. Nelson,
MD, MPH
Ohio University
College of Medicine
Department of
Family Medicine
Grosvenor Hall
Athens, OH 45701
mnelson1@ohiou.edu

Ohio University College of Medicine
TB Control Project
In the mid-1980s, international students at Ohio University College of Medicine were identified as a major risk group for tuberculosis (TB), and the large number of students with active TB was a threat to county residents in general. With CDC funding, the head of the Preventive Medicine/Public Health Section of the Department of Family Medicine and a CDC officer, who was available to the project for technical assistance, established a TB chemoprophylaxis program for students. The program reduced the rate of active TB infection among the students from 97/100,000 to 14/100,000, helping to keep the county rate of 5/100,000 constant. Now, the college operates two TB-prevention clinics, which serve both international students and persons incarcerated in a local prison, and it is fully supported by local funds. The clinic is also a training site for Preventive Medicine/Public Health predoctoral medical students. Careful interpretation and regular reports to local health department staff, county commissioners, and other University staff helped build local support for the program.

OH-2

Partners
LHD, L-GOV, HOSP, CLIN, SOM, VHO, C-OTH

Synergies
5a, 5b, 5c, 5d, 6b-1, 6b-4

Structural Foundations
Contract, Adm/Mgmt, Intraorg

Contact
C. William Keck, MD, MPH
Akron Department of Public Health
177 S. Broadway
Akron, OH 44308
72054.151@compuserve.com

Northeastern Ohio Universities College of Medicine Community Medicine Clerkship

In 1994, the Northeastern Ohio Universities College of Medicine (NEOUCOM) enhanced its emphasis on population medicine and community service by developing a required Community Medicine clerkship for graduating medical students. The Ohio medical school was founded in 1973 as a joint enterprise of three state universities to develop a six-year BA/MD program, with the explicit mission of training community-oriented physicians. Unlike traditional medical schools, NEOUCOM established a Division of Community Health Sciences that stands on equal footing with its Basic and Clinical Sciences Divisions, and in which faculty tenure decisions consider community service as well as research and teaching. The division's director also directs the Akron Department of Public Health, and he has fostered a number of links and affiliations with other regional health departments and community agencies. The Senior Community Medicine Clerkship complements an eight-week community practicum for freshman in which student teams develop community programs and then defend their proposals in a mock legislative hearing presided over by actual state legislators. In the four-week senior clerkship, students and methodologic faculty support the efforts of six regional health departments in community diagnosis and health status improvement. Year-to-year, consecutive teams of students, faculty, and community preceptors analyze and develop strategies for addressing a prioritized community health problem, and then evaluate their interventions. In the City of Akron, for example, clerkship teams targeted the goal of reducing preventable fire deaths. Based on the team's findings and suggestions, the Akron Fire Department changed its prevention strategies by focusing on high-risk neighborhoods identified by epidemiological mapping, improving the availability of working smoke detectors, and endorsing a fire prevention game for elementary school children created by the medical students. As the final piece in NEOUCOM's community-oriented curriculum, the clerkship is designed to increase the students' knowledge of community resources; provide a direct connection between basic science principles of health and disease and their expression in a community; develop better coordination between the medical and public health sectors;

and enhance the students' understanding of how clinicians can influence and affect both individual and community behaviors.

OH-3
Partners
LHD, L-GOV, MDPRAC, HOSP, LAB/RX, RELIG, FNDN

Synergies
2a, 2b

Structural Foundations
Adm/Mgmt

Contact
Randall M. Flint, RS, MPH
Alliance City Health Department
P.O. Box 2504
Alliance, OH 44601
rflint@cannet.com

Alliance Good Samaritan Medical Care Clinic

A physician in Alliance approached her local health department in 1994, interested in establishing a free clinic for indigent care. The public health director echoed her interest in such a clinic, and acknowledged that the health department had tried to organize one but had been unable to muster enough volunteer physicians to staff it. In concert with the health department, church volunteers, and several interested physicians at Alliance Hospital, the physician conducted a feasibility study, solicited financial support and space from a local church, and then incorporated the group as the Good Samaritan Medical Care Clinic. The health department's nursing director and professional health care volunteers from the church helped develop the clinic flow, and the physician recruited 40 nurses and 55 physicians to volunteer their time. Situated within walking distance of the health department, the clinic also refers patients to the health department's services, such as STD and immunization clinics. In the span of only a few years, the clinic has added a prescription program, a dental clinic, and a referral network for specialty and inpatient care.

OH-4
Partners
LHD, MDPRAC

Synergies
2a

Structural Foundations
Adm/Mgmt

Contact
Robert E. Titko, MSW
Zanesville-Muskingum County Health Department
205 North 7th Street
Zanesville, OH 43701

Zanesville Free Clinic

Zanesville is a rural community on the edge of Appalachia, about 50 miles from Columbus. The area's uninsured and underinsured patients have historically been seen at one of the two hospital emergency rooms, with private practitioners accepting patients on a rotating basis. Although this system has not driven either hospital or the physicians to the brink of financial crisis, there has been a growing awareness that patients are presenting at very late stages of an illness, well beyond the reach of good primary or preventive care. A chance encounter in 1995 between the public health director and the senior partner in a local medical practice led to the development of the Zanesville Free Clinic, supported by the health department and staffed by volunteer physicians. Two years later, the clinic has drawn a number of volunteer physicians, and the health department has added a nurse-practitioner to its staff. The health department provides clinical space, a receptionist, a medical technician, a public health nurse, and a nurse-practitioner who provides clinical preventive services. The volunteer physicians staff the clinic and provide sick care. Any follow-up work is done by the public health nurses, who occasionally make home visits or refer patients to other public services. An early effort to "mainstream" the Free Clinic patients into private practices was abandoned when it appeared that the patients preferred the Free Clinic setting. The hospitals report that inappropriate emergency room use has decreased by 20% since the founding of the Free Clinic.

OH-5

Partners
LHD, L-GOV, HOSP, CLIN, MEDSOC, BUS, SCHL, RELIG, MEDIA, FNDN, C-OTH

Synergies
5a, 5d, 5e

Structural Foundations
Coalition, Adm/Mgmt

Contact
Robert E. Titko, MSW
Zanesville-Muskingum
County Health Department
205 North 7th Street
Zanesville, OH 43701

Zanesville PRO-Muskingum

When the chief operating officer of Bethesda Hospital in Zanesville returned from a Healthy Communities workshop in 1995, he enthusiastically promoted the concept to his colleagues at Good Samaritan Medical Center (a competitor) and the local health department. The three administrators agreed to pursue the development of a Healthy Community initiative, and expanded their initial steering committee to include other key administrators from their institutions. The health department director also included his environmental officer in these initial meetings. The group's goal was to change the competitive nature of the community's institutions into a cooperative one, and to stimulate a number of agencies and individuals in the community to address broad determinants of health. Prior to making their initiative public, the initial members spent a year and a half planning the concept and securing a solid financial base. All three institutions committed funding and personnel to the project, entitled PRO-Muskingum (Pride, Respect, Opportunity in Muskingum County). After the initiative was introduced to the community, several hundred people joined forums and committees to work on specific issue areas. PRO-Muskingum has since opened an office, hired a staff person, and is beginning to explore ways of combining similar community efforts—such as those addressing teen pregnancy—under a single umbrella.

OH-6

Partners
LHD, SHD, FEDHLTH, SOM, AHC, U-OTH

Cincinnati STD/HIV Prevention Training Center

In 1993, the CDC decided to scale back the number of STD/HIV Prevention Training Centers

Synergies
3a, 6b-5, 6c-1

Structural Foundations
Contract, Adm/Mgmt,
Advisory

Contact
Nancy M. Lorenzi, PhD
University of Cincinnati
Medical Center
250 Health Professions
Building
Mail Location 0663
Cincinnati, OH 45267
nancy.lorenzi@uc.edu

and fund only one per region, for a total of ten nationally. The Cincinnati Health Department, which had received CDC funding for its prevention training center for 15 years, faced considerable competition from Chicago and Indianapolis for the regional award. The district health administrator approached a number of people at the University of Cincinnati Medical Center for assistance. A small planning group was formed to "reconceptualize" the prevention training center, and they hired a technical writer to assist them. Their new proposal focused on distance-learning technologies, an affiliation with the university's Office of Continuing Medical Education, greater responsiveness to the needs and interests of the practice community, an increased emphasis on behavioral content in courses, and an updated organizational structure in which the Center's program director received formal input from a regional advisory council and an executive steering committee. The group was awarded the five-year grant, which led to a second collaborative effort—actually implementing what they had proposed. A number of organizational barriers materialized: professionals resistant to changing the status quo, a concern over turf, differences in how quickly to initiate change, even a reluctance to work together. As it happened, the CDC brought together the ten national awardees; the enthusiastic response of the other nine centers regarding Cincinnati's innovative approaches served to reinforce the reconceptualization, and members from both the health department and medical center were able to lay aside their differences. One of the most successful projects undertaken by the reestablished center has been an Internet-based training center, which hosts all the CDC Training Prevention Centers, provides access to slides and curricula, and also offers interactive, multimedia training modules

OH-7
Partners
HOSP, CLIN, SOM, AHC

Synergies
1a, 2c, 5a, 6b-4

Structural Foundations
Contract, Advisory

Cincinnati Community-Oriented Primary Care Program
In 1991, the Lincoln Heights Health Center and the University of Cincinnati Medical Center recognized their complementary needs: the medical center needed a community-based site to train primary care physicians, and the community health center needed qualified medical personnel. The health center first opened its doors in 1967 in an impoverished area in which there were no physicians or

Contact
Laura K. Fidler, MPH
Office of the Senior Vice
President and Provost
University of Cincinnati
Medical Center
250 Health Professions
Building
P.O. Box 670663
Cincinnati, OH 45267
laura.fidler@uc.edu

dentists, and over the years, it struggled to maintain sufficient numbers of qualified providers. The academic medical center, on the other hand, received 10% of its operating revenue from the county to cover care for the medically indigent, and the board of trustees felt they had fiduciary, as well as moral and ethical responsibilities, to support primary care services at a community health center within their catchment area. In March 1991, the community health center and the medical center signed a five-year agreement. Faculty from the medical school were recruited to help staff the health center, and one was appointed associate medical director. The clinical faculty, and several medical center specialists, work alongside the health center's physicians. Other elements of the program included: faculty obstetricians working on the health center's community outreach team; the health center's x-ray room was renovated and a university radiologist was recruited; the previously closed pharmacy was reopened as a university satellite pharmacy; systems of coordinating primary, emergency, specialty, and inpatient care were developed; rotations were established for medical, nursing, and pharmacy students; and a Community-Oriented Primary Care program was instituted. The last involved conducting a medical census and interview for every adult in the community, regardless of where they received care, reviewing all their medical charts, and creating a database of age-appropriate cancer screenings, cardiovascular risk factors, and treatments. The program also provided mechanisms for those without care to receive it. To finance the partnership, the university pays $350,000 a year. Since the agreement's inception, the university has seen specialty referrals more than quadruple, and the health center has regained financial stability.

OH-8
Partners
LHD, HOSP, LAB/RX, SOM, RES,
MEDSOC, FNDN

Synergies
1c, 2a, 2b, 3c, 5a

Structural Foundations
Coalition, Adm/Mgmt

Reach Out of Montgomery County
In 1993, in response to The Robert Wood Johnson Foundation Reach Out initiative, a coalition was formed in Montgomery County that included the county medical society, Wright State University School of Medicine, and the local health department. The three groups incorporated as Reach Out of Montgomery County to provide primary and specialist care to the uninsured. With RWJF funding, the group established free clinics at two neighborhood health centers, using the volunteer ser-

Contact
Syed M. Ahmed,
MD, DrPH
Reach Out of
Montgomery County
Fidelity Plaza
211 South Main Street
Suite 1100
Dayton, OH 45402

vices of 30 primary care physicians, 31 specialty physicians, 12 resident physicians, 36 nurses, 46 medical and nursing students, 2 social workers, and 16 office personnel. The local Reach Out project conducted a door-to-door survey in order to determine who the uninsured were and what barriers they faced, developed a comprehensive patient database, instituted a volunteer recruitment system, and established mechanisms for malpractice and liability insurance coverage and provider credentialing. In the first three years of operation, the group enrolled nearly 2,000 patients, and developed a network for specialty referrals, free or low-cost medications, dental care, and diagnostic and laboratory services.

OH-9
Partners
LHD, L-GOV, HOSP, LAB/RX,
MEDSOC, PROFASSN, BUS, FNDN

Synergies
6a-1

Structural Foundations
Coalition

Contact
See citation

Toledo Physicians' Business Partnership

Initiated in 1995, the Toledo Physicians' Business Partnership was an effort to develop a health care program that would expand insurance coverage for the working uninsured. Funded by The Robert Wood Johnson Foundation's Reach Out Physicians' Initiative, the Partnership had a 30-member consortium, which included the Toledo Academy of Medicine as the lead agency, the Toledo Department of Health, the Lucas County Health Department, the Hospital Council of Northwest Ohio, the Chamber of Commerce, and the Northwest Ohio Health Planning Council. Using data from the Toledo Area Health Insurance Study, the physician-led consortium created a booklet that profiles the area's business community, its working uninsured, and the impact of the uninsured on the medical community. The consortium sought proposals from insurance companies to underwrite coverage for the working uninsured and developed a program through which physicians and health institutions receive reduced reimbursement for caring for this population. While physicians had been very supportive of the plans, and many agreed to accept reduced fees, interest from insurance companies was lacking. The partnership also sought legislation on tax incentives for physicians who would provide care under the reduced rate program. There had been little political interest in cutting taxes for physicians, although the state legislature did consider tax breaks for small employers who provide health insurance for their workers. By 1998, the program had disbanded.

Boyd, EB. Partnership creating plan for uninsured workers. *The Toledo Blade*, August 9, 1995:11–12.

OH-10

Partners
LHD, L-GOV, MEDSOC, PROFASSN, VHO, SCHL, FNDN, C-OTH

Synergies
5b, 5c

Structural Foundations
Coalition

Contact
Valentin Mersol, MD
Cleveland ENT and
Facial Surgery Group
12000 McCracken Road
Suite 550
Cleveland, OH 44125

Northeast Ohio Tobacco Control Coalition

To fight adverse tobacco legislation at the state level, the Northeast Ohio Tobacco Control Coalition was formed in 1994 by the local chapter of the American Heart Association with a grant from the Cleveland Foundation. The membership consists of over 22 medical societies and health agencies, including the Academy of Medicine of Cleveland, local health departments, school boards, and citizen groups. Through extensive lobbying efforts, they successfully stalled the bill. In the spring of 1996, the Coalition sponsored the Tobacco Free Youth Conference to increase awareness of the impact of tobacco use and environmental tobacco smoke on children. Directed at health care and public health professionals, law enforcement officers, and teachers in the public schools, conference topics included why children smoke and the increased rates of smoking among girls, plus specific recommendations for action, such as limiting the tobacco industry's access to children and the power of constituencies in lobbying for tougher tobacco control laws.

OH-11

Partners
LHD, L-GOV, MDPRAC, HOSP, INS, SOM, VHO, SCHL, C-OTH

Synergies
4a, 5b, 5d, 6c-1

Structural Foundations
Coalition, Adm/Mgmt

Contact
Janet L. Zak, MA
Community Health
Injury Prevention Center of
the Greater Dayton Area
32 North Main Street
Suite 1441
Dayton, OH 45402
jzak@gdahin.org

Injury Prevention Center of the Greater Dayton Area

Injury from motor vehicle crashes and accidental falls are leading causes of premature death in Montgomery County. A trauma surgeon on the faculty of the Wright State University School of Medicine sought to address this problem and wrote a proposal describing a center that would reduce the impact of injuries through prevention, acute care, and rehabilitation. The Greater Dayton Area Hospital Association, involving all six member hospitals in the county, a private insurer, and the school of medicine, spearheaded a collaborative effort to develop the Injury Prevention Center of the Greater Dayton Area (IPC). IPC began operation in 1995 as a nonprofit organization, and since then, the local health department, school district, and other community-based organizations have taken part in its design and function. IPC focuses on education and research initiatives in bicycle safety, firearm safety, the prevention of falls in the elderly, and the prevention of teen vehicular trauma.

OH-12
Partners
LHD, MCO

Synergies
2a, 4c

Structural Foundations
Coalition

Contact
See citation

Eastern Ohio L.O.V.E.!
A local managed care health plan in Eastern Ohio, United Healthcare of Ohio, joined with the Columbus City and Franklin County health departments in an immunization campaign, L.O.V.E.! (Love Our kids, Vaccinate Early). The coalition operated a free immunization clinic one Saturday each month, with staff provided by volunteers from the HMO, the health department, and other local providers. The health plan also provided physician office staff training, and articles in both physician and HMO plan member newsletters as part of the L.O.V.E.! immunization effort. As a result of the campaign, the health plan's immunization rates rose from 40% in 1993 to 68.6% in 1996.

American Association of Health Plans. 1996. *Improving the quality of life in local communities.* Washington, DC.

OH-13
Partners
LHD, L-GOV, SHD, FEDHLTH, HOSP, SOM, U-OTH, MEDSOC, VHO, MEDIA, FNDN

Synergies
5a

Structural Foundations
Coalition, Adm/Mgmt

Contact
Maguerite A. Erme, DO, MPH
Healthy Summit 2000
Akron Department of Public Health
177 South Broadway
Akron, OH 44308
mao@neoucom.edu

Healthy Summit 2000
The three health departments that serve Summit County, decided in 1993 to conduct a countywide health prioritization project, called Healthy Summit 2000. As an initial step in the process, the project's Steering Committee created a Statistics Committee to develop a community data document based on Healthy People 2000 objectives. Committee members, who included representatives from the health departments, police, educational, and social service agencies, and the acute care hospitals, quickly recognized that such a task posed two problems: (1) any resulting report with data on 338 objectives would be overwhelming to the community panel, and (2) most of the data were unavailable or incomplete. Instead, the project coordinator (who currently serves as an official at the Akron Department of Public Health and on the medical faculty at the Northeastern Ohio Universities College of Medicine (OH-2)), compiled a *Statistical Health Abstract*, which relied upon selected demographic, educational, and economic data. The shorter document proved more useful to the community panel, who returned to the Statistics Committee for greater detail or more data as they needed it.

OH-14
Partners
LHD, L-GOV, HOSP, CLIN, MCO, SOM, SCHL, RELIG, FNDN, C-OTH

Akron Healthy Connections Network
To assist community residents in this low-income, metropolitan area in accessing needed health and social services, Healthy Connections Network of

Synergies
1c, 5a, 5b, 5e

Structural Foundations
Coalition, Adm/Mgmt

Contact
Barbara Honthumb
Managed Care
Summa Health System
525 East Market Street
P.O. Box 2090
Akron, OH 44309

Akron was established in 1995 to create linkages between existing agencies, services and programs. This CCN finalist partnership, recognized by the W.K. Kellogg Foundation, is a nonprofit corporation founded by the Akron General Medical Center, the Akron Health Department, Children's Hospital Medical Center, Summa Health System, and Healthy Summit 2000. The partnership has done extensive community health and resource assessments to determine the collaborative strategies needed to best utilize existing community services. The Life Link program, which uses an interactive computer database to link clients to the services offered by collaborating organizations, grew out of the collaborative work of the Healthy Connections coalition.

[OR] OREGON

OR-1
Partners
LHD, L-GOV, SHD, FEDHLTH, HOSP, CLIN, MCO, SOM, RES, AHC, PHASSN

Synergies
1a, 2a, 2c, 6b-2, 6b-3, 6b-4

Structural Foundations
Contract, Adm/Mgmt

Contact
Alan L. Melnick, MD, MPH
Oregon Health
Sciences University
School of Medicine
Department of
Family Medicine
3181 S.W. Sam Jackson
Park Road
Portland, OR 97201
melnicka@ohsu.edu

Portland Family Practice and Public Health/Preventive Medicine Residency
In 1996, Oregon Health Sciences University, which offered separate Family Medicine and Public Health/Preventive Medicine residencies, decided to offer a combined four-year residency program. By joining the two graduate programs, the school can train physicians with expertise in primary care, prevention, and population-based approaches— skills needed to care for a defined population as a local health officer or in a managed care organization. As a collaborative effort with the Clackamas County health department, the family medicine/ preventive medicine residency program also increases the supply of primary care physicians in underserved areas in Portland, supplements the clinical staff at the county's community health center, and strengthens the ties between the local health department and the medical school. One organizational link has been that the director of the combined residency program, also serves as the local health department's health officer.

OR-2
Partners
LHD, SHD, S-GOV, MCO, SCHL

Synergies
3b, 4c

Washington County Community Prevention Projects
To encourage MCO participation in local prevention activities, the Oregon Health Plan Administration requires all MCOs that hold contracts with the state to participate in at least two local projects. The Oregon Health Division also notified local

Structural Foundations
Contract, Informal

Contact
Clay Parton
Washington County
Department of Health
and Human Services
155 North 1st Avenue
Mailstop 4
Hillsboro, OR 97124
clay_parton@co.
washington.or.us

health departments about this requirement of MCOs, prompting the Washington County health department to collaborate with two MCOs in its area. In 1996, they began formulating two projects. The first is an effort to increase immunization for preschoolers and school-age children, with MCOs donating staff for health department-organized, school-based immunization clinics, and with schools working on publicity and outreach. The second project is aimed at increasing awareness of the need for breast and cervical cancer screening. The MCOs and health department will jointly do outreach to women over age 50 to intensify the overall campaign. In this collaboration, the public health sector helps local MCOs meet their obligations, while they gain assistance with important community prevention campaigns.

OR-3
Partners
SHD, S-GOV, CLIN, SOM, ARC,
RES, AHC

Synergies
2c, 6a-6, 6b-1, 6b-4, 6b-5,
6c-2

Structural Foundations
Advisory

Contact
David Cutler, MD
Public Psychiatry
Training Program
Oregon Health
Sciences University
3181 S.W. Sam Jackson
Park Road
Portland, OR 97201

Public Psychiatry Training Program
While university and state hospital relationships are important to public mental health staffing, so are links to community mental health centers (CMHCs). In 1973, a partnership of the Oregon Mental Health Division and the Department of Psychiatry at Oregon Health Sciences University created the Community Psychiatry Training Program (now called Public Psychiatry) to improve psychiatric education and placement in CMHCs. A key element of the collaboration was the creation of a Program Advisory Board that guided the university and the state on program issues and served as a platform for joint planning, negotiation, and support as well as a practical link among agencies and program staff. Mirroring the interinstitutional design of the program, the Board had representatives from the university's psychiatry department, the state's mental health department, the dean's office of the medical school, and the community mental health center directors, with faculty and administrators for the program residing in the university's Department of Psychiatry. Partners jointly developed the program's curriculum and established the required six-month community psychiatry rotation in the third year of training with an optional senior elective in the fourth year. A public mental health perspective was incorporated into the curriculum's weekly seminar on community mental health planning and service delivery and in its emphasis on consultation skills within the interdisciplinary community setting of the CMHC. The close working relationship among the partners also stimulated opportunities

for collaborative research. Joint interests and priorities of the university and the state spurred research projects in psychiatric education and administration, community treatment of the mentally ill, and forensic psychiatry. Ongoing follow-up of graduates of the program from 1978 to 1998 indicate that a high percentage (up to 75%) of its graduates remained in public service for communities in the region.

Talbott, JA and Robinowitz, CB. 1986. *Working together: state-university collaboration in mental health.* Washington, DC: American Psychiatric Press, Inc. (NAT-20)

OR-4
Partners
LHD, L-GOV, SHD, HOSP, MCO, INS, SOM, AHC, VHO, BUS, SCHL, RELIG, FNDN

Synergies
2b, 3b, 4a, 5a, 5d, 5e, 6a-1, 6b-5

Structural Foundations
Coalition, Adm/Mgmt

Contact
G. Kent Ballantyne
Oregon Association of
Hospitals and
Health Systems
4000 Kruse Way Place
B2-100
Lake Oswego, OR 97035

Metropolitan Portland Oregon Health Systems in Collaboration

Oregon Health Systems in Collaboration (OHSC) was founded in 1993 to address health problems in three counties of metropolitan Portland: high teenage pregnancy rates, high infant mortality rates, inadequate immunization among children, and inadequate access to medical and dental care. The partners of this CCN demonstration partnership, funded by the W.K. Kellogg Foundation, include Blue Cross/Blue Shield, the Oregon Health Science University, the metropolitan area's county health departments, the Oregon Health Division, Kaiser Permanente, Legacy Health System, and Providence Health System, all of whom contribute to other collaborative activities in Portland, a city that has an active Healthy Communities coalition with representatives from business, schools, social service agencies, and the faith community. Specific projects of OHSC include: (1) the creation of a comprehensive immunization infrastructure, complete with a provider database and patient registry to improve the health tracking of children 0–6 years old; (2) the development of community health improvement projects around domestic violence and teenage pregnancy, including a resource inventory of private and public programs that serve women and children; (3) advocacy for health insurance reform and improved dental care access; and (4) cross-training programs for health care and social service agency staff so that there is better communication and support of client needs. All major initiatives of the OHSC use a collaborative process that involves the community in identifying problems, prioritizing them, and working toward solutions.

OR-5
Partners
LHD, L-GOV, SHD, S-GOV,
FEDHLTH, MDPRAC, HOSP, MCO,
INS, U-OTH, MEDSOC, BUS,
SCHL, RELIG, MEDIA, FNDN,
C-OTH

Synergies
1c, 3b, 4c, 5b, 5d

Structural Foundations
Coalition, Contract

Contact
Eleanor Miller
The Child Health Initiative
3180 Center Street, NE
Salem, OR 97301
emiller@open.org

OR-6
Partners
LHD, SHD, S-GOV, MCO

Synergies
4a, 4c, 5a, 5d, 6a-3, 6a-4,
6b-5

Structural Foundations
Contract, Advisory

Contact
Helen H. Schauffler, PhD
School of Public Health
University of California
at Berkeley
406 Warren Hall
Berkeley, CA 94720
helenhs@uclink2.berkeley.
edu

Marion County Child Health Initiative
With funding from The Robert Wood Johnson Foundation, a coalition of parents, neighborhood associations, schools, local and state governments, private health care providers, and the religious and volunteer communities in Marion County developed a Child Health Initiative to provide access to health and social services for children from low-income families. Care coordinators, with offices in the local schools and the county health department, meet families in their homes, at school, or at work to help them identify and gain access to providers and an array of donated services. The partnership also sponsors annual Community Health/Safety Fairs with prizes donated by local insurance companies, health plans, businesses, and community groups, and has launched such projects as annual bicycle safety rodeos with free children's bicycle helmets, and programs providing home smoke detectors, blankets, clothing, emergency dental services, and free dental sealant. One improvement tracked by the partners has been an increase in the percentage of children remaining in school for the entire year from 50% to 83%. In addition, 100% of the children in the county school system are completely immunized, and only one child has been excluded from school for insufficient immunization in the past four years.

Oregon Medicaid Managed Care Plans
As the state with the highest proportion of its population in private HMOs (41%), and as one of the first states to qualify for an 1115 waiver to develop a Medicaid managed care program, Oregon has a number of health promotion programs involving managed care plans. In order for health plans to contract with the state, each must participate in at least two community-wide prevention projects. Participation in the immunization registry is required, and then health plans can select from projects involving tobacco, breast and cervical cancer, or diabetes. The health plans are required to coordinate these prevention activities with their local health departments. In addition, the state's Medicaid agency regularly convenes the medical directors of all the health plans, and is coordinating the development of required clinical preventive services based on the US Preventive Services Task Force recommendations. Because of the state's ongoing relationship with the health plans' medical

directors and quality assurance coordinators, health promotion initiatives have extended beyond the Medicaid population to cover the entire community. The health plans have worked with the state on community assessments, community interventions, provider training, and guidelines development for specific health promotion services.

Schauffler, HH, Hennessey, M, Neiger, B. 1997. *Health promotion and managed care.* Report prepared for the Association of State and Territorial Directors of Health Promotion and Public Health Education. Washington, DC.

[PA] PENNSYLVANIA

PA-1
Partners
LHD, HOSP, MCO, SOM, SPH, AHC, U-OTH, SCHL, C-OTH

Synergies
6b-1, 6b-2, 6b-3, 6b-4, 6c-2

Structural Foundations
Intraorg, Informal

Contact
William Welton
Center for Health
Management and Policy
Allegheny University
of the Health Sciences
School of Public Health
1505 Race Street
11th Floor
Bellet Building
Mailstop 660
Philadelphia, PA 19102
weltonw@allegheny.edu

Allegheny University School of Public Health
In 1993, two Philadelphia medical schools, Hahnemann University and the Medical College of Pennsylvania, merged to form the Allegheny University of the Health Sciences. Senior administrators at the newly formed health sciences university regarded the transition as an opportunity to instill a population focus in its health professions education and research programs and expand its community orientation. In 1996, Allegheny admitted its first class to its new school of public health. The school developed its curriculum based on case studies presented in the context of community problems. Furthermore, the school drew from its own faculty and from the faculties of the medical, nursing, and allied health professions schools to create an integrated faculty base, and in turn supplemented each school's faculty with a population-oriented teaching staff. The school of public health also has served as the organizational linchpin for developing collaborative research and service projects with the local health department, local school system, affiliated teaching hospitals, managed care organizations, other community-based agencies, and three university-community partnerships.

PA-2
Partners
AHC, VHO, FNDN

Synergies
4b, 6b-3, 6b-4, 6b-6, 6c-2

Structural Foundations
Contract

Greater Philadelphia Alliance for Academic Home Care
To improve the connections among nursing practice, education, and research in the home care field, the University of Pennsylvania School of Nursing (SON) and the Visiting Nurse Association of Greater Philadelphia (VNA) formed the Alliance for Academic Home Care in 1995. For many years, the two organizations have worked together informally; SON faculty sit on the VNA Board of

Contact
Kathryn H. Bowles,
PhD, RN
University of Pennsylvania
School of Nursing
1435 Wynnemoor Way
Fort Washington, PA 19034
bowles@dolphin.upenn.
edu

Trustees, and VNA supports research and clinical training sites for the SON's undergraduate and graduate students. Discussions among executive-level staff from VNA and two professors from the SON led to the development of the Alliance, which has an advisory board with joint membership. The interchanges among "practice" (from VNA staff) and "academia" (from SON faculty) are concrete. First, faculty members have been appointed as liaisons with agency staff for consultations and research, while agency staff have received joint appointments to the SON to conduct undergraduate and graduate classes. One result is that three university courses on home care nursing are now being offered. Second, formal clinical practice arrangements have been formed for students and staff, and VNA preceptors have been trained as mentors for nursing students. Third, a full-time researcher, who is a nurse, holds a joint appointment to create and conduct research involving both the VNA and the SON. Through this researcher, the VNA now has access to current research findings in the literature and consultation on study design, data collection, and analysis.

PA-3
Partners
LHD, SHD, FEDHLTH, HOSP,
CLIN, MCO, INS, SOM, SPH,
AHC, U-OTH, MEDSOC, VHO,
BUS, SCHL, RELIG, FNDN, C-OTH

Synergies
1a, 5a, 5b, 5d, 6b-3, 6b-4,
6b-6

Structural Foundations
Coalition, Adm/Mgmt

Contact
Lucy Wolf Tuton, PhD
Community Health
Internship Program
Bridging the Gaps
Consortium
423 Guardian Drive
Blockley Hall
Room 911
Philadelphia, PA 19104
tuton@cceb.med.upenn.
edu

Bridging the Gaps
In 1991, a Philadelphia medical school developed a summer internship program to give first-year medical students an opportunity to explore their interest in community health while providing service to their surrounding urban community. Over time the program grew to include seven academic health institutions in the state, up to 15 health and social service disciplines, and multiple community organizations and agencies. The Bridging the Gaps: Community Health Internship Program requires each participating academic health institution to sustain a relationship with an underserved community, provide meaningful service, and train a cadre of community-responsive health and social service providers. The six key elements of the program model require each institution to: (1) identify an underserved community with which they plan to collaborate; (2) provide continuity of contact between the students and faculty at the academic institution and the identified community and its organizations; (3) develop and integrate didactic and skill-building components for students, based on the assumption that there is a set of skills necessary to provide health care to underserved populations;

(4) ensure supervision by both academic and community-based preceptors; (5) regularly evaluate the program; and (6) inform the community of the progress of the program through a public forum and an annual report. The coalition of participating academic institutions is staffed by a central program office.

PA-4

Partners
LHD, L-GOV, FEDHLTH, MDPRAC, HOSP, CLIN, INS, U-OTH, VHO, FNDN, C-OTH

Synergies
5a, 5d

Structural Foundations
Coalition

Contact
Louis Bonilla, MA, MPH
The Consortium for
Latino Health
Delaware Valley Health
Education & Research
Foundation
121 South Broad Street
North American Building
20th Floor
Philadelphia, PA 19107
lbonilla@dvhc.org

Philadelphia Consortium for Latino Health

To identify specific health needs in the Latino Community and to develop community-based strategies to address them, the Latino Health Issues Forum was initiated in 1992 as a joint effort of the Delaware Valley Hospital Council, the Philadelphia Department of Public Health, the North Philadelphia Health System, and the Latino community. The Forum is committed to involving the community in a comprehensive analysis of health and health care access issues facing Latinos and taking action to implement recommendations. With participants from the community, the health department, health care providers, and social service agencies, eight task forces gathered information on specific health areas, such as maternal and child health and senior citizens' health, for more than a year, using interviews, public health and medical literature, and community-based data. A major symposium was held to present findings in 1993; afterward, a Consortium for Latino Health was created to implement the recommendations. Working with the city health department, eight hospitals and three insurers contributed seed money to establish the Consortium.

PA-5

Partners
L-GOV, S-GOV, HOSP, SOM, SPH, AHC, C-OTH

Synergies
2c, 6a-5, 6a-6, 6b-4

Structural Foundations
Contract, Advisory

Contact
George Board
Forbes Tower
Suite 11090
Pittsburgh, PA 15213

Pennsylvania State-University Collaboration on Mental Health

Pennsylvania has one of the largest public mental health systems in the nation; in the early 1980s, a survey raised concerns about the number and quality of psychiatrists in the state's psychiatric hospital system. To better recruit and retain staff for the system, the state mental health office embarked on collaborative residency programs with the state's six university-based departments of psychiatry. The state realized that financial incentives, such as increased salaries for board-certification and performance-based bonuses, were important, but so were affiliations with medical school departments of psychiatry, improved physical plants, and interesting clinical assignments. Despite challenges, both in distance and professional approaches, there have been many productive relationships: (1) The University of Pittsburgh has committed all its full-time faculty to provide service in public mental health programs, and it supports paid residency rotations if the graduate returns to work in the public system. (2) East Pennsylvania Psychiatric Institute (EPPI), which has supported research and training in mental health for more than 20 years as a state-run agency, is now operated by the Medical College of Pennsylvania under contract with the state. (3) Hahnemann School of Medicine, which has joined with the Medical College of Pennsylvania as a single school, contracts directly with the Philadelphia State Hospital and the city to provide facilities and services for forensics, on-call coverage of the public hospital, and for a prison mental health program. Factors responsible for the success of these programs include the development of mutually compatible goals for the university and the public sector, and a recognition of the realities under which each partner operates, be it binding laws and regulations or differences in professional philosophies.

Talbott, JA and Robinowitz, CB. 1986. *Working together: state-university collaboration in mental health.* Washington, DC: American Psychiatric Press, Inc. (NAT-20)

PA-6
Partners
LHD, VHO

Synergies
1c

Structural Foundations
Contract

Contact
Lynn T. Rinke, MS, RN
The Visiting Nurse
Association of Greater
Philadelphia
Monroe Office Center
One Winding Drive
Philadelphia, PA 19131

Philadelphia High-Risk Infant Follow-Up Program

To improve outcomes for low-birthweight babies and those born to teenage mothers or mothers without adequate prenatal care, the Visiting Nurse Association of Greater Philadelphia and the Maternal and Child Health Department of the City of Philadelphia's Health Department have jointly administered a High-Risk Infant Follow-Up Program since the mid-1980s. For all infants identified as high-risk, a registered nurse visits the infant and family once a month until the first birthday The program ensures that infants are enrolled and receive medical care from the city's Primary Health Care or Early Intervention programs, and the nurses check the infants for normal developmental milestones and for timely immunizations. In addition, the nurses speak to the parents about good parenting skills and other social and support services available in the community. The program started with visits only from nurses, but later included home visits from lay women in the community and from social workers. The success of this collaboration led the partners to work on other projects together (PA-7, PA-8, PA-9, PA-10). Overall, these collaborative initiatives have improved maternal and child health in the city in measurable ways, such as increased primary care to infants, earlier involvement in the early intervention program for developmentally delayed infants, increased immunization rates, decreased infant mortality, increased prenatal care, improved birth outcomes, better family planning and safer sexual practices, decreased congenital syphilis, and increased collaboration among community-based organization serving this population.

PA-7
Partners
LDH, VHO

Synergies
1a, 4c

Structural Foundations
Informal

Contact
Lynn T. Rinke, MS, RN
The Visiting Nurse
Association of Greater
Philadelphia
Monroe Office Center
One Winding Drive
Philadelphia, PA 19131

Philadelphia Response to Measles Outbreak
When Philadelphia had a measles outbreak in 1991, the city health department enlisted the Visiting Nurse Association to lend nurses to help immunize thousands of children at public assistance offices, WIC offices, clinics, and at other locations where there were large numbers of parents with children. Their previous working relationship helped the two organizations mobilize quickly when a crisis occurred.

PA-8
Partners
LHD, HOSP, MCO, INS, VHO

Synergies
1c, 6a-3

Structural Foundations
Contract

Contact
Lynn T. Rinke, MS, RN
The Visiting Nurse
Association of Greater
Philadelphia
Monroe Office Center
One Winding Drive
Philadelphia, PA 19131

Philadelphia Home Care Program for Infants with Congenital Syphilis
In 1990, the incidence of congenital syphilis had increased among infants in Philadelphia, with over 300 cases reported in the city. In addition to being costly for the city, since treatment entails ten days of hospitalization, congenital syphilis causes traumatic separation of mothers and children. The Visiting Nurse Association (VNA) contracted with the City of Philadelphia's health department to treat the infants in their homes so they could be cared for by their mothers, with close supervision by a registered nurse. During the home visit, nurses gave penicillin injections to the infants and health counseling to the family about the disease, safe sex, family planning, treatment options for parents, and about general infant care and safety. The pro-

gram was originally funded through Title V monies and is now a mandatory support service under Medicaid managed care; the services are provided by VNA just like any other case for skilled home nursing. The program has reduced hospitalization rates among affected infants and the prevalence of congenital syphilis has dropped to 35 reported cases in 1997.

PA-9
Partners
LHD, VHO

Synergies
1c, 4c, 5b

Structural Foundations
Coalition, Contract

Contact
Lynn T. Rinke, MS, RN
The Visiting Nurse
Association of Greater
Philadelphia
Monroe Office Center
One Winding Drive
Philadelphia, PA 19131

Philadelphia Healthy Start Consortium and Lay Home Visiting Program

In the early 1990s, the Healthy Start Initiative of West and Southwest Philadelphia started as part of the larger federal initiative to reduce infant mortality. The Healthy Start Consortium is a collaborative coalition of more than 60 agencies, and the Visiting Nurses Association (VNA) is represented on the Steering Committee and in each of the work groups that address key issues associated with infant morality. As part of the Healthy Start Initiative, VNA has initiated a Lay Home Visiting Program where registered nurses and lay home visitors, who are female employees from the community, follow high-risk mothers from pregnancy until their infant's first birthday. This program works in conjunction with Philadelphia's High-Risk Infant Follow-Up Program (PA-6).

PA-10
Partners
LHD, CLIN, VHO, C-OTH

Synergies
1c, 6a-2

Structural Foundations
Coalition

Contact
Lynn T. Rinke, MS, RN
The Visiting Nurse
Association of Greater
Philadelphia
Monroe Office Center
One Winding Drive
Philadelphia, PA 19131

Maternal and Child Health Alliance of Greater Philadelphia

With changes in funding streams and the shift to Medicaid managed care in Philadelphia, the Visiting Nurse Association (VNA) and others became concerned about their ability to continue to provide nursing and support services to high-risk families. In October 1996, the directors of Maternal and Child Health of VNA, LaSalle University Neighborhood Nursing Center, and the Maternal and Child Health Department of the City of Philadelphia met to discuss a possible collaboration to support these services, with specific interest in lobbying local managed care organizations to cover them. After the initial meeting, the VNA and eight other community-based organizations established a coalition, which brought together agencies that were funded by the city health department to provide outreach and home visiting to high-risk women and children in Philadelphia. This coalition, called the Maternal and Child Health Alliance of Greater Philadelphia, has begun talks with four local managed care organizations to obtain funding for the outreach and home visiting services. The coalition has hired a consulting group to direct the first phases of the collaboration and to assist in developing recommendations for future action.

PA-11
Partners
LHD, FEDHLTH, MCO, VHO, FNDN

Synergies
1a, 4a, 4c

Structural Foundations
Contract, Adm/Mgmt

Contact
See citation

Philadelphia Immunization Registry

After the measles outbreak of 1989–91 the CDC approached six cities, including Philadelphia, to develop action plans to improve their immunization rates for children. The Philadelphia plan, led by the local health department and a coalition of health care agencies and providers, involved three interconnected strategies: the development of an immunization registry and tracking system; public health nurses administering "express lane" immunizations at district health centers; and an outreach program in which public health nurses performed in-home immunizations for individuals who failed to respond to traditional outreach methods. Despite incentives such as free computer hardware and vaccines for physicians who participated in the registry, the health department generated little response at first to their request for immunization data. The health department then attempted a regulatory approach, declaring immunizations a "reportable event." That too proved unsuccessful. The health department appealed to Medicaid HMOs to work voluntarily with them on the registry, but divergent organizational missions and competition among the organizations derailed the strategy. Finally, one health plan negotiated separately with the health department, agreeing to provide data and $1.3 million in financial support. In return, the health plan obtained better information on the immunization status of its members (particularly inner-city Medicaid clients), was protected from the liability problems it might face if it operated the program directly, and increased access for its members to express-lane immunizations at the district health center, which also contracted with the plan as primary care providers. The health department also received funding from The Robert Wood Johnson Foundation All Kids Count program and from the CDC. Immunization rates for the health plan's members increased by 11% in the first year. Since then, the health department has reached agreements with all the major managed care plans to provide data to the registry.

Knight, W. 1996. *Improving the public's health: collaborations between public health departments and managed care organizations.* Washington, DC: The Joint Council of Governmental Public Health Agencies.

PA-12

Partners
LHD, L-GOV, S-GOV, MDPRAC, HOSP, RELIG, FNDN

Synergies
1c, 5a

Structural Foundations
Coalition, Adm/Mgmt

Contact
See citation

Lancaster Community Health Plan

The health problems of rural Lancaster County have been changing continually over the last decade due to changing sociodemographics in the area, making access to primary care and coordination of behavioral health and physical health services a pressing need, especially for minority populations. Lancaster Community Health Plan, which began operating in 1995, is a primary care case management program that encompasses all county health and human service providers and includes medical providers, hospitals, health systems, local government, community-based organizations, churches, and foundations to create a community-wide integrated service delivery system. Through this partnership, which is a CCN demonstration partnership funded by the W.K. Kellogg Foundation, the Plan creates a "single-point entry" system into an extensive network of community services and increases coordination among these service agencies while preserving the identity of each organization. Since its inception, the Community Health Plan has connected over 11,000 Medicaid clients to appropriate medical homes through its network of 260 providers and receives over 1,000 calls per month regarding benefits, eligibility, and coverage. Future plans include expanding the service population to include the entire Lancaster community, not just the medical assistance population, and there are efforts to incorporate small and large employers into the network. The partnership has also created a community health assessment report, *The Health of Lancaster*, which was widely disseminated in the community.

Community Care Network Demonstration Program. 1997. *The 25 Community Care Network demonstration partnerships: profiles in progress.* Chicago: Hospital Research and Educational Trust.

PA-13

Partners
LHD, L-GOV, SHD, MDPRAC, HOSP, CLIN, INS, AHC, U-OTH, BUS, SCHL, RELIG, FNDN, C-OTH

Synergies
1c, 5a, 5e

Tioga County Partnership for Community Health

The Tioga County region of Pennsylvania has a longstanding tradition of community-based integrated service delivery; the six federal community health centers in the region were the first to become part of an integrated system of care. Today,

Structural Foundations
Coalition

Contact
See citation

tapping community needs is still an important part of planning services. In 1995, the Laurel Health System and Tioga County Health and Human Services Agencies, along with more than 125 individuals and 20 community organizations, formed the Partnership for Community Health (a CCN demonstration partnership funded by the W.K. Kellogg Foundation) and collaborated on the design and implementation of a countywide health survey. The results have been the basis for six working groups on elderly services, adolescent health, mental health, health status, and resource needs, and two groups on the delivery systems of health and human services. Through the Partnership, the county's health care and human service providers are working with businesses, churches, schools, and the local university to develop solutions to address identified problems. Laurel Health Systems, in particular, is planning to adapt its programs to the expressed needs of the people of Tioga County.

Bogue, R and Hall, Jr, CH, eds. 1997. *Health networks innovations: how 20 communities are improving their system through collaboration.* Chicago: American Hospital Publishing, Inc.

[RI] RHODE ISLAND

RI-1
Partners
SHD, S-GOV, SOM, MEDSOC

Synergies
3a, 6b-5

Structural Foundations
Contract, Advisory

Contact
Particia A. Nolan,
MD, MPH
Department of Health
State of Rhode Island and
Providence Plantations
Cannon Building
Three Capitol Hill, 401
Providence, RI 02908

Medicine & Health Rhode Island
In the early 1990s, the editor of the Rhode Island medical journal approached the leadership of the Rhode Island Department of Health and the Brown University School of Medicine with a novel proposal: the tripartite co-sponsorship of the journal in partnership with the state medical society, the journal's publisher. His goal was to involve all three institutions in the funding, management, editorial guidance, and substantive editorial contributions to *Medicine & Health Rhode Island*. The leaders of the three institutions readily agreed that such an arrangement could present the spectrum of population and clinical perspectives to the state's physicians. The medical school and the state health department provide core financial support to the journal, and have also become involved in strategic planning for the journal, including plans to increase subscribership and advertising. Each institution takes turns serving as "guest editor" for the journal. Moreover, the health department contributes three regular features: a "Public Health

Briefing," covering the latest in health promotion/ disease prevention and control strategies; "Health by Numbers," a contemporary analysis of health statistics; and "Vital Statistics," a summary of sentinel natality, mortality, and morbidity data. The statewide peer review organization has also joined the group, and is using the journal as a medium to promote continuing education.

[SC] SOUTH CAROLINA

SC-1
Partners
LHD, SHD, MDPRAC, MEDSOC

Synergies
1a, 1c, 2d

Structural Foundations
Contract, Adm/Mgmt

Contact
Jan Cauthen, RN
South Carolina DHEC
2600 Bull Street
Columbus, SC 29201

South Carolina Partnerships for Children
In 1993, over half the babies born in South Carolina were Medicaid-eligible, but fewer than half of the physicians accepted Medicaid. In an effort to find "medical homes" for Medicaid babies, the state invited five pediatricians and their respective local health officers to participate in a demonstration project. Public health nurses would be assigned to the private pediatricians' offices to assist the doctors with Medicaid infants up to age two. The state funded these partnerships as special Child Health Initiatives; specific strategies were left to the discretion of each partnership. In rural Lancaster, public health nurses recruited Medicaid mothers, who had just given birth, into the voluntary program, then functioned as the family's primary medical liaison, arranging for office visits with the participating pediatrician, providing clinical preventive services at the baby's home or the pediatrician's office, and assisting the mothers in keeping appointments and accessing health and social services. As a result, one of the pediatrician's "show" rate for appointments increased from 50% to over 90%, his immunization coverage of 2-year-olds increased from 62% to 95% over three years, and the nurses detected several serious medical problems at an early stage. The state's original five partnerships were so successful that the state medical association worked with the health department to expand the public-private partnerships statewide, an enterprise facilitated by the original pediatricians persuading their colleagues to join. Since there was no fixed model for a partnership, the specific arrangements varied by practice. In some offices, a physician contracted for the services of a public health pediatric nurse-practitioner to provide both sick care and well care in the office; in others, the pediatrician referred high-risk families to the health department for family support services. Statewide,

the program aided local public health agencies in finding medical homes for Medicaid babies, and the physicians benefitted by the complementary care provided by the public health nurses.

SC-2

Partners
LHD, L-GOV, SHD, FEDHLTH, MDPRAC, HOSP, U-OTH, MEDSOC, BUS, SCHL, RELIG, MEDIA, FNDN, C-OTH

Synergies
2a, 4c, 5a, 5b, 5d, 5e, 6b-6

Structural Foundations
Coalition, Adm/Mgmt

Contact
Karen Papouchado
Growing Into Life
7 Burgundy Road
Aiken, SC 29801
kchado@aiken.net

Aiken Infant Mortality Task Force

In 1989, Aiken's infant mortality rate was 12.0 per 1,000 live births, one of the highest among any county in the state. The commissioner of the state health department provided $90,000 over three years to a local social service agency to coordinate a community-wide effort to address the problem. The service agency first organized an Infant Mortality Task Force, which included social scientists from the nearby university, the district attorney, school leaders, clergy, local business, the county coroner, physicians, nurses, and public health officials, among others. The Task Force quickly settled on a three-pronged approach. They convened a fetal and infant mortality review team that analyzed every baby's death. They surveyed the prenatal experiences of 477 new mothers (it turned out that 60% did not want their babies, and 43% reported using birth control when they got pregnant). In addition, they sent university students into public health clinics posing as prospective family planning clients. The public report of this undercover operation detailed the indignities and barriers experienced by the "decoys," leading to a massive retraining program for the health department, and to a public-private partnership that raised money to refurbish the clinics. A number of other community-wide projects to promote healthier babies also arose from the Task Force, which changed its name to Growing Into Life. These include: (1) a local community effort in which police officers provided pregnant women with information about prenatal care (the program was called MOMS and COPS); (2) a prenatal ID card with appointment dates, risk factors from the patient's medical history, and indications of preterm labor; and (3) a 24-hour Pregnancy Care Telephone Line staffed by nurses from the hospital. During the time the infant mortality project was underway, the local government and economy of Aiken were undergoing great changes. The mayor and city manager were both retiring after 40 years of public service, and the area's largest employer was laying off 10,000 workers. What began as two separate initiatives—one to address the specific health objective of achieving healthier births, and the other as an economic and community planning and development effort—eventually merged into a broad Healthy Community initiative that has involved a number of local providers and citizens. The group has achieved success in its infant mortality campaign. Between 1989 and 1996, the infant mortality rate dropped over 50%; the 1996 rate was 4.9 per 1,000 live births.

SC-3

Partners
LHD, L-GOV, MDPRAC, HOSP, CLIN, SOM, VHO, SCHL, RELIG

Synergies
1c

Structural Foundations
Coalition

Contact
See citation

Bamberg County Multidisciplinary Committee
Situated in a rural, economically depressed community, the Bamberg County Multidisciplinary Committee was created to restructure the county health delivery system, using "virtual integration" to maximize limited budget resources among its community providers. The Committee, which has representatives from the county hospital, a medical center, the visiting nurses association, local government and the county's health, social service, and education agencies, has several initiatives to enhance existing primary and preventive health systems. Early efforts of the Committee (a CCN demonstration partnership funded by the W.K. Kellogg Foundation) have focused on information-gathering for a community health information network (CHIN), which delayed other efforts of the group. After an evaluation of their partnership, done with assistance from the Medical University of South Carolina at Charleston, the Committee has been reinvigorated and has a new plan for developing a coordinated system for the wide array of public and private services available throughout the county.

Community Care Network Demonstration Program. 1997. *The 25 Community Care Network demonstration partnerships: profiles in progress*. Chicago: Hospital Research and Educational Trust.

[TN] TENNESSEE

TN-1

Partners
LHD, SOM, SCHL, FNDN, C-OTH

Synergies
1b, 5a, 5b, 5d

Structural Foundations
Coalition, Adm/Mgmt

Nashville I Have A Future Program
In the late 1980s, the Meharry Medical College Department of Obstetrics and Gynecology led a community-based effort to reach Nashville's high-risk teenagers. Entitled "I Have A Future," The Robert Wood Johnson-funded program involved the establishment of school-based clinics and "residential venues"—coordinated services centers located in local housing projects. The medical school de-

Contact
John E. Maupin, Jr.,
DDS, MBA
Meharry Medical College
1005 D.B. Todd Boulevard
Nashville, TN 37208
maupin37@ccvax.mmc.edu

partment began by surveying the heads of households in the housing projects to determine the biggest problems facing the youth of the community. The reduction of teen pregnancy was identified as a community health objective, and a multipronged effort to educate teens, increase their access to services and contraception, help them develop "socially adaptive behaviors," and promote better self-esteem was initiated by the medical school and its community partners. The local health department played an active role in developing youth programs, and lent their facilities to the project. By providing the services in the housing projects, the program directors hoped to overcome such obstacles as limited access to services after school and low family participation. The five-year pilot project demonstrated that the families became more involved with their children, more at-risk teenagers remained in school; and a number of the adolescents continued on to college. The program continues as an effort sponsored by the Meharry Department of Obstetrics and Gynecology but is housed at a high school in the community served. Plans are underway to transfer administration of the program to the local health department over the next year.

TN-2
Partners
LHD, L-GOV, SHD, S-GOV,
MDPRAC, HOSP, CLIN, MCO,
SOM, SPH, RES, U-OTH, VHO,
BUS, SCHL, RELIG, MEDIA,
FNDN, C-OTH

Synergies
3b, 4c, 5a, 5b, 5d, 6b-1,
6b-3, 6b-4

Structural Foundations
Adm/Mgmt, Advisory,
Intraorg

Contact
Bruce Behringer, MPH
Office of Rural and
Community Health
East Tennessee
State University
Box 70412
Johnson City, TN 37614
behringer@washington.xtn.net

East Tennessee State University Interdisciplinary Curriculum

With funding provided by the W.K. Kellogg Foundation in 1991, the Division of Health Sciences at East Tennessee State University developed an interdisciplinary curriculum that brought together medical, nursing, and public health students. In order to develop a meaningful program for students, faculty, and the rural communities they served, the university made a number of organizational commitments. They created "academic community health systems" in two rural counties, recruiting local community health and human service providers to advisory boards and establishing clinical sites at local health departments, physicians' offices, schools, state prisons, day care centers, nursing homes, community health centers, and hospitals. They developed a two-year curriculum of 19 required courses on topics such as, rural and community health, patient communication, and health assessment that are taken jointly by the medical, nursing, and public health students. They created interdisciplinary faculty teams, who provide lectures, clinical supervision, and support at the community sites. And they established a program of community projects responsive to assessed community needs. The first interdisciplinary cohort of students conducted a community needs assessment which revealed a high prevalence of cardiovascular disease. Another cohort identified school-age children as the group with the greatest amount to gain from behavioral change and preventive efforts. Other student cohorts established links with schools and industry throughout the counties, and conducted health fairs and screenings. The students reported that 17% of the school-age children were significantly overweight, over-consumed high-calorie beverages, and did not exercise regularly. Interdisciplinary students have targeted the high prevalence of smoking among children. Subsequent cohorts of students will develop clinical and community-based nutrition, smoking, and exercise interventions and evaluations.

TN-3

Partners
MDPRAC, HOSP, CLIN, INS, LAB/RX, MEDSOC, BUS, RELIG, FNDN, C-OTH

Synergies
2b, 6a-1

Structural Foundations
Contract, Adm/Mgmt

Contact
Jenny Bartlett-Prescott
Church Health Center
1210 Peabody Avenue
Memphis, TN 38104

The MEMPHIS Plan
In 1991, a group of health care providers led by the Church Health Center created the MEMPHIS Plan to provide affordable insurance to uninsured, near-minimum-wage workers. The collaboration involves the clinic (an ecumenical health clinic serving the medically underserved), which acts as the plan's administrator; the Memphis and Shelby County medical societies, which recruit physicians and diagnostic facilities; the Methodist Hospitals, which provide inpatient facilities; and Blue Cross Blue Shield of Memphis, which serves as underwriter. The process of enrollment mirrors that of any insurance program: a Church Health Center staff member sends information to interested businesses and follows up with a worksite visit; eligible workers are enrolled and receive primary, specialty, and hospital benefits. For the first four years, the plan had 200 enrollees. Using a Robert Wood Johnson Foundation Reach Out grant, the plan expanded its membership to 700 enrollees in 1995 and presently has over 1,100 enrollees. Over 130 self-employed individuals have taken advantage of the MEMPHIS Plan as well.

TN-4

Partners
MDPRAC, HOSP, LAB/RX, RES, VHO, RELIG, FNDN, C-OTH

Kingsport Friends in Need Health Center
In the early 1990s, a local surgeon from Kingsport visiting a free clinic in Memphis was struck by the

Synergies
1b, 2a, 3b, 5b

Structural Foundations
Coalition, Adm/Mgmt

Contact
Catherine A. Harvey
Friends in Need Health
Center, Inc.
618 Watauga Street
Kingsport, TN 37660

TN-5
Partners
LHD, FEDHLTH, SOM

Synergies
5a, 6b-4, 6b-6

Structural Foundations
Contract

Contact
Anthony Chapdelaine,
MD, MSPH
Directors Office
Metropolitan
Nashville/Davidson County
Health Department
311 23rd Avenue, North
Nashville, TN 37203
tchapdel@nashville.org

TN-6
Partners
LHD, L-GOV, MDPRAC, HOSP,
CLIN, MCO, MEDSOC, VHO,
BUS, FNDN, C-OTH

Synergies
3c, 4c, 5a, 5d, 5e, 6a-4

Structural Foundations
Coalition, Advisory

need for a similar primary care clinic for the working poor of his community. Back home, he convened a group of health care professionals. They incorporated as Friends in Need, Inc., and recruited board members from a number of public and private agencies in the community. The meetings led to a successful grant proposal to The Robert Wood Johnson Foundation under its Faith in Action program, and in 1995 the Friends In Need Health Center was opened. The Center provides medical, dental, and counseling services on a sliding-fee scale, and also coordinates volunteer help for community members who need transportation, lawn care, painting, carpentry, plumbing, electrical work, or filling out insurance or Medicaid forms. The Center has also coordinated several community-wide campaigns, including projects promoting smoking cessation, annual mammograms for women, and skin cancer screening. In its first year of operation over 650 patients were seen for over 2,000 office visits.

Nashville Health Department and School of Medicine Joint Initiatives
With funding from the Agency for Health Care Policy and Research, Vanderbilt University Medical Center and the Metropolitan Nashville/Davidson County Health Departments have several programs that support collaboration among the organizations. To better acquaint students with public health practice, the health department will be a training site for doctoral-level students of the Vanderbilt Department of Preventive Medicine's inaugural masters in public health program. In turn, the academic medical center will provide technical assistance to the health department for better monitoring of key health conditions. The medical and public health organizations are also exploring possible collaborative research activities that would benefit population health goals.

Kingsport Area Health Improvement Project
Kingsport began its community-wide "quality-improvement" activities in 1986, when the local Chamber of Commerce sponsored a 16-week training program for local business leaders and agency administrators. Participants in the program, which focused on data collection and analysis tools, included key administrators from the community's two hospitals. Two years later, many of these business, health care, and community

Contact
Curtis P. McLaughlin, DBA
Kenan-Flagler
Business School
University of North
Carolina at Chapel Hill
Carroll Hall, CB #3490
Chapel Hill, NC 27599

leaders developed a proposal for the Kingsport Area Health Improvement Project (KAHIP), which received foundation funding. The group's goal was to reduce variations in health care practice in the community by instituting quality reviews at local health care institutions and assessments of health care practices. A year later, local business and government agencies financed a nonprofit community agency, Kingsport Tomorrow, to stimulate community and economic development. KAHIP became its health care task force, and over the next several years the group focused on several major community health initiatives (such as smoking cessation and reducing preventable injuries resulting from motor vehicle accidents). Major economic changes in the health care marketplace affected the group's cohesiveness—when the area's largest HMO began selectively contracting with specific specialists and hospitals, and the marketplace became more competitive, the physician and hospital communities withdrew their active participation in activities associated with utilization review and clinical process improvement. After a major reorganization of KAHIP, the providers and agency representatives acknowledged they were more willing to tackle community-wide projects rather than efforts focused on institutional or provider practices. Two of these projects were a major vaccination effort for children and an analysis of community health data provided by the health department and area industries. Population-based projects and regional efforts aimed at accident prevention, substance abuse, and wellness campaigns have continued to expand under KAHIP's direction, with greater governmental and provider representation involved. A number of these projects have attracted government and foundation support.

McLaughlin, CP. 1995. Balancing collaboration and competition: the Kingsport, Tennessee experience. *Joint Commission on Quality Improvement.* 21(11):646–655.

[TX] TEXAS

TX-1
Partners
SOM, SPH

Synergies
3c, 6b-2, 6b-3

University of Texas-Houston Primary Care Fellowship
To encourage cross-training of primary care physicians in public health, the University of Texas-Houston Health Science Center designed a fellowship program which allows resident physicians to assume both clinical and teaching duties at the

Structural Foundations
Intraorg

Contact
Judith Booker, MEd
The University of Texas-
Houston Health
Science Center
P.O. Box 20036
Houston, TX 77225
jbooker@admin4.hsc.uth.
tmc.edu

TX-2
Partners
LHD, SOM

Synergies
2c, 6a-6, 6b-4, 6b-6

Structural Foundations
Contract

Contact
Anthony B. Way, MD, PhD
Division of Occupational
and Preventive Medicine
Texas Tech University
Health Sciences Center
School of Medicine
Lubbock, TX 79340
pvmabw@ttuhsc.edu

TX-3
Partners
AHC, FNDN

Synergies
6b-1, 6b-3, 6b-6, 6c-2

Structural Foundations
Intraorg

same time as they are working toward an MPH degree. The fellows are residents in General Pediatrics, Internal Medicine, or Family Practice and Community Medicine. The president of the University of Texas and the deans of the school of medicine and the school of public health, along with the chairs and faculty of three medical school divisions were involved in designing the program, which arose from strategic planning efforts around better integration of the medicine and public health activities of the institution. University leaders agreed to allocate funding to this program. At its inception in 1996, three fellows were recruited to serve terms of more than three years.

Lubbock Joint Health Department and Preventive Medicine Appointment
In 1983, the Lubbock City Health Department needed a physician health director, but could not afford a full-time salary. At the same time, Texas Tech University-Health Sciences Center had its Chair of Preventive Medicine available for part-time subcontract. An MD/PhD-trained physician served both positions for eight years, with each institution contributing to his support in a contractual arrangement. The health department was able to obtain a director with a high level of expertise, and the medical center had the opportunity to serve the city visibly. The arrangement ended in the face of city budget cuts and a changing political climate, when, in a move toward privatization, the health department eliminated most of its clinical services and transferred most of its environmental services to another city department.

University of Texas-Houston Task Force on Medicine and Public Health
The University of Texas-Houston (UT-H) Task Force on Medicine and Public Health consists of more than 30 faculty members representing the health-related schools and programs of UT-H. They have met monthly since March 1997 to discuss health problems and potential solutions for the health needs of the people in the community. The mission of the Task Force is to devise and communicate an integrated view of health and illness; engage the academic health center and its surrounding communities in health promotion/disease prevention efforts; develop shared concepts of responsibility for health among all health professions (including

Contact
Judith Booker, MEd
The University of Texas-
Houston Health
Science Center
P.O. Box 20036
Houston, TX 77225
jbooker@admin4.hsc.uth.
tmc.edu

public health, medicine, dentistry, nursing, and allied health); and foster a better understanding of the roles of each health professional. The initial objectives of the Task Force are to change, through curricular review, the content of health professions education to reflect these concepts, to articulate strategies by which the health professions can and should work together, and to promote collaborative projects and joint research efforts among the health professions. Accomplishments include an orientation of all UT-H students to population health and the determinants of health, a student essay contest on the question "What Is Health?", and the development of collaborative research proposals. In the summer of 1998, the Task Force will sponsor a multidisciplinary team of ten UT-H students who will compile an anthology of health-related writings, participate in a weekly seminar, collaborate on group projects, and develop a plan for organizing a student medicine/public health initiative.

TX-4
Partners
HOSP, AHC, C-OTH

Synergies
1a, 5a, 5b, 5d, 6b-3, 6b-4

Structural Foundations
Coalition, Intraorg

Contact
Judith Booker, MEd
The University of Texas-
Houston Health
Science Center
P.O. Box 20036
Houston, TX 77225
jbooker@admin4.hsc.uth.
tmc.edu

University of Texas–Houston Acres Homes Community Health Projects

To foster greater involvement of the academic health center with surrounding communities and to create community-based experiences for its students, University of Texas-Houston designated the Acres Homes neighborhood in Northwest Houston as its primary site for community-based clinical training, health promotion, and health education. Acres Homes is an historically African-American community, with citizen advocacy groups interested in working with the university to improve access to health services and health information. As part of the Acres Homes project, a community health educator has been appointed and located centrally in the community. Urban family medicine residents have been assigned to a local hospital clinic, and dental students, nursing students, and public health students have done practica and other projects in the community, including a community health needs assessment. Faculty from all the major health professions training programs (medicine, dentistry, public health, and nursing) were involved in the design of the program and continue to participate in various aspects of the community-oriented efforts.

TX-5

Partners
LHD, SHD, FEDHLTH, MDPRAC,
HOSP, CLIN, MCO, LAB/RX, SOM,
RES, AHC, U-OTH, MEDSOC,
PHASSN, SCHL, C-OTH

Synergies
3a, 6b-4, 6b-5, 6b-6

Structural Foundations
Contract, Adm/Mgmt,
Advisory

Contact
Thomas J. Davis
STD/HIV PTC
Dallas County Health and
Human Services
2377 N. Stemmons
Freeway, Suite 430
Dallas, TX 75207
tjd1@dallas.net

Dallas Regional STD Training Center

In 1978, the Dallas County Department of Health and Human Services partnered with the University of Texas Southwestern Medical School at Dallas, the state health department, and the CDC to develop a Regional STD Training Center. The ongoing mission of such centers has been to establish strong links between public health agencies and academic medical centers, and to provide specialty clinician training to public and private physicians and physician extenders. The CDC contributes funding, broad guidance, consensus guidelines, and oversight, while the academic medical center provides faculty, didactic instruction, and the "authority" of the medical school. The health department contributes clinical and laboratory practicum instruction, surveillance, contact-tracing, specialty referrals, patient counseling, and clinical and laboratory support in partnership with private providers. Faculty from the Training Center, which has expanded to include HIV as well as STD, travel throughout the community lecturing to physicians in a variety of community settings—including prisons and border towns with large immigrant populations—and send mailings to practicing physicians in its region. At the CDC's southwest site, the Training Center covers Texas, Arkansas, Oklahoma, Louisiana, and New Mexico.

TX-6

Partners
LHD, SHD, S-GOV, HOSP, CLIN,
LAB/RX, SOM, AHC, PHASSN,
VHO

Synergies
6a-2, 6a-6

Structural Foundations
Advisory, Intraorg

Contact
Robbie J. Davis, PhD
Bureau of Children's Health
Texas Department
of Health
1100 W. 49th Street
Austin, TX 78756
rdavis@wcl.tdh.state.tx.us

Texas Title V Futures Project

Spurred by escalating program costs, the growth of Medicaid managed care, and concern over the disproportionate share of Title V funds used for clinical care as opposed to population-based services, the Texas Title V Futures Project was established in 1994 to recommend policies that would improve the program and lead to improvements in the health status of women and children. The Texas Department of Health (TDH) convened a Steering Committee and three subcommittees with representatives from state and local health departments, universities, professional organizations, community-based organizations, advocacy groups, and consumers to evaluate short- and long-term strategies to improve the administration of Title V and related state programs. During an eight-month process, the Steering Committee developed and refined several recommendations including a performance-based reimbursement methodology for maternal and child health (MCH) services, a fully competitive request for application process for MCH services and for population-based health projects, and the development and phase-in of an objective, needs-based allocation formula to guide the regional distribution of Title V funding. Attention to partnership issues was important in the success of the project. TDH recruited a diverse group of stakeholders for each committee, and each member made the project a priority, giving it time and effort. The Steering Committee gave biweekly reports to TDH senior management, keeping them up-to-date on progress as well as providing a means of feedback and dialogue with the three subcommittees. Extensive public input from providers and consumers was gathered through nine public hearings and legislative briefings to test the viability of each recommendation as it was being developed. In the end, TDH staff presented the recommendations to the Texas Board of Health, which approved them, even though some were controversial.

TX-7

Partners
FEDHLTH, MDPRAC, SOM, ARC, RES, VHO, BUS, SCHL, MEDIA, C-OTH

Synergies
5b, 5d, 6c-1

Structural Foundations
Coalition, Adm/Mgmt, Advisory

Contact
Jackie Pugh, MD
Department of Medicine
University of Texas-
San Antonio
ALMMVAH
San Antonio, TX 78285

San Antonio Diabetes Campaign

In rural Texas, diabetes is prevalent among Mexican-American children and adults. In the mid-1990s, the Mexican American Effectiveness Research Center at the University of Texas–San Antonio School of Medicine initiated a number of interventions and outcomes research studies focused on reducing risk behaviors and improving health in these communities. In one study, which was an extension of several cancer prevention studies among Hispanics, the research center used local role models and social reinforcements to promote primary and secondary prevention of diabetes. The local Mexican-American role models presented their experiences with diabetes self-management, weight control, and exercise through a number of media formats. Local businesses (approximately 175) helped distribute health education material, community volunteers disseminated information to their neighbors, and there were presentations at schools and at nutrition sites for the elderly. Another study involved recruiting Mexican-American children at risk of developing diabetes along with their diabetic parent or grandparent into a project focusing on nutrition, exercise, and diabetes knowledge. A third intervention involved an overweight prevention program targeting fourth-grade Mexican-Americans, which included individual dietary consultations, Mexican vegetarian cooking classes, a health newsletter written by the children, and a theatrical production acted by the children. Across all the studies, the research center's strategy is to use community leaders and organizations to carry the educational message, assure its cultural appropriateness, and reinforce the importance of healthy diets and adequate exercise. All of the interventions are being evaluated as to their effectiveness.

TX-8
Partners
LHD, L-GOV, MDPRAC, HOSP, MEDSOC, VHO, BUS, SCHL, MEDIA, C-OTH

Synergies
5b

Structural Foundations
Coalition

Contact
Dennis Dawson
Bexar County
Medical Society
P.O. Box 12678
202 West French Place
San Antonio, TX 78212
ddawson@icsi.net

San Antonio Domestic Violence Prevention Information Cards
The Domestic Violence Prevention Information Card is a tool to help victims of domestic violence become aware of their situation, of things that can be done, and whom they can call for help. A coalition, formed in 1996, of the Bexar County Medical Society, the San Antonio Health District, the San Antonio Police Department, the Battered Women's Shelter, Rape Crisis Center, and Emergency Medical Services (EMS) worked collaboratively on a small information card that provides referrals, phone numbers, and instructions for what to do when leaving an abusive relationship. Written in English and Spanish, the text on the card was designed to be understandable and accurate. Over 100,000 cards (50,000 in each language) were printed and distributed to all coalition members and all primary care physicians in San Antonio. The partnership also facilitated wide distribution of the card, and all interested organizations not involved in the original partnership, such as schools and the suburban police departments, were invited to reproduce, distribute, and use the card as they wished. Public media coverage was extensive, with all English and Spanish television stations covering the story as well as the regional newspapers and magazines. Follow-up is planned to measure the effectiveness of the cards; each domestic violence crisis agency will be polled to estimate whether they have received increased calls based on the distribution of the cards.

TX-9
Partners
LHD, L-GOV, SHD, S-GOV, MDPRAC, HOSP, CLIN, LAB/RX, SPH, U-OTH, MEDSOC, PROFASSN, BUS, MEDIA, C-OTH

Houston/Harris County Senior Wellness Days
To meet the health needs of the elderly of Houston, the Houston/Harris County Area Agency on Aging contracted with a private provider, Neighborhood Centers Inc. (NCI), to provide nutrition counseling and socialization opportunities for

Synergies
1a, 5b, 5d

Structural Foundations
Contract, Advisory

Contact
Ruby Toliver Porter,
MA, LMSW
Health and Elderly Services
Neighborhood Centers Inc.
P.O. Box 271389
Houston, TX 77277

the elderly. NCI is a private nonprofit United Way agency that has provided social services to the needy in the Greater Houston area since 1907. Its Health and Elderly Services Department has twenty-one senior citizen centers that provide meals and activities for seniors and one adult day care facility that provides additional services of medication assistance, nursing care, and podiatry. Additional funding from the local government allowed NCI to provide clinical preventive services for their clients, and the services were offered as Senior Wellness Days events. Some available services were: physical, vision, and hearing exams; screenings for cancer (prostate exams and mammography), diabetes, and high cholesterol; and nutrition and exercise advice. A planning committee for these events was headed by NCI's director and consisted of other NCI staff, business professionals, nursing professionals, nursing assistants, health educators, exercise instructors, senior citizens, and professionals from voluntary health organizations. The City of Houston Health and Human Resources Agency, working through the Agency on Aging, provided funding for the effort, and the local health department contributed one of its staff and cholesterol screening equipment.

TX-10
Partners
LHD, MCO

Synergies
3c, 4c

Structural Foundations
Informal

Contact
See citation

Houston Immunization Campaign
A local HMO, Sanus Houston Healthplan, approached the immunization department at the City of Houston Department of Health, for assistance in assessing its immunization rates and to strategize about ways of improving its immunization coverage.

American Association of Health Plans. 1996. *Improving the quality of life in local communities.* Washington, DC.

TX-11
Partners
SHD, MCO, C-OTH

Synergies
5b

Structural Foundations
Coalition

Contact
See citation

Shots Across Texas Immunization Campaign
A statewide HMO, Anthem Health Plan of Texas, supports the statewide Shots Across Texas infant immunization program by providing direct mail promotions and newsletter printings for the campaign.

American Association of Health Plans. 1996. *Improving the quality of life in local communities.* Washington, DC.

TX-12

Partners
SHD, S-GOV, MDPRAC, HOSP, AHC, VHO, MEDIA, FNDN, C-OTH

Synergies
1c, 3b, 5b, 6b-5

Structural Foundations
Coalition, Adm/Mgmt

Contact
See citation

West Texas Community Care Consortium on Cancer

In West Texas, small towns are scattered across a vast region, making access to hospitals, primary care physicians, or public clinics a challenge, and impeding routine cancer screening and medical treatment. Four groups (The Cancer Consortium of El Paso, Texas Tech University Health Sciences Center, Texas Cancer Council (a state health agency), and the West Texas Coalition for Cancer Control) created the West Texas Community Care Consortium with the goals of integrating care for people with cancer, providing preventive health care and services, and promoting lifelong wellness programs. Each partner in the Consortium, which is a CCN demonstration partnership funded by the W.K. Kellogg Foundation, has specific roles in four key areas of their mission: prevention/education, screening/diagnosis, treatment/follow-up, and administration of the Consortium's activities. In its first year (9/95–8/96), two medical professional training programs were implemented (one for nurse oncologists and one for physicians), a computer network system for communication across the region was installed, and a mobile mammography van service was launched, accompanied by full media coverage, special events, and an "open-house" at each county hospital.

Bogue, R and Hall, Jr, CH, eds. 1997. *Health networks innovations: how 20 communities are improving their system through collaboration.* Chicago: American Hospital Publishing, Inc.

TX-13

Partners
LHD, L-GOV, SHD, S-GOV, MDPRAC, HOSP, MCO, SOM, SPH, U-OTH, MEDSOC, PROFASSN, VHO, BUS, SCHL, RELIG, FNDN, C-OTH

Synergies
1b, 1c, 2a, 3c, 4c, 5a, 5b, 5d, 5e, 6b-6

Structural Foundations
Coalition, Contract, Advisory, Intraorg

Parkland Community-Oriented Primary Care Clinics

In 1985, Dallas's Parkland Memorial Hospital decided to "decentralize" and move its high-volume primary care practice to community-based centers. After an intensive review of various ambulatory care models, the Parkland executives developed a network of Community-Oriented Primary Care (COPC) clinics, based on the work of South African physician Sidney Kark. Parkland's COPC clinics were designed to assess and treat both the community and the patient, and key to their organization of clinical services were population data: knowing a market, the health needs that could be addressed by clinical or community programs, and the clinical staffing requirements. The hospital employed such population sciences as demography,

Contact
Sue Pickens, MEd
Strategic Planning &
Population Medicine
Parkland Hospital
5201 Harry Hines
Boulevard
Dallas, TX 75235
spicke@parknet.pmh.org

epidemiology, and sociology, among others, to analyze the effects of socioeconomic factors and health utilization on its clinical practice needs. The information they gathered was applied directly to clinical and programmatic services. It also served as the foundation for community organizing around health and social issues. During one recent community survey, for example, Parkland's Department of Population Medicine and Strategic Planning found a high prevalence of hypertension, diabetes, and hypercholesterolemia, so they facilitated a community-wide intervention—led by the local political leader—to address these problems. The planning department has also supported a number of community-assessment projects in the clinic neighborhoods, convening forums with residents and community leaders to help identify health priorities. Additionally, Parkland has used its COPC planning to develop Youth and Family Centers located in the public schools, the Greater Dallas Injury Prevention Center, and the Wynnewood Village Senior Health Center, among others.

TX-14
Partners
LHD, L-GOV, SHD, FEDHLTH,
MDPRAC, HOSP, SOM, SPH,
U-OTH, SCHL, RELIG, FNDN,
C-OTH

Synergies
1b, 1c, 2a

Structural Foundations
Coalition, Contract,
Adm/Mgmt

Contact
Bill Schlesinger
Project Vida
Comprehensive
Community Health and
Services Program
3607 Rivera Avenue
El Paso, TX 79905
pvida@whc.net

El Paso Project Vida
Project Vida is a community and economic development agency serving the Hispanic population of El Paso's border community. As part of its Community Health and Services Program, Project Vida has developed a "one-stop" health and human services center. The center includes primary health care, education, housing improvement, a food co-op, a thrift store, and a Christmas shop, among others. Using core funding from local Presbyterian churches and program funding from contracts and grants, Project Vida has registered over 1,300 families for health and social services. By working with public health agencies, medical and nursing students, church volunteers, and private health care providers, Project Vida is able to offer health care to 350 patients monthly who have no primary health care provider. As two measures of the agency's success, 97% of registered infants and children are on schedule for their immunizations, and Project Vida has documented saving the local hospital over $150,000 in 1995 by preventing avoidable emergency room usage.

[UT] UTAH

UT-1

Partners
LHD, SOM, RES, AHC, VHO

Synergies
1a, 2c, 6b-4

Structural Foundations
Contract

Contact
Thomas Schlenker,
MD, MPH
Salt Lake City-County
Health Department, S-2500
2001 South Lake Street
Salt Lake City, UT 84190
tschlenker@hs.co.slc.ut.us

Salt Lake City Primary Care Collaboration

In the mid-1990s, the Salt Lake City-County Health Department determined that it needed to assure the clientele in its primary care clinics more comprehensive primary care. This meant finding physicians who could oversee the public health nursing and support staff, provide 24-hour on-call service, and coordinate specialty referrals and inpatient care. The health department director approached the chairs of the University of Utah Medical Center Departments of Pediatrics and of Obstetrics/Gynecology, both of whom agreed to conduct full-time primary care teaching clinics at the health department's multiuse health center. Patients are seen by medical center attending physicians and residents, with support provided by health department nurses, laboratorians, and administrative staff. The collaborative arrangement has worked to everyone's benefit. The state was entering into mandatory Medicaid managed care in 1996, and the medical school needed to increase its presence and expand its patient base among Medicaid clients. They also needed to establish community-based teaching sites for their growing number of primary care residency programs. The arrangement has freed health department personnel who now focus on core public health functions, rather than delivering primary care. The partnership has proved so successful that the model is being duplicated at a second Salt Lake City health center.

UT-2

Partners
S-GOV, SOM, RES, U-OTH

Synergies
6b-4

Structural Foundations
Advisory

Contact
Meredith Alden, MD
Utah State Division
of Mental Health
120 N. 200 W., 4th Floor
Salt Lake City, UT 84103
malden@email.state.ut.us

State Academic Collaboration Committee

In Utah, the academic mental health sector and the public mental health system collaborate via the State Academic Collaboration Committee, which meets quarterly. This Committee is chaired by the director of the Utah Division of Mental Health and includes representatives from academic programs in psychiatry, nursing, social work, and psychology as well as from the public mental health sector. The education subcommittee addresses education and human resource needs in the public mental health system. The research subcommittee is responsible for reviewing applications for service system grants, which must demonstrate academic/public mental health linkages in order to be funded.

[VA] VIRGINIA

VA-1

Partners
LHD, L-GOV, SHD, HOSP, SOM, VHO, RELIG, FNDN, C-OTH

Synergies
1b, 2a, 3c, 5a, 6a-1

Structural Foundations
Contract, Advisory

Contact
Christopher M. Buttery, MD, MPH
Medical College of Virginia
Virginia Commonwealth University
HCR 76, Box 3535
Urbanna, VA 23175
kimro@crosslink.net

Richmond Primary Care Center

Under the guidance of a newly appointed director in the early 1990s, the Richmond City Health Department conducted a survey of the health needs of Richmond's inner-city residents in conjunction with the Medical College of Virginia. Despite the presence in the city of a major medical center, a large number of physicians, and a progressive health department, the survey identified a significant lack of access to primary care services among inner-city residents. At about the same time, the city manager wanted the health department to relinquish its direct provision of primary care services. The health department director used the opportunity to forge a collaborative partnership with the medical school to develop a community health center. Using city and state monies, as well as funding from The Robert Wood Johnson Foundation, they renovated an abandoned market in the inner city, transferred all of the health department clinical staff to the medical school, and agreed to establish an interdisciplinary case management model that would link the services of both institutions under the new health center's roof. After a series of key personnel changes, though, the terms of the collaborative venture changed. Rather than operate as a joint venture, it was decided that the Medical College of Virginia would run the center as part of its ambulatory care network, contract with the health department for specific services (such as case management), and co-locate public health programs at the health center. The health department assisted the medical school in developing a community advisory board for the health center, and also in establishing a tracking and reporting system that would meet state health department requirements. Since opening its doors in 1994, the health center has served over 8,000 patients each year.

VA-2

Partners
LHD, L-GOV, MDPRAC, HOSP, CLIN, MCO, SOM, VHO, SCHL, FNDN, C-OTH

Synergies
1a, 1c, 2a, 3b, 4a, 5a, 5b

Nelson County Rural Health Outreach Program

During a joint community health assessment by the Blue Ridge Medical Center and the district health department in 1991, the Rural Health Outreach Program (RHOP) was founded in Nelson County to increase access to health care by providing community-based services, case management, and health education. A CCN demonstration partner-

Structural Foundations
Coalition, Contract,
Adm/Mgmt

Contact
Peggy Whitehead
Nelson County Rural
Health Outreach Program
4038 Thomas Nelson
Highway
Arrington, VA 22922
rhoppw@aol.com

ship funded by the W.K. Kellogg Foundation, RHOP is a collaboration of several area hospitals and medical centers, the county health department and social service agencies, a managed care company, and community-based organizations. RHOP's community-wide initiatives include: linking referral and patient information across three separately owned primary care practices and the local health department; enhancing access to health and social services through a dedicated care coordinator and an Outreach Team, which includes a program manager, a nurse-practitioner, a nurse's aide and a community care worker; and developing a prepaid primary/preventive care program for the underserved, underinsured, and uninsured with a local managed care company. Another major initiative is the Health Depot program in which regularly scheduled, primary and preventive care clinics are held at nontraditional sites like museums, firehouses, and community centers. Tracking and evaluation of patient encounters are an integral part of the RHOP program. SF-36 health evaluation forms are used, along with other assessments forms, at Health Depot encounters as the basis for a personal health interview, and a database is maintained of clinical, demographic, and financial data on patients. With this information, the RHOP partners hope to show that these primary and preventive care activities are keeping patients out of the emergency room and out of the hospital, thus saving money and preserving community resources.

VA-3
Partners
SHD, S-GOV, FEDHLTH, MDPRAC, MEDSOC

Synergies
6a-1, 6a-4, 6a-6, 6b-6

Structural Foundations
Advisory

Contact
Lisa Smith, MS
Division of Women's
Health Issues
The American College of
Obstetricians and
Gynecologists (ACOG)
409 12th Street, S.W.
P.O. Box 96920
Washington, DC 20090
lsmith@acog.org

Virginia Providers' Partnership
In Virginia, a Providers' Partnership meeting hosted by the American College of Obstetricians and Gynecologists (ACOG) in the fall of 1995 and supported in part by a grant from the federal Maternal and Child Health Bureau (NAT-6), led to the creation of an advisory committee that reviews Medicaid managed care issues related to maternal and child health and provides input to the state Department of Medical Assistance. The committee, composed of private medical providers and public health professionals, developed specific recommendations for improving perinatal health outcomes under publicly funded systems of managed care. One approved recommendation was the creation of a permanent Medicaid Physicians' Advisory Committee to provide the state health department with regular advice and input from practicing physicians whose speciality is women's health.

VA-4

Partners
LHD, L-GOV, MDPRAC, HOSP,
CLIN, SOM, RES, U-OTH,
MEDSOC, FNDN, C-OTH

Synergies
2a, 2c, 5a, 6a-5, 6b-4

Structural Foundations
Coalition, Contract,
Adm/Mgmt, Advisory

Contact
C. Donald Combs, PhD
Planning and Program
Development
Eastern Virginia
Medical School
P.O. Box 1980
Norfolk, VA 23501
combs@planning.evms.edu

Portsmouth Community Health Center
A study in Portsmouth, conducted in 1990 by the Old Dominion University Research Foundation and the Eastern Virginia Medical School, confirmed emerging trends across the country: poor access to medical care for the uninsured, poor access to prescription medication, overburdened emergency rooms, delays in primary care treatment leading to more acute problems, and rising levels of uncompensated care carried by area hospitals. Led by the medical school and the local health department, a coalition of community leaders approached the US Public Health Service for help in developing a federally qualified community health center. Although funding for community health centers was on the decline and few new centers were being approved, the coalition persisted. In 1994, the center received federal funding for planning and development, and it opened its doors to patients in May 1995. The medical school provided organizational training for the fledgling board of directors, and both the medical school and the health department provided administrative support. The medical school also contributed its medical faculty, residents, and students to help staff a free clinic that provided services until the community health center could begin delivering health care services, and has since used the center as a training site for the medical students and primary care residents. The coalition that organized around the center's development evolved into the Mayor's Health Services Advisory Committee (VA-25), providing a forum for engaging the political leaders in discussions about diverse health and social service issues.

VA-5

Partners
LHD, L-GOV, SHD, FEDHLTH,
MDPRAC, HOSP, CLIN, MCO, INS,
LAB/RX, SOM, ARC, U-OTH,
MEDSOC, VHO, BUS, SCHL,
RELIG, FNDN, C-OTH

Synergies
1a, 3a, 4a, 4c, 5a, 5b, 5d

Structural Foundations
Coalition, Adm/Mgmt

Norfolk Consortium for Infant and Child Health
In 1992, the CDC National Immunization Program funded the Norfolk Department of Public Health and the Center for Pediatric Research, a joint program of the Eastern Virginia Medical School and Children's Hospital of The King's Daughters, to organize a community-based coalition to increase childhood immunization. Representatives from service organizations; academic, civic, and religious institutions; public, private, and military providers; and local citizens were recruited to form the Consortium for the Immunization of Norfolk's Children, which became the Consortium for Infant and Child Health. A needs assessment undertaken by coalition members in 1993 identified parent, provider,

Contact
Ardythe L. Morrow, PhD
Center for
Pediatric Research
Eastern Virginia
Medical School
855 West Brambleton
Avenue
Norfolk, VA 23510
amorrow@chkd.com

and health system factors contributing to the problem of underimmunization. Based on these data, a citywide strategic plan was developed and implemented. Some of the projects undertaken by the coalition include: (1) encouraging health care providers to send parents reminder messages when immunizations were due; (2) assessing physician rates; (3) providing immunizations in school-based clinics; (4) linking the health department's WIC clients with immunization services; (5) developing a computerized immunization registry; and (6) establishing a multifaceted immunization promotion campaign that included businesses, the schools, and community police officers. From 1993 to 1996, immunization rates for 2-year-olds increased from 49% to 66%.

VA-6

Partners
LHD, SHD, FEDOTH, MDPRAC, HOSP, SOM, MEDSOC, FNDN

Synergies
3c, 4c, 5a, 6a-2, 6a-4, 6a-5, 6b-5, 6b-6

Structural Foundations
Coalition, Contract, Adm/Mgmt

Contact
C. Donald Combs, PhD
Planning and Program
Development
Eastern Virginia
Medical School
P.O. Box 1980
Norfolk, VA 23501
combs@planning.evms.edu

Eastern Virginia Regional Perinatal Coordinating Council

In 1989, faced with fetal and infant mortality rates in a nine-county area that were 40% higher than the national average, Eastern Virginia Medical School convened a Perinatal Study Group. This coalition of academic medical faculty, community service providers, obstetricians, neonatologists, and public health officials was organized to provide policy and program recommendations to public and private providers. After a pilot infant mortality review project in 1992, the coalition evolved into the Eastern Virginia Regional Perinatal Coordinating Council, a state-funded entity incorporating a formal infant mortality review process with community outreach, policy and programmatic input, and education programs. Operating under the Council's supervision, the fetal infant mortality review program works with the region's health departments, hospitals, and physicians to randomly select four fetal and infant deaths each month for investigation. A nurse trained in perinatal bereavement counseling conducts a home interview with the mother, an obstetrical nurse collects information from the medical records, all identifying data are stripped from the case, and then a multidisciplinary Case Review Team considers the factors involved in the baby's death, particularly those related to community health care gaps. The team's recommendations are deliberated by a community review board, which monitors the implementation of any proposed solutions. Some of the recommendations instituted in the community have included faster administrative processing of Medicaid applications, a review of military clinic procedures and retraining of military medical residents, and greater emphasis on assessing each pregnant woman's psychosocial risks and supports at the first prenatal visit. Since instituting this process, the area's infant mortality rate has dropped from 13.1 per 1,000 births in 1991 to 9.2 per 1,000 births in 1996. More recently, the Council helped the state health department develop a successful application to the federal government to implement the Virginia Healthy Start Initiative, which will expand the review program statewide and link the reviews to improvements and expansions of perinatal services.

VA-7

Partners
LHD, FEDOTH, CLIN, MCO, SOM, RES, U-OTH

Synergies
6b-2, 6b-3, 6b-4, 6b-5

Structural Foundations
Contract, Adm/Mgmt, Advisory

Contact
C. Donald Combs, PhD
Planning and Program Development
Eastern Virginia Medical School
P.O. Box 1980
Norfolk, VA 23501
combs@planning.evms.edu

Eastern Virginia MPH Program

As part of an internal strategic planning process in 1994, Eastern Virginia Medical School began exploring the development of additional "collaborative" programs, including graduate training in public health. The medical school convened an advisory committee that included medical school faculty, all the local health department directors in Eastern Virginia, the dean of Old Dominion University's health sciences college, and a representative of the Navy Environmental Health Center. The group developed an MPH-degree granting program that would be offered jointly by the medical school and Old Dominion, and which would be marketed to professionals already working in the health care field. All the health department directors are actively involved in the implementation of the MPH program, including input on curriculum development, practicum opportunities, and recruitment of public health professionals. Recently, the program implemented a joint MD/MPH program as well.

VA-8

Partners
LHD, MDPRAC, HOSP

Synergies
1a, 2b, 2d, 4c, 6a-1, 6a-2

Structural Foundations
Contract, Adm/Mgmt

Virginia Beach Public-Private Partnership on Prenatal Care

In Virginia Beach, enhanced Medicaid reimbursement for prenatal care has led to an increased number of private physicians willing to care for Medicaid patients, which in turn has dramatically reduced the caseload in the local health department. To reduce competition among these sectors, and to improve care, a public-private partnership was established in 1994 by the director of the health department, involving two local hospitals

Contact
Venita Newby-Owens,
MD, MPH
Virginia Beach Department
of Public Health
Pembroke Corporate
Center III
4452 Corporation Lane
Virginia Beach, VA 23462
vnewbyowens@vdh.state.
va.us

VA-9
Partners
S-GOV, SOM, U-OTH

Synergies
6b-1, 6b-3, 6b-4, 6c-2

Structural Foundations
Contract

Contact
King Davis, PhD
Virginia Commonwealth
University
School of Social Work
Raleigh Building
1001 West Franklin Street
Room 230
Richmond, VA 23284
kdavis@saturn.vcu.edu

and the obstetricians on their staffs. All Medicaid-covered women were shifted to the private sector with case management support from the health department's public health nurses for high-risk pregnancies. The health department has a particularly good track record providing case management to this population, evidenced by low rates of low-birthweight deliveries among high-risk women under their care. In the system, a single source of care is assured from prenatal care to delivery for most women, and the city was able to reduce clinical staff and save over $300,000 annually on deliveries. The health department now provides clinical prenatal services only for uninsured women, a decrease in caseload from 600 women to 60 per year, and these women make direct arrangements with their physician concerning payment for the delivery. To share more equally the burden of uncompensated care, uninsured clients are assigned to private physicians for delivery in a strict rotation. There is continuing dialogue among the private physicians and the health department to assess the program and make suggestions for improvement.

Galt Visiting Scholar Program
In order to better connect the practice of public mental health to academia, Virginia's Galt Visiting Scholar (GVS) program was established as a joint academic/practice position in 1982. The program was created in response to a Virginia State General Assembly resolution that state-supported universities involved in training mental health professionals should develop cooperative relationships with the state mental health department. The goals were to improve staffing of mental health facilities and to better train the medical, psychology, social work, nursing, and other allied health professional students who would become the state's mental health workforce. To engage leaders from the various schools, a cooperative agreement was developed among the University of Virginia, Virginia Commonwealth University, the Eastern Virginia Medical School, the state mental health department, and the Governor. State funding was used to create the Visiting Scholar's position to serve as a link for the state mental health department and the three university departments of psychiatry, and to strengthen clinical, educational, and research ties among these institutions. Some accomplishments of the GVS Program, which won an award from the

State/University Collaborations Project in 1990 (NAT-20), include the development of an integrated residency program, changes in curriculum, initiation of collaborative research activities, recruitment of well-credentialed professionals to key positions in the state mental health facilities, and a general sense of partnership among the academic and state mental health institutions. In 1993, the program changed from a two-year tenure to a monthly workshop and lecture series, and in 1995, the program was discontinued entirely, due to budget constraints.

VA-10
Partners
LHD, L-GOV, HOSP, MCO, U-OTH, MEDSOC, VHO, SCHL

Synergies
1c, 4c, 5a, 5b, 6b-6

Structural Foundations
Coalition, Adm/Mgmt

Contact
Robert Stroube, MD, PhD
Fairfax Health District
10777 Main Street
Suite 203
Fairfax, VA 22030

Fairfax County Partnership for Healthier Kids
In 1993, the Fairfax County Health Department helped initiate the Partnership for Healthier Kids to improve access to primary care medical homes and increase the provision of age-appropriate preventive services in children from birth to age 12. Partners in this project include INOVA Health Systems, Kaiser Permanente, the George Mason University College of Nursing and Health Science, the county medical society, public schools, community groups, and social service agencies. The target population includes 17,500 children in 17 elementary schools in the often poor and ethnically diverse neighborhoods of the Mason district. A multitiered strategy was used to collect baseline data on the health status and needs of community children, including focus group-style interviews in over six languages with young mothers in the Mason area, a survey of households with young children, a study of Fairfax Hospital's Emergency Department records on children under age 12, and an audit of immunization records of local elementary schools and Head Start programs. While INOVA Health Systems contributed significant funds to the project in 1996, each partnering organization has provided in-kind services to support planning, assessment, and community development. The Partnership has been promoted with extensive briefings among government officials, health, education, and social service professionals, and community groups. Despite these efforts, reaching and informing citizens of the available services for their children still has been difficult, due to the large size and cultural diversity of the targeted community.

VA-11

Partners

LHD, L-GOV, MDPRAC, CLIN, FNDN

Synergies

1b, 2a

Structural Foundations

Contract

Contact

Susan McLeod, MD, MPH
Thomas Jefferson
Health District
1138 Rose Hill Drive
P.O. Box 7546
Charlottesville, VA 22906
smcleod@vdh.state.va.us

Charlottesville Shared Clinic Facilities

In 1992, the volunteer-staffed Charlottesville Free Clinic (CFC) began operations. A year later, as CFC was preparing to begin a new dental program using a grant from the Virginia Health Care Foundation to purchase and install new dental equipment, it received notice that it would lose its donated space at the end of the coming year. Wishing to avoid an expensive renovation for short-term use, CFC planned to defer the dental program grant. The Charlottesville-Albermarle Health Department stepped forward with an offer to have the equipment installed in its dental clinic to replace their outdated equipment. CFC volunteer dentists were then able to use the equipment when the health department clinic was closed. In 1995, CFC was operating in a second donated space, nearing a deadline to decide on its future location, and was unable to find space for renovation and long-term rental. Again, the health department stepped forward and offered use of its newly expanded medical clinic space at night. The health department also was aware that CFC required space for offices, records, and a pharmacy adjacent to the clinic rooms. So, the health department arranged with officials from local government, which owned the building, to provide the needed administrative space as part of the last phase of its building project. CFC was required to raise the extra funds needed for renovation, which it obtained from the Virginia Health Care Foundation, the Perry Foundation, and many small donors. The new facilities opened for business in early 1997. The arrangement to share space and operating expenses is covered by a long-term license agreement through which each entity maintains its own operations and identity. Nonetheless, there is a strong cross-referral pattern facilitated by the co-location, making clients aware of the other's services and outreach efforts of each attract clients to both of the partners' offices.

VA-12

Partners

LHD, L-GOV, MDPRAC, HOSP, CLIN, MCO, SOM, RES, U-OTH, PROFASSN, VHO, BUS, SCHL, RELIG, C-OTH

Peninsula Health District Cancer Prevention Program

Concerned that cancer is the second leading cause of death in the district, the Peninsula Health District has established the Cancer Prevention Program to determine local strategies to address this problem. Started in 1996, the health department conducted a needs assessment and invited key stakeholders

Synergies
3b, 4b, 4c, 5b, 6b-5

Structural Foundations
Coalition

Contact
Daniel Warren, MD, MPH
Peninsula Health District
416 J. Clyde Morris
Boulevard
Newport News, VA 23601
dwarren@vdh.state.va.us

from the community to build a coalition, including representatives from the health care sector, the schools of medicine and nursing, voluntary health organizations, schools, local government, community groups, and businesses. Goals of the program are to increase public awareness and health education, to improve professional education, and to enhance screening and referral programs, while assuring quality of care. The District's cooperative budget funds a public health nurse to coordinate partnership activities, and partners in the coalition incur the costs of any activities they sponsor. Cancer risk-reduction programs of the Coalition target all ages from children to senior citizens and include health promotion, health education, and screening efforts. To date, the Coalition has offered four free screenings. Two were held at a hospital-sponsored OB/GYN center and focused on detecting breast and cervical cancer, and two were held at an inner-city clinic and included skin, oral, breast, cervical, and prostrate cancer exams. Follow-up, referral, and treatment were arranged through staff of member agencies in the Coalition. The Coalition also is involved in raising public awareness about breast cancer, prostrate cancer, and the cancer risks of tobacco use, mounting public education campaigns, developing and placing materials in physicians' offices, and distributing smoking-cessation kits in schools and businesses.

VA-13

Partners
LHD, FEDHLTH, MDPRAC, HOSP, LAB/RX, PHASSN

Synergies
1a

Structural Foundations
Contract

Contact
Molly Rutledge, MD
Roanoke City Health
Department
515 Eighth Street, S.W.
Roanoke, VA 24016

Roanoke Veterans Health Administration Exchange of Space for Home Health Services
In a mutually beneficial exchange of services, the Veterans Administration (VA) provides office space to the Roanoke City Health Department's home visiting staff, who, in turn, provide home health services to veterans at no charge. Trading occurs at the fair-market value of each commodity. The health department uses space at the VA Medical Center, which also encourages interoffice referrals and helps the medical staff be aware of their services. An evaluation of the arrangement demonstrated more efficient use of local resources and increased physician awareness of the benefits (financial, medical, and psychosocial) of home health services for the veterans served. This partnership began in 1991, and currently, negotiations are underway to expand the collaboration.

VA-14

Partners

LHD, MDPRAC, HOSP, CLIN, MCO, SOM, VHO, BUS, SCHL, RELIG, MEDIA, C-OTH

Synergies

3b, 4a, 4c, 5b, 6b-5

Structural Foundations

Coalition, Adm/Mgmt

Contact

Daniel Warren, MD, MPH
Peninsula Health District
416 J. Clyde Morris Boulevard
Newport News, VA 23601
dwarren@vdh.state.va.us

Peninsula Health District Immunization Coalition

The Peninsula Health District organized an Immunization Coalition in 1994 to increase the percentage of children who are adequately immunized by age two. The partnership of medical providers, hospitals, community groups, local businesses, and the media focuses on increasing public awareness, educating providers, and coordinating activities on immunization in the community. Each partner assumes the financial cost of their health promotion or provider education activity, but membership in the coalition provides a common forum for sharing information, pooling support for related activities, and coordinating existing efforts, such as the mobile clinic schedules, to avoid duplication. The Coalition implemented a community-wide immunization database, which currently has over 400,000 records and 61 providers who use the system. Other projects of the Coalition have been geared to increasing public awareness about the importance of immunization, and encouraging medical and social service providers of strategies to avoid missed vaccination opportunities in their practices. The Coalition has hosted teleconferences, such as CDC's "Epidemiology and Prevention of Vaccine-Preventable Diseases" program, and has trained WIC staff to evaluate immunization records and refer children to the on-site immunization clinic. For public education, the Coalition received a donation of a full-page telephone book advertisement from regional Bell Atlantic to print the immunization schedule and it coordinated the distribution of immunization reminders to 195,000 families with their utility bills and 33,000 households printed on the monthly school lunch menu. At local day care and Head Start centers, health district staff review immunization records and refer children in need of immunization to their physicians, to on-site clinics, or to the Coalition-sponsored effort Saturday Shots for Tots, held monthly throughout the community.

VA-15

Partners

LHD, L-GOV, MDPRAC, HOSP, CLIN, LAB/RX, SPH, BUS, RELIG, MEDIA, FNDN, C-OTH

Lenowisco Pharmaceutical Indigent Program

To assist indigent patients in obtaining needed medications, the Lenowisco Health District created the Pharmaceutical Indigent Program in 1994 to connect patients, physicians, and pharmaceutical companies. Mount Empire Older Citizens, Inc. (MEOC), the local Area Agency on Aging, now

Synergies
1c, 3a

Structural Foundations
Contract, Adm/Mgmt

Contact
Eleanor S. Cantrell, MD
Lenowisco Health District
134 Roberts Street, S.W.
Wise, VA 24293
ecantrell@vdh.state.va.us

works with the health district to operate the program, which helps uninsured and underinsured patients apply for free or low-cost medications. The health district developed specialized computer software, which facilitates the collection of all information needed to apply for the numerous pharmaceutical programs (over 60) for the indigent elderly. Publicized through social service agencies, home health agencies, doctor's offices and nursing homes, the program has been in great demand, and MEOC assists the health district in handling applications. This program helps participants comply with their medical regimens, and also allows them to shift money previously spent on medications to other basic living expenses, such as food and housing. The computer program acts as a case management system, helping the agencies keep track of patients' medications and assisting them in the coordination of other needed services. In a survey about the impact of this program on their patients' health, 90% of area physicians reported that medication compliance had improved. Anecdotally, these physicians also noted that improved use of medication for chronic diseases, like Black Lung, led to decreases in disability claims and applications for Medicaid, decreased emergency room use, and reduced hospital stays.

VA-16

Partners
LHD, L-GOV, S-GOV, FEDHLTH,
HOSP, ARC, VHO, C-OTH

Synergies
1c, 5b, 5e

Structural Foundations
Coalition, Adm/Mgmt

Contact
Jessica Falkos
Chesterfield Health District
9501 Lucy Corr Drive
P.O. Box 100
Chesterfield, VA 23832

Chesterfield-Colonial Heights Families First Coalition
The large number of high-risk families with young children in Chesterfield County and the City of Colonial Heights could not be served by existing community-based services, and in 1995, the Chesterfield and Colonial Heights Departments of Health, the Chesterfield-Colonial Heights Community Services Board, and Johnston-Willis Hospital held a series of meetings to discuss how they could collaborate to provide an expanded network of services to this population. These partners created the Families First Coalition. Inviting other health and human service providers and citizens in the community to work with them, the Coalition developed a pilot program to provide education and support services to families with children under age five. The program has three components: a comprehensive, long-term home visitation service for high-risk families, a parent newsletter, and Family Resource Centers housed in local libraries. With the support of the Chesterfield-Colonial Heights

Policy and Management Team, the Coalition submitted and was awarded funding from the federal Family Preservation Act. In 1996, through this grant and other federal, state, and local funding, the program began operation and now has a director, two professional staff with training in family assessment and early childhood development, and three family support workers. The home visitation program, which is based on the Healthy Families America (HFA) model, targets first-time, high-risk parents who are expecting a child and provides service until the child is five years old. An evaluation of the program will be conducted following HFA standards, with specific objectives of improving child health, enhancing child development, promoting positive, nurturing parenting, and reducing the incidence of child abuse and neglect.

VA-17
Partners
LHD, SHD, MDPRAC, VHO

Synergies
1a, 1c

Structural Foundations
Contract, Advisory

Contact
Sheila M. Spelman,
MSN, CNS
Eastern Shore
Health District
23191 Front Street
P.O. Box 177
Accomac, VA 23301
sspelman@vdh.state.va.us

Eastern Shore Coordinated HIV Care

In 1996, the Eastern Shore's local infectious disease physician was very concerned about his HIV-positive patients' lack of adherence to medical regimens and their risky sexual behavior. Together with a public health nurse at the Eastern Shore Health District, he initiated a program of HIV/STD care coordination and case management. Two days a month, the nurse works in the physician's private office. They jointly assess the patients' physical and psychosocial needs and develop a care plan with the patient. The nurse maintains contact with patients through home visits, assisting them with referrals for financial or Medicaid assistance, obtaining medication and monitoring compliance, securing dental care and nutritional supplements, and providing counseling and education, In addition to the patients receiving their primary care services from the infectious disease specialist, all persons reported to the health department with HIV infection are referred to the public health nurse for epidemiological investigation and a needs assessment. Since the inception of this case management program, show rates for medical office visits have risen from 50% to over 90%, no secondary HIV or STD infections have been attributed to case-managed patients, and the number of hospital admissions has decreased.

VA-18

Partners
LHD, L-GOV, SHD, HOSP, CLIN, LAB/RX, RES, SCHL, C-OTH

Synergies
1b, 2a, 5b, 5d, 5e, 6b-6

Structural Foundations
Coalition, Contract, Advisory

Contact
Darhyl B. Jasper, RN, MSN
Alexandria Health Department
517 N. St. Asaph Street
Alexandria, VA 22314

Alexandria Interagency Consortium on Adolescent Pregnancy

In 1991, a coalition of public and private youth-serving agencies in Alexandria formed the Interagency Consortium on Adolescent Pregnancy (ICAP). The group's objectives were to reduce adolescent pregnancy and to promote services to adolescent parents. After two years of coalition-building and strategizing, the group developed the Teen Pregnancy Prevention Program, encompassing five components: (1) an after-school life skills development program; (2) a Male Teen Responsibility project; (3) a Postponing Sexual Involvement program for teens 13 to 15 years old; (4) Project Stepout/Manhood; and (5) a Resource Mothers program, which works with first-time teen mothers to prevent a second pregnancy. The consortium also linked all of its programs with free comprehensive medical services offered at the city's Adolescent Health Center. The group has promoted and implemented its joint activities through an interagency collaborative agreement, and they have received some grant funding from the Virginia General Assembly.

VA-19

Partners
LHD, L-GOV, SHD, HOSP, VHO, BUS, MEDIA, C-OTH

Synergies
3b, 4c, 5b, 6b-5, 6b-6
Structural Foundations
Coalition, Adm/Mgmt, Advisory

Contact
Carolyn Winkler, RN, BSN
Alexandria Health Department
517 N. St. Asaph Street
Alexandria, VA 22314
cwinkler.alexander@vdh.state.va.us

Alexandria Committee on Breast Cancer Issues

Alexandria's Office of the City Manager initiated the Committee on Breast Cancer in 1994 as a means of increasing public awareness regarding the early detection of breast cancer, making information available to women diagnosed with breast cancer, and raising funds to cover the costs of screening and diagnostics for uninsured women. Among the committee members, the local health department provides public and professional education through its Breast and Cervical Cancer Early Detection Program; the Office on Women provides staff support to carry out fund-raising and promotion; the INOVA Alexandria Hospital's Northern Virginia Cancer Center maintains the funds for the mammogram program; and a number of other public agencies and private organizations work on volunteer recruitment, fund-raising, and event promotion. The state health department has provided $25,000 to fund a program coordinator at the local health department, and all other funds are raised locally. Although the committee's educational efforts are targeted at all women in the community, the local health department specifically targets low-income, minority women over age 50 for free mammograms.

VA-20

Partners
LHD, S-GOV, FEDHLTH, MDPRAC, HOSP, BUS, SCHL, RELIG, MEDIA, FNDN, C-OTH

Synergies
1a, 1c

Structural Foundations
Adm/Mgmt, Advisory

Contact
Nancy Welch, MD, MHA
Chesapeake Health Department
748 Battlefield Boulevard, N. Chesapeake, VA 23320

Chesapeake Comprehensive Health Investment Project

To improve access to and coordination of medical and social services for low-income children, the Chesapeake Health Department opted to become a replication site for Comprehensive Health Investment Project (CHIP) of Virginia in 1993. This program provides case management and coordination services for families with children under age six who are covered by Medicaid. CHIP's mission is to develop, operate, and expand a network of public-private partnerships to serve young children and their families, and to improve parents' self-sufficiency and involvement in managing their families' and children's health. The Southeastern Tidewater Opportunity Project, a nonprofit organization, serves as the fiscal and administrative agency for employees of the CHIP program, while the health department provides space for the program staff. Families involved in CHIP must meet federal guidelines for Medicaid and must be committed to make a conscious effort to improve their families' health. Over 300 children were enrolled by 1995. An evaluation of enrolled families shows increased use of a private pediatrician as a "medical home," increased medical access, increased employment among mothers, and reduced use of the emergency room for medical care. Despite the program's success, limited funds and staff vacancies have prevented the expansion of the program. For example, in 1996, staffing and funds allowed only 300 children to be enrolled, though over 5,500 were eligible for this program in the city. CHIP was created with support from the W.K. Kellogg Foundation, federal grants (Family Resources and Support Program and the Maternal and Child Health Bureau), an appropriation from the Virginia's General Assembly, in-kind services from the Chesapeake Health Department, and donations from the community.

VA-21

Partners
LHD, PROFASSN, SCHL

Synergies
1a

Loudoun County Dental Screening Program

A 20-year-old partnership of the Loudoun County Health District and the Loudoun County Dental Society assures that all children from kindergarten through fifth grade obtain free dental screenings through their school. School officials notify parents

Structural Foundations
Adm/Mgmt

Contact
Peter Van Sickels, DDS
Loudoun Health District
102 Heritage Way NE
Suite 101
Leesburg, VA 20176
pvansickels@vdh.state.va.
us

VA-22
Partners
LHD, HOSP

Synergies
1a

Structural Foundations
Contract

Contact
Robert Stroube, MD, MPH
Fairfax Health District
10777 Main Street
Suite 203
Fairfax, VA 22030

VA-23
Partners
LHD, SHD, S-GOV, FEDHLTH,
MDPRAC, HOSP, CLIN, MCO, INS,
LAB/RX, SOM, ARC, U-OTH,
MEDSOC, PROFASSN, VHO, BUS,
RELIG, C-OTH

Synergies
3a, 4a, 4c, 5a, 5b, 5c, 5d,
6b-5, 6b-6

Structural Foundations
Coalition, Contract

of the program at the beginning of the school year, and send out parental authorization forms. In December, the schools notify the public health dentist of the number of students who will be screened at each school. The public health dentist assigns a volunteer dental society member to each school to provide free screenings. The school system pays for the cost of the parental authorization forms, tongue blades, and gloves. The program serves between 3,000 and 5,000 children per year, and parents are notified of any dental problems that require treatment.

Fairfax County Nutrition Program
In a cooperative agreement between INOVA Health Systems and the Fairfax County Health Department begun in 1994, the two agencies agreed to hire a part-time nutritionist to provide counseling and food vouchers to WIC clients at the hospital's Pediatric Center. The health department supplies the nutritionist and the hospital system pays the part-time salary. The program was designed to increase the enrollment of eligible women and children in the WIC program, provide more comprehensive counseling and services at the site where they normally receive care, and link the women to other public health and social services that might prove helpful. Since the program was initiated, the WIC caseload has increased by 9%.

Project Immunize Virginia
Project Immunize Virginia (PIV) is a public-private partnership that brings together more than 100 representatives from the Commonwealth to promote immunization for all Virginians. Established in 1995 with funding from the Virginia Department of Health (VDH), Project Immunize Virginia is coordinated by the Center for Pediatric Research, a joint program of Eastern Virginia Medical School and Children's Hospital of The King's Daughters. Members of PIV include VDH and other state agencies, local health departments, local immunization coalitions, service organizations, academic institutions, public, private and military health care providers, insurers and managed care organizations, pharmaceutical companies, state-level professional organizations, and others. According to the National Immunization Survey, 76% of Virginia's 2-year-olds were up-to-date for diphtheria-tetanus-pertussis, polio, and measles-containing vaccines in 1996.

Contact
Frances D. Butterfoss, PhD
Center for
Pediatric Research
Eastern Virginia
Medical School
855 West Bambleton
Avenue
Norfolk, VA 23510
fbutterf@chkd.com

The mission of PIV is to link providers, parents and children, payer and community coalitions with the technical support, public and professional education, and community resources needed so that all Virginians of all ages will be fully immunized by the year 2000. Action-oriented work groups of PIV focus on specific strategies designed to improve immunization rates. The Immunization Information System Work Group promotes and supports collaborative, public-private development of the Virginia Information System Integrated, On-line Network (VISION) tracking system. The Professional Education Work Group focuses on improving the immunization knowledge and practices of current and future health care providers. This group has developed a provider immunization "tool kit" and sponsors vaccine update courses for residents and medical students. The Community Partnerships Work Group links communities with state and local resources and develops local partnerships to promote immunization campaigns. This group also organizes PIV's annual statewide conference and is responsible for its National Infant and Adult Immunization Awareness Week campaign. Lastly, the Legislative and Advocacy Work Group supports legislative action that promotes immunization delivery. The PIV project is nationally recognized as a model of academic/public health collaboration at the state level.

VA-24
Partners
MCO

Synergies
3a, 3c

Structural Foundations
Intraorg

Contact
See citation

MetraHealth Institute for Health Services Research

A Virginia managed care organization developed its own in-house capacity for health services research. The Institute for Health Services Research conducts studies in health policy analysis, health promotion, clinical epidemiology, and health services administration. The unit's main objectives are the compilation and dissemination of information designed to improve the effectiveness and efficiency of health care delivery.

American Association of Health Plans. 1996. *Improving the quality of life in local communities.* Washington, DC.

VA-25
Partners
LHD, L-GOV, FEDHLTH, MDPRAC, HOSP, CLIN, INS, LAB/RX, SOM, RES, MEDSOC, BUS, SCHL, RELIG, MEDIA, FNDN, C-OTH

Portsmouth Mayor's Health Services Advisory Committee

In response to a state mandate, in 1990 the Mayor of Portsmouth organized the Mayor's Health Services Advisory Committee to conduct a health care needs assessment and to address health problems

Synergies
1c, 5a, 5b, 5d, 6a-5

Structural Foundations
Coalition, Advisory

Contact
Alan E. Gollihue
Portsmouth General
Hospital Foundation
P.O. Box 1053
Portsmouth, VA 23705
pghfdn@pilot.infi.net

across the city's agencies and service areas in a co-ordinated way. The Committee, recognized by the W.K. Kellogg Foundation as a CCN finalist partner-ship, includes representatives from several local medical centers and clinics, the local health de-partment, other city agencies, the public schools, a school of medicine, a foundation, the medical so-ciety, clergy, and other community providers (VA-4). After completion of the assessment and strategic planning around the community's health needs, the Committee, under the authority of the mayor, be-came the foundation for collaboration around the health needs identified. The partnership works by setting up task forces to address specific health is-sues, such as obstetric care for single mothers, the development of a community health center, or health and social services for people with HIV/AIDS. Once an issue is resolved, the task force may disband, but the Committee remains intact. The Committee, then, serves as a way both to spur action on health problems that are important to the membership and the community, and to sustain collaborative activity for ongoing community health interventions.

[VT] VERMONT

VT-1
Partners
SHD, S-GOV, HOSP, PROFASSN, FNDN

Synergies
6a-5, 6a-6

Structural Foundations
Advisory

Contact
Peter Holman
Vermont Association of
Hospital & Health Systems
148 Main Street
Montpelier, VT 05602
peteholman@aol.com

Integration Task Force
In January 1996, the governor of Vermont charged a group of hospital CEOs and state officials to ini-tiate a public-private effort to create a vision of the state's future health services system. Known as the Integration Task Force, the group developed a broad vision of how health and human services could be locally organized throughout the state. The Task Force considered the principles on which such a system should be founded, and identified the measurable outcome data which already ex-isted. The group envisioned a locally developed and governed system of physical, mental, and so-cial health services which are integrated with other economic, educational, and community systems. The governance structure, over time, would as-sume responsibility for the health of a defined pop-ulation and, within the resources available, would coordinate the availability of and access to health education, preventive health services, acute care for physical and mental health problems, chronic care, social services, and economic development. Comprehensive information systems, with ade-

quate privacy protections, would be used to help direct the network's development and coordination, and would provide the population data necessary for program development and evaluation. The health of each region would be measured in educational, social, physical, mental, and economic terms. Furthermore, each network would be linked with, and have the ability to influence, state political and administrative processes.

[WA] WASHINGTON

WA-1

Partners
FEDHLTH, MDPRAC, MCO, SPH

Synergies
3a, 4b, 5d, 6c-2

Structural Foundations
Contract

Contact
Shirley A. Beresford, PhD
Department of
Epidemiology
University of Washington
School of Public Health
and Community Medicine
Box 357236
Seattle, WA 98195
beresfrd@u.washington.
edu

Seattle Nutrition Counseling Study
In 1995, an epidemiology professor at the University of Washington School of Public Health and Community Medicine approached colleagues at Group Health Cooperative of Puget Sound, a Seattle-based HMO. Together, they conducted a randomized controlled trial investigating the effect of a brief physician endorsement of a nutritional self-help booklet introduced in the course of a primary care visit. Twenty-eight physician practices participated, half of whom were randomized to the intervention, and over 2,000 patients completed the study. The research team from the school of public health, led by the epidemiologist in collaboration with the behavioral scientist, wrote and produced the booklet, trained the physicians to introduce the booklet in the brief counseling intervention, and interviewed the patients before and after their primary care visit. The physicians spent between one to three minutes during the visit promoting the health-enhancing value of good nutrition, and then provided the patients with the self-help booklet. At both three and twelve-month follow-up periods, the public health researchers determined that the intervention resulted in significantly lower fat intake and greater fiber consumption among the patients who were in the intervention group. Aside from demonstrating the benefits of the specific nutritional health promotion, the researchers also validated the approach of applying behavioral science and epidemiological principles to clinical practice, and of using clinical practice to inform public health science.

WA-2

Partners
LHD, INS, MEDSOC

Pierce County Tobacco Control and Fluoridation Campaigns
In 1984, in coordination with the Tacoma/Pierce County Health Department, the Pierce County

Synergies
5b, 5c

Structural Foundations
Coalition

Contact
Doug Jackman
Pierce County Medical
Society
223 Tacoma Avenue South
Tacoma, WA 98402
doug@pcmswa.org

WA-3
Partners
LHD, L-GOV, HOSP, U-OTH,
MEDSOC, BUS, SCHL, RELIG,
MEDIA, FNDN, C-OTH

Synergies
5a, 5b, 5d, 5e

Structural Foundations
Coalition, Adm/Mgmt

Contact
Torney Smith, MS
Spokane Regional Health
District
1101 West College Avenue
Spokane, WA 99201
tsmith@spokanecounty.org

Medical Society spearheaded efforts to bring about control or regulation of tobacco smoking in public and at workplaces. The medical society's efforts were initiated by its Public Health/School Health Committee. Similarly, in 1987 and 1988, the county medical society worked with the local health department and the county dental society to press for countywide water fluoridation. Both the tobacco control and the fluoridation campaigns were successful, in part attributable to the coalition of public and private interests expressing a common concern.

Spokane Health Improvement Partnership
The Health Improvement Partnership (HIP) is a growing alliance of citizens, health care providers, county health and human service agencies, and over 100 other local organizations dedicated to improving the health of Spokane County through a process of community assessment and mobilization of citizens on local health problems. In 1994, four hospitals, which were traditionally competitors, joined together with the county health department, the county medical society, and the Washington State Health Foundation in a shared goal of improving community health by focusing on broad determinants of health and community development. To date, the Partnership has conducted a community needs assessment, identified six health priority areas, and developed a process of training and support for local citizens who want to take part in improving the health of their community. Another goal of the Partnership is to tap into citizens' own resources to stimulate a myriad of local projects (called "Discoveries") around the priority areas. The community-based projects recognized as Discoveries range from adolescent outreach and case management programs to a "Buckle Bear" health education program designed to increase the use of car seat safety restraints for 3 to 5-year-olds. The Partnership has an Implementation Team (the "I-Team") which consists of executive-level staff from the hospitals and the health department as well as individuals from the community. The I-Team oversees the central coordination of the projects in the field, and partners dedicate staff for training, resource development, communications, and assessment. As of 1997, HIP had several initiatives including the development of a community report card, a job-preparedness program for the mentally

and physically challenged, and community forums on strategies to promote health and well-being among the elderly. The Partnership is currently funded by the four participating hospitals, with significant in-kind support from the health department and community volunteers.

WA-4
Partners
LHD, SHD, FEDHLTH, MDPRAC, HOSP, CLIN, MCO, LAB/RX, SOM, SPH, RES, MEDSOC, VHO, SCHL, RELIG, MEDIA

Synergies
2a, 2c, 4c, 5c, 6a-4

Structural Foundations
Coalition, Contract, Advisory

Contact
Max Bader, MD, MPH
2 S.W. Del Prado
Lake Oswego, OR 97035

WA-5
Partners
LHD, L-GOV, HOSP, CLIN, MCO, SPH, U-OTH, VHO, RELIG, FNDN, C-OTH

Synergies
5a, 5d, 6b-6

Structural Foundations
Coalition, Contract, Adm/Mgmt, Advisory

Contact
Bill Beery
Group Health/Kaiser Permanente Community Foundation
Group Health Cooperative of Puget Sound
1730 Minor Avenue
Suite 1520
Seattle, WA 98101
beery.b@ghc.org

Seattle-King County Historical Collaborations
A retired local health officer with forty years of experience recalled a variety of programs in which the private medical sector worked with the Seattle-King County Health Department. Examples include: public STD clinics involving consultations with private practicing physicians; implementation of vaccine programs; advocacy efforts regarding fluoridation and environmental clean-up of Lake Washington; protection of the Seattle watershed; development of children's clinics in poverty areas; and publicly promulgated standards for sports medicine trainers.

The Washington Consortium
The Washington Consortium was formed in 1991 in response to a four-year funding opportunity under the W.K. Kellogg Foundation's Community-Based Public Health Initiative. Composed of representatives of several county health coalitions, the Lummi Indian Nation, the University of Washington schools of nursing and public health, the Group Health Cooperative of Puget Sound, several local health departments and local colleges, a children's clinic, a vocational institute, and the Seattle Indian Health Board, the Consortium provided capacity-building resources and technical assistance to local community efforts. Each community identified needs and priorities through health assessments, surveys, and focus groups. The university, health departments, and other Consortium members provided technical assistance and support as requested by the communities. In addition, the school of public health and the local health departments identified ways of increasing the number, quality, and relevance of educational and professional development opportunities for all the community partners.

WA-6

Partners
LHD, L-GOV, FEDOTH, HOSP, MCO, LAB/RX, SOM, RES, U-OTH, VHO, SCHL, RELIG, FNDN, C-OTH

Synergies
1b, 1c, 2a, 3b, 6b-5

Structural Foundations
Contract

Contact
Paul Barry
Homeless Youth Clinic
45th Street Clinic
1629 N. 45th Street
Seattle, WA 98103
tfwelsh3@msn.com

Seattle Homeless Youth Clinic

In 1996, there were hundreds of homeless and run-away youth on Seattle's streets on any given night. A local health clinic developed the Homeless Youth Clinic as a free walk-in clinic that provides primary health care services, health education, HIV counseling and testing, and mental health counseling two nights per week. In collaboration with the Group Health Cooperative of Puget Sound, Swedish Medical Center, YouthCare, the Seattle-King County Health Department, and other health and human services organizations, the Homeless Youth Clinic serves as a central access point for youth needing direct services or referrals to specialty care. Through its own funding sources, the Clinic also funds services at a naturopathic university and an alternative high school. The number of patients seen at the clinic tripled in three years, from 217 in 1993 to 548 in 1995. As a consequence of the clinic's programs, there has been reduced reliance on emergency rooms among the homeless youth, and there has been increased training of clinic-based resident and volunteer physicians.

WA-7

Partners
LHD, L-GOV, SHD, S-GOV, MDPRAC, HOSP, CLIN, LAB/RX, ARC, RES, MEDSOC, SCHL, MEDIA, C-OTH

Synergies
1a, 1c, 3a, 4b, 5a, 5b, 6b-5, 6b-6
Structural Foundations
Coalition, Advisory

Contact
Mamae Teklemariam
Community House Calls
Program
Harborview Medical Center
325 Ninth Avenue
Box 359977
Seattle, WA 09814
mamae@u.washington.edu

Harborview Community House Calls Program

In response to waves of immigrants from Southeast Asia, East Africa, and Latin America, the Harborview Medical Center established the Community House Calls Program in 1994. In partnership with the University of Washington Medical Center, the Cross Cultural Health Care Program, the state health department, county public schools, state social services, and local community associations, the program provides cultural mediators who help patients negotiate the health and social services systems. The program provides interpretation, case management, community health education, cultural advocacy, cultural training for health care providers, and access to the national on-line EthnoMed database. Program partners and their clients have received a number of measurable benefits as a result of being part of Community House Calls Program: increased access to primary care services; a reduction in risk factors; improved clinical outcomes; greater rates of state managed care enrollment by target populations; enhanced cultural competency among providers; and increased patient and provider satisfaction. A recent partnership with the Fred Hutchinson Cancer Center extends the model by addressing cancer risk through educational outreach and evaluation in high-risk immigrant women and their families.

WA-8

Partners
LHD, MDPRAC, HOSP, MEDSOC

Synergies
1c, 2a, 4c, 6a-1, 6a-2

Structural Foundations
Contract

Contact
Bonnie J. Kostelecky,
MS, MPA, RN
Assessment &
Epidemiology
Southwest Washington
Health District
2000 Fort Vancouver Way
P.O. Box 1870
Vancouver, WA 98663
bkostele@swwhd.wa.gov

Vancouver First Steps Clinic
Washington state developed the First Steps program in 1990 as an early access prenatal program which provided outreach, prenatal care, and delivery services to high-risk and poor pregnant women up to 200% of the federal poverty line. In the Southwest Washington Health District, a three-county public health jurisdiction, the First Steps legislation provided an opportunity to resolve persistent problems among the health department, the Southwest Medical Center, and physician groups. The delay in getting early prenatal care was the major problem. Prior to the legislation, the health department would screen for pregnancy and attempt to refer women to private practitioners, many of whom were reluctant to care for higher-risk patients because of the limited reimbursement received. The hospital provided uncompensated care to these women, but also transferred those with the highest risk to Portland hospitals with neonatal intensive care units. As a result of the First Steps program, and its more favorable reimbursement schedule, the health department, hospital, and physician groups developed a clinic as a department of the hospital, which was staffed by nurse-midwives for both the prenatal and delivery components of care. The health department maintained its maternity case management and support services (such as home visits, outreach, and case finding), and worked with high-risk women in the First Steps Clinic. The improved emphasis on early prenatal care, access, and outreach allowed the community to improve its management of high-risk patients and to enroll more women in early prenatal care. Furthermore, the health department and medical center developed a closer team approach to managing the care of the pregnant women since they were working side by side in the community. Since the clinic's inception, the medical center has also added to its own capacity to provide case management and support services, and has expanded the First Steps clinic to include pediatrics and primary care to its clients.

WA-9

Partners
LHD, SHD, FEDHLTH, MDPRAC, MCO, INS, ARC, MEDSOC, VHO, BUS, MEDIA, C-OTH

Synergies
5b, 5d, 6c-1

Structural Foundations
Coalition, Adm/Mgmt

Contact
Frederick P. Rivara, MD
Harborview Injury
Prevention and
Research Center
325 Ninth Avenue, ZX-10
Seattle, WA 98104
fpr@u.washington.edu

Seattle Bike Helmet Campaign

In 1985, Seattle's Harborview Injury Prevention and Research Center led a coalition to encourage bicycle helmet use among school-aged children. Based on survey research data, the campaign organizers identified three barriers to bike helmet use: (1) parents were unaware of the risks of unhelmeted cycling and the consequences of a bike-related head injury; (2) children's helmets often were more expensive than the bikes themselves; and (3) children were unwilling to wear the helmets because it was "uncool." The Harborview planners recruited coalition partners from the medical community, the cycling community, public health, insurers, and the media. Among the partners, the state medical society promoted the campaign to its physician membership and raised money; the Seattle-King County Health Department developed educational materials and organized bicycle rodeos; the Cascade Bike Club provided community promotion and contributed a health educator; Group Health of Puget Sound adopted the bike helmet campaign as a "clinical preventive service"; the PEMCO Insurance Company mailed a flier to all of its subscribers and provided funding for an evaluation; and a local television station sponsored events and provided an outlet for the campaign's message. Using rigorous observational studies, the researchers documented an increase in helmet use in Seattle from 5% in 1987 to 16% one year later, rising to 55% in 1994. The coalition demonstrated other important results as well. The Harborview Research Center and Group Health monitored both the injury rates and the helmet campaign's cost-effectiveness. The rate of head injury in ambulatory care and emergency department settings dropped by two-thirds, and the researchers estimated that a helmet subsidy of $5 to $10 cost less than the medical treatment and hospitalization that would have been incurred in unhelmeted children. Campaign organizers attributed their success to the simplicity of the campaign, the narrowness of its focus (they did not attempt to persuade teens to modify their behavior, only younger children), the broad base of their partnership, the use of mass media, and the lowering of helmet costs.

WA-10

Partners
LHD, L-GOV, MDPRAC, HOSP,
MCO, VHO, BUS, SCHL, FNDN,
C-OTH

Synergies
5a, 5b, 5d, 5e

Structural Foundations
Coalition, Adm/Mgmt

Contact
Bonnie J. Kostelecky,
MS, MPA, RN
Assessment &
Epidemiology
Southwest Washington
Health District
2000 Fort Vancouver Way
P.O. Box 1870
Vancouver, WA 98663
bkostele@swwhd.wa.gov

Clark County Community Choices 2010

In 1992, a small group of community residents protested the addition of several social service programs planned by the local hospital, the health department, and a health plan in their neighborhood in Vancouver. Although some of the drug and mental health services were ultimately sited in the neighborhood, this protest prompted the health department's director, the medical center's executive director, and the vice president for community affairs at the health plan, to reconsider their approach to community health planning. A community partnership group, Community Choices 2010 (CC 2010), was formed. CC 2010 was composed of residents, agency leaders, health care providers, local business people, and representatives from such governmental entities as the school district, the sheriff's department, the transportation department, and the economic development agency. The group's goals were to evaluate the health of their community and to prioritize its health needs. After a year-long assessment process, the community partnership settled on six "upstream" domains in which to intervene: youth and families, economic opportunity, access to health and social services, health and safety practices, positive community norms, and education. The implementation of these prioritized strategies evolved into a Healthy Communities project, which garnered the financial support of the Southwest Washington Medical Center and Kaiser Permanente. The hospital and health plan each contributes $50,000 annually to CC 2010, which organized itself as an affiliate of the Vancouver Chamber of Commerce. Strategies implemented by the group include mentoring programs for young men and teenage boys using clergy and police officers, anti-violence campaigns disseminated in the workplace, and efforts to promote affordable housing, among others. The group holds public forums, and its publishes community report cards and assessment reports that are developed and produced through the work of its partners, including the health department's Division of Assessment and Epidemiology. The group's strategy is to use assessment and advocacy, rather than governmental regulation, to promote voluntary action among community members and agencies.

WA-11

Partners
LHD, HOSP, MCO, SOM, SPH,
U-OTH, VHO, C-OTH

Synergies
5b, 5d, 6c-2

Structural Foundations
Coalition, Adm/Mgmt

Contact
See citation

Seattle Minority Youth Health Project

Working with a five-year grant from NIH, a partnership of Seattle and King County agencies and providers attempted to address minority youth health problems. The partnership included the University of Washington Schools of Social Work, Medicine, and Public Health and Community Medicine; the Minority Health Coalition; the Center for Health Studies and Health Promotion at Group Health of Puget Sound; the Seattle-King County Health Department; and the Harborview Medical Center. The partners received $3.5 million to target preventable health problems among 10- to 14-year-old African-Americans, Asian-Americans, Pacific Islanders, Latinos, and Native Americans. The group's strategy involved identifying four related areas—interpersonal youth violence, adolescent pregnancy, STDs, and substance abuse—and then selecting five neighborhoods as "cases" for interventions and matched neighborhoods as "controls." Initiatives involved community education and health promotion campaigns, capacity-building, and leadership development. Despite the experience and expertise of the partners, the group's efforts foundered over several issues: some members of the minority communities resisted the notion of being research subjects; communication among the participating partners was not clear enough regarding respective roles and responsibilities; and the community was not engaged sufficiently as an equal partner with the researchers and policy experts.

Knight, W. 1996. *Improving the public's health: collaborations between public health departments and managed care organizations.* Washington, DC: The Joint Council of Governmental Public Health Agencies.

WA-12

Partners
LHD, SHD, S-GOV, FEDHLTH,
HOSP, FNDN

Synergies
1b, 1c, 2a

Structural Foundations
Coalition, Contract,
Adm/Mgmt, Advisory

Lincoln County Public Health Coalition

When the state of Washington passed its Health Care Reform legislation in 1993 the intent was to develop universal access to health care, a uniform set of health benefits, portability of coverage, small business subsidies for employee coverage, and Medicaid managed care. Medicaid eligibility for children up to 18 was expanded to include families up to 200% of the federal poverty line. In addition, the legislation called for performance-based funding of core public health functions. The health reform prompted the principal health care institutions in rural Lincoln County, in the state's north-

Contact
Diane Martin
Lincoln County Public
Health Coalition
P.O. Box 1207
90 Nichols Street
Davenport, WA 99122
dmartin@co.lincoln.wa.us

eastern corner, to begin considering how they might work together. The two hospitals, both tax-supported, had traditionally been business competitors, but both had seen revenues drop precipitously. The local health department had likewise suffered federal and state cutbacks. The directors of the three institutions hired an accountant and lawyer to provide recommendations, and the result was an interlocal agreement which provided for shared administrative, personnel, and capital costs, as well as linked boards, committees, and advisory structures. The partners received funding for their initial planning from a Rural Health Systems development grant, then from a $225,000 Federal Rural Outreach grant, and they received $135,000 to implement their strategies as a Community Care Network. Although much of the state's reform legislation was repealed in 1995, the coalition continued. The coalition implemented an "800" information/ referral line, established a centralized data management system, and used a mobile clinic for outreach, providing immunization, nutrition, and Medicaid enrollment services throughout the county. As managed care companies continue to dominate the local marketplace, the coalition has also begun to explore ways of working with local clinics to meet the requirements of managed care plans.

WA-13
Partners
LHD, FEDHLTH, MCO, FNDN

Synergies
3a, 3c, 4a, 4c

Structural Foundations
Coalition, Contract

Contact
Angela Salazar
Center for
Health Promotion
Group Health Cooperative
of Puget Sound
1730 Minor Avenue
Suite 1520
Seattle, WA 98101
salazara@ghc.org

Seattle Immunization Registry
In 1991, the CDC funded five sites across the country, including Group Health of Puget Sound, to develop electronic registries for tracking adverse events resulting from immunizations. When several local health departments in the Seattle area wanted to develop a regional immunization database, Group Health agreed to participate in the exchange of immunization data with the local immunization registry. Using funding from The Robert Wood Johnson Foundation All Kids Count program, the health departments developed a registry and a "reminder" system that generates letters to parents in one of 14 languages. Since Group Health covers approximately 40–50% of the population in the Seattle area, its contribution of over one million records to the regional database quickly populated the start-up registry.

WA-14

Partners
LHD, L-GOV, S-GOV, MDPRAC, HOSP, CLIN, MCO, VHO, BUS, SCHL, RELIG, MEDIA, FNDN, C-OTH

Synergies
5b, 5d

Structural Foundations
Coalition

Contact
P.J. Watters
Center for
Health Promotion
Group Health Northwest
5615 West Sunset Highway
Spokane, WA 99224
pjwatter@ghnw.ghc.org

Spokane Teen Pregnancy Prevention Coalition

A local MCO, Group Health Northwest, has participated in a variety of programs to reduce teen pregnancy in the Spokane area, including participation in the Teen Pregnancy Prevention Coalition. As a Coalition member, the MCO interviewed teens, compiled a resource guide, and developed a report on the reasons for and the impact of teen pregnancy in the community. Group Health Northwest also initiated several community-based programs, including a screening tool to identify high-risk teenagers; a summertime evening sports physical program; a pediatric case management program; and an outreach program to educate teenagers about lifestyle choices. All programs were available to both members and nonmembers of the health plan.

WA-15

Partners
LHD, L-GOV, MDPRAC, HOSP

Synergies
5c

Structural Foundations
Informal

Contact
Karen Steingart, MD, MPH
Southwest Washington
Health District
2000 Fort Vancouver Way
P.O. Box 1870
Vancouver, WA 98663

HIV/AIDS Policy in Southwest Washington

Public health officials at the Southwest Washington Health District were faced with a particularly difficult case in the early 1990s. It was apparent that there was an HIV-infected individual in the community who was purposefully and maliciously transmitting the virus to unwitting individuals through sexual contact and needle-sharing. He was unwilling to change his behavior. The people he had infected were unwilling to cooperate with prosecutors interested in pursuing a criminal case against him. A single local physician who was caring for the "index" case as well as for his infected contacts worked with the local health department to identify strategies to prevent further infections. They also worked with policymakers to modify public health reporting laws to allow for criminal prosecution within the state, and to allow local health jurisdictions and physicians to share needed information with their local justice systems.

WA-16

Partners
LHD, HOSP, SOM, RES

Synergies
2c, 6b-4

Structural Foundations
Contract

Clark County Medical Residency Program

In the early 1990s, Clark County was designated as a health professional shortage area. Although the local hospital was able to recruit 15 new physicians to the area each year, as many as 20 physicians moved out. The shortage was acutely felt by the local health department since their public health clinics were treating an ever-increasing number of uninsured patients and individuals who did not

Contact
Marilyn Darr, MD
Family Practice
Residency Program
Southwest Washington
Health District
8716 E. Mill Plain
Boulevard
Vancouver, WA 98663

WA-17
Partners
LHD, L-GOV, HOSP, CLIN,
LAB/RX, SCHL, FNDN

Synergies
1b, 1c

Structural Foundations
Coalition, Contract,
Adm/Mgmt

Contact
See citation

have adequate access to primary care. The local medical center was suffering because it was unable to attract enough physicians or to fill its beds without an adequate physician base. The health department and medical center first strategized about developing a community health clinic, but no state or federal funds materialized. Their solution was to approach the University of Washington in Seattle and apply to be a medical residency program. Neither of the agencies could have supported such a program on its own, but together they were able to contribute sufficient financing, space, and academic resources to sustain a family practice resident.

Seattle Central Area Health Care Center
The Central Area of Seattle has many of the health and social problems associated with an urban community—high rates of poverty, high hospitalization rates for virtually all causes of disease and a disproportionate amount of violence, drug abuse, and mental health problems. Opened in the spring of 1995, the Central Area Health Care Center was created to address health problems in the community by co-locating the services of Odessa Brown Children's Clinic, Carolyn Downs Family Medical Center, and the Seattle-King County Department of Public Health. Realizing that co-location was not enough, the original partners in the Center began developing a vision for a more collaborative and coordinated system of care (as part of a CCN demonstration partnership funded by the W.K. Kellogg Foundation), bringing Garfield High School and its on-site teen health center into the partnership. Current initiatives include efforts to expand adolescent health services, to create a Family Support Center for parenting education and other support programs, and to improve disease management of asthma in clinic and home settings. Each of the partners has independent relationships with a wide variety of social and health service providers, but the partnership provides an opportunity for increased coordination among the service providers of the area.

Bogue, R and Hall, Jr, CH, eds. 1997. *Health networks innovations: how 20 communities are improving their system through collaboration.* Chicago: American Hospital Publishing, Inc.

[WI] WISCONSIN

WI-1

Partners
LHD, MDPRAC, MEDSOC, FNDN

Synergies
3a, 4a, 4c

Structural Foundations
Contract, Advisory

Contact
Betsy Adrian, MED, MPH
Medical Society of
Milwaukee County
1126 S. 70th Street
Suite S-507
Milwaukee, WI 53214
betsy@district-1.org

**Milwaukee Connect & Protect
Immunization Campaign**

In 1996, the City of Milwaukee Health Department approached the county medical society and the Cream City Medical Society (the National Medical Association's local affiliate) to help develop an interactive immunization registry. Seven Milwaukee physicians, including the health department medical director and a group of private pediatricians and family practitioners, formed the Connect & Protect Work Group. The doctors served as a focus group for the registry's software designers, providing feedback on the needs of practicing physicians (such as accurate information, quick response from the database, and a user-friendly interface) and the ways in which the registry is likely to be used in a medical practice (for example, which support staff would utilize the database, what additional software would be useful, and how a database might be integrated into practice operations). The Work Group was also involved in a project to equip a select group of private physicians in Milwaukee with the necessary tools, training, and technical support to access the registry. Physicians selected for this program—those serving children at highest risk for not being immunized—received a "package," including all necessary hardware and software to connect to the registry, training in the use of the registry for themselves and their office staff, and ongoing technical support. To make the system even more attractive, the software for the registry came with clinic management and record-keeping tools. Data in the system is provided through birth certificates, physician entries, reimbursement claims, and schools. Medical practitioners obtain a particular child's immunization history through searches based on name and date of birth. In addition, the Wisconsin Health Information Network, an electronic conduit for claims from physicians to insurance companies, will include the registry as a "menu item" on its network.

WI-2

Partners
LHD, L-GOV, HOSP, CLIN, SOM,
VHO, FNDN, C-OTH

South Madison Health and Family Center

Despite an idyllic dairyland setting and a well-deserved reputation as one of the best cities in which to live, Madison was plagued by intractable health access problems among impoverished city residents. In 1992, the Madison Public Health Depart-

Synergies
1b, 2c, 6b-4

Structural Foundations
Adm/Mgmt

Contact
Gay M. Gross, MPA
Madison Department
of Public Health
210 Martin Luther
King Boulevard
Room 507
Madison, WI 53709
ggross@ci.madison.wi.us

ment spearheaded the development of the South Madison Health and Family Center. This "one stop center" for primary health, public health, and family support services brought together the city and county health departments, a neighborhood health center, Planned Parenthood, Head Start, a city library, and Family Enhancement, which is a parenting and family resource center. The seven independent agencies cooperatively manage the Center, which was recognized by the W.K. Kellogg Foundation as a CCN finalist partnership. As a group, they developed governance structures for providers and consumers; a coordination office providing centralized outreach, benefits counseling, transportation, translation, building management, and collaboration staffing; and interdisciplinary teams composed of staff from the different agencies. The University of Wisconsin academic health center donated physicians to staff the clinic, administrative personnel to help with construction and strategic planning, and financial assistance to help the clinic meet its operating expenses. Although the Center was designed to anchor health and social services for a low-income neighborhood, it has also attracted a number of uninsured patients from around the county and beyond. Approximately one-third of the medical clinic's patients are Spanish-speaking; no other clinic in the area—which is on the northern stream of the Mexican migrant farm worker circuit—provides Spanish translation services to its clients.

WI-3
Partners
LHD, SHD, S-GOV, FEDOTH,
MDPRAC, HOSP, LAB/RX, SOM,
VHO, SCHL, RELIG, MEDIA

Synergies
2a

Structural Foundations
Adm/Mgmt

Contact
Jan Schneider, MA
Wisconsin State Laboratory
of Hygiene
465 Henry Mall
Madison, WI 53706
jmschne4@facstaff.wisc.edu

GuardCare Program in Rural Wisconsin

The 13th Medical/Dental Detachment (MEDD) of the Wisconsin Army National Guard was one of nine National Guard units in the country to participate in the GuardCare program in 1996. The Madison-based unit provided free medical and dental services to nearly 13,000 adults and children at a series of clinics in four medically underserved counties in central Wisconsin. The Wisconsin State Laboratory of Hygiene and local hospitals in the four counties provided laboratory testing for the event and assured that the lab results were returned to patients in a coordinated manner. The Wisconsin Department of Health and Social Services and each local county health department helped with implementation and local involvement of volunteer community organizations. National Guard public affairs specialists conducted an extensive public information campaign to advertise clinic dates and provide clinic-day news coverage. Both state and local public health agencies gained experience in coordinating the multiagency effort at health care delivery, and patients, usually served at local public health agencies and community providers, had increased access to medical services. More GuardCare events were held in the summer of 1997, and four clinic events are scheduled for 1998.

WI-4
Partners
LHD, SHD, S-GOV, FEDHLTH, MDPRAC, HOSP, CLIN, MCO, U-OTH, MEDSOC, PHASSN, PROFASSN, VHO, FNDN, C-OTH

Synergies
4c, 5a, 5b, 5d, 6b-6

Structural Foundations
Coalition, Contract, Adm/Mgmt

Contact
Lisa Monagle
Ambulatory Women's
Health Services
Aurora Health Care
950 N. 12th Street
Milwaukee, WI 53201

Milwaukee Common Ground Project
To address problems with Medicaid managed care, in 1993 a Milwaukee hospital convened a small planning group from the public health sector, hospitals, MCOs, and advocacy organizations to develop new strategies of addressing maternal and child health problems. The group created the Milwaukee Common Ground Project to focus on reducing infant mortality and improving responsiveness of MCOs to the needs of Medicaid-eligible women and children. As a result of a Common Ground conference, a number of collaborative projects emerged: the largest Medicaid MCO in the city collaborated with a federally funded women and infants project to conduct Health Information Parties in inner-city neighborhoods; the city health department established a process that incorporated input and insights from community groups and residents on an infant mortality review project; and one of the city's largest MCOs funded a CBO to conduct a health education campaign on prenatal care. In the last, the MCO justified the cost of sponsorship by determining that it could recover its investment in the health education campaign by avoiding the birth of just one more baby who required intensive care. Many of the original members of the Common Ground Project decided not to continue participating in 1997 when it became clear that certain longstanding issues—such as the inherent imbalance between large institutions and small, minority-run community organizations—required a different forum in which to address matters of race and power.

WI-5
Partners
LHD, SHD, MDPRAC, HOSP, SPH, VHO, BUS, SCHL

La Crosse Health Initiative 2000 and Tobacco-Free Coalition
Responding to the Wisconsin Public Health Agenda for the Year 2000, the CEOs of two major medical centers and hospitals in La Crosse County

Synergies
5b, 5c, 5d

Structural Foundations
Coalition

Contact
Doug Mormann
La Crosse County
Health Department
300 4th Street North
La Crosse, WI 54601
dmormann@compuserve.com

convened a meeting with the director of the local health department and a faculty member of the University of Wisconsin to discuss areas of possible collaboration on community health initiatives. The group chose to focus on reducing disease and illness associated with tobacco use, then took the next step of involving the staffs of their organizations, voluntary health organizations, such as the American Cancer Society and the American Heart Association, and local businesses. The state health department provided the Coalition with information on steps that the community could take to create a tobacco-free environment. The Coalition has worked to educate young people, to stop the sale of tobacco to minors, and to encourage health professionals to become more active in addressing tobacco as a health hazard. It has also campaigned to establish smoke-free restaurants in the area, first with a local ordinance (which did not pass) and then with a voluntary system that provided promotional support to restaurants that went smoke-free. No legislative mandate or large-scale funding drove this collaboration, although small amounts of federal, state, and local funding assisted with the coordination of the Coalition's activities, coupled with funding from the health care institutions.

WI-6
Partners
HOSP, SOM, MEDSOC, VHO, FNDN

Synergies
2a

Structural Foundations
Informal

Contact
Barbara Lindsay, MSW
Human Resources
The Salvation Army
630 East Washington Avenue
Madison, WI 53703

Madison Clinic for the Homeless

Realizing that the homeless families served at their shelter often lacked access to medical care, a group of social workers from the Salvation Army in Madison contacted the University of Wisconsin Medical Center for assistance. In 1990, the social workers, shelter staff, and volunteers organized a free clinic at which University of Wisconsin physicians and medical students provided medical assessment, treatment, referral and education to the homeless, *pro bono*. The physicians have supported this project since it exposes their medical students to low-income patients and provides a needed community service. Donations from a student medical society and a local foundation assist the Salvation Army to purchase consumable medical supplies and other small equipment.

WI-7
Partners
LHD, L-GOV, MDPRAC, HOSP, CLIN, MCO, INS, SOM, RES, U-OTH, VHO, BUS, SCHL, FNDN, C-OTH

Dane County Coalition for Neighborhood Child Health

In 1993, two Dane County HMOs, the local health department, and the Madison Metropolitan School District joined together to provide free physical

Synergies
1c, 2a, 3b, 4b, 4c, 5b

Structural Foundations
Coalition, Adm/Mgmt

Contact
Carmella Glover, RN, MS
Health Management
Group Health Cooperative
HMO of South Central
Wisconsin
8202 Excelsior Drive
P.O. Box 44971
Madison, WI 53744

WI-8
Partners
LHD, SHD, MDPRAC, HOSP, CLIN,
MCO, AHC

Synergies
5a, 5d, 6a-4, 6b-6

Structural Foundations
Contract

Contact
Helen H. Schauffler, PhD
School of Public Health
University of California
at Berkeley
406 Warren Hall
Berkeley, CA 94720
helenhs@uclink2.berkeley.
edu

exams and screenings to area children in low-income neighborhoods. In short order, the Dane County Coalition for Neighborhood Child Health expanded to include other area health plans, hospitals, physician groups, parents' councils, medical and nursing students, and local businesses, among others. Beginning in the spring and continuing through the fall, the Coalition runs free one-day clinics in six different neighborhoods, using volunteer health care and community providers. At each clinic, children are provided with medical and dental assessments, immunizations, diagnostic blood work, and clinical preventive screening services. A common medical record is used, which is then forwarded to the child's health care provider, or to the local community health center, where the uninsured children are referred for care. "Family advocates," community liaisons fluent in Hmong or Spanish, help the families navigate the process and work with the nurse-practitioner who coordinates the clinics to assure that children receive the appropriate follow-up care. The clinics piggyback on other community efforts as well, including a Coats for Kids campaign that uses one clinic to distribute clothing to children in need, immunization campaigns, or school readiness initiatives. Supported by the United Way, the health care community, and local businesses, the Coalition also provides dinner at every clinic for all who attend.

State Seminars on Managed Care
In light of Wisconsin's application for a 1915(b) waiver to expand its Medicaid managed care program to 85% of all eligible enrollees by 1997, the state health department entered into a partnership with the University of Wisconsin to convene a series of seminars involving public and private providers and managed care organizations. To facilitate discussion about the evolving roles of public health, private providers, and managed care organizations, the group focused on tobacco in order to consider how to set priorities and define activities in a comprehensive, coordinated fashion. The state and the university also organized activities around the oversight and dissemination of individual HMO performance, supporting community health assessments, and the integration of health promotion activities into Medicaid managed care practice.

Schauffler, HH, Hennessey, M, Neiger, B. 1997. *Health promotion and managed care.* Report prepared for the Association of State and Territorial Directors of Health Promotion and Public Health Education. Washington, DC.

[WV] WEST VIRGINIA

WV-1

Partners
LHD, SHD, S-GOV, FEDHLTH, MDPRAC, HOSP, CLIN, U-OTH

Synergies
1c, 2a, 2b, 6a-1, 6a-4, 6a-5

Structural Foundations
Coalition

Contact
Mark Vestich
Administration
Bluefield Regional
Medical Center
500 Cherry Street
Bluefield, WV 24701
mvest@aol.com

Southern Virginias Rural Health Network

After release of a statewide study in 1991, the West Virginia Health Care Planning Commission, an advisory committee to the Governor, reported on major roadblocks to the improvement of the health status of West Virginians. The Commission found that health services of all types were fragmented, there was no logical sequence of care in the region, and that preventive, educational, and follow-up treatment measures were inadequate. To address these problems, nonprofit providers in Southern West Virginia, including two major medical centers, three county health departments, rural health clinics, home health and behavioral health agencies, and EMS are collaborating to develop a vertically integrated health services network for their rural catchment area. The intent of the Southern Virginias Rural Health Network is to improve efficiency, reduce duplication of services, and operate under local control based on assessed community needs. A secondary goal is to prepare providers to compete in a managed care environment.

[WY] WYOMING

WY-1

Partners
LHD, L-GOV, HOSP, SCHL, FNDN, C-OTH

Synergies
5a, 5b, 5d, 5e, 6b-6

Structural Foundations
Coalition, Advisory

Contact
Emily Quarterman
Healthier Communities
Wyoming Health
Resources Network, Inc.
P.O. Box 2277
Casper, WY 82602
emquart@trib.com

Natrona County Health Care Advisory Council

As the first step to a healthy communities process, the Casper City Council conducted citywide meetings in 1991 that identified access to health care, job creation, and educational opportunities as key areas of local concern. Next, an advisory committee, with representatives from the City of Casper/Natrona health department, the Wyoming Medical Center, three local foundations, schools, local government, human services, and senior citizen services, was established with a charge of improving the health care system through community involvement and consideration of the social determinants of health. Some changes in organization and mission have occurred, and the group is now called the Natrona County Health Care Advisory Council. The Council was absorbed into the Natrona County Board of Health (though no public funding was attached), but it continues to be coordinated by the Wyoming Medical Center Foundation, an original partner in the planning process. The Council brings the medical center, its foundation, and the city's social and public health services agencies together as partners. During its tenure, this body has conducted community health assessments, which identified leading causes of death and disability in the area and helped establish health priorities, developed targeted health education programs, and served as a resource to connect community medical and social service providers. The Council also fosters professional interaction among the groups represented, which has led to collaboration among members outside the bounds of the Council. For example, SAFE KIDS of Central Wyoming, a coalition that addresses youth risk-taking behaviors, was formed on the basis of one community health assessment. One of its initiatives, Healthy Communities, Healthy Youth, focuses on health and behavioral problems of teens, including substance abuse, violence, and suicide.

Collaborations Involving Multistate Regions

MST-1

Partners
SHD, S-GOV, HOSP, SPH, MEDSOC, PROFASSN

Synergies
3a, 6b-5

Structural Foundations
Coalition

Contact
Michael Meit
National Association of County and City Health Officials
1100 17th Street, N.W.
2nd Floor
Washington, DC 20036
mmeit@naccho.org

Multistate Satellite Broadcast of AZT Guidelines for Pregnant Women

In 1992, when the drug AZT was shown to reduce perinatal HIV transmission, there was an immediate need to provide detailed information to physicians and other clinicians on the counseling and testing of pregnant women, and the treatment of those who were HIV-infected. In Pennsylvania, the state health department's Bureau of HIV/AIDS worked with the Pennsylvania AIDS Education and Training Center, and the schools of public health at Columbia University and University of Pittsburgh, to organize a satellite teleconference entitled "HIV and Pregnancy: Counseling, Testing, and the Use of AZT." The state health department enlisted the help of nine professional organizations, including statewide chapters of pediatricians, obstetrician/gynecologists, nurses, social workers, the medical society, the hospital association, and osteopaths, to publicize the program and encourage their members' attendance. The program was simulcast to nearly 1,500 registrants across four states (PA, NY, NJ, MD), and in Pennsylvania alone there were 73 viewing sites, half of which were at hospitals.

MST-2

Partners
LHD, SHD, MDPRAC, HOSP, CLIN, MCO, SOM, SPH, ARC, AHC, MEDSOC, PHASSN, PROFASSN, MEDIA, FNDN

Synergies
6b-6

Structural Foundations
Coalition

Contact
Gordon H. DeFriese, PhD
North Carolina
Institute of Medicine
725 Airport Road
Chapel Hill, NC 27514
gordon_defriese@unc.edu

North and South Carolina Conference on Medicine and Public Health

The North Carolina Institute of Medicine, in partnership with the medical associations, the hospital associations, the public health associations, the state health agencies, and the managed care associations of both North and South Carolina, as well as the states' six schools of medicine and two schools of public health, hosted a two-day interstate conference in October 1997, with funding from The Robert Wood Johnson Foundation. The first interstate conference of its kind, it explored the possibilities of medicine and public health collaborations in the region. Bringing these diverse health and medical professionals together, the conference organizers outlined areas where medicine and public health intersect and identified potential interdisciplinary projects. The conference was focused on the opportunities and challenges posed by the changing health system and managed care organizations as well as efforts at vertical integration of health services. In the spring of 1998, a second conference was being planned.

MST-3

Partners
LHD, SHD, MCO, VHO, BUS, SCHL

Synergies
5b, 5d, 6b-6

Structural Foundations
Coalition, Adm/Mgmt, Advisory

Contact
Fred Nebel
Community Relations
Kaiser Permanente
Mid-Atlantic States Region
2101 East Jefferson Street
Box 6122
Rockville, MD 20849

Kaiser Permanente Building Hope Initiative

In 1994, the nonprofit Kaiser Permanente HMO approached local public health and school officials in the Baltimore and Washington, DC, metropolitan areas, who identified youth violence as one of their most pressing concerns. In response, Kaiser Permanente developed the Building Hope initiative, which was created to attract regional interest from public and private organizations regarding youth violence. The multiyear initiative received $140,000 from 23 organizations in the area in its first year, with similar support in the following two years, and launched a series of projects: an annual conference showcasing model programs and best practices; a grants program supporting local grassroots efforts, such as mentoring, after-school, and intergenerational programs; and an interactive, educational, live theater presentation called RAVES (Real Alternative to Violence for Every Student), which demonstrates the use of conflict resolution tools to children ages 10–11. The managed care organization has committed to lead the initiative, and to contribute time, skills, and finances over a three- to five-year period. Community participants, drawn from local business, educational, and nonprofit organizations, serve on both the advisory and grants committees.

Collaborations at the National Level

NAT-1
Partners
FEDHLTH, ARC, PROFASSN, BUS

Synergies
3c, 4b, 6a-4, 6b-5, 6b-6

Structural Foundations
Coalition

Contact
Lisbeth Stark
The Center for Clinical
Quality Evaluation
1140 Connecticut Avenue,
NW
Suite 1010
Washington, DC 20036
lstark@ccqe.com

Center for Clinical Quality Evaluation Invitational Workshop on Collaboration

Access to good data is necessary for quality improvement projects, which, in turn, lead to better health practices at the local level. Federal peer review/quality improvement organizations (QIOs) often have access only to public data through state Medicare and Medicaid programs, although other groups, such as businesses, have private employee health data. In January 1997, the Center for Clinical Quality Evaluation hosted a workshop, funded by the Agency for Health Care Policy and Research, to encourage business coalitions and QIOs to work collaboratively on projects, focusing on the potential for data-sharing. In addition, representatives from medical specialty societies, research organizations, and managed care companies were on hand to discuss their perspectives. The structure of the workshop—first presenting a range of collaborative projects, then moving to small sessions, which prompted discussion between the groups—spurred new relationships among the participants. Dialogue between these groups had not existed before the meeting, but within a short time, the business coalitions and QIOs found common ground for several specific projects, including a prenatal improvement project starting in Dallas/Ft. Worth, TX, and a quality improvement study on utilization of right heart catherization in Wisconsin.

NAT-2
Partners
MEDSOC, PHASSN, PROFASSN

Synergies
6a-1, 6a-3, 6a-4, 6a-6, 6b-6

Structural Foundations
Coalition, Advisory,
Intraorg

Contact
F. Douglas Scutchfield,
MD, MPH
The University of Kentucky
Medical Center
121 Washington Avenue
CAPH Building, Room 109
Lexington, KY 40536
scutch@pop.uky.edu

AMA Section Council on Preventive Medicine

In 1975, the American Medical Association opened its policy-making body, the House of Delegates, to representatives of national medical specialty organizations. Several of these organizations, which had delegate status—including the American College of Preventive Medicine, the American Association of Public Health Physicians, the American College of Occupational and Environmental Medicine, and the Aerospace Medical Association—joined to form the Section Council on Preventive Medicine to represent the interests and values of prevention and public health in AMA's policy debates. Over time, the Council has expanded to include the American Society of Addiction Medicine, the American College of Legal Medicine, the American Society of Quality Assurance Physicians, the American Society of Insurance Physicians, and representatives of the Resident and Young Physician sections. Organizationally, the Section Council has provided both a forum and an outlet for advancing discussion of prevention and public health among colleagues more accustomed to clinical, biomedical approaches; has led the effort to seat representatives from national public health associations (NACCHO, ASTHO, and APHA) as observers in the House of Delegates; and has worked to garner support for prevention-oriented health policies. In one recent AMA policy decision regarding graduate medical education, which had "cut out" support for preventive medicine as specialty education, the Council was able to employ its clout within the House of Delegates to restore its support with a single phone call.

NAT-3
Partners
FEDHLTH, MEDSOC, PROFASSN

Synergies
3a, 3c, 6a-4, 6b-5, 6b-6

Structural Foundations
Contract

Contact
Kathleen A. Carey, MS
Division of Cancer
Prevention and Control
Centers for Disease
Control and Prevention
4770 Buford Highway, NE
Mailstop K64
Atlanta, GA 30341
kac@ccdcpc1.em.cdc.gov

CDC and Radiologists Develop Mammography Standards

In October 1990, the CDC entered into a cooperative agreement with the American College of Radiology (ACR) to assess and improve the quality of mammography in the United States. This funding opportunity was the result of a broader legislative mandate, The Breast and Cervical Cancer Mortality Prevention Act of 1990, which established CDC's National Breast and Cervical Cancer Early Detection Program. Under the agreement, the ACR conducted a nationwide quality assurance program on mammography with broad representation from other national medical organizations, state and federal agencies, and industry. The project encompassed a broad professional education effort, and research focused on improving the quality of mammography images. In addition, this cooperative agreement led to the publication of technical documents on equipment standards and professional practices relevant to mammography quality assurance. The team approach adopted by the ACR—which involved recruiting national organizations and recognized experts, as well as practicing professionals—led to the willingness of radiology technicians, medical physicists, radiology residents, and practicing radiologists to adopt the team's educational curricula and practice standards.

NAT-4
Partners
SHD, FEDHLTH, SOM, MEDSOC

Breast and Cervical Cancer Professional Education Material

In 1992, CDC began funding cooperative agreements through their National Breast and Cervical Cancer Early Detection Program. Their strategy

Synergies
3a, 6b-5

Structural Foundations
Contract

Contact
Annie Voigt, CPNP, MPH
Division of Cancer
Prevention and Control
Centers for Disease
Control and Prevention
4770 Buford Highway, NE
Mailstop K64
Atlanta, GA 30341

was to work with professional organizations representing physicians, nurses, and physician assistants in order to support more effective screening and treatment programs. The groups funded by the CDC included the American College of Physicians, the National Medical Association, the American Nurses Association, the American Academy of Physician Assistants, the Duke University School of Medicine, and the American Medical Women's Association (AMWA). Each of the professional organizations chose a slightly different approach to reach their membership with technical information and skills training in early detection of breast and cervical cancer . One chose to implement a study on the effectiveness of office reminder systems, another developed a physicians' clinical notebook to provide current information to its membership. AMWA developed an eight-hour educational program for their members: four hours on breast cancer and four hours on cervical cancer. Two well-known AMWA members developed the text for each of the sections, and AMWA hired a project officer to coordinate the efforts, put the technical material into a training manual, and coordinate the logistics of training courses. Although AMWA did not reach as many of its professional organization members as intended, the training manual was so well received that many state health departments have incorporated the training manual into their professional education programs. Consequently, the training material has reached far more health professionals than originally targeted.

NAT-5
Partners
SHD, FEDHLTH, FEDOTH, U-OTH, MEDSOC, VHO, BUS, LABR, SCHL, MEDIA, C-OTH

Synergies
3a, 5b, 5d

Structural Foundations
Contract, Advisory

Joint Skin Cancer Prevention Campaign
In 1994, the CDC received a small federal appropriation to launch skin cancer prevention efforts. After a careful review of the literature and consultation with experts in dermatology, public health, and education, the decision was made to focus on primary prevention. The CDC entered into a cooperative agreement with the American Academy of Dermatology (AAD), with the immediate objective of educating the American public to the dangers of overexposure to ultraviolet (UV) radiation, its relationship to skin cancer, and ways to protect adults and children from harmful solar radiation. The group's secondary objective was to increase the ability of adults to recognize potentially dangerous skin lesions, particularly melanomas, and generally achieve earlier diagnosis and treatment of the skin

Contact
Barbara A. Reilley, RN, PhD
Division of Cancer
Prevention and Control
Centers for Disease
Control and Prevention
4770 Buford Highway, NE
Mailstop K-52
Atlanta, GA 30241
byr6@cdc.gov

cancers. Together, the CDC and the AAD conducted forums, which provided direction and sought input from experts in health, media, industry, and education in order to set an agenda for sun protection education for young children and their parents and caregivers. The CDC provided scientific and programmatic technical assistance and helped maneuver the federal bureaucracy, and the Academy provided dermatological expertise, an avenue to reach community-based dermatologists, and an authoritative voice in communicating a broad public health promotion message related to skin care.

NAT-6
Partners
SHD, S-GOV, FEDHLTH, MDPRAC,
MEDSOC

Synergies
3a, 6a-1, 6b-5

Structural Foundations
Coalition, Contract,
Advisory

Contact
Lisa Smith, MS
The American College of
Obstretricians and
Gynecologists
409 12th Street, S.W.
P.O. Box 96920
Washington, DC 20090
lsmith@acog.com

ACOG-MCH Bureau Providers'
Partnership Project
Access to health care for low-income women is a problem due in part to a shortage of physicians willing to participate in publicly funded health programs. In 1991, the American College of Obstetricians and Gynecologists (ACOG) entered into a collaborative agreement with the Maternal and Child Health (MCH) Bureau—both nationally and at the state level—to improve provider participation in publicly funded health care programs. Supported in part by an MCH Bureau grant, ACOG has hosted seven Providers' Partnership meetings since 1994. These regional meetings have provided a platform for discussion about collaboration, often bringing together OB/GYN medical providers and MCH Bureau and Medicaid directors who had never met before. All of the meetings have resulted in the identification of critical issues around women's health in each state along with potential collaborative solutions. (DE-1, NJ-2, and VA-3 describe specific activities that were prompted by the meetings.) On the state level, the success of each project is related to both individual leadership and the state's willingness to implement the proposed project. Organizers of the meetings found that if a leader for the project was identified at the state level, either formally or informally, it was more likely to succeed. State government commitment to the activity often led to political leverage and adequate funding. The national partners in this collaboration also produced *A State-by-State Inventory of Programs to Improve Access to Women's Health Care: Provider Participation*, which was distributed to ACOG leaders and others to encourage physician involvement in publicly funded health care programs.

NAT-7

Partners
FEDOTH

Synergies
3c, 6a-4

Structural Foundations
Contract, Intraorg

Contact
Itzhak Jacoby, MD
F. Edward Hébert
School of Medicine
Uniformed Services
University of the
Health Sciences
4301 Jones Bridge Road
Bethesda, MD 20814
ijacoby@usuhs.mil

NAT-8

Partners
FEDHLTH, MEDSOC, PROFASSN

Synergies
6a-6

Structural Foundations
Advisory

Contact
Juanita C. Evans
Office of
Adolescent Health
Maternal and
Child Health Bureau
Health Resources and
Services Administration
5600 Fishers Lane
Room 18A-39
Rockville, MD 20857
jevans@hrsa.dhhs.gov

NAT-9

Partners
LHD, L-GOV, SHD, S-GOV,
FEDHLTH, FEDOTH, MDPRAC,
HOSP, CLIN, MCO, LAB/RX, SPH,
U-OTH, PROFASSN, VHO, BUS,
SCHL, RELIG, MEDIA, FNDN,
C-OTH

Department of Defense National Quality Management Program

In its role as a managed care entity assuring the health of uniformed service personnel and their families, the US Department of Defense has created a data analysis and performance measurement system that ranks health outcomes as a function of morbidity, patient functional status, patient satisfaction, and resource utilization, and then analyzes the patient, provider, and system characteristics that influence these health outcomes. Based on this analysis, the Department of Defense National Quality Management Program has developed practice guidelines that can be tailored to specific subpopulations. The Department's objectives are to apply population-level data to clinical care, and to develop decision-support tools useful for managers and physicians.

HRSA Office of Adolescent Health

Since 1996, HRSA's Office of Adolescent Health (OAH), located in the Maternal and Child Health Bureau, has funded a variety of national membership organizations to assist in developing comprehensive health and mental health care services for adolescents. By 1998, OAH had formal working relationships with the National Association of Social Workers, the American Bar Association's Center on Children and the Law, the American Psychological Association, the American Nurses Association, the American Dietetic Association, the National Assembly on School-Based Health Care, and the AMA's Department of Adolescent Health. Each of the organizations assists OAH in developing programming and overseeing implementation and dissemination of national adolescent health strategies. OAH also has formed the National Adolescent Health Workgroup, which is composed of nationally recognized experts in adolescent health and includes youth representation, to advise the agency on its strategies and programs.

HRSA Healthy Start Program

HRSA's Maternal and Child Health Bureau began funding 15 Healthy Start projects in 1991, adding another seven in 1994. Targeted at communities with high infant mortality rates, the Healthy Start program was based on the formation of community consortia to provide comprehensive health and social services, as well as individual and community

Synergies
1b, 1c, 2a, 4b, 4c, 5e, 6a-6

Structural Foundations
Coalition, Contract,
Adm/Mgmt, Advisory

Contact
Thurma McCann Goldman,
MD, MPH
Division of Healthy Start
Health Resources and
Services Administration
5600 Fishers Lane
Room 11A-05
Rockville, MD 20857
tmccann@hrsa.dhhs.gov

development activities. The consortia used a variety of approaches to reduce infant mortality in their communities: making services more accessible by streamlining eligibility processes, developing one-stop "family resource" centers, providing transportation, and facilitating on-site child care; strengthening and linking comprehensive perinatal care services; making self-help programs available to clients, such as nutrition counseling, smoking cessation, and substance abuse counseling; supplying case management services; employing outreach workers; increasing the cultural competency of local providers; providing education, job training, and employment opportunities; and strengthening local leadership, capacity, and resources. The national program is conducting a multisite evaluation of the initial 15 projects, and each grantee is evaluating its own unique interventions.

NAT-10
Partners
LHD, L-GOV, SHD, FEDHLTH,
HOSP, CLIN, AHC, MEDSOC, VHO

Synergies
1a, 1b, 1c, 4c, 5d, 6a-5,
6a-6

Structural Foundations
Coalition

Contact
Joseph Zogby
Division of Maternal,
Infant, Child, and
Adolescent Health
Health Resources and
Services Administration
5600 Fishers Lane
Parklawn Building
Room 18A-39
Rockville, MD 20857
jzogby@hrsa.gov

HRSA Community Integrated Service System Grants

As part of a federal effort to reduce infant mortality and improve the health of mothers and children, the Omnibus Budget Reconciliation Act of 1989 set aside funds from the Maternal and Child Health Service Block Grant (Title V), to support the development and expansion of community integrated service systems, which are public-private partnerships of health-related and other relevant community organizations addressing community-identified health needs (WI-2 is one example). In 1995, $11 million in funding was available for this purpose. As defined by HRSA, the characteristics of an integrated service system include: collaboration among state-level agencies, community-level partnerships, and families; services based upon community-identified needs; cultural diversity; coordinated comprehensive health and social services, accessibility to all pregnant women, children, adolescents, and families, whether served by private or public providers; and assured feedback on system performance and utilization. As envisioned by HRSA, the home-visiting and one-stop service center models are an important care component of these projects. HRSA has funded community organization projects in 62 locations, and has separate contracts for supporting activities, such as local health planning assistance, coalition-building, and conflict resolution.

NAT-11

Partners

LHD, L-GOV, SHD, S-GOV, FEDHLTH, MDPRAC, HOSP, CLIN, SOM, SPH, MEDSOC, BUS, SCHL, RELIG, FNDN

Synergies

1c, 4c, 5d, 6a-1, 6a-6, 6b-6

Structural Foundations

Coalition, Contract, Advisory

Contact

Latricia C. Robertson
Division of Science, Education and Analysis
Maternal and Child Health Bureau
Health Resources and Services Administration
5600 Fishers Lane
Parklawn Building
Room 18A-55
Rockville, MD 20857
lrobertson@hrsa.dhhs.gov

NAT-12

Partners

FEDHLTH, FEDOTH, MCO, INS, MEDSOC, PHASSN, PROFASSN, VHO, BUS, FNDN, C-OTH

Synergies

6a-1, 6a-2, 6a-3, 6a-4, 6a-5, 6a-6

Structural Foundations

Advisory

Contact

Duncan W. Clark, MD
The Medical Society for the County of Kings, Inc.
165 Cadman Plaza East
Brooklyn, NY 11201

Healthy Tomorrows Partnership for Children

Begun in 1989 as a collaboration between HRSA's Maternal and Child Health Bureau and the American Academy of Pediatrics (AAP), the Healthy Tomorrows Partnership for Children funds community-based programs providing preventive and curative services, particularly for vulnerable children and families with limited access to quality health and social services. The program has funded over 97 local projects since its inception, with a five-year funding period. Projects are required to obtain two-thirds of their operating budgets from non-Federal sources after their first year. The types of services and interventions provided by grantees include: (1) delivery of primary care for uninsured children through state Medicaid programs; (2) coordination of services for special health needs; (3) interventions targeted at risk reduction in families; (4) adolescent health promotion programs including reproductive health, prenatal care, and education services; (5) expanded perinatal care and parenting education; and (6) services for special child and family populations. The initiative utilizes AAP's network of health professionals, including 59 state chapters and 53,000 child health experts across the country.

AMA Health Policy Agenda for the American People

In 1982, the AMA initiated the Health Policy Agenda for the American People (HPA), designed to create a framework for collaborative policy-making. Over 170 national medical, public health, business, consumer, and government-based organizations were invited to develop an agenda of issues and action plans that could be pursued by participants individually or collaboratively. Initially, APHA declined to participate because of the "medical" bias in the agenda items, but later participated, filing a minority report to the main HPA report, as did the American Association of Retired Persons (AARP). In phase one (1982–84), participants met in six work groups, based on health care areas (medical science, health professions education, health resources, delivery mechanisms and processes, evaluation assessment and control, and payment for services), and wrote reports that went to a large advisory committee for comment and final acceptance by a 32-member steering committee. In phase two (1984–86), the same groups tackled policy formulation for 41 issues identified as needing further study. The AMA House of Delegates reviewed HPA's Final Report, and nearly all of the recommendations (185 of 195) were accepted, half of which represented new policy for the AMA. In 1988, a publication on how to implement the recommendations at the state and local level was published and distributed. The HPA continued for a few more years as a nonprofit incorporated entity and dissolved in 1990, soon after the death of its president.

NAT-13

Partners
MEDSOC

Synergies
3a, 6b-5

Structural Foundations
Intraorg

Contact
Duncan W. Clark, MD
The Medical Society for the
County of Kings, Inc.
165 Cadman Plaza East
Brooklyn, NY 11221

JAMA Public Health Reporting and Special Issues

Since the 1980s, the *Journal of the American Medical Association* (*JAMA*) has emerged as an important medical vehicle for public health communications. Through its own editorial process, and with support of AMA Officers and Trustees, *JAMA* has come to incorporate a wide array of public health information in a format that is accessible and relevant to practicing physicians. The Journal presents "In Brief" reports regularly from the major governmental public health agencies, namely CDC, HRSA, HCFA, and the FDA. Also, entire issues have been dedicated to health problems that have a strong "public health" component, such as alcoholism, adolescent health, and substance abuse. The public health perspective is incorporated in stand-alone articles, editorials, and commentary on clinically oriented approaches to health problems. *JAMA* also has issued reports and policy statements on preventive medicine and the uninsured that present perspectives from public health and medicine.

NAT-14

Partners
FEDHLTH, SOM, SPH, AHC,
PROFASSN

Synergies
5d, 6b-5

Structural Foundations
Advisory, Intraorg

AAHC Policy Yearbooks

The Association of Academic Health Centers (AAHC) is a multiprofessional organization that regularly publishes policy yearbooks that consider health issues from a variety of perspectives. The 1992 edition of the policy yearbook, *Promoting Health and Preventing Disease*, was overseen by a multidisciplinary editorial advisory board, which also served as the AAHC Task Force on Health Promotion/Disease Prevention. One goal of the policy book, stated in the introduction, is to encourage academic health centers, which house medical and public health professionals, among others, to take action on health promotion and disease prevention

Contact
Denise E. Holmes,
JD, MPH
Association of Academic
Health Centers
1400 Sixteenth Street,
N.W., Suite 720
Washington, DC 20036
dholmes@acadhlthctrs.org

in their communities. The book consists of abstracts from recently published journal articles on topics such as children's health, workplace wellness, cardiovascular disease, and substance abuse, with commentary relevant to academic health centers. Senior administrators and professors from schools of medicine, schools of public health, and research staff from AAHC are among the contributors listed in the book.

Scherl, DJ, Noren, J, and Osterweis, M, eds. 1992. *Promoting health and preventing disease.* Washington, DC: Association of Academic Health Centers.

NAT-15

Partners
SOM, SPH, AHC, PROFASSN

Synergies
6b-6

Structural Foundations
Informal

Contact
Denise E. Holmes,
JD, MPH
Association of Academic
Health Centers
1400 Sixteenth Street,
N.W., Suite 720
Washington, DC 20036
dholmes@acadhlthctrs.org

NAT-16

Partners
SOM, SPH, AHC, U-OTH

Synergies
6b-3

Structural Foundations
Intraorg

Contact
Denise E. Holmes,
JD, MPH
Association of Academic
Health Centers
1400 Sixteenth Street,
N.W., Suite 720
Washington, DC 20036
dholmes@acadhlthctrs.org

AAHC Annual Policy Forums

Since the early 1990s, the Association of Academic Health Centers (AAHC) has run annual policy forums for selected AAHC members and the deans of schools of public health. The forums are held in conjunction with the Association of Schools of Public Health (ASPH), which is the association of the nation's accredited schools of public health. At the meeting, the public health curriculum is reviewed. Topics of discussion often include strategies for getting physicians to use and appreciate the tools of public health, such as epidemiology, and conversely, ways to teach public health professionals more about the biomedical paradigm.

AAHC Group on Multiprofessional Education

In 1996, the Association of Academic Health Centers (AAHC) established the Group on Multiprofessional Education (GOMPE), which links the persons responsible for interdisciplinary programs in each member institution with one another. Approximately half of the members of AAHC have a designated staff person for interdisciplinary education in their institution. GOMPE has had two national meetings, and its members continue to interact through an Internet forum on the AAHC Web site.

NAT-17

Partners
FEDHLTH, SOM, SPH, AHC,
U-OTH, PROFASSN

Synergies
6b-6

Structural Foundations
Coalition

Contact
See citation

Seminar on Higher Education and the Health of Youth

To encourage group discussion and action around what academic institutions, government, and the community can do to benefit the health of youth, Harvard University and CDC sponsored an invited conference in 1995. The two-day meeting brought together "teams" from nearly 20 institutions of higher learning from across the country with representatives from the federal government, national philanthropies, and other national organizations. A multidisciplinary planning committee for the conference included faculty, researchers and administrators from schools of public health and schools of medicine, plus national associations, including the Association of Schools of Public Health (ASPH) and the Association of Academic Health Centers (AAHC). The central theme was connecting practitioners in the field with researchers and faculty from the institutions of higher education to spur more effective and sustainable partnerships to benefit the health of communities, especially youth. Much of the conference centered on collaborative, small-group discussions, and each group then presented specific recommendations on how to move forward with the relationships.

Higher education and the health of youth: charting a national course in a changing environment. April 6–7, 1995. Conference proceedings sponsored by Harvard University and CDC.

NAT-18

Partners
SOM, SPH, RES, AHC, U-OTH

Synergies
3a, 3b, 4b, 5b, 5c, 6a-4,
6b-5

Structural Foundations
Contract

Contact
Edward Bernstein,
MD, FACEP
Department of
Emergency Medicine
Boston University
School of Medicine
818 Harrison Avenue
Boston, MA 02118
ebernste@bu.edu

Case Studies in Emergency Medicine and the Health of the Public

Case Studies in Emergency Medicine and the Health of the Public, edited by Bernstein and Bernstein, presents a "public health approach to emergency medicine" for emergency medicine practitioners, residents, and medical students. Written by an emergency physician with public health training, a clinical nurse specialist with a doctorate in social policy/health services research, and over 50 other contributors, the book gives emergency physicians (EPs) specific information on public health practices in the areas of STDs, youth and domestic violence, TB, smoking, and substance abuse, as well as specific techniques that EPs can use to address the underlying causes of their patients' health problems. The authors also recognize that the emergency department is a source of primary care for a substantial group of people with special health needs (the homeless, immigrants, at-risk adolescents) and suggest protocols to improve delivery of follow-up medical care and social services. The book highlights the need for medical staff to connect with other health, social service, public safety, and public health professionals to advocate for their patients, to assure necessary follow-up, and to promote changes in the health system to improve care. Case studies that model collaborations between emergency medicine and public health are presented for firearms control, violence and safety interventions, and substance abuse prevention and treatment (MA-9, MA-10, NM-1) The book is an outgrowth of the work of the Public Health Committee of the Society of Academic Emergency Medicine.

Bernstein, E and Bernstein, B, eds. 1996. *Case studies in emergency medicine and the health of the public.* Sudbury, MA: Jones and Bartlett Publishers.

NAT-19

Partners
LHD, SHD, FEDHLTH, MDPRAC, HOSP, VHO, BUS, C-OTH

Synergies
6a-5, 6a-6

Structural Foundations
Coalition, Adm/Mgmt

Contact
Roberto Anson
Federal Office of Rural Health Policy
Health Resources and Services Administration
5600 Fishers Lane
Room 9-05
Rockville, MD 20857

State Rural Health Offices and State Rural Health Associations

Authorized by Congress in 1990 to address health problems in rural areas, the federal Office of Rural Health Policy (ORHP), within the US Department of Health and Human Services, provides matching grants to states that establish and maintain a State Office of Rural Health (SORH). Instituted in 1991, the SORH Grants Program has spurred the development of 50 state offices, and it sponsors forums for exchanging information and successful strategies among states. By administering the state office program, ORHP helps coordinate federal and state strategies in rural health. Under the program, each state office serves its rural communities in four ways: by collecting and disseminating information within the state; by improving recruitment and retention of health professionals into rural areas; by providing technical assistance to attract more federal, state, and foundation funding; and by coordinating rural health interests and activities across a state. Many of the state health offices also have convened state rural health associations, which are broad-based coalitions of consumers, public health professionals and medical providers in the state. The 50 state offices provide an institutional framework that links small rural communities with state and federal resources, and aids in the development of long-term solutions to rural health problems.

NAT-20

Partners
SHD, FEDHLTH, HOSP, CLIN, SOM, RES, U-OTH, MEDSOC, PROFASSN, VHO, FNDN

Synergies
6a-1, 6a-4, 6a-6, 6b-4, 6b-5, 6b-6, 6c-1

Structural Foundations
Coalition, Contract

Contact
John Talbott, MD
Department of Psychiatry
University of Maryland
School of Medicine
701 W. Pratt Street
Suite 388
Baltimore, MD 21201
jtalbott@umpsy.ab.umd.edu

State/University Interdisciplinary Collaboration Project on Mental Health

In 1975, the American Psychiatric Association (APA) formed a task force to foster better relations between public mental health systems and academic psychiatry. This body evolved into the national State/University Interdisciplinary Collaboration Project, which was funded by the Pew Charitable Trusts and is now supported by the Substance Abuse and Mental Health Services Administration (SAMHSA), a federal agency. Within the Project, APA is contracted by the federal Center for Mental Health Services to provide technical assistance that furthers collaboration between state mental health systems and university departments that train mental health professionals. For instance, Project staff offer individualized, on-site consultation on collaboration as well as focused workshops for state mental health commissioners and university deans and chairs on emerging topics in mental health that relate to state/university relations. Prior to 1994, the Project focused on collaborations within psychiatry, but now the focus is more multidisciplinary. The Steering Committee, for instance, now has representatives from the American Nurses Association, the National Alliance for the Mentally Ill, the National Association of Social Workers, the National Empowerment Center, and the National Mental Health Association along with representatives from state mental health programs and from organized psychiatry and psychology. One publication of the Project is *Working Together: State-University Collaboration in Mental Health*, and several cases from it are included in this Pocket Guide (CO-1, GA-9, MD-5, NC-14, NE-2, NY-24, OR-3, PA-5, VA-9).

Talbott, JA and Robinowitz, CB. 1986. *Working together: state-university collaboration in mental health.* Washington, DC: American Psychiatric Press, Inc.

NAT-21

Partners
L-GOV, S-GOV, FEDHLTH, FEDOTH, HOSP, PROFASSN, VHO, BUS, C-OTH

Synergies
3a, 5b, 5c, 5d, 6b-5, 6b-6

Emergency Nurses Motor Vehicle Injury Prevention Programs

In 1994, the head of the National Highway Traffic and Safety Administration (NHTSA) was actively seeking partnerships with health care professionals to improve education about motor vehicle injury prevention strategies. A member of the Emergency Nurses Association (ENA), who had contracted with the NHTSA on another project, became a key contact for bringing representatives of the two organi-

Structural Foundations
Contract, Adm/Mgmt,
Advisory

Contact
Laurie Flaherty, RN, MS
Emergency Nurses
Association
216 Higgins Road
Park Ridge, IL 60068
llfdc@aol.com

zations together. The NHTSA and ENA developed a cooperative agreement for the joint development of an education program for emergency room nurses to improve their role in teaching the general public about how to prevent motor vehicle injuries. The three-year agreement had four specific goals: (1) to increase the number, kind and quality of motor vehicle injury prevention programs delivered by emergency nurses; (2) to promote collaboration between nurses and other groups interested in prevention; (3) to support efforts of law enforcement agencies; and (4) to increase emergency nurse involvement in legislative initiatives. The project was jointly administered by the ENA's Director of Research and NHTSA's National Organization Division's Chief, a jointly staffed working committee, and a project coordinator retained by ENA. Both offices are based in Washington, DC, providing the project coordinator easy access to personnel and resources at NHTSA. During the first year, ENA members were surveyed about their needs as traffic safety advocates, and two education products were developed based on the results: a continuing medical education course titled "A Crash Course in Motor Vehicle Injury Prevention," and a *Safe & Sober* manual outlining ten specific projects nurses can initiate to reduce motor vehicle injury. During year two, over 400 nurses were trained as instructors of the "Crash Course," and additional resources on collaboration, public speaking, and working with law enforcement were also developed and distributed nationwide. During year three, the survey of ENA members was repeated, demonstrating significant increases in levels of nurse involvement in prevention programs, law enforcement programs, and legislative activities.

NAT-22
Partners
FEDHLTH, FEDOTH

Synergies
5b, 5c, 5d, 6b-5

Structural Foundations
Contract, Adm/Mgmt

Native Americans Vehicle Occupant Protection Campaign
In the early 1990s, the National Highway Traffic and Safety Administration (NHTSA) was interested in developing a collaborative and coordinated effort to promote vehicle safety in Native American communities. At the same time, the Indian Health Service (IHS) was interested in expanding their Injury Prevention Program to incorporate child and passenger vehicle safety. Building on a previous collaboration for an anti-drinking and driving campaign ("None for the Road"), representatives from

Contact
Ann E. Mitchell
National Outreach Division
National Highway Traffic
Safety Administration
400 7th Street, N.W.
NOA-01
Washington, DC 20590
amitchell@nhtsa.dot.gov

NHTSA's Office of Occupant Protection and IHS's Injury Prevention Program negotiated a four-year interagency agreement. Representatives from the Native American nations and from other federal agencies, such as CDC, the Bureau of Indian Affairs, and the Federal Highway Administration, were involved in the planning and development of the collaborative products and services. Specific objectives, all targeting Native Americans, include increasing use of seat belts and child restraints, developing culturally relevant education materials, empowering Native American nations to adopt and enforce traffic safety laws, and establishing community-based traffic safety and injury prevention coalitions and programs. During the four-year program, the agencies created a resource guide for conducting community-based programs, conducted assessments of tribal traffic laws and child seat loaner programs, incorporated occupant protection information in health care provider workshops, and developed other educational videos and materials. Factors in the success of this program were a high-level commitment between the NHTSA and the IHS, outreach to associated groups, and an interagency agreement, which allowed them to combine limited resources and technical expertise.

NAT-23
Partners
FEDHLTH, PHASSN, PROFASSN

Synergies
3a, 6b-1, 6b-5

Structural Foundations
Contract, Advisory

Contact
Barbara J. Calkins, MA
Association of Teachers of
Preventive Medicine
1660 L Street, N.W.
Suite 208
Washington, DC 20036
info@atpm.org

ATPM Prevention and Education Activities
The Association of Teachers of Preventive Medicine (ATPM) was formed in 1948 by medical academicians and public health physicians to promote the teaching of population-oriented health sciences in the clinically oriented setting of undergraduate and graduate medical education. ATPM has collaborated with such federal agencies as CDC, HRSA, and the Office of Disease Prevention and Health Promotion (ODPHP) to improve the training of students and health professionals. With CDC, ATPM developed the Inventory of Knowledge and Skills Relating to Disease Prevention and Health Promotion, and is working with HRSA to use the Inventory to enhance prevention education in medical schools. In partnership with CDC, ATPM provides faculty research and training opportunities in public health and preventive medicine. ATPM and the CDC National Immunization Program have developed immunization curricular material for medical students, residents, physicians, and nursing and public health students. In collaboration with

ODPHP, ATPM is developing continuing education opportunities for health care providers to master the materials in the *Clinician's Handbook of Preventive Services.*

NAT-24
Partners
FEDHLTH, FEDOTH

Synergies
3c

Structural Foundations
Contract

Contact
Itzhak Jacoby, MD
F. Edward Hébert
School of Medicine
Uniformed Services
University of the
Health Sciences
4301 Jones Bridge Road
Bethesda, MD 20814
ijacoby@usuhs.mil

NAT-25
Partners
FEDHLTH, FEDOTH, MEDSOC

Synergies
3c

Structural Foundations
Contract

Contact
Itzhak Jacoby, MD
F. Edward Hébert
School of Medicine
Uniformed Services
University of the
Health Sciences
4301 Jones Bridge Road
Bethesda, MD 20814
ijacoby@usuhs.mil

Assessment of Physician-to-Population Ratios

In coordination with the Public Health Service's (PHS) Bureau of Primary Health Care and Bureau of Health Professions, the Department of Defense (DoD) Division of Health Services Administration has been involved in a project to assess physician-to-population ratios that are adequate for primary care. The group has been measuring rates of hospitalizations that could have been prevented by adequate primary care (using a measure known as "ambulatory-care sensitive conditions") and correlating that information with area resource databases. Since a number of federal funding streams depend on accurate measurement of what constitutes a "health professional shortage area," PHS felt that it needed to obtain more directly relevant measures of staffing adequacy. As a direct provider of care, the DoD was independently interested in assuring adequate primary care provision for the families and individuals it covers.

Assessment of Medical and Surgical Practice Patterns

In collaboration with the AMA, HCFA, and the Bureau of Health Professions, the Division of Health Services Administration of the Uniformed Services University of the Health Sciences has been assessing practice patterns of medical and surgical specialists. The objective of the group's work is to clarify both the uniqueness of service provided by specialists, as well as the overlap with services provided among all specialists.

NAT-26
Partners
MDPRAC, SPH, MEDSOC

Synergies
3a, 6a-4, 6b-5

Structural Foundations
Advisory

Contact
Alfred Sommer, MD, MHS
School of Hygiene
and Public Health
Johns Hopkins University
615 North Wolfe Street
Suite 1041
Baltimore, MD 21205
asommer@jhsph.edu

American Academy of Ophthalmology
Preferred Practice Patterns
In 1985, the Board of Directors of the American Academy of Ophthalmology established a Quality of Care Committee, charging it with the very broad mandate of exploring quality of vision care. After much deliberation, it was decided to develop a series of clinical guidelines. The group further designed the process by which a single major ophthalmic problem was selected for review, generally on the basis of the amount of disability, the costs generated, or the level of service required, and then appointed a blue-ribbon review panel composed of ophthalmologists, epidemiologists, and biostatisticians who would review the literature and develop guidelines based on the available evidence. Since that time, 20 *Preferred Practice Patterns* have been published and warmly received by the practice community. Since the original Quality of Care Committee determined these would be published as "patterns" rather than "guidelines," the papers have been used as continuing education tools and are not regarded as prescriptive "recipes" for care, nor as impinging on physicians' autonomy.

Collaborations in Countries Other than the United States

INT-1

Partners
FEDHLTH, SOM

Synergies
3c, 4c, 6c-2

Structural Foundations
Contract, Advisory

Contact
Scott L. Zeger, PhD
Department of Biostatistics
Johns Hopkins School of
Hygiene and Public Health
615 N. Wolfe Street
Baltimore, MD 21205
szeger@jhsph.edu

INT-2

Partners
LHD, FEDHLTH, HOSP, CLIN, INS,
SOM, RES, AHC, U-OTH,
MEDSOC

Synergies
5a, 5e, 6a-5, 6b-2, 6b-4,
6c-1

Structural Foundations
Contract, Advisory

Contact
Simon Weitzman,
MD, MPH
Division of Health
in the Community
Ben-Gurion University
of the Negev
P.O. Box 653
Beer-Sheva, Israel 84105
weitzman@bgumail.bgu.ac.
il

British Medical Research Council Streptomycin Clinical Trial

Tuberculosis was a major medical problem in England immediately after World War II. The British Medical Research Council was struggling to devise an appropriate population-based response to the epidemic. The Council brought together a committee that included a clinician and a biostatistician to test the efficacy of a newly developed drug, the antibiotic streptomycin. The drug was in short supply in the war-ravaged country. Given a scarce resource of unproven efficacy, the pair designed one of the first large-scale randomized clinical trials in a human population, randomly assigning to the treatment groups either the medication plus bed rest or bed rest alone. This linking of clinical medicine and the population-based methods of biostatistics led the randomized clinical trial to become the "gold standard" for testing the value of pharmaceuticals and other clinical interventions.

Ben-Gurion University Division of Health in the Community

In 1974, the Israeli government established the Faculty for Health Sciences at Ben-Gurion University in the Negev Desert. The founding partners of the medical school's innovative Division of Health in the Community were the university, the statewide health insurance fund (Kupat Cholim), and the national health department. The premise of the new Division was to establish a focal point for integrating primary, preventive, and population services as part of the university's mission of teaching, service, and research. Both the medical director of the regional office of the insurance fund and the regional health director have academic appointments, and are involved in strategic planning for the Division's activities. The Division blends an undergraduate and graduate medical education in Family Medicine with the curriculum of a school of public health. The Division is composed of seven departments: Epidemiology and Health Services Evaluation, Family Medicine, Occupational Medicine, Sociology of Health, Health Policy and Management, Primary Care and Bedouin Mobile Unit, and Health Promotion/Disease Prevention. There are also affiliated research programs in health policy, health and nutrition, and family and primary care. Within the medical school, the Division is the leading recipient of research grants and total funding. Organizationally, the structure of the Division allows for numerous cross-sectoral collaborative work among faculty and students within the Division's departments.

INT-3
Partners
FEDOTH, MDPRAC, SOM, SPH

Synergies
6c-2

Structural Foundations
Contract

Contact
Julie Cwikel, PhD, MSW
Department of Social Work
Ben-Gurion University
of the Negev
P.O. Box 653
Beer-Sheva, Israel 84105
jcwikel@bgumail.bgu.ac.il

Health and Psychosocial Effects of Chernobyl

The long-term physical and mental effects of the Chernobyl chemical disaster in Russia in 1985 are unknown, but recent waves of immigration from the former Soviet Union have made it an international health issue. In Israel, for instance, immigrants from Chernobyl were dissatisfied with the government's scientific and medical responses to the incident. The focus was solely on the 1–4% estimated increase in cancer among those exposed rather than morbidity and mortality from other causes such as cardiovascular disease, cataracts, asthma, hypertension, and post-traumatic stress disorder. Responding to political pressure by immigrant advocacy groups and attention to the Chernobyl incident surrounding its tenth anniversary, the Israeli Ministry of Science funded a proposal by a researcher at Ben-Gurion University, who has a doctorate in public health and a degree in social work, to develop a research and intervention protocol to focus on the psychosocial dimensions of the Chernobyl incident. A multidisciplinary research team was formed, including an epidemiologist, a practicing physician and specialist in nuclear medicine, a psychiatrist who had recently immigrated, and academic researchers. In addition to clinical diagnoses and psychological profiles, the researchers held focus groups and open-ended personal interviews with survivors to better understand their health concerns. Additional funding for the research was supplied by the Canadian Ministry of Health and the Israeli Ministry of Absorption.

INT-4
Partners
LHD, SOM, AHC, MEDIA

Synergies
5a, 5b

Structural Foundations
Contract

Hamilton-Wentworth *Fact Book on Health*

As part of the Health of the Public program at McMaster University, a senior faculty member was given a cross-appointment with the local health department. One of the faculty member's first consultations was with the community nutritionist, who had spent several months collecting local health data in order to develop community nutrition programs. *The Fact Book on Health in Hamilton-Went-*

Contact
See citation

worth was first published in 1987 as a 62-page document. The 315-page 1994 edition went beyond health status data to provide information on determinants of health. Chapters included "Living and Working," "Individual Behaviors," "Social Support," and "Genetic Make-Up." To help disseminate the book, the Health of the Public program staff cultivated a relationship with the health reporter at the local newspaper. After a meeting between the editorial staff and *The Fact Book's* authors, the newspaper agreed to publish a weekly table or chart from the book. In developing *The Fact Book* and managing its dissemination, the authors adhered to several guiding principles: basic health information should be known and accessible to both citizens and community leaders; a good graphical display is more powerful than explanatory prose; when appropriate, use local data from a number of sources; and organize the material according to a matrix of determinants of health rather than health status indicators such as morbidity and mortality.

Health of the Public National Program Office. 1995. *Community health improvement through information and action: an anthology from the Health of the Public program.* San Francisco, CA.

INT-5
Partners
MEDSOC, VHO

Synergies
2c, 4c

Structural Foundations
Coalition

Contact
Bradford H. Gray, PhD
Division of Health and
Science Policy
The New York Academy
of Medicine
1216 Fifth Avenue
New York, NY 10029
bgray@nyam.org

World Blindness Organizations and the Medical Profession

In the course of planning for the 1990 International Congress of Ophthalmology in Singapore, an international steering committee of ophthalmologists contemplated a worldwide blindness program as well. Given that cataract is the leading cause of blindness in the world, and that in some developing countries there is only one ophthalmologist for every million patients, the plan was to coordinate volunteer ophthalmic surgeons from the industrialized countries who would spend two to four weeks in the developing countries performing hundreds of cataract operations. The steering committee invited representatives from the world's leading voluntary blindness organizations—many of whom were ophthalmologists themselves, and who had overseen blindness-related programs in Asia, Africa, the Middle East, and India, among others—to participate in the collaborative effort. As became evident in the first planning meeting, the voluntary organizations saw no role in their programs for volunteer ophthalmologists who would spend such limited time doing surgery. A report that analyzed why the collaboration never materialized cited several explanations: the clash of medical and public health cultures, particularly those emphasizing individual benefit versus those considering population-wide benefit (one participant at the meeting reported that for the cost of flying an American ophthalmologist in and out every two weeks, seven full-time ophthalmologists could be hired for a year); fears that the proposed program would reduce the capacity of local practitioners to use available (but older) surgical techniques; the burden on hosting physicians, who would have to spend time orienting their visiting counterparts, treating them when they got sick, and managing their patients after they left; and a fundamental ideological difference around either providing relief (whether food or medical care) or developing self-sufficiency.

Gray, BH. 1992. World blindness and the medical profession: conflicting medical cultures and the ethical dilemmas of helping. *The Milbank Quarterly.* 70(3):535–556.

Part III
Indexes

[INT] International

For each type of partner, cases identifiers are organized geographically—first alphabetically by state postal code, then multistate (MST), national (NAT), and international (INT) collaborations. The partners are listed in the same groupings and order as in the Introduction (page 7).

GOVERNMENT AGENCIES
Local health department

AL-1	CT-3	ID-1	MA-9	MN-4	NE-1	NY-28	PA-8
AL-2	CT-4	ID-2	MA-10	MN-5		NY-30	PA-9
AL-3			MA-11	MN-6	NJ-3	NY-31	PA-10
AL-4	DC-2	IL-1	MA-12	MN-7	NJ-6	NY-32	PA-11
AL-6		IL-3	MA-13	MN-8	NJ-7	NY-33	PA-12
AL-7	FL-1	IL-4	MA-14	MN-10	NJ-8		PA-13
AL-8	FL-2	IL-5	MA-15	MN-12		OH-1	
	FL-3	IL-6		MN-16	NM-4	OH-2	SC-1
AZ-1	FL-4	IL-7	MD-1	MN-17		OH-3	SC-2
AZ-2	FL-6	IL-8	MD-2		NV-1	OH-4	SC-3
AZ-3	FL-7	IL-9	MD-3	MO-1		OH-5	
	FL-8	IL-10	MD-4	MO-2	NY-1	OH-6	TN-1
CA-1	FL-9	IL-11	MD-7	MO-4	NY-3	OH-8	TN-2
CA-2	FL-10		MD-8	MO-5	NY-4	OH-9	TN-5
CA-3	FL-12	IN-3	MD-9	MO-6	NY-5	OH-10	TN-6
CA-4	FL-13		MD-11		NY-7	OH-11	
CA-5		KS-1		NC-1	NY-8	OH-12	TX-2
CA-7	GA-1	KS-2	ME-2	NC-2	NY-10	OH-13	TX-5
CA-8	GA-2	KS-3		NC-3	NY-11	OH-14	TX-6
CA-9	GA-5	KS-4	MI-2	NC-4	NY-12		TX-8
CA-10	GA-6		MI-3	NC-5	NY-13	OR-1	TX-9
CA-11	GA-7	KY-6	MI-4	NC-6	NY-15	OR-2	TX-10
CA-12	GA-8		MI-5	NC-7	NY-16	OR-4	TX-13
CA-13		LA-2	MI-7	NC-8	NY-19	OR-5	TX-14
CA-14	IA-1	LA-3	MI-8	NC-10	NY-20	OR-6	
CA-15	IA-2		MI-9	NC-11	NY-21		UT-1
CA-20	IA-3	MA-4	MI-10	NC-12	NY-22	PA-1	
CA-21	IA-4	MA-5		NC-13	NY-23	PA-3	VA-1
CA-22	IA-5	MA-6	MN-1	NC-15	NY-25	PA-4	VA-2
	IA-6	MA-7	MN-2	NC-17	NY-26	PA-6	VA-4
CT-1	IA-7	MA-8	MN-3	NC-18	NY-27	PA-7	VA-5

VA-6	VA-14	VA-21	WA-4	WA-11	WI-1	WV-1	NAT-9
VA-7	VA-15	VA-22	WA-5	WA-12	WI-2		NAT-10
VA-8	VA-16	VA-23	WA-6	WA-13	WI-3	WY-1	NAT-11
VA-10	VA-17	VA-25	WA-7	WA-14	WI-4	———	NAT-19
VA-11	VA-18		WA-8	WA-15	WI-5	MST-2	
VA-12	VA-19	WA-2	WA-9	WA-16	WI-7	MST-3	INT-2
VA-13	VA-20	WA-3	WA-10	WA-17	WI-8		INT-4

Other local government agency

AL-6	FL-2	IN-2	MN-1	NC-17	OH-1	TN-2	WA-5
AL-8	FL-8		MN-5	NC-18	OH-2	TN-6	WA-6
	FL-12	KS-1	MN-6		OH-3		WA-7
AZ-2	FL-13	KS-2	MN-11	NJ-3	OH-5	TX-8	WA-10
AZ-5			MN-12	NJ-7	OH-9	TX-9	WA-14
AZ-6	GA-2	KY-5	MN-14	NJ-8	OH-10	TX-13	WA-15
	GA-3		MN-16		OH-11	TX-14	WA-17
CA-5	GA-6	LA-2		NM-1	OH-13		
CA-9	GA-8	LA-3	MO-2	NM-3	OH-14	VA-1	WI-2
CA-12			MO-4			VA-2	WI-7
CA-14	IA-1	MA-7	MO-5	NY-7	OR-1	VA-4	
CA-15	IA-3	MA-8	MO-6	NY-9	OR-4	VA-5	WY-1
CA-20	IA-4	MA-10		NY-12	OR-5	VA-10	
CA-21	IA-6	MA-12	NC-1	NY-13		VA-11	NAT-9
CA-22		MA-13	NC-2	NY-14	PA-4	VA-12	NAT-10
	ID-2	MA-15	NC-3	NY-15	PA-5	VA-15	NAT-11
CO-1			NC-7	NY-16	PA-12	VA-16	NAT-21
	IL-1	MD-3	NC-8	NY-25	PA-13	VA-18	
CT-1	IL-6	MD-7	NC-10	NY-26		VA-19	
CT-4	IL-7		NC-11	NY-30	SC-2	VA-25	
	IL-9	MI-2	NC-12	NY-31	SC-3		
FL-1		MI-3	NC-13			WA-3	

State health department

AL-5	AZ-6	CA-15	DE-1	FL-12	IA-1	IL-7	LA-1
AL-6		CA-16			IA-2	IL-10	
AL-7	CA-4		FL-5	GA-1	IA-4		MA-1
AL-8	CA-11	CT-3	FL-7	GA-4	IA-5	IN-3	MA-4
	CA-12	CT-4	FL-8	GA-7			MA-5
AZ-2	CA-13		FL-9	GA-9	IL-2	KS-1	MA-7
AZ-3	CA-14	DC-2	FL-11		IL-6	KS-2	MA-9

Other federal government agency

MEDICAL PROVIDERS/INSURERS

Solo or group medical practice

Hospital or health system

MST-1 NAT-9 NAT-11 NAT-20 INT-2
MST-2 NAT-10 NAT-19 NAT-21

Community health center or other publicly funded clinic

AL-5	CT-2	IL-5	MA-13	MO-6	NY-16	TN-2	WA-5
AL-7		IL-9	MA-14		NY-19	TN-3	WA-7
	DC-1	IL-10	MA-15	NC-1	NY-27	TN-6	WA-14
AZ-3	DC-2	IL-11		NC-5	NY-30		WA-17
AZ-5			MD-5	NC-13	NY-33	TX-5	
AZ-6	FL-1	IN-1	MD-9	NC-14		TX-6	WI-2
	FL-2			NC-17	OH-2	TX-9	WI-4
CA-2	FL-4	KS-2	MI-2	NC-18	OH-5		WI-7
CA-3	FL-7		MI-4		OH-7	VA-2	WI-8
CA-4	FL-8	KS-3	MI-5	NJ-3	OH-14	VA-4	
CA-7	FL-10		MI-7			VA-5	WV-1
CA-9		KY-6	MI-9	NM-2	OR-1	VA-7	———
CA-12	GA-1		MI-10	NM-4	OR-3	VA-11	MST-2
CA-13	GA-7	LA-2				VA-12	
CA-14	GA-8		MN-4	NY-7	PA-3	VA-14	NAT-9
CA-21		MA-3	MN-6	NY-8	PA-4	VA-15	NAT-10
CA-22	IA-1	MA-5	MN-13	NY-10	PA-10	VA-18	NAT-11
	IA-2	MA-6	MN-16	NY-12	PA-13	VA-23	NAT-20
CO-1		MA-7		NY-13		VA-25	
	ID-2	MA-9	MO-2	NY-14	SC-3		INT-2
CT-1		MA-11	MO-5	NY-15		WA-4	

Managed care organization

AZ-2	FL-8	MD-10	MN-9	NV-1	OR- 4	VA-2	WA-13
AZ-3	FL-10		MN-10		OR-5	VA-5	WA-14
AZ-7		ME-3	MN-11	NV-2	OR-6	VA-7	
	IA-4		MN-12	NY-5		VA-10	WI-4
CA-3		MI-1	MN-13	NY-8	PA-1	VA-12	WI-7
CA-9	KS-3	MI-5	MN-14	NY-12	PA-3	VA-14	WI-8
CA-12	KS-4	MI-7	MN-1/	NY-15	PA-8	VA-23	———
CA-13		MI-8		NY-23	PA-11	VA-24	MST-2
CA-17	MA-1	MI-9	NC-17	NY-28			MST-3
CA-18	MA-2	MI-11		NY-29	TN-2	WA-1	
CA-19	MA-7		NH-2		TN-6	WA-4	NAT-9
CA-20	MA-11	MN-3		OH-12		WA-5	NAT-12
CA-21	MA-13	MN-4	NJ-2	OH-14	TX-5	WA-6	
	MA-14	MN-5	NJ-3		TX-10	WA-9	
CT-1		MN-6	NJ-7	OR-1	TX-11	WA-10	
CT-4	MD-9	MN-7		OR-2	TX-13	WA-11	

Health insurance company

AZ-2	HI-1	MA-2	MN-10	NH-2	OR-5	VA-5	———
		MA-13	MN-11	NY-5		VA-23	NAT-12
CT-4	IA-4	MA-14	MN-12	NY-15	PA-3	VA-25	
	IA-5		MN-14	NY-31	PA-4		INT-2
FL-8		MD-7			PA-8	WA-2	
	IL-8		NC-7	OH-11	PA-13	WA-9	
GA-6		MN-4	NC-17				
	KY-5	MN-6			OR-4	TN-3	WI-7

Laboratory or pharmacy

AL-1	GA-2	MA-2	MN-12	NY-10	TN-3	VA-13	WA-7
	GA-7	MA-11		NY-12	TN-4	VA-15	WA-17
CA-7		MD-1	NC-8	NY-15		VA-18	
CA-11	HI-1		NC-13		TX-5	VA-23	WI-3
	IL-10	ME-2	NC-17	OH-3	TX-6	VA-25	———
CT-3			NC-18	OH-8	TX-9		NAT-9
FL-4	KS-1	MI-4		OH-9		WA-4	
FL-8			NJ-6		VA-5	WA-6	

ACADEMIA

School of medicine

AL-1	CT-2	KS-3	MD-11	NJ-4	NY-24	PA-3	UT-1
AL-2	CT-3			NJ-5	NY-25	PA-5	UT-2
AL-3		KY-5	MI-3	NJ-7	NY-26		
AL-4	FL-8			NJ-9	NY-27	RI-1	VA-1
AL-5		LA-1	MO-2				VA-2
AL-7	GA-1	LA-2	MO-4	NM-1	OH-1	SC-3	VA-4
AL-8	GA-2		MO-5	NM-2	OH-2		VA-5
	GA-3	MA-2	MO-6	NM-3	OH-6	TN-1	VA-6
AZ-5	GA-5	MA-3			OH-7	TN-2	VA-7
CA-2	GA-7	MA-5	NC-6	NV-1	OH-8	TN-5	VA-9
CA-4	GA-9	MA-6	NC-9		OH-11		VA-12
CA-6		MA-7	NC-14	NY-8	OH-13	TX-1	VA-14
CA-7	IA-6	MA-10	NC-16	NY-11	OH-14	TX-2	VA-23
CA-8		MA-11		NY-12		TX-5	VA-25
CA-12	IL-1	MA-13	NE-2	NY-15	OR-1	TX-6	
CA-13				NY-16	OR-3	TX-7	WA-4
	IN-3	MD-5	NH-1	NY-19	OR-4	TX-13	WA-6
CO-1		MD-6		NY-20		TX-14	WA-11
	KS-2	MD-8	NJ-3	NY-21	PA-1		WA-16

WI-2	WI-7	NAT-4	NAT-15	NAT-18	INT-1	INT-4
WI-3	————	NAT-11	NAT-16	NAT-20	INT-2	
WI-6	MST-2	NAT-14	NAT-17		INT-3	

School of public health

AL-5	GA-1	KY-5	MD-6	NC-16	PA-5	WA-4	NAT-15
AL-8	GA-3		MD-8			WA-5	NAT-16
	GA-5	LA-2		NY-15	TN-2	WA-11	NAT-17
CA-1	GA-7		MN-4	NY-19			NAT-18
CA-6		MA-2	MN-5	NY-20	TX-1	WI-5	NAT-26
CA-12	HI-1	MA-5	MN-6	NY-23	TX-9	————	
		MA-6	MN-15	NY-27	TX-13	MST-1	INT-3
CT-2	IL-7	MA-7		NY-30	TX-14	MST-2	
	IL-11	MA-10	NC-1	NY-32			
DC-2		MA-11	NC-5			VA-15	NAT-9
FL-5	KS-2	MA-12	NC-6	PA-1			NAT-11
FL-8		MA-13	NC-9	PA-3	WA-1		NAT-14

Academic research center

AL-3	IL-7	MD-6	MN-5	NC-16	OR-3	VA-16	————
AL-5		MD-10	MN-6			VA-23	MST-2
	KY-5		MN-10	NY-12	TX-7		NAT-1
CA-13		MI-3	MN-12	NY-14		WA-7	
	MA-2				VA-5	WA-9	

Residency program

AL-1	FL-4	IL-1	MD-5	NM-3	TN-2	VA-12	NAT-18
AL-2	FL-6	IL-5			TN-4	VA-18	NAT-20
AL-3	FL-7		MI-4	NY-15		VA-25	
	FL-8	KS-2	MN-12	NY-17	TX-5		INT-2
AZ-1	FL-10	KS-3		NY-24	TX-7	WA-4	
			MO-2			WA-6	
CA-4	GA-1	MA-10		OH-8	UT-1	WA-7	
	GA-9	MA-13	NC-14		UT-2	WA-16	
CO-1				OR-1			
	IA-4	MD-1	NE-2	OR-3	VA-4	WI-7	
DC-1	IA-7	MD-2			VA-7	————	

Academic health center

AL-1	CT-3	MA-2	MO-5	NY-11	OH-7	TX-4	NAT-15
AL-2		MA-5		NY-15		TX-5	NAT-16
AL-8	FL-8	MA-6	NC-14	NY-17	OR-1	TX-6	NAT-17
		MA-8	NC-16	NY-18	OR-3	TX-12	NAT-18
AZ-3	GA-7	MA-13	NC-17	NY-19	OR-4		
				NY-22		UT-1	INT-2
CA-4	IA-5	MD-8	NJ-3	NY-25	PA-1		INT-4
CA-12				NY-26	PA-2	WI-8	
CA-13	KS-2	MI-4	NM-1	NY-27	PA-3		
	KS-3		NM-2	NY-30	PA-5	MST-2	
CO-1		MN-16	NM-3	NY-31	PA-13		
	LA-1					NAT-10	
CT-2		MO-4	NY-1	OH-6	TX-3	NAT-14	

Other university-level academic institution or department

AL-4	DC-1	IL-8	MI-2	NE-2	OR-5	UT-2	WI-7
AL-8		IL-9					
	FL-8	IL-11	MN-5	NJ-3	PA-1	VA-4	WV-1
AZ-2			MN-15	NJ-6	PA-3	VA-5	
AZ-3	FL-13	IN-3	MN-16	NJ-8	PA-4	VA-7	NAT-5
AZ-5				NJ-9	PA-13	VA-9	NAT-9
	GA-2	KS-2	MO-2			VA-10	NAT-16
CA-3	GA-3	KS-3	MO-4	NM-1	SC-2	VA-12	NAT-17
CA-6			MO-5	NM-3		VA-23	NAT-18
CA-12	IA-1	KY-5			TN-2		NAT-20
CA-14	IA-3		NC-6	NY-11		WA-3	
	IA-7	LA-2	NC-12	NY-14	TX-5	WA-5	INT-2
CT-1			NC-13	NY-15	TX-9	WA-6	
CT-2	ID-2	MA-2	NC-16		TX-13	WA-11	
CT-3		MA-8	NC-17	OH-6	TX-14		
CT-4	IL-1	MA-10		OH-13		WI-4	

PROFESSIONAL ASSOCIATIONS

Medical/specialty society or other clinician association

AL-5	CA-5	CA-14	FL-2	FL-9	HI-1	IN-3	MA-5
AL-6	CA-6	CA-15	FL-3	FL-11			MA-7
	CA-7	CA-16	FL-4	FL-12	IA-2	KS-2	MA-11
AZ-3	CA-11		FL-5				
	CA-12	DC-2	FL-7	GA-4	IL-2	LA-1	MD-1
CA-2	CA-13		FL-8	GA-7	IL-3	MA-4	MD-3

MD-7   NC-10   NJ-2   NY-16   RI-1   VA-3   WA-9   NAT-6
      NC-12   NJ-3   NY-19   VA-4   NAT-8
MI-2   NC-13   NJ-5   NY-23   SC-1   VA-5   WI-1   NAT-10
MI-6   NC-14   SC-2   VA-6   WI-4   NAT-11
      NC-17   NV-1   OH-5   VA-10   WI-6   NAT-12
MN-3   NY-2   OH-8   TN-3   VA-23   ———   NAT-13
MN-5   ND-1   NY-3   OH-9   TN-6   VA-25   MST-1   NAT-20
MN-10   NY-6   OH-10   MST-2   NAT-25
MN-15   NE-1   NY-8   OH-13   TX-5   WA-2   NAT-26
MN-16   NY-9   TX-8   WA-3   NAT-2
      NH-2   NY-10   OR-5   TX-9   WA-4   NAT-3   INT-2
MO-3   NY-12   TX-13   WA-7   NAT-4   INT-5
    NJ-1   NY-15   PA-3   WA-8   NAT-5

Public health association

AZ-3   DC-2   GA-2   MA-7   MN-4   NJ-3   TX-5   ———
                MA-11   TX-6   MST-2
CA-11   FL-5   IN-3   MO-3   NY-19
CA-12   FL-8   MI-6   NY-23   VA-13   NAT-2
CA-15   FL-11   MA-2   ND-1   NAT-12
             MA-5   MN-3   OR-1   WI-4   NAT-23

Other professional association

AL-5   FL-5   IN-3   NC-14   NV-1   VA-12   MST-2   NAT-15
      FL-8   NY-2   VA-21   NAT-17
AZ-3   MA-5   ND-1   NY-19   VA-23   NAT-1   NAT-20
    GA-7   MA-7   NAT-2   NAT-21
CA-6   MA-11   NJ-1   OH-9   VT-1   NAT-3   NAT-23
    IA-2   MA-15   NJ-3   OH-10   NAT-8
CA-11   NJ-6   WI-4   NAT-9
CA-12   IL-1   MN-5   NJ-8   TX-9   ———   NAT-12
CA-13   IL-10   MN-9   TX-13   MST-1   NAT-14

COMMUNITY GROUPS

Voluntary health organization or advocacy group

AL-5   CA-4   CA-14   CT-1   DC-1   GA-3   IA-3   IL-1
AL-7   CA-10   CA-15   CT-2   GA-5   IA-5   IL-2
      CA-11   CA-19   CT-3   FL-8   GA-7   IA-6   IL-4
AZ-3   CA-12   CA-20   CT-4   FL-9   IL-7
    CA-13   CA-22   IA-2   ID-2   IL-9

IL-10	MA-15	MN-17	NM-1	OH-2	SC-3	VA-10	WI-3
IL-11			NM-3	OH-10		VA-12	WI-4
	MD-1	MO-2		OH-11	TN-2	VA-14	WI-5
IN-2	MD-8	MO-4	NY-1	OH-13	TN-4	VA-16	WI-6
IN-3			NY-8		TN-6	VA-17	WI-7
	ME-1	NC-2	NY-9	OR-4		VA-19	
KS-2		NC-3	NY-10		TX-6	VA-23	MST-3
	MI-2	NC-7	NY-12	PA-2	TX-7		
KY-5	MI-4	NC-8	NY-13	PA-3	TX-8	WA-4	NAT-5
		NC-10	NY-19	PA-4	TX-12	WA-5	NAT-9
MA-1	MN-6	NC-11	NY-21	PA-6	TX-13	WA-6	NAT-10
MA-2	MN-9		NY-23	PA-7		WA-9	NAT-12
MA-7	MN-10	ND-1	NY-25	PA-8	UT-1	WA-10	NAT-19
MA-9	MN-12		NY-27	PA-9		WA-11	NAT-20
MA-11	MN-13	NJ-3	NY-29	PA-10	VA-1	WA-14	NAT-21
MA-12	MN-15	NJ-7	NY-30	PA-11	VA-2		
MA-14	MN-16	NJ-8	NY-33		VA-5	WI-2	INT-5

Business

CA-4	FL-8	IL-11	MI-3	NJ-6	OH-9	TX-8	WA-10
CA-5	FL-13			NJ-8		TX-9	WA-14
CA-7		KS-2	MN-10		OR-4	TX-13	
CA-10	GA-1		MN-12	NM-3	OR-5		WI-5
CA-13	GA-6	KY-5	MN-14			VA-5	WI-7
CA-14			MN-16	NV-2	PA-3	VA-12	
CA-20	IA-1	MA-5			PA-13	VA-14	MST-3
CA-21	IA-4	MA-7	MO-2	NY-5		VA-15	
		MA-10		NY-8	SC-2	VA-19	NAT-1
CT-1	ID-2	MA-13	NC-1	NY-10		VA-20	NAT-5
CT-3		MA-14	NC-2	NY-15	TN-2	VA-23	NAT-9
CT-4	IL-1		NC-7	NY-16	TN-3	VA-25	NAT-11
	IL-7	MD-11	NC-13	NY-31	TN-6		NAT-12
DC-2	IL-9		NC-17			WA-3	NAT-19
		MI-2		OH-5	TX-7	WA-9	NAT-21

Labor organization

CA-15	FL-8	MA-2	MN-5	NY-10	
		MA-5	MN-16		NAT-5

School below the college level

CA-3	GA-2	KY-5	MN-6	NJ-7	OR-4	VA-2	WI-3
CA-5	GA-5		MN-12	NJ-8	OR-5	VA-5	WI-5
CA-9	GA-6	MA-1	MN-13			VA-10	WI-7
CA-10		MA-2	MN-16	NM-1	PA-1	VA-12	
CA-14	IA-4	MA-5			PA-3	VA-14	WY-1
CA-15	IA-5	MA-7	MO-1	NY-10	PA-13	VA-18	———
CA-21		MA-8	MO-2	NY-13		VA-20	MST-3
	ID-2	MA-9	MO-4	NY-18	SC-2	VA-21	
CT-1		MA-11	MO-5	NY-27	SC-3	VA-25	NAT-5
CT-3	IL-1	MA-12		NY-29		WA-3	NAT-9
CT-4	IL-6	MA-13	NC-1		TN-1		NAT-11
	IL-7		NC-2		TN-2	WA-4	
DC-1	IL-9		NC-7	OH-5		WA-6	
	IL-11	MD-8	NC-8	OH-10	TX-5	WA-7	
		MD-9	NC-12	OH-11	TX-7	WA-10	
FL-8		MD-11	NC-13	OH-14	TX-8	WA-14	
FL-12	IN-2		NC-17		TX-13	WA-17	
FL-13		MI-2			TX-14		
	KS-2	MI-5		OR-2			

Religious organization or clergy

AZ-3	FL-8	IL-9	MD-7	NC-7	OH-3	TN-2	VA-23
	FL-12	IL-11	MD-8	NC-8	OH-5	TN-3	VA-25
CA-5				NC-12	OH-14	TN-4	
CA-6	GA-2	IN-2	MI-1	NC-13			WA-3
CA-10	GA-5		MI-2		OR-4	TX-13	WA-4
CA-15		KS-2		NJ-3	OR-5	TX-14	WA-5
CA-19	IA-4			NJ-7			WA-6
		MA-7	MN-6	NJ-8	PA-3	VA-1	WA-14
CT-1	ID-2	MA-9	MN-12		PA-12	VA-5	
CT-4		MA-11		MO-4	PA-13	VA-12	WI-3
	IL-1	MA-14	MO-5	NY-8		VA-14	———
DC-1	IL-7	MA-15		NY-10		VA-15	NAT-9
	IL-8		NC-1	NY-12	SC-2	VA-20	NAT-11
				NY-29	SC-3		

Media

CA-4	CT-3	FL-2	GA-7	IA-5	IL-11	MI-2	MO-2
CA-6	CT-4	FL-8				MI-4	MO-4
CA-14		FL-13	HI-1	ID-2	KS-2		
	DC-1					MN-15	NC-1
CT-1	DC-2	GA-2	IA-4	IL-1	MA-11		NC-2

MO-2	NJ-1	NY-8	OH-10	SC-2	TX-11	VA-18	WA-14
	NJ-2	NY-9	OH-11		TX-12	VA-19	
NC-3	NJ-3	NY-10	OH-14	TN-1	TX-13	VA-20	WI-2
NC-6	NJ-7	NY-12		TN-2	TX-14	VA-23	WI-4
NC-7	NJ-8	NY-13	OR-5	TN-3		VA-25	WI-7
NC-8		NY-17		TN-4	VA-1		
NC-11	NM-1	NY-22	PA-1	TN-6	VA-2	WA-3	WY-1
NC-12	NM-2	NY-27	PA-3		VA-4	WA-5	———
	NM-3	NY-29	PA-4	TX-4	VA-5	WA-6	NAT-5
NE-1		NY-30	PA-5	TX-5	VA-12	WA-7	NAT-9
	NV-2		PA-10	TX-7	VA-14	WA-9	NAT-12
NH-1		OH-2	PA-13	TX-8	VA-15	WA-10	NAT-19
	NY-5	OH-5		TX-9	VA-16	WA-11	NAT-21

For each type of synergy model, cases identifiers are organized geographically—first alphabetically by state postal code, then multistate (MST), national (NAT), and international (INT) collaborations.

Synergy 1 Models: Improving health care by coordinating medical care with individual-level support services

1a: New personnel to site

AL-1	CA-9	MA-8	MO-1	NJ-4	OH-7	TX-4	VA-17
AL-2		MA-9		NJ-7		TX-9	VA-20
AL-3	FL-6	MA-10	NC-4		OR-1		VA-21
AL-4			NC-5	NM-1			VA-22
AL-7	IA-1	MD-2	NC-10			UT-1	
			NC-15	NY-7	PA-3		
AZ-1	IL-5	MN-8		NY-33	PA-7	VA- 2	WA-7
AZ-4	IL-10	MN-12	NE-1		PA-11	VA-5	
AZ-5		MN-13				VA-8	———
				OH-1	SC-1	VA-13	NAT-10

1b: "One-stop" center

CA-10	IL-7	MD-8	NY-17	TN-1	VA-1	WA-12	NAT-9
CA-18			NY-18	TN-4	VA-11	WA-17	NAT-10
	IN-2	NC-4	NY-25		VA-18		
IL-1		NC-18	NY-26	TX-13		WI-2	
IL-4	KY-6		NY-32	TX-14	WA-6		———

1c: Coordination across sites

AL-3	CT-1	GA-8	IL-9	MD-1	MI-9	NC-10	NV-2
AL-7			IL-10	MD-2	MI-10	NC-13	
	FL-4	IA-1		MD-4		NC-15	NY-1
AZ-2	FL-7	IA-5	IN-2	MD-8	MN-7		NY-8
AZ-4	FL-8	IA-7		MD-9	MN-10	NE-1	NY-13
AZ-6	FL-12		LA-3	MD-11	MN-11		NY-17
		ID-1			MN-16	NJ-4	NY-21
CA-9	GA-2		MA-7	ME-1		NJ-7	NY-28
CA-19	GA-5	IL-3	MA-13	ME-2	MO-1		NY-30
CA-21	GA-6	IL-5	MA-14				NY-31
CA-22	GA-7	IL-8	MA-15	MI-5	NC-5	NM-4	NY-32

NY-33	OR-5	PA-10	SC-3	VA-2	VA-20	WA-8	WV-1
		PA-12		VA-10	VA-25	WA-12	———
OH-8	PA-6	PA-13	TX-12	VA-15		WA-17	NAT-9
OH-14	PA-8		TX-13	VA-16	WA-6		NAT-10
	PA-9	SC-1	TX-14	VA-17	WA-7	WI-7	NAT-11

Synergy 2 Models: Improving access to care by establishing frameworks to provide care for the un- or underinsured

2a: Free clinic

CA-2	FL-12	MA-7	NY-17	OH-12	TX-14	WA-6	———
CA-9		MA-14	NY-18			WA-8	NAT-9
CA-10	GA-6		NY-25	OR-1	VA-1	WA-12	
	GA-8	MD-8	NY-26		VA-2		
CT-2			NY-33	SC-2	VA-4		WI-3
	IL-4	MN-8			VA-11		WI-6
DC-1	IL-6		OH-3	TN-4	VA-18		WI-7
		NC-7	OH-4				
FL-8	IN-2	NC-10	OH-8	TX-13	WA-4		WV-1

2b: Referral network

AL-7	FL-3	GA-7	KS-1	MD-7	NE-1	OH-3	WV-1
	FL-4	GA-8				OH-8	
CA-2	FL-7		MA-7	MI-4	NV-2		
CA-7	FL-8	ID-1	MA-15	MI-10			
CA-10	FL-9				NY-8	OR-4	
	FL-12	IN-1	MD-1	NC-13	NY-10	TN-3	
FL-2			MD-3			VA-8	

2c: New clinical staff at public health facilities

AL-1	CA-3	FL-10	MD-2	NE-2	OR-1	UT-1	WI-2
AL-2			MD-5		OR-3		———
AL-3	CO-1	GA-6		NY-4		VA-4	INT-5
		GA-9	MI-5	NY-24	PA-5		
AZ-1	FL-2		MI-7			WA-4	
	FL-6	IA-1				WA-16	
				OH-7	TX-2		
CA-2	FL-8		NC-14				

Synergy 3 Models: Improving the quality and cost-effectiveness of care by applying a population perspective to medical practice

Synergy 4 Models: Using clinical practice to identify and address community health problems

4a: Population database

AL-5	FL-1	IL-9	ME-1	MN-12	NJ-6	OR-4	VA-14
			ME-2	MN-17		OR-6	VA-23
AZ-2	GA-3	MA-9			NV-1		
AZ-3		MA-14	MI-9	ND-1		PA-11	WA-13
	IA-2		MN-4		NY-1		
CA-16		MD-4	MN-7	NJ-1	NY-31	VA-2	WI-1
	IL-5		MN-9	NJ-3	OH-11	VA-5	

4b: Risk assessment and intervention

AZ-4	CA-13	IL-3	MD-10	MN-8	NC-5	VA-12	———
AZ-5		IL-6		MN-10			NAT-1
AZ-6	FL-1		MI-2	MN-11	NY-13	WA-1	NAT-9
		MA-8	MI-10	MN-12	NY-28	WA-7	NAT-18
CA-1	GA-3	MA-9			NY-32		
CA-11		MA-10	MN-5	MO-2	PA-2	WI-7	

4c: Clinical community health objective

AL-7	DC-1	MA-14	MN-17	NY-12	PA-11	VA-10	———
	DC-2	MA-15		NY-15		VA-12	NAT-9
AZ-2			MO-1	NY-23	SC-2	VA-14	NAT-10
AZ-5	FL-8	MD-8		NY-25		VA-19	NAT-11
AZ-7			NJ-3		TN-2	VA-23	
	GA-7	ME-2	NJ-4	OH-12	TN-6		INT-1
CA-5			NJ-8			WA-4	INT-5
CA-12	IA-1	MI-4		OR-2	TX-10	WA-8	
CA-13		MI-9	NV-1	OR-5	TX-13	WA-13	
CA-19	IL-5		NV-2	OR-6			
CA-22		MN-4				VA-5	WI-1
	KS-4	MN-7	NY-8	PA-7		VA-6	WI-4
CT-3		MN-8	NY-10	PA-9		VA-8	WI-7

Synergy 5 Models: Strengthening health promotion and health protection by mobilizing community campaigns

5a: Community health assessment

AZ-5	CA-9	CA-22	DC-1	FL-12	GA-5	IA-1	ID-2
	CA-10			FL-13	GA-6	IA-4	
CA-4	CA-15	CT-1	FL-8			IA-7	IL-8

5b: Public education campaign

5c: Health-related law or regulation

5d: Community health promotion objective

AL-8	GA-5	KY-5	MN-5	NJ-7	PA-3	VA-23	———
	GA-6		MN-6	NJ-8	PA-4	VA-25	MST-3
CA-11		LA-2	MN-10				
CA-14	HI-1		MN-14	NM-2	SC-2	WA-1	NAT-5
CA-15		MA-12	MN-15			WA-3	NAT-10
CA-22	IA-1	MA-14	MN-17	NY-23	TN-1	WA-5	NAT-11
	IA-3			NY-27	TN-2	WA-9	NAT-14
CO-1	IA-4	MD-8	NC-1		TN-6	WA-10	NAT-21
	IA-5	MD-10	NC-6	OH-2		WA-11	NAT-22
CT-1			NC-7	OH-5	TX-4	WA-14	
CT-4	ID-2	MI-1	NC-12	OH-11	TX-7		
		MI-2	NC-13		TX-9	WI-4	
DC-1	IL-1	MI-10	NC-16	OR-4	TX-13	WI-5	
DC-2	IL-7			OR-5		WI-8	
		MN-1	ND-1	OR-6	VA-5		
GA-3	IN-2	MN-4			VA-18	WY-1	

5e: "Healthy Communities"-type initiative

CA-9	IA-1	KS- 2	MI-2	NC-8	OH-14	TX-13	———
CA-10	IA-4			NC-11			NAT-9
CA-17	IA-6	KY-5	MN-2	NC-12	OR-4	VA-16	
CA-21	IA-7		MN-6	NC-13		VA-18	INT-2
		MA-6	MN-14	NC-17	PA-13		
CT-1	ID-2	MA-14					WA-3
				NC-1	NJ-7	SC-2	WA-10
FL-13	IL-7	ME-1		NC-2	NJ-8		
	IL-8	ME-3		NC-3		TN-6	WY-1
GA-6				NC-7	OH-5		

Synergy 6 Models: Shaping the future direction of the health system by collaborating around health system policy, health professions training, and health-related research

SYN 6a: Health system policy
6a-1: Access to care policy

AL-3	DE-1	FL-12	LA-1	MD-7	MO-6	NY-6	OH-9
						NY-14	OR-4
CA-20	FL-2	GA-8	MA-13	MN-7	NC-10	NY-16	
	FL-7					NY-31	TN-3
CO-1	FL-8	KS-1	MD-4	MO-1	NV-2		

6a-2: Provider reimbursement policy

6a-3: Insurance benefit policy

6a-4: Quality of care policy

6a-5: Regional organization of health care services

6a-6: Organization/financing of public health

SYN 6b: Cross-sectoral education and training

6b-1: Cross-sectoral perspective in curriculum

KS-3	NC-14	NJ-9	OH-2	PA-1	TX-3	———
						NAT-23
MA-3	NH-1	NM-2	OR-3	TN-2	VA-9	

6b-2: Dual-degree program

GA-1	MA-2	OR-1	TX-1	———
				INT-2
LA-2	NJ-9	PA-1	VA-7	

6b-3: Cross-sectoral connection between schools or departments

AL-8	CT-2	NC-6	NM-2	PA-2	TX-1	VA-9
		NC-9		PA-3	TX-3	———
AZ-3	GA-1	NC-14	OR-1		TX-4	NAT-16
		NC-16		TN-2		
CO-1	LA-2		PA-1		VA-7	

6b-4: Involvement of community organizations in academic training

AL-1	CT-2	KY- 5	MO-4	NY-20	PA-1	UT-1	NAT-20
AL-2			MO-5	NY-21	PA-2	UT-2	
AL-3	FL-6	LA-2		NY-24	PA-3		INT-2
			NC-6	NY-27	PA-5	VA-4	
AZ-1	GA-1	MA-2	NC-14			VA-7	
AZ-3	GA-6	MA-3		OH-1	TN-2	VA-9	
	GA-9	MA-6	NE-2	OH-2	TN-5		
CA-8				OH-7		WA-16	
	IL-6	MD-2	NM-2		TX-2		
CO-1		MD-5	NM-3	OR-1	TX-4	WI-2	
	KS-3	MD-8		OR-3	TX-5	———	

6b-5: Cross-sectoral training for practicing professionals

AL-2	CA-11	GA-4	MA-10	MN-7	NJ-2	OR-3	\VA-6
AL-8	CA-12	GA-7		MN-9	NJ-4	OR-4	VA-7
			ME-1	MN-10	NJ-5	OR-6	VA-12
AZ-2	DC-2	IA-2		MN-12			VA-14
AZ-3		IA-7	MI-11		NY-15	RI-1	VA-19
AZ-6	DE-1			NC-11			VA-23
		MA-6	MN-3	NC-17	OH-6	TX-5	
CA-3	FL-8	MA-8	MN-4			TX-12	WA-6

6b-6: Cross-sectoral networking

SYN 6c: Cross-sectoral research

6c-1: Multidisciplinary research center

6c-2: Other research models

Index 4
Cases by Structural Foundation

For each type of structural foundation cases identifiers are organized geographically—first alphabetically by state postal code then multistate (MST) national (NAT) and international (INT) collaborations.

Coalition

AL-4	DC-1	IL-7	MI-2	NC-7	NY-23	TN-6	WA-11
AL-5	DC-2	IL-8	MI-3	NC-8	NY-27		WA-12
AL-8		IL-9	MI-4	NC-11	NY-30	TX-4	WA-13
	DE-1		MI-9	NC-12	NY-31	TX-7	WA-14
AZ-2		IN-2	MI-10	NC-13	NY-33	TX-8	WA-17
AZ-3	FL-5	IN-3		NC-17		TX-11	
AZ-5	FL-8		MN-1		OH-5	TX-12	WI-4
AZ-6	FL-9	KS-1	MN-2	ND-1	OH-8	TX-13	WI-5
AZ-7	FL-11	KS-2	MN-3		OH-9	TX-14	WI-7
	FL-12	KS-3	MN-4	NE-1	OH-10		
CA-2	FL-13		MN-7		OH-11	VA-2	WV-1
CA-3		KY-5	MN-8	NJ-2	OH-12	VA-4	WY-1
CA-4	GA-2		MN-9	NJ-3	OH-13	VA-5	———
CA-6	GA-3	MA-1	MN-10	NJ-7	OH-14	VA-6	MST-1
CA-9	GA-5	MA-5	MN-11	NJ-8		VA-10	MST-2
CA-10	GA-6	MA-6	MN-12		OR-4	VA-12	MST-3
CA-12	GA-7	MA-8	MN-14	NM-1	OR-5	VA-14	
CA-13		MA-12	MN-15	NM-2		VA-16	NAT-1
CA-14	HI-1	MA-13	MN-16	NM-3	PA-3	VA-18	NAT-2
CA-15		MA-14			PA-4	VA-19	NAT-6
CA-17	IA-4	MA-15	MO-1	NV-1	PA-9	VA-23	NAT-9
CA-19	IA-5		MO-2	NV-2	PA-10	VA-25	NAT-10
CA-20	IA-6	MD-1	MO-3		PA-12		NAT-11
CA-21	IA-7	MD-3	MO-4	NY-8	PA-13	WA-2	NAT-17
CA-22		MD-8	MO-5	NY-10		WA-3	NAT-19
	ID-1	MD-11	MO-6	NY-12	SC-2	WA-4	NAT-20
CT-1	ID-2			NY-13	SC-3	WA-5	
CT-2		ME-1	NC-1	NY-14		WA-7	INT-5
CT-3	IL-1		NC-2	NY-15	TN-1	WA-9	
CT-4	IL-5	MI-1	NC-6	NY-16	TN-4	WA-10	

Contract

AL-1	FL-12	KY-6	MN-4	NY-2	OR-1	VA-1	WI-4
AL-2			MN-5	NY-4	OR-2	VA-2	WI-8
AL-3	GA-1	MA-1	MN-6	NY-6	OR-5	VA-4	———
AL-4	GA-3	MA-2	MN-11	NY-7	OR-6	VA-6	NAT-3
AL-5	GA-4	MA-3	MN-13	NY-10		VA-7	NAT-4
AL-6	GA-5	MA-6	MN-17	NY-11	PA-2	VA-8	NAT-5
AL-7	GA-8	MA-8		NY-12	PA-5	VA-9	NAT-6
	GA-9	MA-10	MO-1	NY-14	PA-6	VA-11	NAT-7
AZ-1		MA-12	MO-6	NY-15	PA-8	VA-13	NAT-9
AZ-4	IA-1	MA-15	NC-4	NY-17	PA-9	VA-15	NAT-11
AZ-5	IA-4			NY-18	PA-11	VA-17	NAT-18
	IA-7	MD-2	NC-10	NY-20		VA-18	NAT-20
CA-1		MD-4	NC-14	NY-21	RI-1	VA-22	NAT-21
CA-10	ID-2	MD-5	NC-15	NY-22		VA-23	NAT-22
CA-22		MD-7	NC-18	NY-24	SC-1		NAT-23
	IL-3	MD-9		NY-25		WA-1	NAT-24
CO-1	IL-5	MD-11	NE-2	NY-26	TN-3	WA-4	NAT-25
	IL-6			NY-27	TN-5	WA-5	
FL-1	IL-10	ME-2	NJ-1	NY-28		WA-6	INT-1
FL-2		ME-3	NJ-3	NY-30	TX-2	WA-8	INT-2
FL-3	IN-1		NJ-4	NY-32	TX-5	WA-12	INT-3
FL-4		MI-3	NJ-6		TX-9	WA-13	INT-4
FL-6	KS-1	MI-4		OH-1	TX-13	WA-16	
FL-7	KS-2	MI-5	NM-3	OH-2	TX-14	WA-17	
FL-8	KS-3	MI-7		OH-6			
FL-10		MI-9	NY-1	OH-7	UT-1	WI-1	

Administrative management system

AL-3	CT-1	FL-13	ID-1	KY-6	MD-1	MN-5	NC-14
AL-4	CT-2		ID-2		MD-3	MN-6	NC-15
AL-7	CT-4	GA-3		LA-3	MD-7	MN-11	NC-17
		GA-4	IL-1		MD-8	MN-12	NC-18
CA-2	DC-1	GA-5	IL-4	MA-2		MN-14	
CA-5		GA-6	IL-5	MA-3	ME-2	MN-15	NE-1
CA-6	FL-3	GA-9	IL-8	MA-4			
CA-7	FL-4		IL-9	MA-6	MI-4	MO-2	NJ-1
CA-9	FL-7	IA-1	IL-10	MA-7	MI-9		NJ-3
CA-10	FL-8	IA-2		MA-8	MI-10	NC-5	NJ-4
CA-11	FL-9	IA-4	KS-2	MA-13		NC-10	
CA-17	FL-12	IA-7	KS-3	MA-15	MN-1	NC-12	NV-2

Informal

CA-8	IL-11	MD-2	MI-8	NM-4	OR- 2	TX-10	WI-6
CA-16		MD-6					
	KS-4	MD-10	NH-2	NY-6	PA-1	WA-15	NAT-15
IA-3				NY-9	PA-7		

Part IV
Keys to
Abbreviations

Key 1
Geographic Regions

INT   International

MST   Multistate Region

NAT   National

STATE   Particular States
POSTAL
CODE

Key 2
Organizational Partners
(listed alphabetically by acronym)

AHC	Academic health center
ARC	Academic research center
BUS	Business
C-OTH	Other community group
CLIN	Community health center or other publicly funded clinic
FEDHLTH	Federal health agency
FEDOTH	Other federal government agency
FNDN	Foundation
HOSP	Hospital or health system
INS	Health insurance company
L-GOV	Other local government agency
LAB/RX	Laboratory or pharmacy
LABR	Labor organization
LHD	Local health department
MCO	Managed care organization
MDPRAC	Solo or group medical practice
MEDIA	Media
MEDSOC	Medical/specialty society or other clinician association
PHASSN	Public health association
PROFASSN	Other professional association
RELIG	Religious organization or clergy
RES	Residency program
S-GOV	Other state government agency
SCHL	School below the college level
SHD	State health department
SOM	School of medicine
SPH	School of public health
U-OTH	Other university-level academic institution or department
VHO	Voluntary health organization or advocacy group

Key 3
Synergy Models

SYNERGY 1 — Improving health care by coordinating medical care with individual-level support services (such as home visits, case management services, transportation, translation, child care, and social services).

SYN 1a Link medical and support services by bringing new types of personnel to existing practice sites

SYN 1b Establish "one-stop" centers that locate a broad range of medical and support services in one place

SYN 1c Coordinate medical and support services provided in various locations throughout the community

SYNERGY 2 — Improving access to care by establishing frameworks to provide care for the un- or underinsured

SYN 2a Establish free clinics that provide indigent patients with free or discounted care

SYN 2b Establish referral networks, in which clinicians provide free or discounted care where they usually work

SYN 2c Recruit academic or private medical practitioners to enhance staffing at public health facilities

SYN 2d Shift the care of indigent patients from public health clinics to private medical practices, hospitals, health systems, or managed care organizations

SYNERGY 3 — Improving the quality and cost-effectiveness of care by applying a population perspective to medical practice

SYN 3a Make population-based information to support clinical decision-making more available and useful to medical practitioners

SYN 3b Link community-wide screening programs to follow-up medical care

SYN 3c Apply public health methodologies (such as clinical epidemiology or cost- effectiveness analysis) to clinical practice in order to support quality improvement activities, manage financial risk, or inform organizational planning

SYNERGY 4 — Using clinical practice to identify and address community health problems

SYN 4a Design and/or implement community-wide information systems that incorporate clinical data from hospitals, laboratories, or office-based practices

SYN 4b Take advantage of clinical encounters to identify health risks in patients, to educate patients about health risks, or to address social or environmental causes of health problems in patients

SYN 4c Assure the delivery of a particular clinical service in medical practices throughout the community by combining individual-level and population-based strategies (such as public education campaigns, screening programs, outreach services, and/or practice supports)

SYNERGY 5 — Strengthening health promotion and health protection by mobilizing community campaigns

SYN 5a Conduct community health assessments to identify health problems in the community

SYN 5b Mount public education campaigns to make people in the community aware of important health problems

SYN 5c Advocate health-related laws and regulations

SYN 5d Achieve particular community health promotion objectives by implementing multipronged strategies (including assessments, health education campaigns, laws and regulations, and/or voluntary community initiatives)

SYN 5e Launch "Healthy Communities"-type initiatives

SYNERGY 6 — Shaping the future direction of the health system by collaborating around health system policy, health professions training, and health-related research

SYNERGY 6a	Collaborate to influence health system policy
SYN 6a-1	Influence access to care policies
SYN 6a-2	Influence provider reimbursement policies
SYN 6a-3	Influence insurance benefits policies
SYN 6a-4	Influence quality of care policies
SYN 6a-5	Influence policies related to the regional organization of health care services or facilities
SYN 6a-6	Influence policies related to the organization and financing of public health services or activities

SYNERGY 6b — Collaborate for the explicit purpose of promoting cross-sectoral education and training of health professionals

SYN 6b-1	Incorporate a cross-sectoral perspective in the curriculum of a health professions degree program
SYN 6b-2	Institute a dual-degree program (such as MD/MPH)
SYN 6b-3	Establish formal, functional connections between medical and public health schools or academic programs
SYN 6b-4	Link academic training to medical and public health practice sites and other organizations in the broader community
SYN 6b-5	Provide cross-sectoral education or training to health professionals in the field
SYN 6b-6	Provide opportunities for cross-sectoral networking

SYNERGY 6c — Bring together multidisciplinary perspectives to conduct cross- sectoral research

SYN 6c-1	Establish a multidisciplinary research center
SYN 6c-2	Promote cross-sectoral research through activities other than a multidisciplinary research center

Key 4
Structural Foundations
(listed alphabetically by index item)

ADM/MGMT
Administrative/management systems are personnel or offices that run some or all aspects of collaborative enterprises, allowing partners to closely coordinate their activities and resources, or to centralize organization or control. Depending on the work involved, such a "system" may be a full-time staff person dedicated to managing a collaboration, a management office within one partner's organization, or a separate, autonomous management office. These arrangements make it possible for collaborations to integrate activities, to reduce duplication of services, and to achieve economies of scale.

ADVISORY
Advisory bodies are groups convened to provide an organization in one sector (such as a government agency or research entity) with input or support from other sectors. Advisory bodies may deliberate independently in constructing recommendations, but they do not have the authority to make operational or policy decisions.

COALITION
Coalitions are formal groups that bring together representatives of autonomous organizations to address a common problem or objective. The authority, responsibility, and capacity to take action lies with the coalition itself rather than with any one partner or external agency. Coalitions are particularly useful in collaborations that benefit from a broad range of community partners, particularly if they do not require equal or consistent involvement on the part of all partners or close coordination of partner activities.

CONTRACT
Contractual agreements are binding agreements (e.g., legal documents, memoranda of understanding, or verbal agreements) that commit one partner in a collaboration to carry out a function or to provide a service for another partner. Contracts are used in collaborations that depend on certain interactions between partners—usually the delivery of various health services to individuals. These agreements clarify partners' roles in critical interactions and assure that they are carried out.

INFORMAL
Informal arrangements are any of a variety of ad hoc relationships among partners, which are generally dependent on personal, rather than structured, interactions.

INTRAORG
Intraorganizational platforms are structural arrangements that allow a single organization to expand its perspective by bringing in professionals with the skills and expertise of another sector. Examples include a managed care organization that establishes a clinical epidemiology branch to assess quality or outcomes, or a section on public health within a medical society.

Key 5
Acronyms in Case Abstracts
(listed alphabetically)

AAHC	Association of Academic Health Centers
AAHP	American Association of Health Plans
AAMC	Association of American Medical Colleges
ACHE	Association of Community Health Educators
ACPM	American College of Preventive Medicine
AFDC	Aid for Families with Dependent Children
AHCPR	US Agency for Health Care Policy Research
AMA	American Medical Association
ANA	American Nursing Association
APEX*PH*	Assessment Protocol for Excellence in Public Health
APHA	American Public Health Association
ASTHO	Association of State and Territorial Health Officials
ATPM	Association of Teachers of Preventive Medicine
AZT	Zidovudine (drug to treat HIV/AIDS)
CBO	Community-Based Organization
CCN	Community Care Network Demonstration Partnerships
CDC	US Centers for Disease Control and Prevention
CEO	Chief Executive Officer
CME	Continuing Medical Education
COPC	Community-Oriented Primary Care
DHHS	US Department of Health and Human Services
EPA	US Environmental Protection Agency
EPSDT	Early Periodic Screening, Diagnosis and Treatment
HCFA	US Health Care Financing Administration
HEDIS	Health Plan Employer Data and Information Set
HIV/AIDS	Human Immunodeficiency Virus/Acquired Immunodeficiency Disease Syndrome
HMO	Health Maintenance Organization
HOP	Health of the Public Program
HRSA	US Health Resources and Services Administration

HUD	US Department of Housing and Urban Development
IHS	US Indian Health Service
JAMA	Journal of the American Medical Association
MCH	Maternal and Child Health
MCO	Managed Care Organization
MDR-TB	Multiple Drug Resistant Tuberculosis
NACCHO	National Association of County and City Health Officials
NIH	US National Institutes of Health
NIMH	US National Institute of Mental Health
NYAM	The New York Academy of Medicine
OB/GYN	Obstetrics and Gynecology
RWJF	The Robert Wood Johnson Foundation
STD	Sexually Transmitted Disease
TB	Tuberculosis
USPHS	US Public Health Service
WIC	Special Supplemental Food Program for Women, Infants, and Children
WKKF	W. K. Kellogg Foundation